Literary and Cultural Alternatives to Modernism

Our collection of essays re-evaluates the much critically contested term of Modernism that, eventually, came to be used as the dominant, or paradigmatic, strain of literary discourse in early twentieth-century culture. Modernism as a category is one which is constantly challenged, hybridised and fractured by voices operating from inside and outside the boundaries it designates. These concerns are reflected by those figures addressed by our contributors' chapters, which include Rupert Brooke, G. K. Chesterton, E. M. Forster, Thomas Hardy, M. R. James, C. L. R. James, Vernon Lee, D. H. Lawrence, Richard La Galliene, Pamela Colman Smith, Arthur Symons and H. G. Wells. Alert to these disturbing voices or unsettling presences that vex accounts of an emergent Modernism in late nineteenth-century and early twentieth-century literary cultures predominately between 1890 and 1939, our volume questions traditional critical mappings, taxonomies and periodisations of this vital literary cultural moment. Our volume is equally sensitive to how the avant-garde felt for those living and writing within the period with a view to offering a renewed sense of the literary and cultural alternatives to Modernism.

Kostas Boyiopoulos is a teaching associate at the Department of English Studies at Durham University.

Anthony Patterson is an Assistant Professor of English at Celal Bayar University in Manisa, Turkey.

Mark Sandy is a Professor of English at Durham University.

Routledge Studies in Twentieth-Century Literature

For more information about this series, please visit: https://www.routledge.com

Literary and Cultural Alternatives to Modernism

Unsettling Presences

Edited by Kostas Boyiopoulos,
Anthony Patterson and Mark Sandy

Routledge
Taylor & Francis Group

NEW YORK AND LONDON

First published 2019
by Routledge
605 Third Avenue, New York, NY 10017

and by Routledge
2 Park Square, Milton Park, Abingdon, Oxon, OX14 4RN

First issued in paperback 2021

Routledge is an imprint of the Taylor & Francis Group, an informa business

Publisher's Note
The publisher has gone to great lengths to ensure the quality of this reprint but points out that some imperfections in the original copies may be apparent.

Library of Congress Cataloging-in-Publication Data
Names: Boyiopoulos, Kostas, editor. | Patterson, Anthony (College teacher of English literature), editor. | Sandy, Mark, 1970– editor.
Title: Literary and cultural alternatives to modernism : unsettling presences / edited by Kostas Boyiopoulos, Anthony Patterson, and Mark Sandy.
Description: New York, NY : Routledge, 2019. | Series: Routledge studies in twentieth-century literature | Includes bibliographical references and index. |
Identifiers: LCCN 2019001694 (print) | LCCN 2019008095 (ebook)
Subjects: LCSH: Modernism (Literature)—Great Britain. | English literature—20th century—History and criticism.
Classification: LCC PR478.M6 (ebook) | LCC PR478.M6 L57 2019 (print) | DDC 820.9/112—dc23
LC record available at https://lccn.loc.gov/2019001694

ISBN 13: 978-1-03-209334-5 (pbk)
ISBN 13: 978-1-138-71021-4 (hbk)

Typeset in Sabon
by codeMantra

In memory of Michael O'Neill (1953–2018);
a true poet, critic and friend.

Contents

Acknowledgements

The editors are appreciative of Durham University and Celal Bayar University, respectively, for their departmental and institutional support of this project at various stages. In particular, Mark Sandy would like to thank Durham University for the granting two terms of research leave in 2018 that helped to bring this collection to completion. We would like to thank all those participants (some of whom contributed to this collection) in the '"We Speak a Different Tongue": Maverick Voices and Modernity, 1890–1939' international conference held in Durham during July 2013. We are especially grateful for the inspiring and instrumental participation of Chris Baldick and Michael O'Neill. Through papers and lively discussion at this event, which focused on many of the similar concerns and issues addressed in the pages that follow, the idea for this present volume began to germinate. We would also like to thank Yoon-joung Choi for her involvement and encouragement at an early stage of a lengthy journey that terminates with the present publication. We are thankful to our contributors for their continued interest in being a part of our volume and their patience and understanding throughout the time it took to bring this book to fruition. We are indebted to Suzannah Evans at Durham for her invaluable editorial assistance in preparing our typescript. We are also grateful to Jennifer Abbott who, initially, commissioned this project for publication and Michelle Salyga at Routledge for all her unstinting support and advice who, with the able assistance of Bryony Reece, assured the transition of this book from typescript to print.

List of Contributors

Kostas Boyiopoulos is a teaching associate in English studies at Durham University. He specialises in aestheticism, decadence and *Fin-de-siècle* literary culture. He is the author of *The Decadent Image: The Poetry of Wilde, Symons, and Dowson* (Edinburgh UP, 2015), funded by the Friends of Princeton University Library Research Grant. He has co-edited the essay collection *Decadent Romanticism: 1780–1914* (Ashgate, 2015) and *The Decadent Short Story: An Annotated Anthology* (Edinburgh UP, 2014). A co-edited volume of essays on *Aphoristic Modernity: 1880 to the Present* will be published by Brill/Rodopi in 2019.

Koenraad Claes is a Research Foundation Flanders (FWO) Postdoctoral Fellow based at Ghent University (Belgium). He has published on several topics related to British literature and print culture of the long nineteenth century, focusing on the Romantic period and the Victorian Fin de Siècle, and serves as the managing editor for the open-access journal *Authorship*. His first monograph, *The Late-Victorian Little Magazine*, came out with Edinburgh University Press in 2018.

Katharine Cockin is a Professor at the University of Essex and currently editing the eight-volume *Collected Letters of Ellen Terry* (Pickering & Chatto, 2010 onwards). She is the author of the biography of Ellen Terry's daughter, Edith Craig (1998) and monograph on Craig's groundbreaking Pioneer Players theatre society. In staging innovative productions ranging from women's suffrage to Expressionist drama in the period 1911–25, the Pioneer Players has been London's forgotten art theatre. Other research interests include contemporary literature, most recently resulting in her editing of a collection of essays, *The Literary North* (Palgrave 2012).

Andrew Hodgson is a Lecturer in Romanticism at the University of Birmingham. He has written essays on English poets from Gray to Larkin and his monograph *The Poetry of Clare, Hopkins, Thomas, and Gurney: Lyric Individualism* is forthcoming with Palgrave Macmillan.

xiv List of Contributors

Sondeep Kandola is a Senior Lecturer in English, Liverpool John Moores University. She published her monograph *Vernon Lee* in 2011 and has also published articles on Vernon Lee and Ouida, Arthur Machen and W. B. Yeats, and Oscar Wilde. She will be editing an essay collection for Ashgate on the vampire for 2015. She also organises a high-profile lecture series at John Moores called 'New Perspectives on National Identity' which has featured speakers such as Tariq Ramadan and Janet Suzman. She began a new research project on D. H. Lawrence in 2014.

Saikat Majumdar is the author of a monograph on global modernism, *Prose of the World* (2013), a finalist for the Modernist Studies Association Book Award in 2014; a general nonfiction title, *College: Pathways of Possibility* (2018), on liberal arts and sciences education in India; and three novels, including *The Scent of God* (2019), and *The Firebird* (2015; published in the US as *Play House*, 2017), one of *Telegraph*'s Best Books and a finalist for the Bangalore Literature Festival Best Fiction Award in 2015, and for the Mumbai Film Festival Word-to-Screen Market in 2016. He is Professor of English and Creative Writing at Ashoka University.

Michael O'Neill was a Professor of English at Durham University, where he worked for nearly forty years, until his recent death in December 2018. He published on many aspects of Romantic literature, especially the work of Percy Bysshe Shelley, on Victorian poetry, and on an array of British, Irish and American twentieth- and twenty-first-century poets. Recent books included, as an editor, *The Cambridge History of English Poetry* (2010), as a co-author (with Michael D. Hurley), *Poetic Form: An Introduction* (CUP, 2012), and as a co-editor, and (with Anthony Howe and with the assistance of Madeleine Callaghan) *The Oxford Handbook of Percy Bysshe Shelley* (2013). His book-length study of *Shelleyan Reimagings and Influences: New Relations* is forthcoming (Oxford UP, 2019). He is the author of four collections of poems, including *Gangs of Shadow* (Arc, 2014) and most recently *Return of the Gift* (Arc, 2018). With a fifth collection forthcoming, *Crash and Burn* (Arc in 2019).

Anthony Patterson is an Assistant Professor at Celal Bayar University in Manisa, Turkey. He has published articles and book chapters on a number of writers in the late Victorian and Edwardian periods. His monograph *Mrs Grundy's Enemies: Censorship, Realist Fiction and the Politics of Sexual Representation* was published by Peter Lang in 2013. He is the co-editor of two recent volumes, *Vile Women: Challenging Representations of Female Evil in Fact Fiction and Mythology* and *We Speak a Different Tongue: Maverick Voices and Modernity 1890–1939*. His chapter 'Social Realism and the Short

Story' was published in the *Cambridge Companion to the English Short Story* in 2016. He is currently working on a monograph on social realism.

Mark Sandy is a Professor of English literature at Durham University. His research interests are in Romantic and nineteenth-century poetics. His publications include *Poetics of Self and Form in Keats and Shelley* (2005) and *Romanticism, Memory, and Mourning* (2013). He has edited and co-edited several critical essay collections on Romanticism and its legacies, the two most recent of which are *Decadent Romanticism 1780–1914* (2015) and *The Persistence of Beauty: Victorians to Moderns* (2015). He is currently co-editing a volume titled *Ghostly Encounters: Cultural and Imaginary Representations of the Spectral from the Nineteenth Century to the Present* and researching a book on *Transatlantic Transformations of Romanticism*.

Luke Seaber taught for eight years in various universities in Italy before moving to University College London, where he was a Marie Curie Research Fellow in the English Department for two years before becoming tutor in Modern European Culture in 2014. He is the author of various articles and chapters on nineteenth- and twentieth-century British literature, and his most recent book is *Incognito Social Investigation in British Literature: Certainties in Degradation* (Palgrave Macmillan, 2017). He is currently working on the early stages of a project on the role of allusion in twentieth-century literature.

Michael Shallcross is an independent researcher, based in York, UK. His first monograph, *Rethinking G. K. Chesterton and Literary Modernism: Parody, Performance, and Popular Culture*, was published by Routledge in 2017. He co-edits *The Journal of Wyndham Lewis Studies*, and is currently editing the scholarly edition of Lewis's novel, *Mrs. Dukes' Million* (c.1908–10), for the forthcoming *Collected Works of Wyndham Lewis* (OUP). He is also working on a second monograph for Routledge, *The Parodic Devil in British Post-Enlightenment Culture: Inscribing Pandemonium*.

Carey Snyder is an Associate Professor of English at Ohio University, the author of *British Fiction and Cross-Cultural Encounters: Ethnographic Modernism from Wells to Woolf* (Palgrave, 2008), and the editor of the Broadview Press edition of *H. G. Wells's Ann Veronica* (2016). Her recent essays have appeared in venues such as the *Journal of Modern Periodical Studies* and the collection, *Brave New World: Texts and Contexts* (Palgrave, 2016).

Margaret D. Stetz is the Mae and Robert Carter Professor of Women's Studies and Professor of Humanities at the University of Delaware. As well as being the author of books such as *British Women's Comic*

Fiction, 1890–1990 and *Facing the Late Victorians,* she has published more than 120 essays and chapters in scholarly journals and edited volumes. She was also the co-curator (with Mark Samuels Lasner) of a 2016 exhibition titled *Richard Le Gallienne, Liverpool's Wild(e) Poet* at Liverpool Central Library. In 2015, she was named by the magazine *Diverse: Issues in Higher Education* to its list of the top 25 women in higher education.

Kate Symondson holds a PhD in English literature from King's College London, supervised by Professor Max Saunders. Her thesis focuses on innovations in representation in the early twentieth century. She looks at what she identifies as the realisation of the abstract aesthetic in the works of Joseph Conrad, E. M. Forster and Virginia Woolf. She has presented numerous papers at conferences where she discusses the parallels between the writing of certain Modernist authors with the concepts and vision of abstract artists.

Introduction

Alternatives to Modernism: Dissonant Voices and Multiple Modernities, 1890–1939

Kostas Boyiopoulos, Anthony Patterson and Mark Sandy

Our collection of essays focuses on the much critically contested term of Modernism that, eventually, came to be used as the dominant, or paradigmatic, strain of literary discourse in early twentieth-century culture. Modernism as a category is one which is constantly challenged, hybridised and fractured by voices operating from inside and outside the boundaries it designates. Alert to these disturbing voices or unsettling presences that vex accounts of an emergent Modernism in late nineteenth-century and early twentieth-century literary cultures between 1890 and 1939, our volume questions established critical mappings, taxonomies and periodisations of this vital literary cultural moment. For Frank Kermode, at least, the spirit of 'modernness' is spawned in the 1890s with its emphasis on both 'apocalyptic' themes and 'transition' inducted by both *The Yellow Book* (1894–1897) and later adopted by *Blast* (1914–1915).[1]

The first half of the twentieth century comprises a series of discordant voices suggestive of a richer and more varied texture of modernity (or modernities) than has been previously recognised. In a rapidly changing world, where literature was trying to find its place, Ezra Pound's slogan 'make it new' was understood in diverse ways by a plethora of writers of wildly different artistic persuasions, ranging from genre fiction of mass popularity to the avant-garde movements of the manifestoes, with perspectives that have been underappreciated and relegated to the margins of so-called 'Modernism'. The colourful and varied mosaic of the literary scene was all but obliterated by an inner circle of authors associated with what is now known as the Modernist movement. Modernism gained its foothold by inciting canon formation and the academic institutionalisation of literary studies. The intelligentsia that emerged in the 1930s privileged a specific assemblage of texts contemporarily as well as retroactively.

Centres and Schisms

Canonical Modernism was not only shaped by constellations and alliances but, equally, by oppositions and mutinies. The plurality of alternative literary and cultural voices that were side-lined can be heard in those critiques of the predictably familiar figures of Modernism. Put differently, insurrection came from within as much as without.[2] A central example of this is Wyndham Lewis, who broke away from the 'Men of 1914', as he famously called them.[3] In *The Apes of God* (1930), a gargantuan satire of the coteries of Modernism, Lewis launched a vituperative and waspish attack on Virginia Woolf, the Sitwells and others, calling them '*prosperous mountebanks who alternately imitate and mock at and traduce those figures they at once admire and hate*'.[4] Lewis expostulates about the '*societification* of art' (123) by the 'select and snobbish club' of '*Bloomsbury*' whose

> foundation-members consisted of monied middleclass descendants of victorian literary splendour. Where they approximate to the citizens of this new cosmopolitan Bohemia is in their substitution of money for talent as a qualification for membership. Private-means is the almost invariable rule. In their discouragement of too much unconservative originality they are very strong. The tone of "society" (of a spurious donnish social elegance) prevails among them. Where they have always *differed* has been in their *all* without exception being Apes of God. That is the first point. All are "geniuses," before whose creations the other members of the Club, in an invariable ritual, must swoon with appreciation. (123)

And the invective goes on. What Lewis targets is the hegemonic and ideological role of the Bloomsbury Group (and its annexes) in claiming exclusive rights to 'originality'. Of course, in an alienating world of cheap mass culture and mechanised industry, the writers and artists under attack wore the attitude of highbrow, hermetic elitism as a badge of honour. But what we can extricate from this passage is what lies beyond Lewis's accusations of partisanship and pretentiousness: a tendency of a specific cultural force to dominate and command the literary scene, set its parameters and edge out dissenting voices. The Bloomsbury group symbolises a centre of gravity, an implicit point of reference against which all other literary voices are pitched. In fact, it was a prominent intellectual Rome that emerged as an iconoclastic cultural centre for a whole variety of lone wolves and niche groups that have been often obliquely perceived or under-represented, and are excluded from the history of modernity. Ironically, for Lewis, it was the Bloomsbury group that exhibited divine authority (aping God), and so placed itself at the top of some sort of pecking order. The 'geniuses' are at the centre with the privileged satellites orbiting their gravitational pull. In the periphery, 'they exercise their influence in the interests of what is virtually their club. A certain network of not very remunerative patronage extends over outsiders who are not too important' (*Apes* 124).

Lewis denigrates the Bloomsbury *parties* in a manner that recalls Woolf's excoriation of popular literature in *Mr. Bennett and Mrs. Brown* (1924), or the kind of work produced by what Rebecca West called 'Uncles' or 'the Big Four': H. G. Wells, Bernard Shaw, John Galsworthy and Arnold Bennett.[5] Similarly, in *Tono-Bungay* (1909)—a text anticipating postmodern sensibilities—Wells sneered at the jingoism of canned popular adventure stories. In *The Apes of God*, Lewis expresses disappointment at the formation of a quasi-organised group whose overshadowing authoritativeness mimics the traditional establishment which it professedly opposes. The shattering of the dominant narratives of Romanticism and Victorian Realism, ironically, led to the making of another dominant narrative. Bloomsbury is not defined by formal rules and programmes; it lacks the vigorous clarity of an unflinching manifesto, as those espoused by Futurism or Surrealism. Instead, Bloomsbury thrives lukewarmly on fluid social interactions among peers, cliquey solidarity and camaraderie. In Britain, pure avant-garde movements such as Imagism and Vorticism, due to their narrow scope, quickly ran their course and fizzled out in their intensity. Instead, Bloomsbury dominated through the flexibility afforded by the '*societification* of art'; it gained ground by providing a framework of self-promotion that safeguarded a pontificating Eliot or an arbitrating Woolf.

The class consciousness and stratification that pervades the literary landscape with Bloomsbury at the centre, signalled unequivocally by E. M. Forster in *Howards End* (1910) and affirmed by Eliot in *Notes Towards a Definition of Culture* (1948), is a phenomenon that Eliot embraces and vindicates. In his obituary of Virginia Woolf in 1941, Eliot acknowledged the symbolic *centrality* of Bloomsbury, writing that she 'was the centre, not merely of an esoteric group, but of the literary life of London'.[6] With her death, 'a whole pattern of culture is broken: she may be, from one point of view, only the symbol of it; but she would not be the symbol if she had not been, more than anyone in her time, the maintainer of it' (*CPTSE* 6, 171). In his cultural diagnosis, Eliot went as far as to map out the pyramidal structure of literary production according to its apportioned value. In 'Modern Tendencies in Poetry' (1920), he writes:

> You produce half a dozen, at most, of respectable poets in a generation; you produce twenty or thirty people who are capable of discovering that these poets are good; a hundred people who can see that they are good when somebody else points it out; a thousand who will admire out of respect for others' opinion; and the rest who will, eventually, believe what they are told.[7]

Eliot's prescribed elitist model acknowledges the existence, as well as ratifying the role, of minor voices, or what Modernist writers would class as second fiddles. In the introduction to *The Sacred Wood* (1921), Eliot deems that 'the poetaster who understands his own limitations will be one of our useful second-order minds; a good minor poet (something which is very rare) or another good critic' (*CPTSE* 2, 297). The notion of the 'minor poet', a figure associated with the Nineties and considered by Ezra Pound in *Hugh Selwyn Mauberley* (1920), implies a hierarchy. Eliot is careful not to use the term 'second-rate' but 'second-order', as opposed to 'first-order' or 'Genius' (*CPTSE* 2, 296). The Victorians believed that culture should preserve only genius and stamp out the rest; nevertheless, for Eliot, artistic genius spearheads culture and defines itself in relation to what might be perceived as inferior voices.

Eliot's division of highbrow and middlebrow literary cultures, through his editorship of *The Criterion* (1922–1939), which succeeded *The Egoist* (1914–1919), enabled the rise of the discipline of literary studies and the literary canon through the groundwork laid by I. A. Richards, Cleanth Brooks and F. R. Leavis. These academics cemented and secured the hegemony of a Modernism that, in the words of Malcolm Bradbury and James McFarlane, was 'less a style than a search for a style'.[8] What became institutionalised was this protean, non-terminal quality that Lewis attacked and which was introduced by those works of High Modernism. This quality comported with Eliot's principle of 'impersonality' in 'Tradition and the Individual Talent' (1919), the hidden layers of meaning beneath a fragmented self. Interestingly, Lewis critiques Eliot's 'impersonality' as a thin 'pretence', 'a bluff or a blasphemy' (*Apes* 125), anticipating Michel Foucault's theory of the author's disappearance as a construct.[9] The conceptual hallmarks of Modernism, Eliot's 'impersonality', James Joyce's stream of consciousness, Woolf's 'moments of being' and shifting viewpoints, are designed to provide a writerly framework of sibylline disjointedness that invites only the cultured reader to participate and thus confirms the canonised status of a given work.

Discrete popular genres such as romance, the detective novel, fantasy fiction and science fiction were excluded from the canon and were marginalised by Modernism's safeguarding against genre fixing and compartmentalisation. In *Mass Civilization and Minority Culture*, published in 1930 (also the year of Lewis's *The Apes of God*), F. R. Leavis quotes George A. Birmingham (Canon Hannay) who had written that '"[t]he detective novel writers have their own clientele, though they make no appeal to the young ladies who throng the counters of Boots' libraries and but little to the sheep-like crowd who follow the dictates of highbrow literary critics"'.[10] On the back foot, Leavis posits that highbrow culture is 'in minority keeping' in a way that it had not been since the works of Shakespeare up to the Victorian period. By highbrow, Leavis identifies '*The Waste Land, Hugh Selwyn Mauberley, Ulysses* or *To the Lighthouse*' (25). These works were not narrowly focused so as to reach an *impasse* but, instead, were riddle-like and allowed for organic expansiveness of meaning in the classroom, thus giving rise to the school of New Criticism in the 1930s. In the antipode, apart from popular genres, extreme avant-gardism was viewed with equal suspicion. Canon formation had a preference for works rigged with enigmas that encouraged expansion of the discourse on meaning rather than one-off artistic *statements* that limited meaning. Pound was quick to realise this, and as a result transitioned from the aggressive experiments of his 'make it new' doctrine to the reflective gestures of the *Cantos* and the Eliot collaboration in the 1920s.

A further retrospective articulation of the dominance of cultural movements is provided by George Orwell in 'Inside the Whale' (1940). In this contemplative assessment of Henry Miller's *Tropic of Cancer* (1934), Orwell offers a lucid diagnosis of literary modernity, contrasting the pessimism and political aloofness of the 1920s highbrows against the vacuous political involvement of the 1930s. His discussion, however, is revealing about the tendency of group formation at the expense of peripheral individual voices, the propensity to homogenise periods by squeezing them into keynotes and slogans, and so steer dominant cultural narratives.[11] He asserts that the Joyce–Eliot axis of the 1920s was 'the movement' in the same way the Auden–Spender group were 'the movement' in the 1930s (with Yeats and Forster traversing both tendencies).[12] Yet, Orwell is quick to note that the highbrows were, initially, just one tendency out of many.[13] Confirming the paradigm of Lewis's heretical stance, Orwell writes that the exponents of High Modernism were not uniform but were united by opposing 'progress' and by being entrenched in tradition as they shared 'a certain tenderness for the Catholic Church' (154, 158). The shift from the 1910s to the 1920s to the 1930s is that of the Georgian 'beauty of Nature', to the ambience of the Church and 'tragic sense of life', to Communism and 'serious purpose' (154, 160). Orwell ruminates on the possibility of a return to passive individualism embodied in Henry Miller who might be 'the starting-point of a new "school"' (174); at the opening of 'Inside the Whale', Orwell deems *Tropic of Cancer* to be one of those books that 'create a world of their own' (134).

The crucial difference between Leavis's and Orwell's analyses of modernity is that the former is prescriptive and the latter descriptive. At any rate, the homogenising approach to summing up culture and the ethos of a group- and in-group-formation are indicative of the presence of a quiet and subcutaneous periphery of voices having the propensity to push towards the centre (Orwell's view of Miller's anticipated future is a case in point). In his characteristic belligerence and bias, Lewis is aware of the group problem. In *Time and Western Man* (1927), he writes against 'groups' and 'movements': 'No collectivity ever conceives, or, having done so, would ever be able to carry through, an insurrection or a reform of any intensity, or of any magnitude. That is always the work of individuals or minorities'.[14]

The schismatic deviations within Modernism itself mirror its disregard for peripheral voices, which unsettle and disorientate by weaving a web of destabilising, crisscrossing perspectives. Consider, for example, the responses of Woolf, Wells and Forster to *Ulysses* (a work that holds a unique position in the history of Modernism). In 'Modern Fiction' (1919), Woolf concludes that 'no "method", no experiment, even of the wildest – is forbidden, but only falsity and pretence'.[15] But in one of her mixed responses to *Ulysses*, she wrote to Lytton Strachey in 1922 that the first 200 pages are 'tosh' and the later chapters she described as '[t]he scratching of pimples on the body of the boot boy at Claridges'.[16] Woolf's desultory metaphor plays on the corporeal style of *Ulysses* itself, framing the work in hyperbolic class distinctions. Wells, in his feedback to Joyce in 1928 for both *Ulysses* and published parts of *Finnegans Wake*, assumes a stern tone, writing: '[Y]ou have turned your back on common men' with '[v]ast riddles'; he acknowledges (perhaps ironically) Joyce's 'extraordinary experiment' and concludes that 'the world is wide and there is room for both of us to be wrong'.[17] Remarkably, Wells here displays sportsmanship towards Joyce despite his role as a literary arch antagonist. For Woolf, the book is too base and vulgar; for Wells, it is too elitist. And in an astonishing turn, Forster interprets *Ulysses* as a species of 'fantasy', describing it disapprovingly as 'an inverted Victorianism'.[18] Even though New Criticism sanctioned Modernism by opting for neat demarcations, the varied responses to *Ulysses* reflect a pandemonium of subjective views that makes balanced innovation a matter of perspective.

Alternative Modernities

This pandemonium of perspectives originates in the muddled, overlapping splicing of two perennial cultural tendencies: 'oscillation in style over periods of time, an ebb and flow between a predominantly rational worldview (Neo-Classicism, Enlightenment, Realism) and alternate spasms of irrational or subjective endeavour (Baroque, *Sturm und Drang*, Romanticism)' (Bradbury and McFarlane, 47). But specifically in Modernism, these tendencies 'cross' and 'interfuse' (48). Productive confusion of unsettling presences partly reigned due to the fact that the term 'Modernism' had not yet entered academic discourse in the interwar years. Aldous Huxley in his essay 'The New Romanticism' (1931) echoes Forster's assessment of *Ulysses* as an example of 'inverted Victorianism'. He turns the perspective around: 'Modern romanticism is the old romanticism turned inside out, with all its values reversed'; that is, Romantic individualism versus Communist collectivism, a sort of 'photographic negative'.[19] Huxley pre-empts the progressive avant-garde: 'The Cubist dehumanization of art is frequently accompanied by a romantic and sentimental admiration for machines' (217). He chooses the 'golden mean' between these two extremes (220), an instance of Bradbury's and McFarlane's *interfusion* of alternate epochs (Classic and Romantic) in Modernism. In the same year, Edmund Wilson's well-known study, *Axel's Castle* (1931), instead chooses the term 'symbolism' and stretches it to describe Eliot, Proust, Joyce and Stein (alongside Yeats and Paul Valéry).

In view of the absence of the 'Modernism' label in the early twentieth century, modern poetry became almost synonymous with the generic tag *vers libre*. Resistances or responses to *vers libre* yielded different versions of counter-Modernist poetics. Thomas Hardy believed that '*vers libre* could come to nothing in England', writing to Robert Graves that '[a]ll we can do is to write on the old themes in the old styles, but to try to do a little better than those who went before us'.[20] Hardy's appeal mirrors Edmund Gosse who, in the Victorian period, issued a 'Plea for Certain Exotic Forms of Verse' (1877), a turn to Medieval French fixed forms as a measure against the careless imitators of blank verse employed by Tennyson and Browning. Eliot himself expands the purview of '*vers libre*' which is 'a collective name for a number of forms'; at 'which it is very easy to do badly [*amphigory*]; and on the other hand some of the best verse is being done in very old forms'.[21] For all the striving of the front-runners of Modernism to ablactate from tradition, Eliot recognised that tradition is essential in achieving the splintering of novelty and original-ity. The critic and editor Raymond Mortimer writes in 1928 that 'there is a romantic poet in Mrs. Woolf, a mystic in Mr. E. M. Forster'; but in comparing these writers 'with any outside the group, great Edwardians like Wells and Bennett, for instance, [...] a certain consonance in the Bloomsbury artists becomes [...] apparent'.[22]

Horace Zagreus, that insurgent gadfly in *The Apes of God*, comments cynically on a poem by the nineteen-year-old Mr Boleyn (modelled on Stephen Spender): 'it is in quite traditional metre. Absolutely the *young-est* generation, sir, do not write in free verse – they have gone back to *quite* traditional forms' (40); only the older generations 'believe in vio-lent experiment – the *very youngest generation* [...] are super-victorian now, if you like – are classical *to a man!*' (40). Zagreus's retort could be a reference to the Sitwells, whom Lewis considered to be old-fashioned Victorian poets in spite of their innovative stylistics, as well as the con-ventionality of the Georgians. *Georgian Poetry* as it was dished out in the five anthologies from 1912 to 1922 edited by Edward Marsh, and further kept alive by J. C. Squire in 1919–1939 in his editorship of *The London Mercury*, promoted traditional forms and rhythms, English-ness, pastoralism and Romantic nostalgia. C. K. Stead and James Reed endeavoured to rehabilitate the Georgians.[23] Reed notes that 'Georgian' was a term at the 'periphery'; yet '[t]o be new, a feeling does not neces-sarily demand radical novelty of expression'.[24]

In the apologetic prefatory note to the final Georgian anthology, Marsh described modern poetry in free verse as 'gravy imitating lava', and argued that its upholders may be thinking in a similar way about the Georgian poets as 'tapioca imitating pearls', adding that '[e]ither view – possibly both – may be right'.[25] With this even-handed attitude to the coexistence of Georgian poetry and *vers libre*, Marsh displays the egalitarianism of Wells, who writes to Joyce that 'the world is wide and there is room for both of us to be wrong'. Far less generously, Eliot in a review (signed with the pseudonym Aptéryx) juxtaposed *Georgian Poetry, 1916–1917* with the avant-garde anthology *Wheels: A Second Cycle* (1917) edited by Edith Sitwell. Eliot described Georgian poetry as 'inbred' yet with 'a technique and a set of emotions all of its own'.[26] He deemed *Wheels* more 'serious', but like a more systematic Horace Zagreus, Eliot noted that 'while the Georgians have the appearance of ignorance, the Cyclists have a little the air of smattering' ('Verse', 44).

It is important to note that already in the 1930s, notwithstanding Leavis's efforts to promulgate a high culture, the concept of anthology emerged as a more inclusive outlet, dulling its manifesto-like character. Yeats's anthology *The Oxford Book of Modern Verse: 1892–1935* (1936) embraced a diverse mix of poets as disparate as Wilde, James Elroy Flecker, Lawrence Binyon, Hardy and Davies, alongside Eliot and Pound. Yeats begins the book by setting Walter Pater's famous Mona Lisa passage in *vers libre* in order to 'show its revolutionary importance'.[27] Yeats argues that Eliot works by 'rejection' of conventions used by the Romantics and this gives 'his work an exaggerated plainness that has the effect of novelty' (xxi). Yeats hints at an expansion of the purview of modernity by way of a genealogical synthesis: certain poets of the 1920s combined Eliot's modern 'vocabulary' with the 'suffering' of the war poets (xxxv), while Cecil Day Lewis, Charles Madge, Louis MacNeice 'are modern through the character of their intellectual passion', they may seem 'obscure' because of 'their interest in associations hitherto untravelled' (xxxvi). He prefers them to Eliot and even to his own attempts 'to be modern' (xxxvi).

A comparable anthological project to Yeats's is Michael Roberts's *The Faber Book of Modern Verse* (1936), setting the beginning of modernity at 1910 (incidentally agreeing with Woolf's statement in *Mr. Bennett and Mrs. Brown* that 'On or about December 1910, human character changed').[28] Roberts divides the poets of his anthology 'into two classes': those whose work is dominated by the 'European' sensibility and those of the 'English' sensibility, or intertextual erudition and the effects of the English language, respectively.[29] He defends his selections on the basis of alternative perspectives. If 'a poet's use of language is valid for some people, we cannot dismiss his way of speaking as mere "obscurity" and idiosyncrasy' (4).

Robert's defence of alternative perspectives regarding poetry is just as pertinent to a consideration of the fiction of the period, much of which was compartmentalised by Modernist critics that followed Woolf's sharp dividing practice between experimental Georgians and outmoded Edwardians. This view of Modernist fiction as protean, innovative and above all dynamically experimental invariably located Realist fiction as the Modernist 'other', as static, staid, artistically naïve and formally predictable, a straw man whose major function was to highlight literary experimentation elsewhere.[30]

This basis of Modernist canon formation has been robustly disputed and the canon itself consequently extended even to the extent that the fiction of Modernism's supposed arch antagonist, the popular Realist Arnold Bennett, has been recovered as more nuanced, complex and perspectival than Woolf's critique of him as merely creating character through external detailing.[31] Bennett's re-evaluation through the lens of Modernist experimentation is part of a more general tendency to expand the Modernist canon by incorporating fiction previously believed to be beyond its pale, a tendency, though, that still invariably fosters the valorisation of Modernist aesthetics, often at the expense and marginalisation of other narrative approaches.

Novels may be designated as proto-modernist and/or as transitional: the most innovative aspects of formal experimentation noted as emergent and the more 'realistic' perceived as residual, and as such meriting minimal attention. Both the linear literary–historical trajectories in which Realism is supplanted by Modernism and, then, in turn, superseded by Postmodernism[32] have increasingly been viewed as providing an inadequate framework for the diversity and creativity of the period's literary production. More significantly, the complex relations, antagonisms and transactions between the marginalised and the established Modernist centres have increasingly come, as this collection demonstrates, under critical pressure and scrutiny.

While the Moderns campaigned for a literature that fragments, twists and streamlines language in order to see moments of feeling in a new way, their contemporaries were searching for the new in alternative contexts, some in already existing narratives such as Romanticism and Realism, and some by reinventing the poetic imagination. Our volume attempts to see those gestations anew without the heavy filters of New Critical and post-1960s academic canon-building and endorsement of the term 'Modernism'. In so doing, we are tacitly responding to what Douglas Mao and Rebecca L. Walkowitz have described as New Modernist Studies, a term describing a fresh academic approach to the field that includes ventures such as the journal *Modernism/modernity*. Through their *Bad Modernisms* (2006), Mao and Walkowitz distended the designation Modernism to make it more inclusive. They posed a felicitous question:

> What effects of synergy or friction result when the many, sometimes contradictory, criteria of high modernism are tested against less evidently experimental texts by principal figures; against principal works by less well known or non-European artists; against texts that seem neither to be art nor to be about art, such as erotic novels, popular films, spy thrillers, melodrama, and ethnography?[33]

In a sense, this aspect of New Modernist Studies speaks to what we envisage in this book. And yet, our collection of essays seems to be at variance with Mao's and Walkowitz's framework. In their foundational text, 'The New Modernist Studies' (2008), they latch onto 'Modernism' and foreground the field's *'expansion'*, its 'temporal, spatial, and vertical directions'.[34] But our volume is aware that the term 'Modernism' is already culturally loaded, historically encumbered and ideologically fraught. We are less interested in an expanded atlas of 'Modernism' and its transcendence of national borders. We seek instead partly to challenge and partly to illuminate what is precisely denoted by the label Modernism within the Anglo-American paradigm. In the seemingly exclusionary context of the politics, practices, aesthetics and beliefs of Modernism, our collection of essays aims at showcasing what might be called *alternativeness*. As the Modernist writers assumed the mantle of highbrow avant-gardism, their contemporaries, astute to the demands of a culture in flux, opted for *alternative* practices, a broader and more ubiquitous category than merely the *avant-garde*. The term 'alternativeness' not only suggests divergent pathways, but it does so in response to a current movement (i.e. Modernism) which tends to cap or overrun other types of cultural activity. Often, alternative voices (unsettling presences) in modernity reinvent, hybridise, or sample nineteenth-century trends, such as Romanticism, Realism and Aestheticism, in unusual ways.

Our collected essays challenge, then, the autocentric view (largely shaped by academic preferentialism) of what Bloomsbury or, a little more broadly, the axis of Woolf, the Sitwells, Katherine Mansfield, Eliot, Pound, D. H. Lawrence, and Joyce represent, with figures such as Yeats, Forster, Hardy, Lewis, Huxley, H. D. and Dorothy Richardson being just off-centre, and other writers, including Galsworthy, Bennett, Wells and Chesterton, standing outside the ambit of high culture. Alternatively, our volume seeks to highlight the idea of a non-hierarchical multiplicity of voices. We do not wish to explore centrifugal forces, but, to use a potent metaphor from a short story by Jorge Louis Borges, we seek to explore the tableau of modern voices as one of multiple centres; a canvas in which the centre is everywhere.[35]

Unsettling Presences

Our edited volume investigates writers and texts chiefly stretching from 1890 to 1939, from both within and outside the Modernist canon. Both individually and collectively, these chapters address the following questions: does a privileging of Modernism undervalue texts that are perceived to operate outside either the parameters of its understood aesthetic and/or periodisation? And are there marginalised or obscure texts whose innovatory or *alternative* practices renew a sense of the plurality of types of modernisms? Our volume also endeavours to register how the *avant-garde* felt for people within the period rather than how

Modernism was defined and redefined retroactively. What it meant, for instance, to be on the edge for Wells and Bennett or, indeed, what is distinctive about this kind of cultural displacement.

Our collection is bound together not by examining a specific group of writers, a specific genre or a specific movement. Neither is it interested in expanding the purview of canonical Modernism. Its central focus explores an all-pervading cultural phenomenon the dominant trends of which were challenged, directly or indirectly, by voices operating in the margin (such as M. R. James), or just off-centre (such as Forster). Our collected chapters explore instances of revision and recasting of the tradition (Romanticism, Victorian Realism and Aestheticism), as well as cultural and literary exchanges and comparisons. A central claim is that the first half of the twentieth century does not herald one movement in opposition to a jaded Realism, even if the Modernist movement is recognised as encompassing a range of practices, but several disparate and often discontinuous cutting-edge developments, some of which occurred within Realism itself.

Our volume does not claim to provide an exhaustive catalogue of all of the literary and cultural alternatives to Modernism but, through a series of case-by-case examples, is indicative of the variegated and potentially inexhaustible nature of these alternatives. The chapters testify to a richer variety of literary experimentation in psychological realism, perceptions of public and private time, the stream of consciousness, fragmentary narratives, than the designation 'Modernism' usually allows. Across the collection as a whole, the genres and forms discussed include Realist fiction, lyric poetry, Symbolist drama, critical essay, heroic fantasy, supernatural fiction, popular and detective fiction, epistolary writing, parody, detective fiction and painting.[36]

Paying close attention to responses to very specific historical periods such as the 1890s, the Edwardian era, the Great War and the interwar years re-sensitises us to the plurality of original voices operating beyond the Bloomsbury cultural elite. Reflecting the multiplicity, varied tones and complex nuances of these innovative voices, our chapters are gathered, in a broadly chronological order, under four main headings that identify the distinctive quality (whether it be 'unsettling', 'dissenting', 'doubling' or 'popular') of the literary and cultural voices discussed.

Our first grouping of essays centres on 'Unsettled Voices: Imaginative and Cultural Encounters' in First World War poetry and the poetic tradition from Thomas Hardy to Stephen Spender. Andrew Hodgson's opening chapter offers a reconsideration of 'Rhetoric and Feeling in Rupert Brooke'. Hodgson's subtle reading of Brooke is alert both to the ways that his poetry can, at moments, give itself over to sentimentality and the ways in which Brooke as a poet is aware of the human tendency (and need for) sentimentality licenced, for example, by his sonnet, 'The Soldier'. Such a licencing of sentimentality, for Hodgson, is a clear indicator of Brooke's opposition to the kind of poetic 'intelligence' avowed by Eliot. If Brooke's poetry is marked by an 'intelligence', it is one of tones which, as Hodgson's attentive reading shows, resides in moments of self-irony and undercutting humour that deflates gestures towards rhetorical aloofness. Ultimately, Brooke is a poet who looks squarely at the tragic limitations of the human condition, but refuses to endow personal feelings with any sense of enduring sentimentality.

Brooke's debt to the poetry of Andrew Marvell is matched by that of Wilfred Owen and Siegfried Sassoon to the Romantics. In our second chapter, Mark Sandy reflects on the diverse ways in which the strange truths of the poetry of Owen and Sassoon are imbued with the poetry of Shelley, Keats and Clare. For Sandy, Owen and Sassoon did not find in their Romantic forebears an aesthetic that was wanting in the wake of their experience of war, but one that was robust enough to communicate the strange truths of the unprecedented catastrophe of the Great War. Owen's nightmarish landscape finds affinity with Shelley's dizzying and tragic vision in *The Triumph of Life* as much as it does with Keats's fragmented 'Hyperion' epics. Equally, Sassoon's poetry is rounded out, according to Sandy, with those imaginary landscapes of Keats's Odes. The fact that the poetry of Owen and Sassoon fractured and fragmented the poetry of the Romantics does not mean that their engagement with Romanticism was a cursory phase, but that both poets were committed Romantics albeit with very tainted sensibilities.

In the final contribution to our 'Unsettled Voices' section, Michael O'Neill focuses on a strain of poetry that runs from Thomas Hardy through Edward Thomas to Stephen Spender. The three poets emphasise, often with an integrity that borders on obstinacy, the unignorable fact of subjectivity. These are poets who do not resort to Modernist uses of personae or quasi-mythic dissimulation. In them, different voices do not melt into Tiresias, or play occult games with daimons, or dwell cryptically among the ruins of literary tradition. Their poetry speaks typically of what the writer feels, even when that feeling is at odds with a culture's more modish values, as when Hardy half-defies sceptical rationalism in 'The Oxen'. O'Neill argues that these poets explore as much as they assert subjectivity; they allow for the mind's mysteries as when Edward Thomas traces back associations of a flower's smell in 'Old Man'; they concede the active role society plays in conditioning the self. Having a self is not a passport to poetic success for these writers. But it is a necessary condition of their work, one that results in powerful and affecting poetry. O'Neill analyses subjectivity as a complex state which they depict, often unsparingly, in order to probe fully the meaning of their experience. As critics such as Donald Davie and Edna Longley have argued, the legacy of Hardy and Thomas to later writers is immense, equally as important as that of the major Modernists. O'Neill's chapter seeks to explain, through precise consideration of the poetry's workings, how and why that is the case, as well as reasserting the poetic value of Spender's work.

Katharine Cockin's chapter opens our next section, focused on 'Dissenting Voices: Aestheticism, Gender, and the Art of Identity', with a reconsideration of W. B. Yeats's involvement in a short-lived hand-coloured little magazine, *The Green Sheaf* (1903). The magazine was edited by the artist Pamela Colman Smith, who became a collaborator in scene design with Ellen Terry's daughter, Edith Craig before designing one of the most famous tarot card packs in the world. The two women (self-styled 'devils') were centrally involved in both this magazine and in The Masquers, a new theatre society organised (and disbanded) in the same period. Little has been made of the relationship between these two cultural organisations. New and ephemeral cultural formations, especially clubs, societies, magazines and journals, as Cockin shows, characterised the challenging aesthetic interventions which have come to be described as 'Modernist'. Cockin rightly points up the fact that narratives of Modernist cultural forms have a tendency for the theatre to be overlooked. For Yeats, the intensity of drama meant that it was the ultimate art form, but Cockin illuminates this pivotal moment in Yeats's turn to the theatre by retrieving the influence exerted by Edith Craig and Pamela Colman Smith.

Drawing on research by Cassandra Laity, Laura Doan and Jane Garrity, Sondeep Kandola discusses the routes and pathways of 'Sapphic Modernity' by taking into account female homosociality that anticipates 'the counter-Decadent and Sapphist strains of the Modernist movement(s)'. She explores new forms of dissidence emerging from complex intertextual responses to Wilde and his generation. The first half focuses on Vernon Lee's lesbian relationship with Clementina Caroline Anstruther-Thomson, and specifically on Lee's response to Thomson's posthumously collected and published *Art and Man* (1924). Kandola reads their turn of the century experiments in 'psychological aesthetics' as a supplementary line of influence from Victorian queer sexualities to the Modernists. Consequently, Kandola explores how Lee and Thomson's theory of psychological aesthetics in its promotion of Art not for art's sake but art (Classical sculpture) as health, invigorated muscles, the psychology of corporeal response and two women in love in 1897 reads uncannily like a patchwork Modernist manifesto. In the latter part of the chapter, Kandola proposes an unlikely successor to Lee's and Thomson's work in D. H. Lawrence. In *The White Peacock* (1911) and *Women in Love* (1920), Lawrence offers a 'counter-Decadence animus' in which male homosociality has a restorative effect. Lawrence as a male writer, Kandola avows, owes a significant, though unwitting, conceptual debt to Vernon Lee and Kit Anstruther-Thomson's inimitable, if forgotten, brand of Sapphic Modernism.

In our third chapter in this section, taking John Betjeman's impromptu lyric 'On Seeing an Old Poet in the Café Royal' (1940) as his point of departure, Kostas Boyiopoulos focuses on the Arthur Symons's post-War period. It is well known that the Symons of the 1890s was a major influence on the Men of 1914. Symons outgrew what Yeats called the 'Tragic Generation' and, although was briefly lost to insanity in 1907–1908, he recovered and carried on writing throughout the Interwar years. Yet, given his earlier penchant for avant-garde cultural politics, Symons became reclusive, stubbornly recycling his Decadent themes, and did not engage in Modernist developments. Boyiopoulos's chapter sheds new light on this question by highlighting Symons's preoccupation with myth and mythmaking, which have an important role in Modernism. Through the prism of Dionysian–Apollonian paradigm (as formulated by Michael Bell), Boyiopoulos investigates Symons's imagery of Judeo-Christian mythology of his volumes *Lesbia and Other Poems* (1920), *Love's Cruelty* (1923) and *Jezebel Mort* (1931), arguing that his utterance is highly subjective and personal, juxtaposed with Eliot's 'depersonalisation'. In a lingering post-Romantic subjectivity, Symons's late verse is that of Satanic posturing, self-mirroring and embodying the object of desire. The myth of Original Sin, in its orthodox and Lilithian variations, becomes a narrative framework through which Symons wrestles with postlapsarian sexuality in its alternation between mysteriousness and crassness as he strives to comprehend and control his fractured self.

Our final chapter grouped under 'Dissenting Voices', by Margaret Stetz, re-evaluates the reputation and poetic achievement of Richard Le Gallienne, a poet known for his allegiance to a Decadent sensibility and aestheticism of the 1880–1890s. Through a series of wide-ranging and dexterous readings of Le Gallienne's poetry, Stetz finds a poet who, in spite of his unwavering Decadent aesthetic sensibilities, has a capacious and malleable imagination, capable of adapting to and accommodating a rapidly changing society and shifting cultural times and tastes. Le Gallienne's *A Jongleur Strayed: Verses on Love and Other Matters Sacred and Profane* (1922) is a kind of provocation against *BLAST*. The Futurists and the moderns disparaged Le Gallienne's nostalgic, anachronistic, Ninetyish posturing. But in his poetry, Stetz argues, he was more ambivalent towards modernity. Stetz shows that in his lyrics, such as 'Brooklyn Bridge at Dawn', Le Gallienne nods to Romanticism and Wilde but also speaks to the present moment through trasantlantism, the metropolis, and images of labouring workers and industrialism. Often branded as a poet of Paterian descent who criticised modern poets for failing to capture beauty, Stetz argues persuasively for Le Gallienne's innovations in style and subject matter as clear indicators of his alertness to the complex cultural, social and political milieus of the modernity in which he found himself.

Such surprising imaginative innovation can also be found elsewhere in the period. Luke Seaber's chapter on M. R. James in our penultimate section, titled 'Double Voices: Central and Peripheral Transactions', demonstrates the extent to which genre fiction, dismissively compartmentalised and neglected by Modernist critics, can also produce significant literary experimentation. Seaber argues that James's ghost stories deserve to be placed beyond the limitations of the 'genre ghetto' in which they are located as James merits consideration amongst those writers more clearly recognised as experimental modernists. James's originality lies in incorporating into his narrative structures 'mechanisms for reproducing textual realities extratextually at the moment of the text's consumption'. Seaber proposes an alternative to Umberto Eco's distinction between open and closed fabulae, one in which 'the end result is imposed by the fabula but the path taken to read it is not', to account for James's literary experimentation. James's extratextuality, 'his ability to foresee and control readers' actions in the world outside the text', not only provokes fear appropriate for a writer of ghost stories, but also locates James as a significant literary innovator of the early twentieth century.

If Seaber revises M. R. James, a writer of ghost stories, as a significant literary innovator, Michael Shallcross reconsiders the rather complex relationship between the anti-modernist and decidedly middlebrow G. K. Chesterton and arch-modernist T. S. Eliot. Chesterton's appeal to popular culture was often situated in binary opposition to the elitist vanguardism of Eliot. By sustaining a key metaphor from dentistry, Shallcross investigates Chesterton's parodying of Eliot and the latter's prevarications and anxieties about self-image. With the image of the gaping mouth of Modernism displaying decayed and unsightly protrusions, Chesterton engages in textual games, playing on the theme of abjection that permeates Eliot's work from *Prufrock, and Other Observations* to *The Waste Land*. The theme is augmented and given depth by the osmotic presence of such figures as E. C. Bentley for Chesterton and Wyndham Lewis for Eliot. The chapter highlights Eliot's snobbery and elitism and Chesterton's subtle critique of Modernist etiquette and 'politeness'. However, Shallcross argues that Chesterton's parodic response to Eliot in 'To A Modern Poet', like much parody, oscillates between criticism of Eliot and a sense of emotional kinship with him. Chesterton's parody attacks Eliot's ontological pessimism, his elitism and his esoteric scholarship, but also reveals identification with Eliot's poetry at the same time as it strains to establish difference.

In sympathy with Seaber and Shallcross, who take as their subject matter 'middle-brow' authors seemingly antithetical to Modernist experimentation, Kate Symondson focuses on the rather liminal Modernist figure of E. M. Forster. Her chapter explores what Virginia Woolf describes as Forster's double vision, his straddling of both Realist and the Modernist traditions as Woolf saw it, a view which in her opinion ultimately judges Forster as a failure. Symondson argues that this rather reductive view of Forster undervalues the author's own aesthetics. Indeed, Symondson argues that Forster's double vision 'is as significant and calculated a response to the conditions of early twentieth-century modernity as any other canonical, established Modernist experiments'. Forster's narrative dualism should be understood in terms of the impact of scientific discovery upon metaphysics 'as science had rendered the visible world unstable, chaotic, relative'. Thus, Forster's double vision can be reinterpreted as 'the reinstatement of the dualism that modern thinking had declared was no longer (ontologically) tenable'.

Saikat Majumdar's 'The Amateur Modernist: C. L. R. James in Bloomsbury' discusses the transactional relationship between the peripheral colonial amateur and the metropolitan centre of Modernism. By considering the figures of the amateur intellectual and the autodidact in light of *bildung* (culture), Majumdar posits that the colonial amateur subverts the 'professionalizing impulse' of the educational model in the Empire. Majumdar argues that Modernist practice was 'haunted by a sense of amateur play' originating in part by Modernism's colonial periphery. Such marginalised 'amateurs' negotiate their privately idiosyncratic worldview with the public world of colonial modernity which is strikingly embodied by literary Modernism. Deploying the figure of C. L. R. James as an example of the colonial amateur, Majumdar explicates how James's aspiration for metropolitan modernity culminates in a 'delicately fractured relationship with the ethos and practices of high Modernism' in which James's passionate engagement with literary culture transmutes into 'a critique of the lifestyle fetishised by the metropolitan literary establishment'. Paradoxically, Majumdar contests, the valorisation of the metropolitan centre in Modernist narratives of artistic migration lies seemingly at odds with a Modernist obsession with provincialism.

Our final section, 'Popular Voices: Questions of Realism, Politics, and Modernity', focuses on the somewhat vexed relationship between Realism and Modernism from three distinct perspectives, suggesting that experimentation is a key presence in popular genres not usually credited with modernist innovation. Carey Snyder argues that Wells's dismissal from the Modernist canon, clearly related to aesthetic differences between Wells and writers such as Henry James and Virginia Woolf, was also predicated on Wells's immense popularity, a popularity which, for many contemporary Modernist writers, was incompatible with serious artistic endeavour. Wells's fiction complicates the seemingly opposing terms of 'popular' and 'modern'. Snyder's analysis of the reception of *Ann Veronica* and its radical politics of 'free love' renders Wells both an outmoded Realist in terms of Modernist aesthetics and, at the same time, a distinctly modern author of cutting-edge fiction. Through charting the reception of the novel and Wells's take on 'New Woman' fiction, however outmoded his fiction might have been perceived, Snyder suggests that he was also a 'rousing, disturbing and potentially revolutionary' author.

Wells's friend, Arnold Bennett, became arguably an even greater straw man for his Modernist contemporaries than Wells. Anthony Patterson's chapter, which concentrates on Bennett's literary journalism, 'Books and Persons' in A. R. Orage's *The New Age* from 1908 until 1911 and Lord Beaverbrook's *Evening Standard* from 1926 until his death, examines Bennett's attitude to literary experimentation generally, and specifically his response to Modernist writing. Patterson maintains that Bennett lauds Chekhov's 'absolute realism' while criticising contemporary British fiction in the same way Woolf discriminates sharply between the Georgians and the Edwardians. In the latter half of the chapter, Patterson focuses on Bennett's tangled response to Joyce, his acknowledgement of *Ulysses* and sceptical assessment of *Finnegans Wake*. Bennett was invariably more open and generous to the Modernists than they were to him; his critical praise of writers such as Lawrence and Joyce, although expressing qualms about the conscious difficulty such writers created for the reader, was often superlative. Taken his career as a whole, Bennett invariably praised, encouraged and promoted innovative fiction. While appreciative of the exciting transformations Modernist writing brought to the novel, Bennett still predominantly sees it as much as part of a continuum with earlier experimentation than as a decisive break with literary tradition.

Finally, Koenraad Claes explores the occasionally overlooked Modernist figure of Ford Madox Ford by examining his tetralogy of novels *Parade's End* (1924–1928). For all of its deployment of a variety of Modernist techniques in what Ford calls 'progression d'effet' as well as pages-long sections of streams of consciousness, *Parade's End*, Claes argues, deploys literary modes from nineteenth-century Realist and 'condition of England' fiction. Through the lens of an ambiguous political ideology and by examining the Tory ideals of the protagonist, Christopher Tietjens, in relation to the disruptive forces of the First World War, Claes notes some of the meaningful parallels and inverted mirroring between the plot structure of *Parade's End* and that of Benjamin Disraeli's *Sybil*, Walter Scott's historical romances and the writings of Humphrey Ward. By so doing, Claes shows that 'the novel's thematic preoccupation with the legacy of the nineteenth-century is also represented in its formal features'. For Claes, *Parade's End* is 'an adaptation of Romantic and Victorian models to the aesthetic demands and political expectations of the post-War era'.

This repurposing of cardinal cultural instances in literary history and questioning of those categories (such as Modernism, Romanticism and Victorianism) that seek to contain and define literary periods and their artistic imaginings in isolated splendour is central to all of the essays collected in this volume. As in our concluding contribution, we as editors are also mindful of the organised plotting of literary forms and genres by Northorp Frye and Alastair Fowler. In Frye's model of 'high mimetic', 'low mimetic' and ironic modes, the Poundian 'make it new' is just another category.[37] Our rereading of pre-Second World War voices finds an apposite model in Fowler's postmodern revisionism of the idea of the canon and his rejection of hierarchical taxonomies:

> [B]eside this more recent canon – which includes Hawthorne, Melville, James, and Conrad (in new aspects), as well as Woolf and Beckett – we already glimpse further "alternative traditions" based on emergent or previously uncanonical genres: the dystopic fantasy (Pynchon, Vonnegut), the fabulation (Barth, Barthelme), the *poioumenon* (*The Golden Notebook*), the historical novel of ideas (*The French Lieutenant's Woman; G*).[38]

Such a notion of 'alternative traditions' resonates with the spirit of our present project. Niche genres and analogous formal phenomena overlapped especially in the first half of the twentieth century. Examples include historical fiction (Robert Graves), utopian/dystopian fiction (Wells, Aldous Huxley, Katharine Burdekin), Neo-Aestheticism (Harold Acton, Evelyn Waugh), Weird Fiction (Arthur Machen), high fantasy (Lord Dunsany), spy fiction (W. Somerset Maugham), popular fantasy magazines and revivalist poetry labelled by prefixes such as neo- and post-. We hold up such peripheral phenomena as the flipside to the Modernist *zeitgeist*, in the same way Steven Marcus in *The Other Victorians* (1966), for example, highlights subcutaneous subversive voices against the canon of nineteenth-century literature and culture. We might not hold entirely that 'things fall apart', but we firmly believe that the 'centre' of Modernism, as Yeats writes in his whirling phantasmagoric, Romantic, apocalyptic, vision of the early twentieth century, 'cannot hold'.[39]

Notes

1 Frank Kermode, 'Modernisms', *Encounter 3* (March 1966): 53–59; 53, 54.
2 Peter Nicholls explores what he calls 'anti-modernism' or an 'often polemic disturbance within the canonical version' of Anglo-American Modernism, by examining phenomena such as William Carlos Williams's New York scene and Mina Loy's verbalism. Peter Nicholls, *Modernisms: A Literary Guide*, 2nd ed. (1995; Basingstoke: Palgrave Macmillan, 2009), p. 193. See chapter titled 'At a Tangent: Other Modernisms', pp. 189–218.
3 Wyndham Lewis, *Blasting and Bombardiering* (1937; Berkeley and Los Angeles, CA: U of California P, 1967), p. 9. See also pp. 249–52.
4 Wyndham Lewis, *The Apes of God* (1930; Santa Barbara, CA: Black Sparrow P, 1984), p. 123. Italics in the original.
5 Rebecca West, *Strange Necessity: Essays and Reviews* (London: Jonathan Cape, 1928), p. 199.
6 Thomas Stearns Eliot, *The Complete Prose of T. S. Eliot: The Critical Edition: The War Years: 1940–1946*, vol. 6, eds. David E. Chinitz and Ronald Schuchard (Baltimore: Johns Hopkins UP, 2017), p. 171. Hereby abbreviated as *CPTSE*. See also Eliot's letter to John Hayward on 21 April 1941 on Woolf. Eliot wrote that Woolf was the 'pin' that held everyone together,

and now that she is gone, he will become a ghost in an 'alien, plebeian and formless society' (*CPTSE* 6, 172, n.4).

7 Thomas Stearns Eliot, *The Complete Prose of T. S. Eliot: The Critical Edition: The Perfect Critic, 1919–1926*, vol. 2, eds. Anthony Cuda and Ronald Schuchard (Baltimore, MD: Johns Hopkins UP, 2014), p. 212.

8 Malcolm Bradbury and James McFarlane, eds., *Modernism: A Guide to European Literature 1890–1930* (London: Penguin, 1976), p. 29.

9 See Michel Foucault, 'What Is an Author?' (1969) in Michel Foucault, *The Foucault Reader*, ed. Paul Rabinow (1984; Harmondsworth: Penguin, 1987), pp. 101–20.

10 F. R. Leavis, *Mass Civilization and Minority Culture* (Cambridge: The Minority P, 1930), p. 24.

11 For a mapping of the multiplicity and variety of writers of the Twenties, loosely united by a sharp sense of time and the past, see Chris Baldick's, *Literature of the 1920s: Writers among the Ruins* (Edinburgh: Edinburgh UP, 2012).

12 George Orwell, *Inside the Whale and Other Essays* (London: Gollancz, 1940), p. 152.

13 See Orwell, p. 153.

14 Wyndham Lewis, *Time and Western Man* (1927; Boston, MA: Beacon P, 1957), p. 25. In this work, by darting his critiques at Joyce, Gertrude Stein and Pound, Lewis criticises the focus of modernity on 'time-cult' initiated by Louis Bergson, favouring discourse of the Romantic impulse of history, change and the past at the expense of the Classical impulse of spatiality.

15 Virginia Woolf, *Selected Essays*, ed. David Bradshaw (Oxford: Oxford UP, 2008), p. 12.

16 Virginia Woolf, *The Question of Things Happening: The Letters of Virginia Woolf: Volume II: 1912–1922*, ed. Nigel Nicolson (London: The Hogarth P, 1976), pp. 550–1.

17 Herbert George Wells, *The Correspondence of H. G. Wells: Volume 3: 1919–1934*, ed. David C. Smith (London: Pickering & Chatto, 1998), p. 277.

18 Edward Morgan Forster, *Aspects of the Novel* (1927; Harmondsworth: Penguin, 1970), p. 125.

19 Aldous Huxley, *Music at Night and Other Essays* (1931; London: Chatto and Windus, 1970), pp. 212–3.

20 Robert Graves, *Good-bye to All That* (1929; London: Penguin, 1960, rpt. 2000), p. 251.

21 Eliot, 'Modern Tendencies in Poetry', *CPTSE* 2, p. 219.

22 Raymond Mortimer, 'London Letter' in *The Bloomsbury Group: A Collection of Memoirs and Commentary*, ed. S. P. Rosenbaum, ed., rev. ed. (Toronto, ON: U of Toronto P, 1995), pp. 309–12, p. 311.

23 Stead in *The New Poetic: Yeats to Eliot* (1964) considered the Georgians and the Imperialists as important as Yeats, Pound and especially Eliot.

24 James Reeves, 'Introduction' [written 1960], in *Georgian Poetry*, James Reeves, ed., (Hamondsworth, Essex; Ringwood, Victoria: Penguin, 1962; rpt. 1968), pp. xi–xxiii, pp. xix–xx.

25 Edward Marsh, ed., *Georgian Poetry: 1920–1922* (London: The Poetry Bookshop, 1922), n.p.

26 Aptéryx [T. S. Eliot], 'Verse Pleasant and Unpleasant', *The Egoist*, 3.5 (March 1918): 43–4, p. 43.

27 William Butler Yeats, chosen by and ed. *The Oxford Book of Modern Verse: 1892–1935* (1936; Oxford: Oxford UP, 1955), p. viii.

28 Virginia Woolf, *Collected Essays, I* (London: The Hogarth P, 1966), p. 320.

29 Michael Roberts, ed., *The Faber Book of Modern Verse* (London: Faber and Faber, [1936]), pp. 7–8.
30 Rachel Bowlby, 'Foreword', *Adventures in Realism*, ed. Matthew Beaumont (Oxford: Blackwell, 2007), p. vii.
31 Robert Squillace, *Modernism, Modernity and Arnold Bennett* (Lewisberg, PA: Bucknell UP, 1997), p. 17.
32 Brian Richardson, 'Remapping the Present: The Master Narrative of Modern Literary History and the Lost Forms of Twentieth-Century Fiction,' *Twentieth-Century Literature* 43.3 (1997): 291–309.
33 Douglas Mao and Rebecca L. Walkowitz, eds., *Bad Modernisms* (Durham, NC: Duke UP, 2006), p. 2.
34 Douglas Mao and Rebecca L. Walkowitz, 'New Modernist Studies', *PMLA*, 123.3 (May 2008): 737–48, p. 737.
35 See Borges, *Labyrinths: Selected Stories and Other Writings*, eds. Donald A. Yates and James E. Irby (1964; London: Penguin, 2000), p. 228.
36 In its conceptual framework and concerns, our volume shares common ground with another, recent collection of essays: Anthony Patterson and Yoonjoung Choi, eds., *We Speak a Different Tongue: Maverick Voices and Modernity, 1890–1939* (Newcastle upon Tyne: Cambridge Scholars, 2015).
37 Northrop Frye, 'Historical Criticism: Theory of Modes' in *Anatomy of Criticism: Four Essays* (Princeton, NJ: Princeton UP, 1957), p. 34 *passim*.
38 Alastair Fowler, *Kinds of Literature: An Introduction to the Theory of Genres and Modes* (1982; Oxford: Oxford UP, 2002), p. 233.
39 William Butler Yeats, *W. B, Yeats: The Major Works*, ed. Edward Larrissy. 1997. (Oxford: Oxford UP, 2001), 'The Second-Coming', p. 91.

Part I
Unsettled Voices
Imaginative and Cultural Encounters

1 Rhetoric and Feeling in Rupert Brooke

Andrew Hodgson

Trying to account for the faculty by which modern poets had 'avoided rhetoric', T. S. Eliot arrived at his celebrated remark about 'the exercise of intelligence, of which an important function is the discernment of exactly what, and how much, we feel in any given situation'. The insight rounds off a review of Harriet Monroe and Alice Corbin Henderson's 1917 anthology *The New Poetry*, a volume Eliot welcomes tepidly for being representative, as much as for being any good. The book, as Eliot observes, gathers a rabble of 'incongruous allies' in a generational effort to 'wring the neck of rhetoric'—a phrase of Verlaine's that ricocheted from writer to writer in the earlier years of the century, and indicated, in the terms of the anthology's editors, an effort to puncture Victorian sonorities on the thorns of 'concrete and immediate realisation of life' and 'absolute simplicity and sincerity'.[1] Enlisted in its ranks are figures of lasting and varied achievement, including Thomas Hardy, D. H. Lawrence and Ezra Pound, alongside many long and justly forgotten: Skipwith Connell, Grace Hazard Conkling and Adelaide Crapsey are among those whose names contain more poetry than their works, and that is only the Cs. Eliot runs through the contents with an eyebrow raised, discriminating favourably (Robert Frost's New England 'is not a New England of ghosts; Mr Frost has done something of his own') and more equivocally (as when he describes Maxwell Bodenheim as having 'not all the qualities of a poet, but some of them in an exceptionally high degree'), before a final, tart survey of the English contribution: 'Of the English poets, Mr [Ford Madox] Hueffer is well illustrated by the only good poem I have met with on the subject of the war; Harold Monro is at his best in the "Strange Companion"; Lawrence, a poet of quite peculiar genius and peculiar faults, comes off badly; and Rupert Brooke is not absent'.[2]

The Rupert Brooke present in the anthology is the poet of the patriotic 1914 sonnets, a group whose defining poem, 'The Soldier', depends upon the opposite of 'intelligence' as Eliot defined it. The famous sonnet twice invites its reader to 'think', but, not in the service of discerning 'exactly what, and how much, we feel in any given situation':

> If I should die, think only this of me:
>   That there's some corner of a foreign field
> That is for ever England.
> [...]
> And think, this heart, all evil shed away,
>   A pulse in the eternal mind, no less
>   Gives somewhere back the thoughts by England given;[3]

It does not matter whether what this poem asks the reader to think is true, only that the reader convinces himself that it is. Brooke offers a patriotic ideal seductive precisely because it repels and eludes thought ('think *only* this'), and because it does not demand 'exactness' at all ('gives *somewhere* back' [emphases added]). The fact that the poem's patriotic blandishments should segue seamlessly into Churchill's *Times* eulogy for Brooke, which praised a man 'willing to die for the dear England whose beauty and majesty he knew' and who 'advanced towards the brink in perfect serenity, with absolute conviction of the rightness of his country's cause',[4] only affirms its proficiency in just the sort of rhetoric whose 'neck' Eliot and his contemporaries were seeking to 'wring'.

But the urge to deride Brooke's sentimentality should be restrained. 'The Soldier' indulges sentimental rhetoric, but there are times when sentimental rhetoric can be sustaining, and at the time of its inclusion in Monroe and Henderson's anthology in 1917, Brooke's sonnet offered thousands of readers consolation. Moreover, the poem shows Brooke's ear for popular feeling; and while 'The Soldier' submits to that feeling with dangerous ease, the way the poem licences sentiment points to a tendency which in Brooke's best poetry becomes part of a more complex mix. At times, Brooke succumbs to sentimentality, but he is also responsive to the human tendency to succumb. The closing lines of 'The Night Journey' envision human life as a flow of delirious individuals, each in an accelerating quest 'to meet the light or find his love' (l. 10):

> The white lights roar; the sounds of the world die;
>
> And lips and laughter are forgotten things.
>   Speed sharpens; grows. Into the night, and on,
> The strength and splendour of our purpose swings.
>   The lamps fade; and the stars. We are alone.
>
> (ll. 24–8)

The final sentence affirms the fruitlessness of the impulse. But Brooke speaks as one of 'end-drunken huddled dreamers' (l. 23) he describes, and the way his rhythms and syntax become whipped up in their excitement generates a vigour which transcends rhetoric through its very liberation from 'intelligence', and which causes the final realisation to arrive with an almost terrifying frisson. The lines expose a sentimental delusion but they also show the thrill of partaking in it. In an essay characteristic of the generally low estimation of Brooke's achievement that followed Eliot into the remainder of the twentieth century, Samuel Hynes records how 'In a rare moment of self-criticism Brooke composed a table of contents for an imaginary anthology, to which his own contribution was to be "Oh, Dear! oh, Dear! A Sonnet"', remarking that it is 'very perceptive, for nearly half of his poems are conventional sonnets, and most of them [...] say little more than "Oh dear!"'.[5] The exercise would more profitably be regarded not as a 'rare moment of self-criticism' but as an instance of characteristic self-awareness. Brooke is often knowing about his abandon. His poems court 'rhetoric', in the *OED*'s sense of 'artificial, insincere, or ostentatious expression' in subtle as well as unsubtle ways: a line like 'the strength and splendour of our purpose' is the more stirring for the way it strains against Brooke's consciousness of its grandiloquence. A supple intelligence, human susceptibility and surrender to feeling lies behind the wit, sympathy and daring of his best writing.

The fact that Brooke should write poetry so antithetical to Eliot is in one respect odd, since Brooke, like Eliot, was an enthusiastic champion of the Metaphysicals, Donne in particular; and the qualities he admired bear striking similarity to the passionate 'intelligence' Eliot held up for approval. The terms of Brooke's enthusiasm in his reviews of Grierson's edition of *The Poems of John Donne* (1912) might well have been Eliot's own: 'He belonged to an age when men were not afraid to mate their intellects with their emotions'; 'He was the one English love-poet who was not afraid to acknowledge that he was composed of body, soul, and mind'; and again: 'when passion shook him, and his being ached for utterance, to relieve the stress, the expression came through the intellect'.[6] This in 1913, eight years before Eliot's 'The Metaphysical Poets'. All of which may be to say no more than that Eliot condensed ideas about English poetry that already existed in the intellectual atmosphere early in the century. And it is true that Brooke's poems never really aim at a Donne-like fusion of thought and passion. The poem in which Donne's influence on Brooke is most apparent, 'Dining-Room Tea', makes clear the difference in their manners. The very un-Donne-like title attests to Brooke's filtering of metaphysical speculation through a distinctively Edwardian setting and sensibility (the poem dates from 1909). 'One imagines a young man who has been reading Donne's "The Ecstasy" in a room upstairs [...] being summoned by a decorous bell to join the family for a meal. He goes down to the dining-room with one of the great love poems of the world still murmuring in the back of his head, enters the Edwardian social scene [...] and walks straight into an imaginative experience which makes a deep impression on him', comments Christopher Hassall.[7] This is helpful as an account both of the action of the poem and its creation, as Brooke translates Donne's impassioned intricacy and intimacy to a more sociable idiom. Brooke's speaker encounters a girl across the table, and the poem catches her impression of him in couplets which are at once graceful and agile:

> And lifted clear and still and strange
> From the dark woven flow of change
> Under a vast and starless sky
> I saw the immortal moment lie.
> One instant I, an instant, knew
> As God knows all. And it and you
> I, above Time, oh, blind! could see
> In witless immortality.
> I saw the marble cup; the tea,
> Hung on the air, an amber stream...
>
>   (ll. 17–26)

Comparison between the two poems might seem to prove Eliot's point about 'intelligence'. Donne's poem thinks through an experience that 'Interinanimates two souls' ('The Ecstasy' (l. 42))[8] with an intensity which drives him to forge a new language for feeling; Brooke's speaker is in thrall to his passions, his voice modulating between genuine wonder and a stock language of 'vast and starless' skies. Rather than scrutinising 'exactly what, and how much, he feels', Brooke celebrates a moment of 'witlessness'—a movement beyond thought of more Keatsian than Metaphysical cast.

But 'Dining-Room Tea' is not straightforwardly rhetorical, or without emotional complexity. The fact that Brooke should have thought admiringly of Donne in the terms that he did hardly suggests a poet blind to the possibilities of bringing the intellect to bear on the emotions; and some of his most suggestive commentators have wondered with more even-handedness than Eliot about his poetry's combination of the head and the heart. Edward Thomas, for instance, wrote to Robert Frost that Brooke 'was a rhetorician' because he 'could only think about his feeling', rather than think through it—or indeed actually feel it[9]; yet Thomas also described Brooke's poetry in a review as 'full of the thought, the aspiration, the indignation of youth; full of the praise of youth',[10] which implies that if anything Brooke felt his feelings all too readily. One route to reconciling the contradiction is to say that Brooke's poems are often interested in the spectacle of feeling, an argument that Peter Howarth has pursued in relation to Brooke's engagement with Roger Fry's idea in his 'Essay in Aesthetics' (1909) that 'In the imaginative life [...] we can both feel the emotion and watch it'.[11] Howarth takes up Fry's argument as a way of thinking about Brooke's poems' 'tacit internalisation' of audience in relation to nascent ideas of celebrity;[12] but Brooke's interest in Fry's conception of art as an agent of detachment as well as expression gestures towards the peculiar self-consciousness of his poetic voice, too. Brooke glimpses the ironic possibilities of self-observation in a whimsical contemplation of his own cannibalisation sent to Violet Asquith in 1913: 'Of the two eyes that were your ruin, / One now observes the other stewing'.[13] 'Dining Room-Tea' is the fruit of a more sustained application of Fry's notion: the poem itself is about the elevation of experience to the status of art, a process which enables its speaker simultaneously to 'feel' and 'watch' his emotions and to speak out of 'witless' rapture while avoiding self-indulgence—preserving what Bernard Bergonzi called Brooke's 'saving irony and detachment of mind'.[14] Brooke's voice marries exuberance with elusive self-irony. The lines above surrender to feeling with an authenticating dexterity which makes it difficult to know how to respond. The rhythms of 'I, above Time, oh, blind! could see' discompose the metre almost entirely, in step with the fluster in their speaker: but whether this fluster is to be laughed at, or to be taken as a token of the veracity of his immersion in an 'immortal moment' which transcends rhetoric is uncertain. Throughout, the poem's attitudes are nimble—now partaking in the ecstasies of its protagonist, now hinting at their incongruity with the situation, and ultimately balancing levity and sadness with surprising dexterity. A suggestion that the speaker's raptures have outgrown their domestic setting is already asserting itself in the imagery at the end of these lines, which even as they begin to elaborate on the way the timeless moment overtakes the whole room dilute its 'immortality' in a rhyme with 'tea'. Howarth draws comparison with an unpublished paper of Brooke's in which he speaks in Keatsian mood of 'The Kingdom of Art' in which 'All things are taken out of the flux for ever. They are themselves. They intensely are'.[15] Framing it in the dizzying comedy of being a work of art about the transfiguration of experience into art, Brooke's poem transfigures the portentousness of that essay into a simultaneously more wondering and more self-aware idiom: as his vision of the woman as 'august, immortal, white, / Holy and strange' (ll. 39–40) works to a climax, the speaker's tangible passion and the scale of his world are made to pull against one another with a deftness which calls to mind a more reserved manifestation of the metaphysical imagination than Donne's—that of Andrew Marvell. Brooke's affinity with Marvell shows above all in 'Dining-Room Tea' as a quality of tone which is intimate with Brooke's handling of Marvell's favoured form, the tetrameter couplet. The verse steps with inscrutable care as Brooke describes how the climactic vision of the poem subsides, and time unfreezes:

> The cup was filled. The bodies moved.
> The drifting petal came to ground.
> The laughter chimed its perfect round.

> The broken syllable was ended.
> And I, so certain and so friended,
> How could I cloud, or how distress
> The heaven of your unconsciousness?
>
> (ll. 49–55)

The self-conscious gait of the couplets (their measured endstopping, the preposterousness of rhyming of 'ended' against 'friended' (in lines which draw attention to syllables)), along with the whimsical precision of the imagery, at once realise and send up the earnestness of Brooke's lover as he steps out of his 'immortal moment' and towards the question of whether to 'distress' his bliss by informing the woman of his infatuation. The question is ludicrous and self-defeating, but it is also genuine. It is difficult to know whether to force a moment to its crisis and risk rejection (a Prufrockian dilemma, in its local way), and the attitude of the poem seems to be that it is better on balance to leave things be: it ends with the speaker rejoining the group in the dining room and living 'from laugh to laugh' (l. 68). Yet, in the light of the speaker's question, it is hard to see the mood as the end of the poem as being quite so happily reconciled. The final thought directed towards the girl is that 'You never knew that I had gone / A million miles away, and stayed / A million years' (ll. 61–3), which makes the escape that has been the occasion for bliss throughout the poem come all of a sudden to seem oddly and sadly isolating. 'The laughter played / Unbroken round me' (ll. 63–4) says Brooke's speaker, observing the hearty spirits resume, but with at least a whisper of an intimation that his mood has the potential to 'break' them.

'Dining-Room Tea' stands both within and without an experience of overwhelming happiness. The poem shows Brooke as the possessor of a deft humour of a sort which is ready to ironise his poetry's commitment to a feeling, but without dispelling that feeling. Brooke's observation that 'as Donne saw everything through his intellect, it follows, in some degree, that he could see everything humorously' applies to his own poetry.[16] Brooke's poems are often self-conscious about their own rhetoric—but that very self-consciousness licenses them to commit to it further. The best-known instance of this ambivalence is the quintessentially 'Georgian' 'The Old Vicarage, Grantchester'. The question surrounding the poem is whether it knows how 'quintessentially Georgian' it is being. Its home thoughts from abroad certainly provoke rhetoric of the most tub-thumping kind—'For England's the one land, I know, / Where men with Splendid Hearts may go' (ll. 73–4), and so on—from which Brooke beat a retreat when he changed the poem's title from the original, straight-faced, 'Home' to 'Fragments of a Poem to be entitled The Sentimental Exile'. But the deliberate underplaying of feeling can be sentimental, too, and the clumsy defensiveness of that second title betrays the veracity of the poem's initial impulse, which manifests itself not only in jingoism but also in couplets of weirdly hypnotic pastoral which evinces a true feeling for place: the description of how the Grantchester chestnuts make 'A tunnel of green gloom, and sleep / Deeply above; and green and deep / The stream mysterious glides beneath, / Green as a dream and deep as a death' (ll. 9–12), for instance, in which the rhyming goes so far beyond excess that its ostensible ludicrousness warps into haunted entrancement with a world that seems to transcend its own reality. The poem's best writing both commits to and mocks the products of its nostalgia, as at the poem's questioning close, in which yearning and embarrassment entwine:

> Say, is there Beauty yet to find?
> And Certainty? And quiet kind?
> Deep meadows yet, for to forget
> The lies, and truths, and pain? ... Oh! yet
> Stands the Church clock at ten to three?
> And is there honey still for tea?
>
> (ll. 137–42)

You will find no shortage of readers lined up to mock these lines for their lack of intelligence; but to do so is to fail to respond to them with sufficient intelligence oneself. 'Grantchester' is a poem, in David Perkins' words, in which 'one both shares and laughs at the emotion'[17]; and it succeeds again for not being quite as sure as it first seems about what it feels. It is not that the lines are to be understood as 'placed' exactly (to disavow the emotion would be just as rhetorical a pose as to back it completely) but rather that, as the questioning is pushed to a crisis, a discrepancy opens up between the urgency of the voice ('Oh! yet') and the tweeness of the questions it poses which it is possible to hear as inviting amusement, as much as endorsement. Again, 'intelligence' enters as a property of tone, a note of humour which enriches rather than corrodes the feeling.

Eliot identified in metaphysical poetry an 'alliance of levity with seriousness (by which the seriousness is intensified)'.[18] If, for all their deftness of tone, neither 'Dining-Room Tea' nor 'Grantchester' achieves the poise or pathos of Marvell, that is because they are not sufficiently serious to begin with. The levity is required because to take the poem's attitudes entirely seriously would expose them to ridicule; Perkins puts it best: 'seriousness is not intensified in Brooke but it is combined with play and joke, perhaps permitted by them'.[19] This is true, too, of what is perhaps Brooke's most accomplished satirical poem, 'Heaven'. But the effect here is different, because the original position is one of levity, into which seriousness intrudes. Brooke's unflattering conceit catches the naïve rhetoric of religious optimism in couplets which move fluidly between keeping a check on sentimental optimism and arriving at momentary glimpses of sympathy with the hopefulness they ostensibly satirise. The opening lines give an instance of how the verse keeps alert intelligence and lyric grace in dialogue, as their syntax and punctuation swim against the tide of apparently over easy rhyming:

> Fish (fly-replete, in depth of June,
> Dawdling away their wat'ry noon)
> Ponder deep wisdom, dark or clear
> Each secret fishy hope or fear.
>
> (ll. 1–4)

It would be stretching it to describe a punctuation mark as 'witty', but the parenthesis that opens up one word into this poem immediately signals an imagination ready to send up its own impulses and deviate from anticipated turns of thought; a more surface-level sort of wordplay perhaps ripples through '*Ponder* deep'. Brooke's register moves with the poem's glancing changes in mood, flitting in these lines from pedantic description to hyperbole to a half-amused, half-indulgent childishness, so that it is never quite clear on what level the voice ought to be engaged. The poem brings adult scepticism to bear on 'fishy' confidence in an afterlife; and yet its tone and language is such that if it mocks the childishness behind such faith, it remains sympathetic to the impulse:

> But somewhere, beyond Space and Time,
> Is wetter water, slimier slime!
> And there (they trust) there swimmeth One
> Who swam ere rivers were begun,
> Immense, of fishy form and mind,
> Squamous, omnipotent, and kind;
> And under that Almighty Fin,
> The littlest fish may enter in.
>
> (ll. 17–24)

The relationship of this writing with 'rhetoric' is slippery. Its target is a kind of sentimental self-delusion; and again Brooke deploys parenthesis to puncture it: his '(they trust)' is a descendent of Marvell's 'I think' in 'To His Coy Mistress' and his cool '(perhaps)' in 'Bermudas'. While the parentheses lack Marvell's urbanity, there remains a delicacy to their deployment: yes, there is the implication that the trust is misplaced, but the remark acknowledges a pathos in the misapprehension, too. The lines show how 'intelligence' might involve not just the curtailment of feeling, but also its considered extension. The easy course would be to satirise the naivety: instead, the lines move between exposing that naivety and courting sympathy for the fishes' hopes. The description of the imagined deity as 'Squamous, omnipotent, and kind' is one example: the play between the grotesque description of the God's scaliness and the more modest vision of him as someone 'kind' is very winning. The last lines quoted again balance humour with pathos: their vision is reductively bland, and yet it is again hard not to be at least in part won round by their innocent wish for a world where even 'the littlest fish' wins acceptance.

Brooke's poems are simultaneously caustic and compassionate about the human propensity for sentimentality. His most persistent theme is Romantic love, a topic which provides no shortage of opportunities for skewering self-delusion. But G. Wilson Knight is only half-right when he describes Brooke's poems as being written 'against' love.[20] Certainly, the poems generate sparks by puncturing starry-eyed rhetoric in a spirit of 'realism', but they are rarely blind, either, to passion's genuine allure—even if that allure is often apprehended negatively, through apertures on the possibility of its disappearance, as in the vision of the love-bereft face 'Lonelier and dreadfuller than sunlight is / And dumb and mad and eyeless like the sky' at the close of 'Town and Country' (ll. 31–2). A more down-to-earth vision of the transience of Romantic feeling is on show in Brooke's neatest account of Romantic self-delusion, 'Sonnet Reversed'. The poem is usually seen as effective if one-dimensional 'squib', in Nigel Jones's words,[21] a literary joke about the materialism and aridity of suburban life framed through a gloomy look into what 'Menelaus and Helen', a double sonnet on a similar theme, calls the 'long connubial years' (l. 16). And there is an inventive literary wit at work in the way the poem upturns the attitudes to feeling associated with the sonnet along with the structure of the form:

> Hand trembling towards hand; the amazing lights
> Of heart and eye. They stood on supreme heights.
>
> Ah, the delirious weeks of honeymoon!
> Soon they returned, and, after strange adventures,
> Settled at Balham by the end of June.
> Their money was in Can. Pacs. B. Debentures,
> And in Antofagastas. Still he went
> Cityward daily; still she did abide
> At home. And both were really quite content
> With work and social pleasures. Then they died.
> They left three children (besides George, who drank):
> The eldest Jane, who married Mr Bell,
> William, the head-clerk in the County Bank,
> And Henry, a stock-broker, doing well.

The writing seems at first almost over-determined to stamp out sentiment. The rhymes that breathe new weariness into the 'moon'/'June' pairing and set the exoticism of 'strange adventures' against the name of an overseas investment fund, the sense, in syntax of the central quatrain, of how the rhythms of a life fall out of and in with the form's established patterns, and the bathos of the ending all mock the overblown promises of Romantic love, whose fruit, eventually, is simply someone 'doing well'. But the humour works, as in 'Heaven', because Brooke leaves breathing space for understanding. The wit is not targeted at the couple themselves. There is no sneering at being 'quite content / With work and social pleasures', for all their meagre charm (partly, perhaps, because as Bristow suggests, Brooke himself was conscious of his susceptibility to being drawn into an urban life after which, as he put it in a 1909 letter, 'we shall swollenly stupidly and uninterestedly—*die!*')[22]; nor is there any sense that the lives are doomed by the bad feeling Hardy called describing a similar scenario with a determined grimness which must have struck even him a bit much, 'wedlock's aftergrinds' ('Honeymoon Time at an Inn' (l. 40)).[23] Instead, the comedy comes from the contrast of life's mundane details with the burst of Romantic feeling with which the poem starts, and which, in marriage, seems to promise or to speak from a plane higher than the everyday circumstances in which life will be carried out. And yet, the poem knows that this plane of feeling also counts. The 'magic' of marriage may be illusory, but people feel it nonetheless; and Brooke's opening lines dramatise it with boldness and sparseness. The impact of the opening ensures that the line on which the tone of the poem pivots, 'Ah, the delirious weeks of honeymoon!', is open to being voiced with genuine wistfulness as well as cynicism. The poem puts its heart into the rhetoric it exposes.

Brooke's most infamous attacks on love invert rather than debunk the intensity of passionate feeling. 'A Channel Passage' is usually seen as a somewhat timid attempt at roughing up the gentility and decorum of literary culture in a manner that matches Brooke's praise of Marston as a writer who 'loved dirt for truth's sake; also for its own'.[24] In this spirit, the poem engages in some no-holds-barred evocations of seasickness: 'Retchings twist and tie me, / Old meat, good meals, brown gobbets, up I throw' (ll. 9–10). The archly inverted syntax hardly matches the down-to-earth spirit of its imagery, you might think—though a case could be made that the speaker is supposed to have thrown natural word order up in the air with the contents of his stomach. But, as critics have long observed, such 'rebelliousness' fails because its unpleasantness reaffirms the codes of refinement it seeks to disrupt (Brooke's publisher Edward Marsh objected to Brooke's attempts at ugliness on the grounds that he favoured poems which he could read over supper).[25] But alongside the poem's surface grotesquery is a more substantial effort to give to a true voice to a feeling which upsets the usual rhetoric and niceties of courtship. 'A Channel Passage' is not just an account of a bout of seasickness, but an effort to draw the feelings of seasickness side by side with those of being in love, or rather of being tortured by lost love; and it is in its passionate expression of this unhappy side of the emotion that the poem succeeds in cutting loose from rhetoric. The comparison is given force by the way Brooke plays the urge to recoil from past feeling against the directness of the poem's address. 'I must think hard of something, or be sick / And could think hard of only one thing – *you*! / You, you alone could hold my fancy ever' (ll. 3–5), says Brooke, grasping for distraction in his opening stanza. The last of those lines might seem to put things in all too mushy a manner, but the 'hold' the lover has on Brooke is not a matter of enchantment but rather 'sharp pain' (l. 6), and, by the end of the poem, disgust. 'Do I forget you?' he asks (l. 9): well then the nausea comes on; 'Do I remember?' well then 'Acrid return and slimy, / The sobs and slobber of last year's woe' (ll. 12–13). The consciousness articulated here is not particularly thoughtful about the nature of feeling, but the language describes a mind buffeted between feelings with a visceral power; 'sobs and slobber' catches in its slippery alliteration a mess of emotions: both infatuation and scorn of infatuation; and the overall effect is of a voice freed from artifice and insincerity not through the exercise of 'intelligence' but rather its sense of how feelings overwhelm the individual. The potency is spoiled by the closing lines, whose attempt at Byronic insouciance tries to engineer a levity that does not come off—in part, because the attempt at colloquialism ('I tell ye') does not ring true, in part because it shows Brooke straining for a flippancy which feels rhetorical in light of the intensity of revulsion in the rest of the poem: ''Tis hard, I tell ye, / To choose 'twixt love and nausea, heart and belly' (ll. 13–14). The poem's vehemence is contained within a situation that is inherently comic; this attempt to diffuse the histrionics is both extraneous and bashful.

'Jealousy' is another poem which proceeds from the principle that corrosive feelings are less likely to provoke rhetoric than warm-hearted ones. The emotions the poem deals with—jealousy that a partner has taken another lover, gleeful contemplation of their future decrepitude—are not admirable ones, but the poem itself is admirable for the honesty with which it confesses them. Any consideration of 'what, and how much one feels in any given situation' goes out of the window here; instead, Brooke's writing exhilarates on account of its expression of a mind in the grip of feeling. And not only that, but a mind in the grip of feeling about another mind in the grip of feeling:

> I know
> You holiest dreams yield to the stupid bow
> Of his red lips, and that the empty grace
> Of those strong legs and arms; that rosy face,
> Has beaten your heart to such a flame of love,
> That you have given him every touch and move,
> Wrinkle and secret of you...
>
> (ll. 5–11)

The power of these lines derives from their entanglement of contraries: the play of the speaker's disgust against the subject's delight, and the poet's intimacy with her thoughts and feeling against the feeling of distance from them. The anguish is relieved by the turn in the poem, which is towards a boastful anticipation of 'the great time when love is at a close' (l. 13) and she starts clocking up his imperfections ('The greasier tie, the dingy wrinkling coat' (l. 18)) and suffering some of her own ('the thickening nose / And sweaty neck' (ll. 14–15)); and then, further:

> When all that's fine in man is at an end,
> And you, that loved young life and clean, must tend
> A foul and sick fumbling dribbling body and old,
> When his rare lips hand flabby and can't hold
> Slobber...
>
> (ll. 21–5)

It is a revolting enjambment, the poem's form asking us to mouth what it describes. No thought checks the feeling here, but there is apparently no rhetoric either: the lines give true voice to the malice.

Yet, for all its ferocity, 'Jealousy' suffers for its single-mindedness. Once the tension between pain and contempt that sustains the first set of lines quoted has vanished, its mood turns ugly—the poem becomes a mean-spirited exultation in the disintegration of 'love, love, love to habit!' (l. 20) without any saving irony. The comedy is all at the service of invective rather than self-awareness. Unlike in 'Channel Crossing', no staging diverts attention between the emotion as felt from within and its effect on the speaker from the outside. Brooke said in a letter to Edward Marsh in 1912 that the idea that poetry should be 'naïve & a cry from the heart' is 'the sort of thing an inspired child might utter if it was in the habit of posing to its elders'.[26] He forgets that principle in 'Jealousy'; the poem is so eager to advertise its 'honesty' that the ugliness becomes in itself a sort of rhetoric. Brooke achieves a more truthful and more humane vision when the feeling in his poems is more ambiguous, and his writing more self-conscious about the human tendency to be swept away by passion. Among the handful of poems which commit a similar energy as 'Jealousy' to healthier emotions, for instance, 'The Hill' is thoughtful about the kind of truth enjoyed by things said and felt in the heat of passion. The poem is ostensibly an exposure of the hollowness of its two 'Breathless' (l. 1) lovers who cast 'intelligence'—and self-consciousness about the veracity of their feeling—to the wind in favour of hedonistic abandonment to the moment:

> 'We are Earth's best, that learnt her lesson here.
>   Life is our cry. We have kept the faith!' we said;
>   'We shall go down with unreluctant tread

Rose-crowned into the darkness!' . . . Proud we were,
And laughed, that had such brave true things to say.
– And then you suddenly cried, and turned away.

(ll. 9–14)

'We must seek in art & immensely in Life for the end here and now. To pass from emotion to emotion, radiantly, for a few years, & then vanish!' Brooke wrote in another unpublished paper described by Howarth.[27] The poem puts such exhilarated enthusiasm sardonically in its place, which is not to say that it disavows it altogether. The lovers' exuberance is held at a distance, in speech marks and in the past tense; and the closing image is surely right to suggest that such hedonism soon sours. The burden of its final line is that any attempt to triumph over time by living in the moment can only be temporary; the necessity of 'vanishing' is recognised as being more painful than it is made to seem in the prose. And yet, it is hard to think of 'The Hill' as a poem simply about the vacuity of what remain in the eyes of the poet even at the end of the poem we 'brave true' sentiments. Indeed, the most persuasive vision of experience offered in the poem is grounded not in the last line, with its curious metrical limp (the wording might easily have been much more snappily in step with the metre, and much worse: 'Then suddenly you cried...') but in the daring and exuberance of the couple's statements: 'Through glory and ecstasy we pass; / Wind, sun, and earth remain, the birds sing still, / When we are old, are old...', the speaker's partner exclaims in the octet (ll. 3–5). And it is this delight in living as an end in itself, as much as the more 'intelligent' one in which it is couched, that finds most exhilarating and persuasive voice in the poem.

Humans are rarely intelligent about feelings in Brooke's poems. Even when they catch themselves in the throes of rhetoric, as in 'I said I splendidly loved you; it's not true', the response isn't to rescind its promises, and arrive at an assessment of 'exactly what, and how much' one feels (love remains in the poem's overblown terms an emotion which 'soars from earth to ecstasies unwist' (l. 5)) but rather to rise to a surprisingly affecting vision of humans as beings who cannot ever know the truth of what they feel:

Wanderers, in the middle mist,
Who cry for shadows, clutch, and cannot tell
Whether they love at all, or, loving, whom...

(ll. 7–9)

Brooke's best poems almost always present human beings subject to a passion which they can seldom command or see beyond. It is the vision affirmed in the sonnet 'Mutability' as the octave's spare, measured voice breaks in against the 'high windless world and strange', 'subject to no change' posited in the sestet (ll. 1, 4):

> Dear, we know only that we sigh, kiss, smile;
> Each kiss lasts but the kissing; and grief goes over;
> Love has no habitation but the heart.
> Poor straws! on the dark flood we catch awhile,
> Cling, and are borne into the night apart.
> The laugh dies with the lips, 'Love' with the lover.
>
> (ll. 9–14)

This is a far cry from Eliot's 'intelligence': indeed, like similar moments from 'Dining-Room Tea' to 'The Hill', it isolates as especially human an inability to say 'exactly how much' one feels—only that one feels it: 'we know only that we sigh, kiss, smile'. And yet, the lines, for all the grandeur and broadness of their own feelings, are far from 'rhetoric', either. What saves them is the sparseness of their rhythms and their language: the balance of sadness and relief at the predicament; the refusal to be sentimental about endurance of personal feeling (the quotation marks in the closing line are bracingly sceptical about 'Love' as anything other than subjective experience); the early caesura in the most sentimental of the lines that sees 'Cling' poignantly clinging to the start of its line; the refusal of the rhyme scheme to arrange itself into any sort of crescendo, so that the closing line has a brisk finality after this grandiose image. This blindness is the human predicament in Brooke's poems. He is often witty about it, sometimes warmly sympathetic. At other times, he treats with humour, seeing its absurdities and our readiness to rise above it. It is not a grand, or intense or especially original vision, but it has dash and sometimes pathos.

Notes

1 Harriet Monroe and Alice Corbin Henderson, *The New Poetry* (New York: Macmillan, 1917), p. xxxix. For a comprehensive account of the debates around poetic 'rhetoric' in the first two decades of the twentieth century, see Peter Howarth, *British Poetry in the Age of Modernism* (Cambridge: Cambridge UP, 2005).
2 Thomas Stearns Eliot, 'Contemporary Poetry' III', *Egoist* 4 (1917), p. 151.
3 Rupert Brooke, *Poetical Works,* ed. Geoffrey Keynes (London: Faber and Faber), p. 19, ll. 1–3; 9–11. All subsequent references to this edition parenthetically in the text.
4 Winston Churchill, 'Death of Mr. Rupert Brooke. Sunstroke at Lemnos.' *The Times* (26 April 1915), p. 5.
5 Samuel Hynes, *Edwardian Occasions: Essays on English Writing in the Early Twentieth Century* (London: Routledge and Kegan Paul, 1972), p. 146.
6 Rupert Brooke, *The Prose of Rupert Brooke*, ed. and introd. Christopher Hassall (London: Sidgwick and Jackson, 1956), pp. 88, 92, 94.

7 Hassall, *The Prose of Rupert Brooke*, pp. xxxviii–xxxix.

8 John Donne, *Complete Poems*, ed. Robin Robbins. (Harlow: Longman-Pearson, 2008), p. 177.

9 Edward Thomas to Robert Frost, 19 October 1916, *Selected Letters of Edward Thomas*, ed. R. George Thomas (Oxford: Oxford UP, 1995), p. 132.

10 Edward Thomas, *A Language not to be Betrayed: Selected Prose of Edward Thomas*, selected and introd. Edna Longley (Manchester: Carcanet in association with Mid-Northumberland Arts Group, 1981), p. 109.

11 Roger Fry, 'An Essay in Aesthetics', *Vision and Design* (London: Chatto, 1925), p. 27.

12 Peter Howarth, 'Rupert Brooke's Celebrity Aesthetic'. *English Literature in Transition, 1880–1920*, 49.3 (2006): 273; 272–92.

13 Hassall, *Rupert Brooke: A Biography* (London: Faber and Faber, 1964), p. 426. Brooke was on a visit to Fiji, and the letter's gently macabre speculations ('Consideration of the thoughts that pour through the mind of the ever-diminishing remnant of a man, as it sees its last limbs cooking, moves me deeply') grow out of racist conjecture about the islanders' supposed reputation for cannibalism.

14 Bernard Bergonzi, *Heroes' Twilight: A Study of the Literature of the Great War* (London: Constable, 1965), p. 42.

15 See Howarth, 'Celebrity Aesthetic', pp. 280–3.

16 Hassall, *The Prose of Rupert Brooke*, p. 95.

17 Perkins, *Modern Poetry*, p. 210.

18 Eliot, 'Andrew Marvell', p. 255.

19 Perkins, *Modern Poetry*, p. 211.

20 Wilson Knight, 'Rupert Brooke', *Neglected Powers: Essays on Nineteenth and Twentieth Century Literature* (London: Routledge and Kegan Paul, 1971), p. 296.

21 Nigel Jones, *Rupert Brooke: Life, Death and Myth* (London: Head of Zeus, 2014), p. 195.

22 Brooke to Jacques Raverat, 3 November 1909, *Selected Letters of Rupert Brooke*, ed. Geoffrey Keynes (London: Faber and Faber, 1968), p. 192.

23 Thomas Hardy, *The Complete Poems of Thomas Hardy*, ed. James Gibson. (London: Macmillan, 1976), p. 515.

24 Brooke, *Prose*, p. 131.

25 For a discussion of the motivation behind and reception of Brooke's attempts to puncture his reputation for the poetical, see Hynes, *Edwardian Occasions*, pp. 147–9.

26 Brooke to Edward Marsh, 25 February 1912, *Selected Letters of Rupert Brooke*, p. 361.

27 Howarth, 'Celebrity Aesthetic', p. 280.

2 Strange Truths
Romantic Reimaginings in Wilfred Owen and Siegfried Sassoon

Mark Sandy

Any exploration of the Romantic legacies bequeathed to the poetry of Wilfred Owen and Siegfried Sassoon is, inevitably, indebted to the paradigmatic models that Jon Silkin established for First World War poetry.[1] Yet, as Michael O'Neill rightly observes, these borrowings of Romantic vocabulary, rhythms and voices by First World War poets are not necessarily or exclusively 'simply "ironic"'.[2] This chapter explores the ways in which the strange truths of the poetry of Wilfred Owen and Siegfried Sassoon are imbued with the poetry of William Wordsworth, P. B. Shelley, John Keats and John Clare. The debt of Owen and Sassoon to these Romantic writers is not in the form, as has often been contended,[3] of an aesthetic that was found wanting and in dire need of demythologising in the wake of their experience of the First World War. Both Owen and Sassoon often fuse together the solidity of Keats's poetic language with the kinetic energy of Shelley's imagination as a means to find a new expressive poetic mode equal to the strange truths of the battlefield.

Retaining something of Shelley's protean elemental imagination 'of flame transformed to marble',[4] 'Spring Offensive' recasts phrases drawn from Keats's autumnal ode to round out and intensify the vernal, anticipatory moment of battle that Owen's poem depicts:

> Halted against the shade of a last hill
> They fed, and eased of pack-loads, were at ease;
> And leaning on the nearest chest or knees
> Carelessly slept.
>   But many there stood still
> To face the stark blank sky beyond the ridge,
> Knowing their feet had come to the end of the world.
> Marvelling they stood, and watched the long grass
>   swirled
> By the May breeze, murmurous with wasp and midge;
> And though the summer oozed into their veins
> Like an injected drug for their bodies' pains,

> Sharp on their souls hung the imminent ridge of grass,
> Fearfully flashed the sky's mysterious glass.
>
> Hour after hour they ponder the warm field...[5]

This temporary haven from the exertions and dangers of battle for the 'halted' soldiers conveys its muted natural music of late spring's 'May breeze' (and 'murmurous' sounds of wasp and midge) through a modulated echo of the musicality of Keats's 'The murmurous haunts of flies on summer eves'.[6] In depicting the ominously cloying atmosphere of a promised anaesthetisation to the threat 'at the end of the world' of the 'imminent ridge of grass' and further action, Owen fractures and reimagines the personified figure of Keats's 'To Autumn', who can be found 'sitting careless on a granary floor' (l. 15), or drugged with the narcotic 'fume of poppies' (l. 17), or else watching 'the last oozings hours by hours' of the 'cyder-press' (ll. 20–1), to point up the increasingly strained relations between humanity and nature.

Owen's lines, thick with Keatsian allusion, finally, settle for a Shelleyan infused portentous image of 'Fearfully flashed the sky's mysterious glass'.[7] In 'Spring Offensive', Owen is closer to Shelley in poetic technique, but not necessarily in sentiment. Responding to *The Triumph of Life*, Owen's line imaginatively commingles Shelley's imagery of the 'opposing steep of that mysterious dell' (l. 470) and 'fragile glass' (l. 226) with an appreciation of Shelley's use of 'flashed' as meaning revelation or insight. This is typified by Shelley's account of the poet-figure's moment of revelation when 'meaning on his vacant / Flashed like strong inspiration' (*Alastor*, ll. 126–7), or the 'sun-like truth / Flashed on his visionary youth' (*Rosalind and Helen*, ll. 618–19).[8]

Here, Owen's 'fearfully flashed' augurs the soldier's apocalyptic experience of their military campaign on an infernal 'world's verge' where 'instantly the whole sky burned with fury against them' and 'the green slope / Chasmed and steepened sheer to infinite space'. The existential and spatial dilemmas of occupying this 'infinite space' and 'world's verge' resonate further with Keats's sonnet, 'When I have fears that I may cease to be', where the speaker finds himself 'on the shore / of the world I stand alone' (ll. 12–13).[9] Surprisingly, unlike Keats's sonnet, the close of Owen's 'Spring Offensive' attests to the possibility of spiritual renewal for those who 'crawling slowly back, have degrees / Regained cool and peaceful air in wonder'. Owen's lines hold out for, even strain after, a recovery of Wordsworth's 'cool air' of 'the unencumbered Mind' ('VIII. Retirement', l. 12). But Owen's final ambiguous question asked of those who have survived the 'fury of hell's upsurge'—'Why speak not they of comrades that went under?'—disturbs with its haunting silence any possibility of recovering an 'unencumbered Mind'.

Within the seasonal and metrical rhythms of Keats's 'To Autumn', human existence ebbs towards its own natural demise and non-existence, coming into being and expiring as naturally as the 'light wind that lives or dies' (l. 29).[10] In this manner, 'To Autumn' is perfectly poised between states of living and dying and as such enacts that eased 'die into life' (*Hyperion*, 3, l. 130) that his *Hyperion* fragments could not effectively bring into being. Keats's transitional twilight of the day, season, year and human existence is the fully and finally realised form of Hyperion's 'grief and radiance faint' (*Hyperion*, 1, l. 304). So saturated with their war experiences are the perceptions depicted in 'Mental Cases' that Owen reconfigures Keats's defiant 'bright Titan' commingled with the twilight into a 'Dawn [that] breaks open like a wound that bleeds afresh'. Owen's imagery is both alert to the latent tragedy within Keats's hushed, muted and dignified autumnal Apollonian light and affirms the Dionysian tragic acceptance of a negatively capable poetic self given over entirely to a 'World of Pains' and 'Things real'.[11]

'Things real' and a 'World of pains' speak directly to the increasing realism of Sassoon's poetry. An early sonnet by Sassoon, printed in the collection *The Old Huntsman and Other Poems* (1917), on the subject of 'October', in spite of its mawkish, often overly ornamental, affectations of Georgian poetry, draws on aspects of the sombre affirmation of Keats's ode:

> Across the land a faint blue veil of mist
> Seems hung; the woods wear yet arrayment sober
> Till frost shall make them flame; silent and whilst
> The drooping cherry orchards of October
> Like mournful pennons hang their shrivelling leaves
> Russet and orange: all things now decay;
> Long since ye garnered in your autumn sheaves,
> And sad the robins pipe at set of day.
> Now do ye dream of Spring when greening shaws
> Confer with the shrewd breezes, and of slopes
> Flower-kirtled, and of April, virgin guest;
> Days that ye love, despite their windy flaws,
> Since they are woven with all joys and hopes
> Whereof ye nevermore shall be possessed.
>
> ('October')

The imaginative ambit of Sassoon's treatment of autumn can be traced in the wholesome promise of Keats's external autumnal landscapes, where the 'harvest's done' and the 'squirrel's granary is full', which can readily translate into dearth, bereft and negative mindscapes, where 'the sedge is wither'd from the lake / And no birds sing' (*La Belle Dame Sans Merci*, ll. 7–8; ll. 47–8).[12] In Sassoon's 'October', we find, instead of Keats's 'moss'd cottage-trees' ('To Autumn', l. 5), 'The dropping cherry orchards of October / Like mournful pennons hang their shrivelling leaves'[13] and the realisation, with overtures of 'a shade of grief'[14] typical of John Clare's late poetry, that 'all things decay; / Long since ye garnered in your autumn sheaves / And the sad robins pipe at set of day' (ll. 6–8). There are also present here recycled elements of the poetry of Thomson and Goldsmith (perhaps, filtered through the language of Keats's ode), but the figure of autumn as gleaner—Sassoon's use of 'garnered' recalling, in Keats's 'When I have fears that I may Cease to be', those who 'Hold like rich garners' the full-ripen'd grain (l. 4)—and the robin's presence at the close of day are certainly indebted to Keats's 'To Autumn'.

Readily identifiable, too, is the Keatsian origin of the volta to Sassoon's sonnet. Sassoon remoulds Keats's self-conscious questioning of 'Where are the songs of spring?' ('To Autumn', l. 23) to ask 'Now do ye dream of Spring' (l. 9) only to conclude that 'all joys and hopes / Whereof ye nevermore shall be possessed' (ll. 13–14). Keats's question, 'Where are the songs of spring?' (l. 23), dissipates the speaker's anxious presence into a cacophony of autumn's mournful whisperings.[15] The question born of a hankering after new beginnings, birth and rejuvenation finds a rejoinder in the funeral orchestra of the season which reaches its climax with the 'treble soft' (l. 31) of the robin. Deliciously bittersweet in its Keatsian aspirations, Sassoon's conclusion resonates with Clare's own mournful sense that even 'summer's prime a leaf / [is] tinged with autumn's visible decay' ('Decay').

A year later (coloured by his experience of trench warfare and stay at Craiglockhart, where he read Shelley voraciously),[16] Sassoon returned to the subject of October in a short lyric poem, titled 'Autumn', published in *Counter-Attack and Other Poems* (1918):

> October's bellowing anger breaks and cleaves
> The bronzed battalions of the stricken wood
> In whose lament I hear a voice that grieves
> For battle's fruitless harvest, and the feud
> Of outraged men. Their lives are like the leaves
> Scattered in flocks of ruin, tossed and blown
> Along the westering furnace flaring red.
> O martyred youth and manhood overthrown,
> The burden of your wrongs is on my head.
>
> ('Autumn')

Sassoon's previous poem, 'October', in spite of its indebtedness to Keats, contained flashes of Shelley's elemental protean brilliance found here and in Sassoon's earlier description of 'the woods [that] wear yet arrayment sober / Till frost shall make them flame' (ll. 2–3). It is the transformative and kinetic energy of Shelley's 'Ode to the West Wind' that powers Sassoon's description of the Scottish landscape of 'Autumn' in which (as in Owen's 'Exposure') the natural world is saturated with the language and experience of war to bear witness to 'battle's fruitless harvest' (l. 4). The 'lives' of those killed in this futile harvesting, Sassoon writes, 'are like the leaves / Scattered in flocks of ruin, tossed and blown / Along the westering furnace flaring red' (ll. 5–7). Here, Sassoon rejects the quintessential harmony and solidity of Keats's English autumn in favour of the chaotic commotions of Shelley's distinctly Italian autumn in 'Ode to the West Wind' where, cutting across the *terza rima* stanziac form, 'the leaves dead / Are driven, like ghosts from an enchanter flee-ing, // Yellow, and black, and pale, and hectic red, / Pestilence-stricken multitudes' (ll. 3–5).

Nature, for Owen, as Sassoon discovered in the poetry of Thomas Hardy,[17] is increasingly indifferent and obdurate to the active hostilities of the soldiers. Such indifference, for these soldier-poets, is expressed through a remodelling of Shelleyan and Keatsian tropes. The Keatsian 'feel of not to feel', condensed in 'as though of hemlock I had drunk' ('Ode to a Nightingale', l. 2), finds a reimagined form in Owen's account of anaesthetised and stumbling soldiers who, in 'Dulce Et Decorum Est', 'All went lame; all blind; / Drunk with fatigue'. Owen's start of 'Expo-sure' explicitly rewrites Keats's opening lines, 'My heart aches, and a drowsy numbness pains / My sense' (ll. 1–2), to 'Ode to a Nightingale' as the painfully visceral and nerve-frayed exhaustion of 'Our brains ache, in the merciless iced east winds that knive us...' in which memory and reality are blurred.[18] Within a space of a few lines, 'knive us' finds its pararhyme with 'nervous' to reinforce Owen's deadly sense of the freez-ing balm that nature pours on the physical and psychological effects of warfare.

Owen is equally capable of translating with biting irony Shelley's credo of 'I shall be one with nature, herb, and stone' into the brutal 'philosophy of many soldiers' in 'À Terre'. Here to be one with the earth is to be interred within it. By contrast, Shelley writes, in his elegy for Keats, *Adonais*, that 'He is made one with Nature' and his 'presence to be felt and known, / In darkness and in light, from herb and stone' (*Adonais*, l. 370; ll. 373–4). Shelley knew the risks, as did the Word-sworth of 'A Slumber Did My Spirit Steal' (the lyric ambiguously closes with the line 'Rolled round in earth's diurnal course / With rocks and stones and trees'),[19] attached to trusting spiritual salvation to the tran-scendent. Owen's 'À Terre' strips away any sense of spirituality or com-fort ('"Pushing up daisies" is their creed you know') to confront the stark reality of the dead corpses of the soldiers, eventually, incarcerated in the ground.

Such infernal sights are gauged by Owen's surreal and nightmarish landscapes 'scooped / Through granites which titanic wars had groined' ('Strange Meeting'). These physical and psychological landscapes speak to, and through, Keats's own scene of 'Spaces of fire, and all the yawn of hell' (*Hyperion*, 1. l. 120) that mark Titanic disaster, as much as they find affinity with Shelley's visionary 'world of agony' (*The Triumph of Life*, l. 295). As has been noted by critics, including Jon Silkin, John Stallworthy and Alan Tomlinson,[20] the visionary strangeness of Owen's poem takes its title 'Strange Meeting' and narrative shape of descent into 'some profound dull tunnel' from Canto V of Shelley's *The Revolt of Islam* and Rousseau's recount of his encounter with 'a shape all light' (l. 352) within 'the deep cavern' of Shelley's final poem, *The Triumph of Life*. The fact that both Shelley's *The Triumph of Life* and Keats's 'Hyperion' projects exist, for very different reasons,[21] as incomplete textual fragments is likely to have appealed to Owen's imaginative struggle to come to terms with the catastrophic, mechanised, mass slaughter of the First World War. Forgoing usual anti-Romantic sentiment, T. S. Eliot's 1922 poetic memorial for the lost generation, *The Waste Land*, with its declaration that 'These fragments I have shored against my ruins'[22] underwrites Owen's artistic inclination towards the fragment and fragmentary. Romantic textual fragments offered up the fragmentary and fractured as an appropriate poetic mode to elegise the death and destruction that Owen, Sassoon and his comrades experienced on such a titanic scale.

Owen's choice of the adjective 'Strange' in his poem's title offers a further allusion to Shelley's description of the dream-narrator's first sighting of the 'strange distortion' (183) that 'was once Rousseau' (l. 204) in *The Triumph of Life*. In this final, unfinished work, Shelley frames Rousseau's elegiac regret for a fled vision as akin to Wordsworth's own. Tellingly, Shelley's description of the birth of Rousseau's 'shape all light' from 'the bright omnipresence / of morning', which 'Burned upon the waters of the well' (*Triumph*, l. 343, l. 346), is infused with those 'Waters on a starry night' and the sunshine's 'glorious birth' that chart Wordsworth's own mourning for the passing of 'a glory from the earth' ('Ode: Intimations of Immortality', ll. 14, 16, 18):[23]

> ...there stood
>
> Amid the sun, as he amid the blaze
> Of his own glory, on the vibrating
> Floor of the fountain, paved with flashing rays,
>
> A Shape all light, which with one hand did fling
> Dew on the earth, as if she were the dawn,
> And the invisible rain did ever sing...
> (*The Triumph of Life*, ll. 348–54)

The fact that Shelley invites parallels between the figure of Rousseau and Wordsworth, as well as the poetic diction of *The Triumph of Life* and

Wordsworth's 'Ode: Intimations of Immortality', testifies to Shelley's desire to draw out the scepticism within Wordsworth's poetry through a process of imaginative revisionism.[24] Shelley's testing of Wordsworthian ideals through these acts of revision marked out the darker contours of Wordsworth's poetic thought and provided an imaginative revisionist model that spoke to the unprecedented situation in which Owen and Sassoon found themselves.

Uncertainty over the exact nature of the visionary state experienced by Owen's soldier-poet-narrator (who feels that 'out of battle' he has 'escaped' and, simultaneously, 'knew we stood in Hell') strongly recalls Shelley's Rousseau, who can no longer tell 'Whether my life had been before that sleep / The Heaven which I imagine, or a Hell' (ll. 332–3). This ontological and epistemological confusion characterises Owen's reimagined and abridged version of the experience of the dreaming narrator in Shelley's *The Revolt of Islam* and *The Triumph of Life*. More significantly, Owen's 'Strange Meeting' reimagines a dominant pattern of vision and sceptical quest that persists throughout Shelley's poetic career:

> 'None,' said the other, 'save the undone years,
> The hopelessness. Whatever hope is yours,
> Was my life also; I went hunting wild
> After the wildest beauty in the world,
> Which lies not calm in eyes, or braider hair,
> But mocks the steady running of the hour,
> And if it grieves, grieves richlier than here.'
>
> ...I would go up and wash them from sweet wells,
> Even with the truths that lie too deep for taint.

>   ('Strange Meeting')

Though striking a distinctly Keatsian register, Owen translates the psycho-biographical quest of the poet-figure into terms that both disavow and avow Romantic ideas. Recalling the opening of *Endymion* and Keats's final axiom, in 'Ode on a Grecian Urn', that 'Beauty is truth, truth Beauty', Owen recalibrates Romantic ideas about beauty and truth. For Owen, the permanence of beauty cannot exist in truth, but must reside in a true poet's ability to be truthful. For Owen, true poets must come to understand that truth is not an idealised form that mocks the 'running of the hour', but must convey that truth is the 'pity of war'. Beauty, in Owen's poem, grieves not for those who are already dead, but for those still living who continue to run the risk of losing their lives. Owen's 'Strange Meeting' implies that if war is able to teach one single lesson—one single 'untold truth'—it is the need for compassion. Other than that, war, as Owen knew all too well, destroys everything else utterly, even our human ability to comprehend eternal beauty or appreciate the beauties of the natural world.

The dilemma may be a very Keatsian one, but the unsettling trajectory of Owen's romance quest, ending in disappointment and disillusion, finds its prototype in the discernible pattern of Shelley's poetry of visionary quest.[25] A late reprisal of the quest motif central to *Alastor* and Shelley's *Epipsychidion* opens with a symbolic record of his youthful poet-figure's encounter with a female 'Spirit [that] was the harmony of truth' (l. 215):

> There was a Being whom my spirit oft
> Met on its visioned wanderings, far aloft,
> In the clear golden prime of my youth's dawn,
> Upon the fairy isles of sunny lawn,
> Amid the enchanted mountains, and the caves
> Of divine sleep, and the air-like waves
> Of wonder-level dream, whose tremulous floor
> Paved her light steps...

> (ll. 190–7)

Typically, for Shelley, this idealised biography of the poet begins in the revelatory mode of visionary dream ('divine sleep') and with a sense of connection between the self and all that is spiritually and intellectually beautiful and good in the universe.[26] Such vision, inevitably, ends with a waking, troubled consciousness that embarks upon a potentially fatal quest to recapture the ideal figure of lost vision in 'one form resembling hers, / In which she might have masked herself from me' (ll. 254–5). Playing out a similar predicament, the poet-figure's unquenchable desire for knowledge of the 'sacred past' (l. 73), in *Alastor*, is a product of his highly individuated consciousness that separates him from both his fellow beings and the material universe.

His quest for self-knowledge becomes a search for meaning across time and space amongst the ruins of civilisation (ll. 109–15). Through uncovering the origins of time itself and translating the hieroglyphs, the poet-figure emerges as a consciousness more independent than the poet-narrator of *Alastor*, who is incapable of deciphering those hieroglyphics or the 'thrilling secrets of time' (l. 128).[27] Restoring significance to these 'speechless shapes' (l. 123) causes the poet-figure of *Alastor* to acknowledge an incongruity between meaning and language and increases his own anxiety that reality will never match up to those idealised visions of his adolescence.

For Owen, the only reality is the inharmonious 'truth untold, the pity of war, the pity war distilled', which in its chiastic formulation both enigmatically takes on shapes of speech and eludes them. Inverting the Shelleyan paradigm of irrecoverable lost vision, Owen's narrating soldier-poet is confronted 'With a thousand pains that vision's face was grained'. Owen's description of this visage is closer verbally and in type to Keats's figure of Moneta, whose 'wan face' (1. 1. 256), as we are told, is 'deathwards progressing / Towards no death' (1. ll. 260–1) in *The Fall of Hyperion*.[28] 'Strange Meeting' revises Shelley's idealised biography of the visionary quest through Owen's depiction of a nightmarish phantasmagorical revelatory encounter.

Recalling Wordsworth's 'fled visionary gleam' ('Ode: Intimations of Immortality', l. 56), Shelley's account of the passage from childhood to adulthood in *Epipsychidion*, by contrast, reveals a painful process of individuation which irrevocably separates the poet-speaker from the once all-pervasive presence of the Spirit of his dream vision. Growing up only teaches the idealised and idealising poet his many limitations. A mortal 'man with mighty loss dismayed' (l. 229) is unable to track the flight of his visionary Spirit, as she departs 'like a God throned on a winged planet.../ Into the dreary cone of our life's shade' (ll. 226, 227). Owen shares in a similar tragic realisation (in which the 'Strange friend' implicates the narrating soldier-poet) of the 'undone years' of 'hopelessness' born of 'hope' that defines a 'life' of 'hunting wild / After the wildest beauty in the world'. The language may be Keatsian, but Owen's vision shares in a dynamic Shelleyan scepticism about the limitations of idealising and idealised fictions in the face of harsh realities. 'Hope', as Shelley has it in *Prometheus Unbound*, 'creates / From its own wreck the thing it contemplates' (IV, ll. 573–4).

Shelley's early poem *Alastor* presents such scepticism, in Wordsworthian terms, through the narrator's love of nature and sceptical search, founded on a 'dark hope' (l. 32), for a power within the natural world that will 'render up the tale / Of what we are' (ll. 27–8). Infused with the language of Wordsworth's commitment to nature, the appeal of Shelley's narrator to the 'Earth, ocean, air, beloved brotherhood!' (l. 1) revises and qualifies Wordsworth's belief in the elemental trinity 'Of something far more deeply interfused / Whose dwelling is the light of setting suns / And the round ocean and the living air' ('Lines Written a Few Miles Above Tintern Abbey', ll. 97–9).[29] Hopeful faith in the revelatory power of nature, enabling us, as Wordsworth assures, 'to see into the life of things' ('Tintern Abbey', l. 49), in the hands of Shelley's narrator gives way to a darker realisation that such revelation is merely an 'incommunicable dream' (*Alastor*, l. 39). The narrator's sense of failed vision and abandonment by the force of nature is reiterated in the description of the broken body of the poet-figure that subjects the sentiment of Wordsworth's 'Ode: Intimations of Immortality' to critical pressure by recognising 'a woe "too deep for tears"' (l. 713). Shelley modifies Wordsworth's closing line of the 'Ode', 'Thoughts that do often lie too deep for tears', exchanging 'thoughts' for 'a woe' and silently dropping the crucially qualifying 'often' to draw out the more negative implications of Wordsworth's sense of loss.

'Strange Meeting' reimagines this same line from Wordsworth and, in the poem's original draft, Owen writes of 'thoughts that lie [...] / Even too deep for taint.' In the finalised version of the poem, Owen substituted 'thoughts' for the more Keatsian 'truths' and, perhaps, refracted through Shelley's own allusion to Wordsworth that does not retain the qualifying 'often' of the Ode's original settling on the line: 'Even with truths that lie too deep for taint'.[30] Owen's choice of taint suggests an investment in a Shelleyan poetic language of 'pestilence' and 'contagion', as well as his own sense of a darker, more tainted, mode of Romanticism.

Compared with Owen, Sassoon's own engagement with Shelley was brief and intense. But Sassoon, whose work is often identified with a Byronic mode of satire,[31] shared with Owen an abiding fascination with the poetry of Keats. Sassoon often echoes the world of Keats's nightingale in his depiction of those soldiers who abandon 'safety [...] and the bird-sung joy of grass-green thickets' ('Prelude: The Troops') for battle or Sassoon's reimagining of Keats's seductively rich synaesthesia of 'embalmed darkness' ('Ode to a Nightingale', l. 43) as nocturnal rainfall 'rustling through the dark; / Fragrance and passionless music woven as one' which 'wash[es] away life' and the thoughts of the dying soldier ('The Death-Bed'). Its 'passionless' nature adds a touch of cold irony (as does the substitution of Keatsian heavenly light for a curtain's 'glimmering curve') to Sassoon's otherwise sensuously and sensually inviting Keatsian 'embalmed darkness' in which the fatally injured soldier is 'blind' to the stars:

> Warm rain on drooping roses; pattering showers
> That soak the woods; not the harsh rain that sweeps
> Behind the thunder, but a trickling peace,
> Gently and slowly washing life away.

As in Keats's 'Ode to a Nightingale', the 'fragrance' of Sassoon's enclosed benighted space presses in upon the poet-speaker and threatens to overwhelm (or stifle) the very act of breathing itself. Keats's poet-speaker strains, as must the waning consciousness of the soldier, to recreate the nocturnal scene ('flickered and faded in his drowning eyes') as a series of precise and wholesome tropes from an inexact approximation of things which, at best, remain uncertain shadowy presences.[32]

In 'The Death-Bed', Sassoon dismembers the personified figure of Keats's autumnal ode to realise a fatally wounded casualty as the one who 'drowsed and was aware of silence heaped'. Sassoon's image, like Owen's 'Spring Offensive', verbally echoes Keats's account of autumn 'on a *half-reap'd* furrow sound *asleep*, / Drows'd with the fume of poppies' ('To Autumn', ll. 15–16). Sassoon's account of the soldier's passing truncates and reverses one of Keats's extended similes—describing the grief-stricken words of the fallen Titans, 'As when upon a tranced summer-night... one solitary gust comes upon the silence and dies off' (*Hyperion*, 1. ll. 71–6; 79–80)—into the matter-of-fact statement,

'So he went, / And there was silence in the summer night'. Through this reworking of Keatsian imagery, Sassoon intends us to register the irony that this young soldier's life is claimed by a Titanic war 'he hated'. Sassoon's echo of Keats's 'half-reaped' tellingly relates to the eventual fate of the dying soldier who, having drifted for hours in and out of consciousness, is eventually claimed (no matter how unjustly as his comrades may feel) by the ultimate reaper, 'death'. For Sassoon and Owen, nature's processes afford both the prospect of an anaesthetic relief from pain to the soldiers and a bleak promise (and fatal judgement on the unnatural act of the war itself) of their extinction.

Published in the interwar years, Wallace Stevens's 'The Death of a Soldier' is an alert to the presence of this existential threat in these post-Romantic responses of Owen and Sassoon to Keats's original homage to autumnal processes. Drawing on the sensibilities of Owen and Sassoon, Stevens casts a sceptical eye over the kaleidoscopic effect of temporal modes, in Keats's own 'To Autumn', which dissolves harvesting activities into the eternity of nature and the annual cycle of the seasons into the single passage of a day. For Stevens, the contraction of life and expectation of death is a symbiotic process that occurs in, and is encapsulated by, the simile 'As in the season of autumn'.[33]

Reserving the verb 'falls' for the deceased soldier (and not the tumbling leaves of the season), Stevens repeats the simile in the third stanza, where the death of a soldier, as the Owen of 'Anthem for Doomed Youth' would have agreed, is 'absolute and without memorial'. With the emphasis on collective loss, Owen's pivotal question in his sonnet, 'What passing-bells for these who die as cattle?', both pluralises and compresses Clare's 'passing bell' ('Graves of Infants') of natural processes with a Keatsian allusion to ritual sacrifice (taken from stanza 4 of Keats's 'Ode upon a Grecian Urn') to press home the point that the mass slaughtering of young soldiers in mechanised warfare is neither a noble sacrifice nor a consequence of natural outcome.

Stevens may permit a fleeting glimpse of spiritual salve or transcendence but, in 'The Death of a Soldier', the ceasing of the wind (doubly emphasised by the repeated 'When the wind stops') is less nature's respectful acknowledgement of the death of the soldier than a reinforcement that all natural processes and life itself come to an 'absolute' end. Such finality can be a consequence of natural or unnatural processes which, like those clouds, indifferently ('nevertheless') pursue 'their direction'.

Owen and Sassoon, like Stevens after them, were committed Romantics albeit with, adapting Owens's own self-description, 'very seared consciences'.[34] These verbal, often unsettling, echoes of Wordsworth, Keats, Shelley and Clare indicate the commitment of Owen and Sassoon to the continuation of the sceptical, imaginative revisionism practised by these Romantic poets, a practice itself born of colossal upheaval, historical and experiential crisis in the early nineteenth century. By fracturing the tropes, diction and imagery of their Romantic inheritors, Owen and Sassoon trusted that the Romantic poetics of the fragment might afford an elegiac mode that could speak to, and of, the tragedy of modern warfare. Owen and Sassoon also found within Romanticism itself a resilient scepticism and spirited interrogation of ideals that remained robust enough to survive and communicate the unsettling, strange truths of the unprecedented catastrophe of the First World War.

Notes

1 Jon Silkin, *Out of Battle: The Poetry of the Great War.* 1972. (London: Ark, 1987).
2 Michael O'Neill has Owen particularly in mind. See O'Neill, *The All-Sustaining Air: Romantic Legacies and Renewals in British, American, and Irish Poetry since 1900* (Oxford; Oxford UP, 2007), p. 1.
3 For a recent view dissenting from those of Bernard Bergonzi and Jon Silkin, see Nils Clausson, '"Perpetuating the Language": Romantic Tradition, Genre Function, and the Origin of the Trench Lyric', *Journal of Modern Literature* 30 (2006): pp. 106–7; pp. 104–28.
4 Percy Bysshe Shelley, *Shelley's Poetry and Prose.* 1979. Eds. Donald H. Reiman and Neil Fraistat (New York: Norton, 2002), *Adonais*, ll. 447, 425. Hereafter *SPP*. Subsequent references to this edition.
5 Wilfred Owen, *The Complete Poems and Fragments by Wilfred Owen.* Ed. Jon Stallworthy. Vol 1. (London: Chatto, 1983), 'Spring Offensive', pp. 192–3. Subsequent quotations from this edition.
6 John Keats, *Poems of John Keats.* 1978. Ed. Jack Stillinger (Cambridge, MA: Belknap, 1979), 'Ode to a Nightingale', p. 371, l. 50. Subsequent references to this edition. For an alternative and persuasive reading of Owen's 'Spring Offensive' that places Keats's 'Nightingale' ode as the key precursor text, see Emma Suret, '"Among the Unseen Voices": The Influence of Shelley and Keats on the Poetry of Wilfred Owen'. PhD Diss. U of Sheffield, 2017, Chapter 5.
7 Paul Fussell notes that life in the trenches offered a renewed awareness of the sky, an awareness that 'was a cruel reversal of that sunrise and sunset, established by a century of Romantic poetry and painting, as the tokens of peace and hope and rural charm should now be exactly moments of heightened ritual anxiety' (p. 59). See Fussell, *The Great War and Modern Memory: An Illustrated Edition.* 1975. (Oxford: Oxford UP, 2000). Shelley's tropes of light, however, often unsettle Wordsworth's sublimely soothing fiction of the trinity of light, water and air as expressed, for example, in 'Lines Written a Few Miles Above Tintern Abbey'.
8 See Frederick Startridge Ellis, *A Lexical Concordance to the Poetical Works of Percy Bysshe Shelley: An Attempt to Classify Every Word Found Therein According to its Signification* (London: Quaritch, 1892), p. 439.
9 For an astute reading of Owen's poetic apprenticeship to Keats in art of the sonnet as open-ended form, see Emma Suret, 'John Keats, Wilfred Owen, and Restriction in the Sonnet' *English* 66 (2017): 145–62.
10 Compare with Jon Silkin's reading of the metrical emphasis on 'bloom' in Keats's line 'While barred clouds bloom the soft-dying day' ('To Autumn', l. 25) to stress the enmeshing of the 'three cycles of nature, day, and man' in the ode. See 'Introduction', *The Penguin Book of First World War Poetry.* 1979. Ed. Jon Silkin (Harmondsworth: Penguin, 1981), pp. 70–1.

11 John Keats, *The Letters of John Keats, 1814–1821*, ed. Hyder Eward Rollins. 2 vols. (Cambridge, MA: Harvard UP, 1956), 2, p. 102.

12 For a discussion of 'negative fiction' in Keats, see Mark Sandy, *Poetics of Self and Form in Keats and Shelley: Nietzschean Subjectivity and Genre* (Aldershot: Ashgate, 2005), pp. 48–9.

13 Siegfried Sassoon, *Siegfried Sassoon: Collected Poems 1908–1956* (London: Faber, 1986), p. XX, ll. 4–5. Subsequent quotations taken from this edition.

14 John Clare, *John Clare: Selected Poems*. 1990. Ed. Geoffrey Summerfield (Harmondsworth: Penguin, 2000), p. 178.

15 Helen Vendler observes that 'the perpetuity of nature's music … is based on the cyclicity of nature. There is something false in the metaphor: human life reaches, as seasons do not, an utmost verge; human music ends.' (p. 236). *The Odes of John Keats*. 1983. (Cambridge, MA, 2003).

16 See Patrick Campbell, *Siegfried Sassoon: A Study of the War Poetry* (Jefferson, NC: Macfarland, 1999), pp. 74–5.

17 See Oindrila Gosh, '"How Curious and Quaint War is": Thomas Hardy and the First World Poets' *The Thomas Hardy Journal* (2015): 133–4; 130–9.

18 See O'Neill, *The All-Sustaining Air*, p. 1.

19 William Wordsworth, *William Wordsworth: The Major Works*, ed. Stephen Gill (1984; Oxford, 2000), p. 147. All quotations from this edition.

20 See Jon Silkin, 'Introduction', *Firslt World War Poetry*, p. 28 and see Jon Stallworthy, *Wilfred Owen*. 1977. (London: Pimlico, 1988), p. 256. See also Alan Tomlinson, "Strange Meeting in a Strange Land: Wilfred Owen and Shelley", Studies in Romanticism 32:1 (1993): 75–95.

21 Shelley's *The Triumph of Life* is left incomplete after the poet's accidental drowning off the coast of Lerici on 8 July, 1822. Keats abandoned the first *Hyperion* for artistic reasons and recasts it in Dantean mode as *The Fall of Hyperion: A Dream*, which was also left unfinished.

22 Thomas Stearns Eliot, *The Complete Poems and Plays* (London: Faber, 2004), p. 75, l. 431. For further resonances of Eliot's *The Waste Land* with survivors of the First World War see Peter Lowe, '"Exploring Sunken Ruinous Roads": The First World War Poet as Archaeologist', *English Studies* 97:1 (2016): 51; 42–60.

23 Mark Sandy, *Poetics of Self and Form in Keats and Shelley* (Aldershot: Ashgate, 2005), p. 118.

24 See J. Hillis Miller, 'Shelley's "The Triumph of Life"', in *Shelley*, ed. Michael O'Neill (London, 1993), p. 233, pp. 218–40. For a detailed account of the imaginative responses of Byron and Shelley to Wordsworth's 'Ode: Intimations of Immortality' see Mark Sandy, "Lines of Light:" Poetic Variations in Wordsworth, Byron, and Shelley', *Romanticism* (3) 22: 260–8. Bernard Bergonzi recognises that an importance of 'The Wordsworthian theme of the obscuring of early innocence' (78) for war poetry (in particular the work of Herbert Read). See Bergonzi, *Heroes' Twilight: A Study of the Literature of the Great War* (London: Constable, 1965). Michael O'Neill observes that 'Owen reminds us how important Wordsworth's ode' (p. 69) is for poetry of the early twentieth century. See also O'Neill, 'English Poetry, 1900–1930', *William Wordsworth in Context*. 2015. Ed. Andrew Bennett (Cambridge: Cambridge UP, 2017).

25 The account that follows is indebted to my discussion of Shelley and 'Quest Poetry' in *The Oxford Handbook of Percy Bysshe Shelley*, eds. Michael O'Neill and Anthony Howe, with the assistance of Madeleine Callaghan (Oxford: Oxford UP, 2013), pp. 272–88.

26 Such an idealised biography of the poet's life would have appealed to Owen, who read Keats's *Endymion* as an 'autobiography' that spoke of the Romantic poet's experience and his own. See James Najarian, *Victorian Keats: Manliness, Sexuality and Desire* (London: Palgrave Macmillan, 2002), p. 177. Owen responded in an equally empathetic way to reading Shelley's poetry and biography. See Guy Cuthbertson, *Wilfred Owen* (New Haven, CT: Yale UP, 2014), pp. 76–77.

27 See Ronald Tetreault *The Poetry of Life: Shelley and Literary Form* (Toronto, ON: U of Toronto P, 1987), p. 51.

28 Alternatively, Alan Tomlinson finds a 'pre-echo' for Owen's description in Shelley's remark about the poet that 'pains and pleasures of his species must become his own'. See Tomlinson, 'Wilfred Owen and Shelley', p. 84. See also Shelley, *A Defence of Poetry, SPP*, p. 517.

29 'Lines Written a few miles above Tintern Abbey' hereafter 'Tintern Abbey'.

30 Compare with Michael O'Neill's sense that Owen's revisionism 'raises the stakes (Wordsworth had spoken of "thoughts" rather than 'truths", "tears" rather than "taint") and suggests his speaker's risky idealism; perhaps belief in such untainted "truths" was among the inadvertent causes of the war.' (p. 79). See O'Neill, 'English Poetry, 1900–1930'.

31 Jon Silkin, *Out of Battle*, p. 207.

32 For an account of the 'speaker's dark guesswork' in Keats's ode, see Jacques Khalip and Forest Pyle, eds. *Constellations of a Contemporary Romanticism* (New York, 2016), pp. 5–6.

33 Wallace Stevens, *Collected Poems*. 1984. (London: Faber, 2006, p. 89). Subsequent references to this edition.

34 Owen describes himself to his mother, Susan Owen, in a letter (26? May, 1917) as 'conscientious objector with a very seared conscience.' See Wilfred Owen, *Wilfred Owen: Selected Poetry and Prose*. Routledge Revivals Ser. Ed. Jennifer Breen (London: Routledge, 1988), p 183.

3 'Now I Climb Alone'

Poetic Subjectivity in Thomas Hardy, Edward Thomas and Stephen Spender

Michael O'Neill

'The woman whom I loved so, and who loyally loved me'; 'And yet I still am half in love with pain, / With what is imperfect, with both tears and mirth, / With things that have an end, with life and earth, / And this moon that leaves me dark within the door'; 'Well, well, I carry on'.[1] These snippets of poetry, which come, respectively, from Thomas Hardy's 'Beeny Cliff', Edward Thomas's 'Liberty' and Stephen Spender's 'Thoughts During an Air Raid', have in common a quiet conviction that the first-person pronoun is still a serviceable staff on which a poem can prop its weight of significance. I've chosen examples in which the poem's 'I' seems assimilable to some sense of the poet speaking in propria persona, a Latin tag which profitably suggests that 'I' is always a version of the empirical self, never quite reducible to it.

In each case, the poem depends for its effect on 'I' used as a divining stick, a conduit, an instrument for concentrating and dispatching rays of otherness. Hardy's elegy in rollicking, romping, deftly metrical lines summons and empowers the 'I' to serve as a guide, sufferer and witness. It is the first-person singular pronoun that brings into reckoning external realities that are at the same time known only as they are internalised: whether these realities consist of the exclaimed-into-being, 'O the opal and the sapphire of that wandering western sea', in which the apostrophe and bejewelled nouns tell us that the line expresses feeling as much as it essays objective description, or whether they include 'The woman whom I loved so, and who loyally loved me', at once wholly other, very much 'The woman' as in the poem's affecting penultimate line ('The woman now is – elsewhere – whom the ambling pony bore'), yet surrounded by an aura because of her continued life in the consciousness of the speaker, who is touchingly sure that she 'loyally loved me' as the line traces its intimate circle, restoring her, in that last phrase, as the subject of 'love'.

In Thomas's 'Liberty', the use of 'I' crystallises and takes forward the poem's preoccupation with the nature of 'liberty'. The poet imagines scenarios of utter fullness and complete loss of awareness, before he arrives at a more partial conclusion, in which, implicitly, value attaches itself to the fact that he can occupy an in-between state, one in which he vividly enters the present tense of the poem's own lyric meditation. 'And yet I still am half in love with pain', Thomas writes, the debt to Keats freely admitted in this poem about freedom, even if something of the nigglingly corrective instinct that's part of the allusive process inheres in the word 'still', as though to imply that, while Keats's semi-falling in love with death in 'Ode on a Nightingale' was a mood, Thomas's half-love for pain is closer to a persistent existential, even ethical stance.[2]

As the syntax unfolds, it moves outwards, able to do so precisely because of the 'I' at the centre of the poetic web, syllables tracing along conversationally iambic filaments, a connection between self 'and things that have an end'—such as, one's prompted to speak back to the poem, the lyric 'Liberty' itself. Thomas dramatises not only a return to the present, but also the intuition that the poem's 'I' will stay in the verbal artefact's imagined space, helping to make a permanent treaty with process, 'with life and earth', with, that is, words that are at one 'With what is imperfect'. Helping the 'I' escape any pit of solipsism are the resources of rhyme, here linking the 'imperfect' 'life and earth' with the mingled yarn of human existence, 'with both tears and mirth'. But the poem's sign-off holds any too easy reconciliation with the 'imperfect' at arm's length, since it moves back to the real yet symbolic post-Romantic moon, which, throughout the poem, has been imagined as a fellow meditative presence: 'Both have liberty / To dream what we could do if were free / To do some thing we had desired long, / The moon and I'. That confederacy, entirely shaped by the need of the poet to have a companion in his voyage of thought and feeling, falls away in the striking rift between moon and self that opens up the last line and leaves the poet 'dark within the door'; briefly brought back to a point of seeming original loss and 'darkness'.

Stephen Spender's 'Thoughts during an Air Raid', my final opening exhibit, takes the word 'I' as its self-mocking fulcrum. Lying in a 'hotel bedroom' during an air raid (in the Spanish Civil War) on 'This girdered bed, which seems more like a hearse', the poet amusingly and half-unavailingly tries to put aside thoughts of imminent extinction. Readily, in and through his ironic manner, the poet concedes the self-concern which makes it both impossible and only too plausible to imagine that a 'bomb should dive / Its nose right through this bed, with me upon it'. The reader might imagine the 'me' there as uttered with a squawk of impotent indignation that finds refuge in a self-protective indifference in which 'all the "I"s should remain separate / Propped up under flowers, and no one suffer / For his neighbour'. Christ's teachings (see Matthew 22:39, 'Thou shalt love thy neighbour as thyself') are neatly sidestepped as the poet examines what it means to say 'Well, well, I carry on'. Keeping calm and carrying on emerge both as exhibiting a nonchalant sangfroid and displaying wryly an almost necessary callousness to and about the fate of others.

Thus, the three poets on whom the present chapter focuses emphasise what is for them the unignorable fact of subjectivity. As I trust has already been brought out, this central dimension to their work should not be confused with self-indulgence, narcissism or narrowness of perspective. These poets explore as much as they assert subjectivity. Having a self is not, for them, a passport to poetic success. But it is a necessary condition of their work, one that results in powerful and affecting poetry that delights in evolving its own particularities of form and structure: tercets, each monorhymed with virtuosic dash, in Hardy; a twenty-seven-line piece of fluid and unexpectedly rhyming iambic pentameter in Thomas, recalling the rhyming surprises of poems such as Milton's *Lycidas* and Arnold's 'Dover Beach', and cheating the ear into half-expecting yet failing to detect a double sonnet (lines 12–13 constitute a final couplet rhyme in the Shakespearean manner, though line 13—one short of a sonnet anyway—is hesitantly enjambed, while lines 22–27 compose a sestet rhyming *abaccb*), a twenty-two-line paragraph of unrhymed and irregular pentameter in Spender that exploits, as do the other two poems, the possibilities of abrupt caesurae. The use of 'I' in these poems—and poets—goes hand in hand with a daring willingness to let experience find its appropriate shape.

Hardy's Self-Hauntings

Hardy trusts in the observations made by the perceiving self, a trust made in the full knowledge that these observations are likely to be partial and untrustworthy. 'The poetry of a scene', he writes in his ghosted autobiography, 'varies with the minds of the perceivers. Indeed, it does not lie in the scene at all'.[3] 'Scene' recovers its association with drama in Hardy's poetry. Revisiting a scene, he formerly went to with his now dead wife in 'At Castle Boterel', he writes of the 'Primaeval rocks' that 'much have they faced there, first and last', geological phenomena that seem in touch with the Alpha and Omega. Magnificently and irrationally, magnificent because the irrationality accords with the heart's best truth, Hardy asserts: 'But what they record in colour and cast / Is – that we two passed'. The dash after 'Is' allows for let-down and recovered nerve, and the passing stays, is held in and as part of the 'Primaeval' 'cast' of things: where the 'cast' is that of a statue or indeed the dramatis personae of a play, and the passing is also a remaining. What matters in the end, as an archpriest of Modernism will have it, is 'the quality / of the affection':[4] 'affection', in Hardy's case, that is able to allow for a diminuendo, almost a confession that he hangs, in his assertion of sustained significance, on to the merest shred of a once-brilliant garment. Of his wife's now 'phantom figure', he writes:

> I look and see it there, shrinking, shrinking,
>   I look back at it amid the rain
> For the very last time; for my sand is shrinking,
>   And I shall traverse old love's domain
>   Never again.

The repeated, if uninsistent, use of 'it' there concedes much to the reality of death, the fact of extinction that makes a nonsense of the poet's attachments, and yet the reader responds with immense empathy to the resonance of Hardy's words earlier in the previous (penultimate) stanza, 'And to me'. Hardy's employment of a Wordsworthian signature ('To me did seem', say, from the opening stanza of the 'Ode: Intimations of Immortality') has its own original force. Wordsworth locates the subjective pain and loss in himself; Hardy says, 'what I know may have no objective value, yet without it there would be no knowledge of the kind that proves me to be a human being capable of valuing another person even after that person has served the purposes of a purposeless Nature'. The two 'for's in the quoted (final) stanza's third line display a stylistic trait prized by Hardy, namely, indifference to mere elegance: the first 'for' is bound up with a temporal construction; the second 'for' is a word meaning 'because' and allows for the poet's awareness of his own near-obliteration from a 'scene' he has sought to stamp with meanings conferred by memory and emotion.

And stamped it is and remains, for all the poet's authentic faltering of confidence, his recognition that 'my sand is sinking'. A similar trajectory curves through one of the most famous 1912–1913 elegies for his dead wife Emma, 'The Voice', where, again, another person's existence flashes itself upon us through the poet's subjective involvement. 'Woman much missed, how you call to me, call to me': the opening line almost fuses 'you' and 'me' and through its alliterative hypnotism fuses, too, 'me' with the fact of the woman being 'much missed'. Even the shock of the close when direct address is no longer available to the poet who now, in an extraordinary metrical key change, stands back and half-ironises the electrifying endearments, hopes and fears of the opening three stanzas— even here, the very existence of the self depends on fugitive belief in the continued existence of 'the woman calling':

> Thus I; faltering forward,
> Leaves around me falling,
> Wind oozing thin through the thorn from norward,
> And the woman calling.

'Thus I' may cast a look of resigned scepticism at the poetic performance that precedes it, scepticism possibly alleviated by a dash of something like severe compassion. But the poem's 'I' makes clear too his commitment to possibly futile speculation and questioning, a futility that's turned into tears such as angels weep as memory takes over like an inspired force of inspiration in the second stanza:

> Can it be you that I hear? Let me view you, then,
> Standing as when I drew near to the town
> Where you would wait for me; yes, as I knew you then,
> Even to the original air-blue gown!

The stanza opens with a barely credible hope that wholly binds any belief in Emma's posthumous existence to the mortal sensory apparatus of the poet. That apparatus, in conjunction with memory and imagination, will take us back to the stanza's yearningly positive if enigmatic last line and a half: yearningly positive in its epiphanic recovery of '*the* original air-blue gown' (emphasis added); enigmatic in the full implications of 'yes, as I knew you then', the line containing as an unspoken subtext the questions, 'how and how well did I know her then'? The next stanza will, in dispirited mood and mode, half-undo the exalted conviction here. In that third stanza, Hardy wonders whether all he hears is 'the breeze, in its listlessness', and yet when he republished the poem, a revisionary impulse persuaded him to confer upon Emma 'wan wistlessness' rather than the more agnostically bare 'existlessness'.[5] What's for sure is that 'The Voice' achieves its own poetic voice by deploying the self's capacity for intimations of otherness.

Often in Hardy a former, experiencing self is second-guessed, has shown to it something that a later self discovers, retrospectively and in the process, it would seem, of poetic composition, was or might have been the case. 'We Sat at the Window' contrasts past unawareness with present recognition of waste:

> We were irked by the scene, by our own selves; yes,
> For I did not know, nor did she infer
> How much there was to read and guess
> By her in me, and to see and crown
>   By me in her.
> Wasted were two souls in their prime ...

What there was 'to read and guess' we don't know, but that there was 'waste' the poem is in no doubt, and has much to do with 'our own selves'. Still, as the lines unfurl their haunting mix of simple diction and complicated syntax, we sense the poem sponsoring the possibly futile consolations of retrospective interpretative construction—it's able at least to break through to the majestic assertion (albeit of the triumph of negation), 'Wasted were two souls in their prime'. 'I' again is the enabler, permitting the poem to occupy the space hinted at as existing between the rhyme-coupling of 'yes' and 'guess', between certainty and speculation; the very errors of the former self are essential, ironically enough, to the truth-finding of the latter person.

The same collection *Moments of Vision* reminds us that Hardy's understanding of the first-person pronoun incorporates insights derived from Darwin and others. In 'Heredity', 'I' accommodates a persistent 'family face', a constant 'trait and trace' that passes on through generations, and turns the tables on the idea of the self as merely born to live and die; the same ideas that interrogated orthodox religion kindle disembodied belief in what allows the poet to 'Despise the human span / Of durance' and place his trust in 'I; / The eternal thing in man, / That heeds no call to die'. As the consciously oxymoronic 'eternal thing' concedes, there's not exactly a resurrection of the immortal soul being imagined here—more a kind of inhumanly human constant that persists, dominant genes inscribed across lifetimes. The poem exemplifies Hardy's ability to unsettle our sense of perspective, here disrupting any too easy or cosy a comprehension of the meaning of 'I'.

A comparable manipulation of viewpoint occurs in 'To the Moon', a dialogue poem between the poet and the much stared-at lunar phenomenon. In this ballad-like piece, 'I' is used only by the moon, the poem's addressee and it's the moon's experiences which have the character of subjective report: so, in the second stanza, asked what it has 'mused upon', the moon replies:

> 'O, I have mused on, often mused on
>   Growth, decay,
> Nations alive, dead, mad, aswoon,
>   In my day!'

Worth noticing here is the bravura with which the moon's swashbucklingly ironic speech rhythms are caught: in the first line's repetition, the second's metrical deepening (still trisyllabic, but here with two contrapuntal strong stresses), and the third's growingly mocking run of epithets. The human speaker and the moon occupy the same cosmos and poetic stanza, the cunningly wrought echo between each stanza's second line (spoken by the human being) and final line (spoken by the moon) binding their subjectivities together. Of course, we're witnessing projection of human feeling onto the inanimate, but such is the poetry's verve and nerve that it gifts what is usually the object of feeling with a capacity to speak for itself, not least in the poem's final words where the moon suggests that life is 'a show / God ought surely to shut up soon, / As I go'. There, the effect of 'surely', at once reinforcing the good riddance to bad rubbish attitude of the moon and hinting too at a tacit note of disquiet, again interests us in the moon as though it possessed its own identity.

In so doing, the poem hints at a metapoetic link with another poem from the same collection, 'On A Midsummer Eve', a seeming trifle of a poem that shows how a Hardy poem rhymes to see itself, and set alterity echoing[6], to adapt phrases from Seamus Heaney's 'Personal Helicon':

> I idly cut a parsley stalk,
> And blew therein towards the moon;
> I had not thought what ghosts would walk
> With shivering footsteps to my tune.

I went, and knelt, and scooped my hand
As if to drink, into the brook,
And a faint figure seemed to stand
Above me, with the bygone look.

I lipped rough rhymes of chance, not choice,
I thought not what my words might be;
There came into my ear a voice
That turned a tenderer verse for me.

'I idly cut a parsley stalk': subject, verb, object—the simplest of opening lyric gambits setting up a metre (iambic tetrameter) which holds with variations throughout the sturdily familiar three-stanza form, a form suited to triadic possibilities and resolutions. Only an adverb 'idly' affects our reading, pushing us in the direction of 'chance, not choice', and yet, in miniature, the poem dramatises its own creative emergence as words that finally accept that out of chance comes choice, the design shaped from the very idleness and thoughtlessness displayed by the poem's 'I'. It could be the case, as has been noted, that folkloric associations gather round the cutting of the parsley, 'a sign that the person so occupied will sooner or later be crossed in love',[7] and the very title reminds of the harum-scarum events of Shakespeare's *A Midsummer Night's Dream*. But Hardy plays his allusive hand coolly, as though rhythm and rhyme led him against any conscious intention to imagine 'what ghosts would walk / With shivering footsteps to my tune'.

The phrase 'my tune' almost mocks itself as rhyme-induced, but it earns its place pleasingly in the story, as the ghosts obey the poet's whim, one turning before the reader's eyes and in his or her ears into a poem. Further active verbs in the second stanza seem less sure that they are without purpose: 'scooped my hand / As if to drink' implies an action half-conscious that it isn't what it seems, lending the following 'And' a 'shivering' impression of conjuration, 'As if' the poet had called up the 'faint figure' that 'seemed to stand / Above me'. An echo of Shelley's *Alastor*—'A Spirit seemed / To stand beside him' (pp. 479–80)[8]—immediately brings in the poem's purview associations with the tale of Narcissus and Echo, and among other things 'the bygone look' is directed towards Hardy's Romantic ancestor, even as it retains a link to the poem's commerce with age-old, immemorial customs.

While Shelley's Poet receives no answer to his questioning calls, however, Hardy's 'I' records in the final stanza the coming of a successful reply that justifies the process of lyric thoughtlessness, blowing new tunes on an old, cut stalk, vouchsafed some vision of the future: 'There came into my ear a voice / That turned a tenderer verse for me': 'verse' emerges from 'voice', voice', in turn, arising from the 'choice' to marry subjectivity to the chances involved in poetic composition. The result is a 'tenderer verse' than might have been expected after the first stanza's 'ghosts'; yet, the poem is haunted by their 'shivering footsteps' and by the fear that tenderness will prove to be illusory. As often in Hardy's hands, reliance on the 'I' opens a door into richer experiential dimensions.

Thomas's Self-Communion

Edward Thomas's poetry struck Walter de la Mare on account of the 'intensity of solitude' that shines through it, an intensity revealed through his companionship with 'things natural, simple', a fellow feeling for the shy, the forgotten and overlooked.[9] His brother poet also noticed Thomas's way of making poems from what seems an extended process of 'quiet self-communion': 'They are not drops of attar in a crystal vase', not so much self-admiring verbal icons as structures expressive of 'inmost being'.[10] The comments are illuminating, the more so when one allows for the poems as searching for what that 'inner being' might be, whether of the self or the natural world. Or in the case of the poem 'Beauty' of a concept, though an idea inseparable from its sensuous incarnations and the poet's subjective approach to it. Thomas breaks through to a renewed discovery of the notion—'Beauty is there' is the poem's close, the first time, after the title, the great Kantian/Keatsian abstraction is deployed—by way of navigating a mood of some intricacy.

It's a mood that begins with a mocking and self-mocked caricature of Keats's famous 'epitaph': Thomas writes, 'Here lies all that no one loved of him, / And that loved no one', before immediately dismissing the self-dismissive lines, 'Then in a trice that whim / Has wearied'. He moves on in a long sentence that takes it in nuanced, continually rebalancing couplet rhymes to present himself as a river unwarmed or unlit by the sun, then as a birdlike presence, floating 'through the window even now to a tree / Down in the misting, dim-lit, quiet vale'. This presence may only be 'some fraction of me', but it is a fraction of his 'heart', and it turns out, with the unexpectedness of lyricism's grace and gift, not to be 'content with discontent', as 'The Glory' has it, or in love with loss, but to be in touch with some newly recovered awareness of value, the poet comparing himself to 'a dove / That slants unswerving to its home and love'. The phrase 'slants unswerving' captures in its weave of deviation and directness the journey towards 'Beauty' made by the poem's 'I'.

Thomas is careful, as are all three poets discussed, not to suppose that the self is merely a straightforward point of departure for embrace of the universe. Poem after poem by all three poets suggestively inhabit a liminal space where self loses absolute definition and to that degree negotiates with otherness. But what's entered into, at its close, by a poem such as 'It Rains' is an even more intense 'intensity of solitude' than its first two stanzas had evoked. Contrasting the happiness of previous companionship with the precarious happiness of being 'alone', Thomas concludes the poem with what feels like an allusion to Hardy's 'On A Midsummer Eve':

> When I turn away, on its fine stalk
> Twilight has fined to naught, the parsley flower
> Figures, suspended still and ghostly white,
> The past hovering as it revisits the light.[11]

Hardy 'idly cut a parsley stalk'; Thomas has a strong sense of the parsley flower assuming a symbolic function when 'I turn away', as though walking off from and yet remaining on his chosen path and leaving behind in his wake a welter of 'suspended and ghostly white' possibilities; that the parsley 'Figures . . . / The past hovering as it revisits the light' springs into virtual poetic life as a result of the writer's imagination. At the same time, it involves a turning away, a letting go, as temporal abstractions subsume personal identity.

Altogether sturdier in its grasp of difference is 'The Owl', one of Thomas's finest poems, exemplary in its demonstration of how the self can serve as a lantern to light up the experience of others. The poem opens with a refusal to melodramatise: the poet may be cold, hungry and tired, but 'at the inn I had food, fire, and rest'. There's much art, apparent in the nicely judged, self-checking 'yet's' that feature in each of the first three lines, in the poem's way of preparing us for its major turn, when the poet's attention is broken in upon by 'An owl's cry, a most melancholy cry // Shaken out long and clear upon the hill'. The clean pentameter, with initial stress reversal, in that last line summons us to attend, despite any faltering wish to suppose we can dismiss the effect as pathetic fallacy, to the fact that the poet's been told 'plain what I escaped / And others could not, that night, as in I went'. 'And others could not' is terse with something close to necessary guilt, a guilt that sees in any one moment of warmth or happiness a likely shadow award to 'others' of cold and misery.

Thomas avoids self-congratulation or transcendence of the difficult truth told him by the owl's cry. His energies as a poet are devoted in a crucial final stanza to securing and living with recognitions that are almost impossible fully to accept:

> And salted was my food, and my repose,
> Salted and sobered, too, by the bird's voice
> Speaking for all who lay under the stars,
> Soldiers and poor, unable to rejoice.

'Salted' means something like given pungency and even added relish, on the one hand; yet on the other hand, it can suggest salt rubbed in a wound, and the medley of meanings carries over into the sibilant-shaped words that dominated the stanza:[12] 'sobered' marks a movement into deeper responsiveness to the plight of those who come into view in the final line, 'Soldiers and poor, unable to rejoice', though able to suffer and endure, or so that strong stress reversal on 'Soldiers' may indicate. The bird's voice, surrogate in some ways of the poet's own, sets up the expectation that 'rejoice' will come as a rhyme word. Thomas's poem ends on a firm rebuttal of the idea that 'rejoicing' is available to all, without discrediting it wholly.

The poem comports itself with the subtlest of tact towards the others that 'intensity of solitude' brings to the poet's mind, comparable in its uncondescending recognitions to Baudelaire's reaching out from beyond his own melancholy in 'Le Cygne' to a sense of the defeated and lost throughout history. Baudelaire's great poem may have more flair and 'attack', but it's a tribute to 'The Owl' that it can be spoken about in the same breath. Elsewhere, bird song can speak to Thomas of a dimension close to the source of poetry, as in 'The Unknown Bird', quintessential in what might be called its rapidity of hesitation, its quickness to mobilise qualifications of voice and perspective, the light, sure touch it brings to its handling of a blank verse ready to switch caesural positions, to mix its registers, to strew the poem with words that question statement such as 'If', 'Yet' or 'but', to introduce parentheses that turn out to be central, as when the bird's 'La-la-la!' is described as 'seeming far-off – / As if a cock crowed past the edge of the world, / As if the bird or I were in a dream'. The bird is the poet's restlessly other-worldly Romantic self and harbinger of an enchanted realm that the poet is one side of or another: the effect of 'or' in that second line is to suggest that one of the two, but not both, 'were in a dream'. Yet, the poem concludes with a greater sense of conviction than Thomas's self-monitoring investigations tend to express:

> This surely I know, that I who listened then,
> Happy sometimes, sometimes suffering
> A heavy body and a heavy heart,
> Now straightway, if I think of it, become
> Light as that bird wandering beyond my shore.

Even here, the writing cannot wholly surrender to the transcendence of self-promised by the last line with its identification between poet and 'that bird wandering beyond my shore': subjectivity and its possible limits, and the possible positives of those limits, reappear as a subtext below the phrase 'beyond *my* shore' (emphasis added). The words 'surely I know' are not without a doubt signalled by the hint of over-assertion. And chance and inspiration seem equally at play in the conditional mood that re-enters the poem in the second-to-last line, 'if I should think of it', a reminder, should we need it, that transcendence of self, merging with an idealised other who represents something buried in the self, is no easy business. It requires the intervention, an intervention not simply at the disposal of the will, of the very self that finds fulfilment in the idea of self-transcendence.

In 'Lights Out', Thomas explores the point at which self must pass into non-self, into some larger otherness which he figures as a forest that all must enter.

> I have come to the borders of sleep,
> The unfathomable deep
> Forest where all must lose
> Their way, however straight,
> Or winding, soon or late;
> They cannot choose.

The writing has candour and boldness that make it individual, even as one senses affinities with the opening of Dante's *Inferno* and roughly contemporary Freudian ideas of the 'id' or the Jungian notion of the 'collective unconscious', a phrase used by Jung in an essay of 1916, the same year as the composition of Thomas's poem. Without the opening gambit 'I have come', the exploration of 'The unfathomable deep / Forest where all must lose / Their way' would not be possible. In other words, 'I' provides the starting point for a meditation on what 'all' must experience. Such shifts find a mirror in the poem's technique: rhyme, with its promise of pattern, delivers a surprise as of missing a step as the enjambment between 'deep' and 'Forest' performs itself. The poem comes close to showing what is stake for Thomas in his use of 'I': the word is the imperilled guarantor of a hard-worn and often painful freedom, a freedom opposed starkly in 'Lights Out' to a state in which 'They cannot choose'.

The poem's true battle is to make of this inability to choose a state that can be, if not chosen, at least understood, or at least negotiated with imaginatively, as the final two stanzas bring out:

> There is not any book
> Or face of dearest look
> That I would not turn from now
> To go into the unknown
> I must enter, and leave, alone,
> I know not how.
>
> The tall forest towers;
> Its cloudy foliage lowers
> Ahead, shelf above shelf;
> Its silence I hear and obey
> That I may lose my way
> And myself.

The short lines give an air of resolution even as the poet seems almost too long for loss of clarity. Active verbs recover a sense of agency in

'I would not turn from now', 'That I may lose my way'; at the same time, the modal words 'would' and may' imply an element of wish and hope. In the first stanza, the poet presents himself as free yet compelled 'To go into the unknown', any way of exiting from which is itself something that 'I know not how'.

That not knowing is the poem's unspoken goal and derives from a rhyming scheme in which 'And myself', with uncanny irony, appears as the last word of a piece devoted to an imagining of loss of self. It's as though the poet was telling himself and his reader that the word 'I' names both centre and circumference of his endeavours, so far, at any rate, as the process of poetic creation is concerned. This is less to reduce the pursuit of otherness to a fundamental solipsism than to authenticate a poem as a place where self, language and form triangulate their mutually inflecting claims.

In 'The Long Small Room', Thomas plays with the place he evokes and commemorates—'The long small room that showed willows in the west'— as an implicit emblem of a poem.[13] If the four, seemingly four-square stanzas suggest the poem as a space for housing thought and memory, its chief lodger feels as though he never owned the place: 'When I look back I am like moon, sparrow, and mouse / That witnessed what they could never understand'. With a hint of yearning communicated through the sensitively roughened rhythms ('never', for example, chosen in preference to the more regular 'not'), the poem rises here to an acuter awareness of the not knowing, the never quite understanding that is among Thomas's major contributions to fuller comprehension of what a truthful reliance on subjectivity might feel like. Understanding, we suppose mistakenly, or so the poem hints, may develop across time, and in a sense it does.

But the understanding that develops here is of never fully grasping the nature of experience. 'The Long Small Room' is threaded through with currents of temporality: a pure pastness ('I liked it'); an explicitly present process of recollection ('When I look back'); the occupation of a now that feels recurrent, and involves almost tragic commitment to the endless conversion of wordlessness into shaped poetic designs (we note the return at the close to the willow, now a symbol of deciduous loss) that are always at the same time incomplete, in process:

One thing remains the same – this my right hand

Crawling crab-like over the clean, white page,
Resting awhile each morning on the pillow,
Then once more starting to crawl on towards age.
The hundred last leaves stream upon the willow.

There is an effect of resolution created by the verbal 'stream' set against the three participles that precede it, and yet the resolution involves a recognition of loss, too, as 'The hundred last leaves' cling to the tree. The 'I' reduces to a part of itself, the 'right hand' seen by the poet as 'Crawling crab-like over the clean, white page', almost driven by a force beyond will or identity, yet serving a function of expression, too: the self's persistent wish to track the adventures of consciousness, which, like the hand itself, is said to 'crawl'—piteously, yes, but also with 'crab-like' determination—'towards age'.

Spender's Self-Possession

Stephen Spender is the heir of poets such as Hardy and Thomas in his preoccupation with the self. In relation to the political pressure exerted on writers by events to conform to an ideological line, Spender writes memorably: 'The majority of artists today are forced to remain individualists in the sense of the individualist who expresses nothing except his feeling for his own individuality, his isolation'.[14] The cost exacted by such individualism shows in the phrasing: 'are forced', 'expressed nothing but'. In a sense, he sells his own achievement short here; he is alert in his critical work to ways in which the self can function in poetry, drawing attention (for example) to Yeats's quest 'for a mysterious symbol which would contain everything outside the writer's self' and to the difference between the same poet's art of 'self-dramatizing' and T. S. Eliot's mastery of 'self-criticism'.[15]

In his poetry, he covers a spectrum of tones and attitudes in his handling of the self that make his work, for this reader, truthful and beautiful. He sees off gibes about his alleged protestations of sincerity and candour in poems that don't so much defend the self as bring out the pathos of its inevitable existence. 'My parents kept me from children who were rough' only superficially seems to invite us to sympathise uncritically with the snobbish, vulnerable speaker. The last line captures perfectly the blind spot in the boy's assumption of superiority: 'I longed to forgive them, yet they never smiled' achieves a singular mingling of tones; ventriloquising the child's belief that it's for him to 'forgive them', it captures too the way in which the self shapes and is shaped by interpretation, seeing here the absence of smiles as justification for near-paranoid isolation and rejection of others. The reader is left in possession of a song of innocence blighted by experience, of the way in which experience leads to the formation of personal myths and social judgements.

'Moving through the silent crowds' tears up the second-imagery triggered by sincere, heartfelt but hackneyed responses to the plight of the unemployed and becomes a searing and unsettling poem about the poet's relationship to his imaginings:

> I'm jealous of the weeping hours
> They stare through with such hungry eyes.
> I'm haunted by these images,
> I'm haunted by their emptiness.

The poem uses the first-person pronoun to plunge in upon itself and uncover forbidden sources of inspiration: jealousy of those experiencing first-hand, authentic suffering; inward self-haunting by 'images', modes of representation; a sense of their final 'emptiness', despite their allure. That 'emptiness', the final word in this calculatedly self-thwarting ballad of driven iambic tetrameters, suggests the bankruptcy of the poem's love affair with the aesthetic and restores, in an eleventh-hour, oblique way, sympathy with the poor.[16]

Spender is a poet of the self's complications. 'Subject: Object: Sentence' explores the ambiguous meanings of each noun in its title, noting that 'subject' can mean both ruler and being ruled. What is semi-amused abstraction here, in this later poem, serves as a wry coda to many of Spender's more lyrically impassioned poems in earlier decades, as in works concerned with the 'real' such as 'Rolled over on Europe' which conveys something close to isolated estrangement from contemporary culture and politics: 'Only my body is real', the poet asserts in the final lines, where rough-hewn phrases and rhythms establish less a boastful candour than a beleaguered form of affective bare life: 'Only this rose / My friend laid on my breast, and these few lines / Written from home, are real'. The inflections are transgressively homosexual, and the 'few lines' seem inscribed by a self both cerebral and corporeal.

Few poets convey so powerfully what it means to have and live inside a self, a process given near-physical force in 'Not to you I sighed', in which nothing is said to 'you', but in which inanimate objects 'All splintered in my head and cried for you', 'you' ending up as the poem's final word, held in a significant rhyme with 'I knew'. 'Acts passed beyond the boundary of mere wishing' looks as though it's turning from 'wishing' to action; yet, the poem derives from the touch of hands the feeling that 'I must have love enough to run a factory on, / Or give a city power, or drive a train'. The exuberant conceit (half-mocked by the last off-rhyme) suggests a connection between erotic impulse and the contemporary technological world, and also that any such connection lies firmly within the bounds of 'wishing'. 'An "I" can never be great man' (later entitled 'Trigorin', a character from Chekhov's *The Seagull*, whose passion for fishing is alluded to) explores the ways in which self is composite, and how in a person of genius 'The "great I" is an unfortunate intruder', having to compete with 'all those other "I"s who long for "We dying"'.

Freudian death-wish theory seems at work in that final line, and Spender, like other writers of the period, can trace connections between private neurosis and public disturbance. But while Auden uses 'I' warily, Spender grounds his work in territory staked out by the pronoun. He accepts that his is a subjective poetry, and, therefore, a poetry of quest, process and development, and, in 'Never being, but always at the edge of Being', he writes an eloquent defence of his commitment to becoming. His gerundival, participial phrasing, alongside a syntax and rhythm that never come to rest until the crucial last line, concedes and exults in the fact of always being in pursuit of being; he is no claimant to any Heideggerian posture of 'dwelling', and is the more impressive, for this reader, for not being so. That last line reads in what amounts to an ethics as well as a poetics: 'I claim fulfilment in the fact of loving'. The line ripples with a subliminal, consciously embraced paradox: since 'loving' involves—if one recalls Socrates's and Diotima's definitions in Plato's *Symposium*— desire for what is not possessed, 'fulfilment' on Spender's reckoning is likely to go hand in hand with acceptance of being unfulfilled. The line's emotional colouring is nuanced: it suffuses its tone of hard-won affirmation with something close to acceptance of loss.

Interplay between past and present selves, between expectation and outcome, brings a necessarily historical dimension to the writings of all three poets. In 'What I expected', Spender plays his own variation on such interplay by returning in the poem's concluding stanza to the very ideal whose erosion has been lamented in the second and third stanzas. So at the close, we swim against the current of personal experience and public events to recover what the poem both knows can no longer be attained and yet can be rearticulated as a potent absence: 'For I had expected always', writes Spender,

> [...] Some final innocence
> To save from dust;
> That, hanging solid,
> Would dangle through all
> Like the created poem
> Or the dazzling crystal.

Those final images, emerging from rhythms that at once 'solid' and intricately dangling, reward creator and receiver: the poem is 'created', putting in mind the fact of an inventor, while the crystal is 'dazzling', reminding us of the effect of something that is beautiful. The fact that they exist in the virtual space created by the self's expectations underscores the way in which such expectations, possibly blemished by over-idealism, possibly doomed to be disappointed, serve to keep before us aspirations and hopes we would not wish to see ignored.

In 'The Room above the Square', Spender holds in a near-single act of mind a past 'light' and a present 'dark', a past 'certainty' and a present state of solitude, isolation and a sense of other lovers connected to the poet through kinship of situation and now, it's implied, metaphorically and perhaps literally buried, a square above a room and 'sunbright peninsulas of the sword'. The poem moves between 'I' and 'you' and extends its amorous and geographical/historical scope to accommodate other lovers and conflict-torn Europe. A near-single act of mind, and yet the poem is also triadic in its structure, shifting its gaze until it ends with a process that feels 'perpetual', though differently 'perpetual' from the opening 'light': 'Now I climb alone', the opening words of the last stanza describe a lonely climbing that is an image for the way in which the poets discussed in this essay locate their inevitable predicament, their imaginations' almost tragic, often enabling end and origin. Their pursuit of their individual tracks gives their work a capacity to unsettle and disturb that in equal measure complements and clashes with the more evident ambitiousness of great Modernist masters. Certainly, it suggests the many paths open to and taken by poets writing in the first few decades of the twentieth century, poets who neither reject wholly the lyric ego, nor unquestioningly cosset it either, but deploy it for questioning, adventurous purposes.

Notes

1 Qtd, respectively, from Thomas Hardy, *The Complete Poems*, ed. James Gibson (London: Palgrave Macmillan, 2001); Edward Thomas, *Collected Poems*, with a foreword by Walter de la Mare (London: Faber, 1974); Stephen Spender, *New Collected Poems*, ed. Michael Brett (London: Faber, 2004). Unless indicated otherwise, all poems by Hardy, Thomas, and Spender are quoted from these editions, none of which has line numbers.

2 The echo of Keats is noted in Edward Thomas, *The Annotated Collected Poems*, ed. Edna Longley (Tarset: Bloodaxe, 2008), p. 262.

3 Qtd from Thomas Hardy, *Selected Poems*, ed. Tim Armstrong (London: Longman, 1993), p. 348.

4 Ezra Pound, *The Cantos* (New York; New Directions, 1996), Canto 76, p. 477.

5 See Thomas, *Annotated Collected Poems*, p. 165.

6 Seamus Heaney writes, in 'Personal Helicon', 'I rhyme / To see myself, to set the darkness echoing', *Death of a Naturalist* (1966; London: Faber, 1976), p. 57.

7 Ruth Anita Firor, *Folkways in Thomas Hardy* (1931), qtd from Hardy, *Selected Poems*, ed. Armstrong, p. 206.

8 Qtd from *Percy Bysshe Shelley: The Major Works*, ed. Zachary Leader and Michael O'Neill (Oxford: Oxford UP, 2003).

9 Thomas, *Collected Poems*, p. 8.

10 Thomas, *Collected Poems*, p. 10.

11 For the idea that the poem displays 'parallels (rain, lovers walking, ghostliness) with Hardy's "At Castle Boterel"', see Thomas, *Annotated Collected Poems*, p. 294.

12 See Vernon Scannell for the view that 'the word *salted* certainly means *flavoured* or *spiced*, but at the same time less comfortable connotations are invoked: the harshness of salt, the salt in the wound, the taste of bitterness, and of tears', qtd in Thomas, *Annotated Complete Poems*, p. 198.

13 Edna Longley finds 'hints of a coffin-shape' about the poem which for her 'seems spoken posthumously: as by a ghost who haunts "the dark house" of life with unfinished business', Thomas, *Annotated Complete Poems*, p. 316.

14 Stephen Spender, 'Poetry and Revolution', in *The Thirties and After: Poetry, Politics, People 1933–1975* (Glasgow: Collins, 1978), p. 53.

15 Stephen Spender, *The Destructive Element: A Study of Modern Writers and Beliefs* (London: Cape, 1935), pp. 125, 121.
16 For discussions of this poem and other poems by Spender treated in this present essay, see Michael O'Neill, 'Poetry and Autobiography in the 1930s: Auden, Isherwood, MacNeice, Spender', in *A History of English Autobiography*, ed. Adam Smyth (Cambridge: Cambridge UP, 2016), pp. 31–44 (esp. 334–5); that essay argues that 'At times Spender uses the word "I" less as a means of telling us about himself than about what it is to have a self', p. 334.

Part II

Dissenting Voices

Aestheticism, Gender and
the Art of Identity

4 Pamela Colman Smith, Anansi and the Child

From *The Green Sheaf* (1903) to *The Anti-Suffrage Alphabet* (1912)

Katharine Cockin

Little magazines have a significant place in the cultural practices of Modernist artists and writers. Often short-lived, magazines were launched with great enthusiasm and zeal and acted as a catalyst for emerging aesthetic innovations. When the artist Pamela Colman Smith launched *The Green Sheaf*, a new hand-coloured magazine, on 30 January 1903, it was a pivotal moment for many of the individuals closely involved.[1] For a not insignificant investment in an annual subscription of thirteen shillings, readers were promised thirteen issues, postage included.[2] At the end of its first, and ultimately only, year of publication, *The Green Sheaf* had published an intriguing and idiosyncratic collection of poetry, short stories and artwork, with an eclectic series of occasional supplements. The quality of the publication is striking: several thick, cream paper pages are fastened with green ribbon. This is echoed by the self-referential image on the front cover, depicting printed green pages tied up in a bundle with red ribbon, in the manner of sheaves of corn.[3] Its style, method of reproduction and emphasis on decorative arts, folk art and symbolism place *The Green Sheaf* in the arts and crafts tradition. It is also characterised by mysticism and a distinctively (and deceptively) whimsical mode. This essay is concerned with the significance of this curious, childlike aesthetic adopted by Smith in *The Green Sheaf* and throughout her life and work, from the 1890s to the period of women's suffrage campaigning.

Pamela Colman Smith's work as an artist was difficult to locate: in various ways, it was innovative, disturbing and eclectic. Melinda Boyd Parsons laid the ground for subsequent studies of Smith's work, with her analyses of its mysticism and experiments with synaesthesia.[4] In 1907, Smith's artwork was exhibited in New York by the photographer Alfred Stieglitz, who became the leading promoter of modern art. Kathleen Pyne has examined Smith's association with female artists, such as Gertrude Käsebier, in some detail, concluding that they 'shared in common this feminine paradigm of the unconscious as a mystical voice'.[5] Smith was singled out by Stieglitz for exhibition in 1907 at his Little Galleries of the Photo-Secession, where she exhibited several times, in 1907–1909. An entire article on her art was published in *Camera Work*, a journal founded by Stieglitz to explore photography as an art form.[6] In his gallery and in the journal, other visual arts (such as Smith's) were included as a point of comparison for the different techniques and effects available in different media. More recently, Elizabeth O'Connor has examined the 'female networks' and 'performative primitiveness' of Smith's work, noting that: 'She seems to have styled her public and private personae as a distinctive fusion of the Jamaican trickster Anansi and the Irish pixie, both of which she appears to have been drawn to because of their gender indeterminacy, unconventionality and fearlessness'.[7] Although Irish cultural references seem to have become relevant, it was the internationally renowned actor Ellen Terry who was responsible for naming her 'Pixie'.[8] In building on my research on Pamela Colman Smith's associations with theatre practitioners, Ellen Terry and her children, Edith Craig and Edward Gordon Craig,[9] I will focus here on the child as a sustained figure in her artwork and how it becomes amenable to the challenging gender politics of the women's suffrage campaign. The androgynous aspects of Smith's artwork noted by Pyne[10] lend themselves to a more challenging interpretation when considered in wider contexts. Androgyny or markers of gender resistance as a challenge to heteronormativity were a feature of a developing lesbian aesthetic and way of life associated with Edith Craig and her circle of female partners and friends. Ellen Terry also became associated with challenges to the institution of marriage and free love, featuring in the editorial of the notorious periodical *The Freewoman*, with its later modernist transformations as *The New Freewoman* and *The Egoist*. The queerness of 'Pixie' Smith therefore signifies beyond the attributes of individual quirkiness and accumulates the force of association with wider movements for social reform and gender equality. It is in this context that I place Smith's adoption of a childlike, mystical persona as a storyteller and collector of Jamaican folk stories. Hyacinth Simpson has noted that Smith was responsible for publicising Jamaican short stories at a critical moment with her edition, *Annancy Stories* (1899).[11] The destabilising potential of Anancy the spider was somewhat overshadowed by the childlike mode in Smith's visionary and mystical artwork and poetry. It created a new way of seeing that was ahead of its time but it also recreated an orientalising perspective to which she was at some points herself subjected. Smith made a great impression on those who met and worked with her, in the fields of art, theatre, the occult and women's suffrage politics; she was often described and presented herself in terms of her difference and strangeness.[12]

Details about Smith's family history are gradually becoming clearer. Although she was born in London, she grew up in Jamaica and lived at times in New York and London and, in her later years, in Cornwall.

She was heavily influenced by Jamaican folk stories, the Arts and Crafts aesthetic and Japanese visual arts. Her artistic contribution to the tarot has brought her appreciation in that field of interest. In 1909, Smith's artwork was commissioned by A. E. Waite for a set of tarot cards which has become world-famous. Her artwork has been shown to have innovative and idiosyncratic features.[13] With Waite and W. B. Yeats, Smith was actively involved with the Order of the Golden Dawn and interested in mysticism and the occult. As an artist, she trained at the Pratt Institute, Brooklyn where she came into contact with Gertrude Käsebier and learned about a style informed by Japanese techniques of notan-massing.[14] Her landscapes, figures and decorative motifs are boldly described in thick black outline and later hand-coloured. She had established herself as an artist and illustrator in USA before returning to Britain in 1899 under the patronage of the actor Ellen Terry. For Terry, Smith was at that time a role model for her son Edward Gordon Craig, who was developing his skills in art and design but needed guidance on the practicalities of making his own living. It is from Terry's recommendations to her son of Smith's applied art and business methods that some insights are provided into Smith's range of works: decorated boxes, cards and lampshades and, more importantly for Terry, that these were selling in USA.[15] Smith diversified with publications of books and magazines, both contributing to them and editing them. In 1902, Smith had co-edited with Jack B. Yeats, the brother of the poet W. B. Yeats, a little magazine entitled the *Broadsheet*. The circumstances of that collaboration, and Smith's decision to launch a new magazine on her own at all, is one of the intriguing elements of the story of *The Green Sheaf*.

Although *The Green Sheaf* was indeed her project, it has instead been associated with the Yeats brothers, if it is mentioned at all. It is therefore relevant to consider this framework briefly at the outset. In a private letter from W. B. Yeats to his patron, Lady Augusta Gregory, on 9 December 1902, claims credit for his influence over Smith's new magazine project:

> I had almost forgotten to tell you that Pamela Smith is bringing out a Magazine to be called the 'Hour-Glass' after my play. I am to write the preface in order to define the policy which I have got them to take up. The Magazine is to be consecrated to what I called to their delight, the Art of Happy Desire. It is to be quite unlike gloomy magazines like the Yellow Book [*sic*] and the Savoy [*sic*]. People are to draw pictures of places they would have liked to have lived in and to write stories and poems about a life they would have liked to have lived. Nothing is to be let in unless it tells of something that seems beautiful or charming or in some other way desirable. They are not to touch the accursed Norwegian cloud in any way, even though they may be all good Ibsenites, and they are not to traffic in Gorky.[16]

Under two months later, Smith's *The Green Sheaf* magazine was published, with content similar to that described by Yeats. although, as will be established later, some of the contributions including even the two by Yeats tended more towards the sombre if not even the nightmarish. The new magazine also had a different title and an unsigned editorial verse statement or manifesto which highlighted eclectic forms united by their aim of 'pleasure':

> My *Sheaf* is small ... but it is green.
> I will gather into my *Sheaf* all the young fresh things I can –
> *pictures, verses, ballads*, of *love* and *war*; tales of *pirates* and the
> *sea*.
> You will find ballads of the *old world* in my *Sheaf*. Are they not
> green for ever...
> Ripe ears are *good* for *bread*, but green ears are good for *pleasure*.

In his study of W. B. Yeats, Roy Foster described *The Green Sheaf* as the 'house journal' of the 'circles of ninetyish aestheticism'.[17] This essay begins with a reconsideration of the extent to which this overlooked magazine did follow the agenda Yeats had planned for *The Hour Glass*. The assumption of necessary links between *The Hour Glass* and *The Green Sheaf* seems to be based on Yeats's own account and may have overemphasised his role in *The Green Sheaf*.

Although *The Green Sheaf* was listed in Alvin Sullivan's *British Literary Magazines: The Victorian and Edwardian Age 1837–1913* (1984), it was omitted from James G. Nelson's checklist of publications by Elkin Mathews since it was a publication 'for which Matthews acted for a time as London agent'.[18] It was also sold at Brentano's in New York and directly by Pamela Colman Smith. Matthews was the publisher of W. B. Yeats, James Joyce and Ezra Pound and various little magazines, so the association of *The Green Sheaf* with his name would have generated expectations and provided access to an existing market of readers. Since Edith Craig's costumier business was advertised in every issue and Craig was a close friend of Smith, it is not surprising that a full run of *The Green Sheaf*, as well as some of Smith's artworks, have survived in Craig's archive.[19] As Mark S. Morrison (2001) has noted, 'little magazines [operated] as a public forum',[20] and *The Green Sheaf* shared a common hostility towards the mass market and a turning away from the material world. Pamela Colman Smith's role as the editor of *The Green Sheaf* becomes clearer in view of what Churchill and McKibble have described as the new 'conversational model' of Modernism rather than the 'competitive framework' which had hitherto dominated.[21] In the *Broadsheet* (1902), Smith had reportedly been distressed by the volume of work in production which fell to her in the hand-colouring of the artwork required for each issue. Lily Yeats described Smith's physical exhaustion and reference to her treatment as bullying.[22] Bruce Arnold notes that in the second year of publication, in January 1903, 'mainly because of the burden of hand-colouring, [Pamela Colman Smith] pulled out'.[23] In a private letter, Jack Yeats described Smith's 'erratic' behaviour and his own dissatisfaction with a lack of control over the magazine:

> Between you and me and the wall, as they say, Miss Pamela Smith (though I think a fine imaginative illustrator with a fine eye for colour, and just the artist for illuminating verse) is a little bit erratic, and she being a woman I can't take a very high hand with things, so there is often a lot of bother about the numbers, and I don't like being responsible for anything that I have not got absolute control of.[24]

This scenario is reminiscent of Jayne Marek's conceptualisation of the orthodox gendered designation of Modernism which presumes that men are the bold experimenters and women are driven by the personal and emotional.[25]

The mood in which *The Green Sheaf* emerged is reminiscent of the character Bridget, in W. B. Yeats's play *The Hour Glass*, who expresses frustration with the Wise Man who is insistent on a tiresomely adversarial pedagogical style: 'It is a hard thing to be married to a man of learning that must always be having argument'.[26] If *The Hour Glass* was an influence on the development of *The Green Sheaf*, as Yeats had claimed in a private letter to Lady Augusta Gregory, it may also appear to imply the stealing of some thunder from the editor. Christopher St John confided in Ellen Terry some details about Yeats's view of this new magazine, as conveyed by Smith:

> Pixie is starting another paper – an affected, dilettante sort of affair, but as her Irish god "Mr Willie" has blessed it, she thinks it will be the most original journal ever produced.[27]

Some indication is provided here of the extent to which Pamela Colman Smith and her associates tended to posture and declaim. This consequently presents a difficulty for others to arrive at a definitive account of their motives or attitudes on the basis of the surviving records. In private correspondence, especially a hyperbolic and confrontational style is adopted which makes it difficult to determine the explicit from the ironic meanings. Ellen Terry was unambiguous about her opinion of W. B. Yeats's poetry; in weights and measures, Yeats's quantity was overtaken by Tennyson's and Swinburne's quality, as she confided to her son Edward Gordon Craig:

> [...] after Tennyson the wee-est bit of old Swinburne for me before bucketsful of Yeats – I've tried for a whole year to "acquire the taste" for Yeats, & can't <Yeats> – Phillips – Watson all good, but not good enough I feel.[28]

In her idiomatic evaluation, the hyperbolic quality perceived in Yeats's poetry is relevant also for an understanding of Christopher St John's reporting
that Smith's 'Irish god "Mr Willie" has blessed' *The Green Sheaf*. St John
seems to be alluding to the shared extravagance of expression in which one
may support another's work as if in religious devotion and service when
he reported that Smith thought 'it will be the most original journal ever
produced',[29] as if Yeats's blessing conferred a guarantee of originality.

In spite of the reported difficulties between the co-editors of the *Broadsheet*, related to uneven workloads, difficulties in communication and
clarity about areas of responsibility and control, there was a productive
relationship between the two magazines, demonstrated by shared contributors such as Lady Augusta Gregory, W. B. Yeats, Frederick York
Powell, the 'Oxford scholar and neighbour of the Yeats family in Bedford
Park since 1887',[30] AE (George William Russell) whose three-act play
Deirdre was a supplement to issue seven. Christopher St John, the author
and historian, with whom Edith Craig had established a relationship by
this point, contributed several short stories. They were drawn to Smith's
approach, described in *Camera Work* by Benjamin De Casseres: 'To such
minds what is practical is vulgar, what is utilitarian is ugly'.[31] In its pursuit of pleasure, *The Green Sheaf* published material concerned with folk
revival, fictionalised transcription of oral narrative (short stories told to
the author by...), short enigmatic lyrics and long narrative poems concerning archaic subjects and settings. It has been suggested that the magazine
was influenced by the Pre-Raphaelites in its 'integration of art forms'.[32]
This is typical of little magazines, where text and artwork are often inte-
grated, so it is difficult to analyse either separately. Art was also published
in *The Green Sheaf* as supplements such as an unknown drawing of the
actress Mrs Stirling (1815–1895) by Dante Gabriel Rossetti (issue three)
and, most notably perhaps, a pastel sketch by W. B. Yeats of 'The Lake at
Coole' reproduced in black and white on silver paper (issue four).

Contributions to the magazine were eclectic but some themes are apparent. Numerous contributions to issue six focus on the sea, neptune,
a mermaid.[33] Yeats's description of 'the Art of Happy Desire' does not
accurately describe his own short story in the second issue, entitled 'The
Dream of the World's End' which is more of a nightmare. However, the
dream vision aesthetic is a dominant feature and characterises Yeats's
other contribution, one of the few supplements, his pastel sketch. I have
argued elsewhere that the place depicted has a great significance for
Yeats as a site associated with mysticism and elucidated by his essay
'Magic'.[34] The absence of any framing editorial statement in each issue
makes interpretations generally more complex, specifically with regard
to the rationale for the various supplements. However, this place is for
Yeats a portal to ancient times, a visionary place.

Several contributions to the first issue focused on mountainous landscapes (Lady Gregory's translation of 'The Hill of Heart's Desire' from

'the Irish of Raferty a peasant poet', Alix Egerton's poem 'A Song of the Pyrenees') and journeys (Cecil French's poem 'The Parting of the Ways' and Christopher St John's short story 'How Master Constans Went to the North'). Other contributors incorporate the terms 'dream' or 'vision' in their titles. In the second issue, several contributions meditated, like Yeats's 'Dream of the World's End', on dreams: short stories by J. M. Synge, 'A Dream on Inishmaan' and John Masefield's 'Jan a Dreams' and the poem by Cecil French, 'A Prayer to the Lords of Dream'. The three short stories by Yeats, Synge and Masefield present themselves as autobiographical, non-fictional records of actual dream experiences. Masefield's 'Jan a Dreams' begins: 'This dream, like all my intenser dreams, commenced with a noise as of the beating of many wings, the rush of water, and the roaring of a sea-wind' (9). Smith's illustration to the story depicts a long swirl of water with leaves above as if caught by the wind. Synge's 'A Dream on Inishmaan' begins with a reflective analysis of the significance of place: 'Some dreams I have had in a cottage near the Dun of Conchubar on the middle island of Aran, seem to give strength to the opinion that there is a psychic memory attached to certain neighbourhoods' (8). Like Yeats's dreamer, Synge's wakes trembling. Synge's story provides a link to Yeats's sketch of 'The Lake at Coole' if it is read alongside Yeats's essay on 'Magic' where he establishes the lake at Coole as a mystical site: 'I think I now know why the gamekeeper at Coole heard the footsteps of a deer on the edge of the lake where no other deer had passed for a hundred years'.[35]

In issue 4, Pamela Colman Smith's poem 'Alone' exemplifies the introspective and individualist experience of the dream/vision. The isolated figure, usually androgynous, is presented in a landscape which is both empty and, under the brooding surveillance of the figure, presented as if in a provisional state, waiting for something to happen. The lone woman in the poem (and accompanying illustration by the poet) is presented intently gazing at a far horizon:

Alone and in the midst of men,
Alone 'mid hills and valleys fair;
Alone upon a shop at sea;
Alone—alone, and everywhere.

O many folk I see and know,
So kind they are I scarce can tell,
But now alone on land and sea,
In spite of all I'm left to dwell.

In cities large – in country lane,
Around the world – 'tis all the same;
Across the sea from shore to shore,
Alone – alone, for evermore.

Although Conolly associates the solitude in the poem with Smith's own perceived isolation,[36] the situation of the figure in relation to the landscape is a recognisable configuration. The positioning of relative powerlessness (of the child or the isolated figure) as objects of attention in Smith's artwork appears to be a complex acting out and a speaking back to power. The conceptualisation of a blank landscape lends itself to the visionary but risks homogenising other places and peoples in an orientalising perspective.

This kind of vision is nevertheless embraced by a diverse group of contributors from Ireland and Japan as well as England. Transnational perspectives are provided by contributors such as Yone Noguchi (1875– 1947), who was active in New York and London. He contributed three poems to *The Green Sheaf*: 'The Violet', issue eleven and 'Evening', and 'Mugen' to issue twelve.[37] Laurence Irving's short story 'Prince Siddartha' in issue four is a short story based on the life of Gautama Siddartha who became Buddha. Pamela Colman Smith's storytelling work was advertised in several issues of *The Green Sheaf*. She adopted the persona of Gelukiezanger, teller of 'West Indian folk stories'. This performance work positioned her as a transatlantic mediator and prophet, disseminating the stories of Anansi the trickster. Smith seems to have celebrated creolisation in an innovative aesthetic and mystical mode which used the dream visions of *The Green Sheaf* as a portal to another world of experience. Her experiments with paintings which translated music share this aesthetic of translation and transportation, engaging with the unconscious in their automatic response and moving between modes in a synaesthesia.

Before *The Green Sheaf* came to an end, Smith was already planning to open up a shop and had even created an advertisement, as she announced in a letter:

> I have a shop! Observe circular! "The Green Sheaf" as a periodical is to be discontinued! After number 13 which will be out shortly (also no 12) – And the shop's the thing – Any stencils or drawings or watercolours of yours or Jacks I should be so pleased to have – on sale – at 10 per cent. You fix price – I had not heard of Lilly & Lolly's great move – of taking on all Dun Emer – good!!!!' [...].[38]

The innovative work in Ireland which brought together folk and traditional crafts with new perspectives on national cultures was taking place in theatre and the textile arts. In 1905 when Lily Yeats founded the Dun Emer Guild, she enlisted Smith on the design of banners.[39] In London in 1903, Pamela Colman Smith had been involved with W. B. Yeats and Edith Craig in theatrework. They were all involved in The Masquers theatre society, led by Craig in 1903, and Craig and Smith collaborated on scene designs for W. B. Yeats's play *Where There is Nothing*. Smith's correspondence suggests a competitive attitude towards the actor Florence Farr who seemed to be more successful in forming her own society, The Dancers.[40] The volatility in these various cultural organisations was intense and in the occult societies, various factions seemed to have vied for power. The rift in the Order of the Golden Dawn seems to have been the inspiration for a dramatic farce entitled *Nicandra*, on which Edith Craig and Pamela Colman Smith seem to have collaborated.[41]

The year 1909 was for Pamela Colman Smith one of new opportunities. The women's suffrage movement was diversifying even further in its use of arts and crafts to promote the arguments and enlist support. Edith Craig had become the leading director of women's suffrage plays, working as a freelance and for the Actresses' Franchise League. The militant campaigns were building momentum but the visual arts continued to be a priority as the posters and postcards ensured that memorable images and messages were kept in the public eye. Smith's artwork was used in various posters produced by the Suffrage Atelier at this time.[42] The timing, in the same year as her women's suffrage artwork, of what became one of her most significant commissions deserves some consideration. In 1909, she was invited to create eighty illustrations for a set of tarot cards for A. E. Waite, her colleague from the Order of the Golden Dawn. Joan Coldwell has established the extent to which the artist elaborated on the instructions provided by Waite and some of these amendments related to the facial resemblances of figures on the cards to Smith's friends.[43] The temptation to create subversive elements in such powerful images must have been hard to resist. Her graphic design work for the women's suffrage movement may have given her some motivation to inscribe and transmit through the tarot cards some aspect of her own interpretations.

Through her continued friendship with Edith Craig and her mother, Ellen Terry, Colman Smith received other commissions of various kinds which make up the freelance artist's life. Bram Stoker, the author and business manager for Henry Irving at the Lyceum Theatre, enlisted her to illustrate his remarkable gothic novel, *The Lair of the White Worm* (1911). It provided some challenges for the illustrator which I have discussed elsewhere,[44] but the temptation to incorporate friends into the images which she succumbed to in the tarot cards seems to have been repeated in her depiction of the sinuous form of Lady Arabella. In her white gown and wearing thick-lensed glasses and long fingers, Lady Arabella seems to resemble Ellen Terry in some of her stage roles.[45] By 1913, Ellen Terry's health had deteriorated and the publication of an illustrated book entitled *The Russian Ballet* was an emergency project designed as a rescue package by Edith Craig and Christopher St John to save the family income by catching the potentially lucrative wave of interest in Russian dance.[46] At very short notice, Pamela Colman Smith provided the illustrations and Christopher St John wrote the text, a rapid response demonstrating their willingness to come to the aid of Ellen Terry on a confidential basis to preserve the illusion of Terry's authorship.

When, in 1911 Edith Craig founded the Pioneer Players theatre society in London, with Ellen Terry as its president, Pamela Colman Smith was on hand to collaborate on some productions. The society operated from Craig's Covent Garden flat at 31 Bedford Street. Smith was a member from 1915 to 1920 and responsible for designing the society's logo which was used to decorate the play programmes, posters and annual reports. The distinctive design showed a number of figures in silhouette, suggesting perhaps a cast of actors assembling or processing. Smith also designed souvenir programmes in 1915 for Craig's Pioneer Players productions of Nikolai Evreinov's *The Theatre of the Soul*.[47]

During the First World War, Smith was involved in commissions for charities associated with the war. She designed posters for the Red Cross and became involved in the manufacture of toys. As a contribution to the war effort, this appears to be a fairly conventional response in its use of needlework skills and the production of items for the care of children. It was however an activity associated with women's suffrage and social reform interventions. In November 1914, Christopher St John reported to Ellen Terry that her daughter and Smith were busy making dolls.[48] Toy-making was associated with charitable organisations at this time but it was also part of a radical socialist venture in London's East End. Sylvia Pankhurst had founded the East London Toy Factory, creating work for women in a way which would provide satisfying work and opportunities for development: if a woman developed a new design which became successful, she would receive the benefits.[49] Pankhurst had also been instrumental in founding a creche for working women: a revolutionary solution to a fundamental problem. These powerful forces were encapsulated in its name, the Mothers' Arms. Although it repurposed the site of the Gunmakers' Arms public house, the new name captured the forcefully nurturing embrace of the community as 'the mothers' arms' which liberated individual women from childcare, making them armed and ready to labour to create a new world. It is not clear whether the toy production with which Smith and Craig were involved was connected with the Mothers' Arms, but they had the opportunity of learning about it from Norah Smyth, who was a Pioneer Players member, and had ubiquitous presence at the Mothers' Arms.[50]

Pamela Colman Smith bridged various traditions and cultural practices with her childlike persona and her subversive comedy. As a trickster figure, in the persona of the storyteller Gelukiezanger, Smith brought stories from the West Indies to Western Europe. The revolutionary potential of the comic mode had become a powerful force for dramatists and artists producing thought-provoking and effective works to sustain interest and enlist new recruits to the women's suffrage movement and to challenge the hegemony which held that women were indeed to be classified with children as subordinate to patriarchal control and protection. Nursery rhymes, fairy tales, children's literature and memorable oral forms were appropriated for political purposes with deadly ideological intent. Postcards depicted the Houses of Parliament as 'The House that Man Built',[51] adapted from the nursery rhyme 'This is the house that Jack built'. An anthology of verse written by suffrage prisoners, *Holloway Jingles*,[52] drew on the memorable oral tradition, yoking the authority of naïve innocence with a revolutionary cultural force reminiscent of the Romantic period of revolutionary zeal. As a revolutionary force, women were explicitly promoting the creation of the new era, and at times appealed to mothers of the new generation to create a new world. The postcard emblazoned with the emotive image of a crying baby with the caption 'Mummy's a suffragette' disseminated an anti-suffrage warning of the damage inflicted by a politically active mother on her child.[53] The photographs which documented events and street processions provide evidence that the children of suffrage activists were present. They accompanied their mothers, posed for photographs with promotional materials and attended plays. Some of the propagandist merchandise appropriated whimsical, witty or childlike references. Pamela Colman Smith was one of three artists who collaborated with Laurence Housman on *The Anti-Suffrage Alphabet*, a gift book produced by Leonora Tyson, the organiser of the Lambeth and Southwark branch of the WSPU at a high price (at 10s 6d) and advertised in the WSPU newspaper, *Votes for Women*, for publication in time for the Christmas period.[54] It therefore seems to have been aimed to raise the maximum for the limited outlay which the hand-printing production involved and in this respect may have been influenced by Smith's experiences of the American market. The design of the stencilled artwork for the book incorporated the WSPU colours by printing the images and the text in purple and green ink on cream paper.[55] The appeal of linking each letter of the alphabet to a fact or phenomenon related to women's suffrage derives from the implications of the decorative gift book as a child's alphabet book: equality is as fundamental as ABC. This sentiment was articulated by Lady Constance Lytton when she recalled in her autobiography the insights provided by Olive Schreiner's *Dreams* (1891) which acted like 'an ABC railway guide to our journey'.[56] The discourse of the child in the women's suffrage movement therefore activated a powerful emotive response, drew on the didactic modes of representation from children's education, and spoke back to the ideological force of the anti-suffragists' biological essentialism. For Smith, it was a coherent and consistent application of the childlike as a dynamic and revolutionary mode of representation which she had tested extensively for several decades in her own work and, seemingly, created a gateway to access the ancient wisdom of Anansi.[57]

Notes

1 An account of the involvement of Edith Craig, Ellen Terry and William Butler Yeats is provided in Katharine Cockin, 'Bram Stoker, Ellen Terry and Pamela Colman Smith: The Art of Devilry', in *Bram Stoker and the Gothic: Formations and Transformations*, ed. Catherine Wynne (Basingstoke: Palgrave, 2016), pp. 59–71; and Katharine Cockin, *Edith Craig and The Theatres of Art* (London: Bloomsbury Methuen, 2017), Chapters 2 and 3.

2 A flyer was distributed to publicise the new publication; John Johnson Collection, Bodleian Library.

3 A complete run of *The Green Sheaf* is held in the National Trust's Ellen Terry and Edith Craig archive and the John Johnson Collection, Bodleian Library; a partial run is held at the British Library. An original watercolour sketch, possibly unique, depicting a tree is inserted in the copy of *The Green Sheaf*, no. 11 held in the John Johnson Collection, Bodleian Library.

4 Melinda Boyd Parsons, 'Pamela Colman Smith and Alfred Stieglitz: Modernism at 291', *History of Photography* 20.4 (1996): 285–92.

5 Kathleen, Pyne, 'The Photo-Secession and the Death of the Mother: Gertrude Käsebier and Pamela Colman Smith', in *Modernism and the Feminine Voice: O'Keeffe and the Women of the Stieglitz Circle* (Berkeley: U of California P, 2007), p. 58.

6 Benjamin de Casseres, 'Pamela Colman Smith', *Camera Work* 27 (July 1909): 18–20.

7 Elizabeth Foley O'Connor, 'Pamela Colman Smith's Performative Primitivism', in *Caribbean Irish Connections: Interdisciplinary Perspectives*, eds. Allison Donell, Maria McGarrity, and Evelyn O'Callaghan (Kingston, Jamaca: U of Cork P and U of the West Indies P, 2015), pp. 157–73; Elizabeth O'Connor, '"We Disgruntled Devils Don't Please Anyone": Pamela Colman Smith, *The Green Sheaf* and Female Literary Networks', *South Carolina Review* 48.2 (Spring 2016): 72–89.

8 Ellen Terry letter [4 June 1900] in *The Collected Letters of Ellen Terry*, Vol. 4, ed. Katharine Cockin (London: Pickering & Chatto, 2013), p. 119. Hereafter *CLET*.

9 An account of the involvement of Edith Craig, Ellen Terry and William Butler Yeats is provided in Cockin, 'Bram Stoker, Ellen Terry and Pamela Colman Smith', pp. 159–71; and Cockin, *Edith Craig and The Theatres of Art*, Chapters 2 and 3.

10 Pyne argues that in the exhibition of her work, Pamela Colman Smith 'appears as an androgynous sorceress, a prophetess who seeks and finds the cosmic, heroic voice in nature'; Pyne, *Modernism and the Feminine Voice*, p. 48.

11 See Hyacinth M. Simpson, 'The Jamaican Short Story: Oral and Related Influences', *The Journal of Caribbean Literatures* 4.1 (Fall 2005): 11–21. Simpson notes that collections such as *Annancy Stories* (1899) removed the 'moral ambivalence of the trickster tales' because they were aimed at 'young audiences'.

12 See Ellen Terry's characterisation of her as a 'Japanese toy' discussed in Cockin, 'Bram Stoker, Ellen Terry and Pamela Colman Smith', p. 171. Smith's self-portraits of herself with Edith Craig are reproduced in Katharine Cockin, 'New Light on Edith Craig', *Theatre Notebook* XLV.3 (1991): 139; and Katharine Cockin, *Edith Craig (1869–1947): Dramatic Lives* (London: Cassell, 1998), p. 123.

13 Joan Coldwell has pointed out that Colman Smith had freedom in designing the minor arcana and that Waite failed to notice that she had indeed adapted

his designs in different ways; Joan Coldwell, 'Pamela Colman Smith and the Yeats Family', *Canadian Journal of Irish Studies* 3.2 (1977): 27–34.

14 Melinda Boyd Parsons, 'Mysticism in London: The "Golden Dawn": Synaesthesia and Psychic Automatism', in *The Spiritual Image in Modern Art*, ed. Kathleen J. Regier (London: The Theosophical Publishing House, 1987), pp. 73–101. Mary K. Greer, *Women of the Golden Dawn: Rebels and Priestesses* (Rochester, NY: Park Street P, 1995), pp. 405–9.

15 Ellen Terry letter to Edward Gordon Craig [30 October 1899], *CLET*, p. 69.

16 Letter from William Butler Yeats to Lady Gregory [9 December 1902]; John Kelly and Ronald Schuchard eds., *The Collected Letters of W. B. Yeats* (Oxford: Oxford UP, 1994), pp. 271–72.

17 Roy Foster, *W. B. Yeats: A Life* (Oxford: Oxford UP, 1997), p. 258.

18 See Katharine Cockin, 'Addendum to "British Literary Magazines: The Victorian and Edwardian Age 1837–1913"', *Victorian Periodicals Review* XXIII.2 (Summer 1990): 68; James G. Nelson, *Elkin Mathews, Publisher to Yeats, Joyce, Pound* (Madison: U of Wisconsin P, 1989), p. 195.

19 Cockin, 'Addendum'.

20 Mark S. Morrison, *The Public Face of Modernism: Little Magazines, Audiences and Reception 1905–1920* (Madison: U of Wisconsin P, 2001), p. 7.

21 Suzanne W. Churchill and Adam McKible, eds., *Little Magazines and Modernism: New Approaches* (London: Ashgate, 2007), p. 12.

22 Lily Yeats qtd in Bruce Arnold, *Jack Yeats* (New Haven, CT & London: Yale UP, 1998), p. 103.

23 Arnold, *Jack Yeats*, p. 103.

24 Jack Yeats, qtd in Arnold, *Jack Yeats*, p. 103.

25 Jayne Marek, *Women Editing Modernism: Little Magazines and Literary History* (Lexington: Kentucky UP, 1985), p. 8.

26 William Butler Yeats, *The Hour Glass* (Dublin: Cuala P, 1914), p. 28.

27 Christopher St John qtd in Cockin, *Edith Craig and the Theatres of Art*, p. 60.

28 Ellen Terry qtd in Cockin, *Edith Craig and the Theatres of Art*, p. 60.

29 Christopher St John qtd in Cockin, *Edith Craig and the Theatres of Art*, p. 60.

30 Arnold, *Jack Yeats*, p. 101.

31 De Casseres, 'Pamela Colman Smith', p. 20.

32 Sullivan, 'The Green Sheaf', p. 156.

33 Pamela Colman Smith, 'The Rime of the Sea'; 'The Mermaid of Zennor'; John Masefield, 'A Deep Sea Yarn'; Dorothy Ward, 'The Tidal River'; Thomas Campion, 'A Hymn in Praise of Neptune'; Cecil French, 'The Waters of the Moon'.

34 Cockin, 'Bram Stoker, Ellen Terry and Pamela Colman Smith', pp. 159–71.

35 William Butler Yeats, "Magic" (1901), in *Essays and Introductions* (London: Macmillan, 1961), p. 518.

36 Conolly bases this on Smith's marital status, being an only child whose parents have died and her deteriorating relationship with W. B. Yeats; p. 169.

37 The Japanese author was to become closely involved with W. B. Yeats and was published in New York and London at this time.

38 Pamela Colman Smith qtd in Arnold, *Jack Yeats*, p. 105.

39 At the Women's Museum of Ireland, there are records of Colman Smith's designs for vestments and banners for Loughrea Cathedral, County Galway, produced by the Dun Emer Guild, founded in 1902 by Susan ('Lily') and Elizabeth ('Lolly') Yeats and Evelyn Gleeson; http://womensmuseumofireland. ie/articles/susan-and-elizabeth-the-yeats-sisters [accessed 13 February 2018].

40 For a detailed account of these collaborations, see Cockin, *Edith Craig and the Theatres of Art*, Chapters 2 and 3. The scene designs, two paintings by Colman Smith depicting Edith Craig as 'The Puck' and Colman Smith and Craig as 'The Devils' and a photograph of a group in which Colman Smith is included are reproduced in Cockin, *Edith Craig (1869–1947): Dramatic Lives.*

41 A signed sketch of the costume worn by Nicandra, the Egyptian spirit, is extant in Edith Craig's archive; see Cockin, *Edith Craig (1869–1947): Dramatic Lives*, pp. 45–6. An account of *Nicandra* 1901 is given in Cockin, 'Bram Stoker, Ellen Terry and Pamela Colman Smith', pp. 169–70.

42 Lisa Tickner, *The Spectacle of Women: Imagery of the Suffrage Campaign 1907–1914* (London: Chatto & Windus, 1987), pp. 247–8.

43 Coldwell, 'Pamela Colman Smith and the Yeats Family', pp. 27–34.

44 Cockin, 'Bram Stoker, Ellen Terry and Pamela Colman Smith', p. 166.

45 Terry as Ophelia was the subject of portraits by various artists, including G. F. Watts. As Margaret in *Faust* she was photographed for publicity and theatrical merchandise.

46 See *Cockin, Edith Craig and the Theatres of Art*, pp. 145–7.

47 Smith's involvement in the Pioneer Players theatre society accounts for a significant period hitherto overlooked by critics who have examined her artwork.

48 Christopher St John letter to Ellen Terry, 30 November 1914, ET-Z1, p. 433; National Trust Ellen Terry and Edith Craig archive, British Library.

49 Sylvia Pankhurst, *The Home Front: A Mirror to Life in England During the First World War* (London: Cresset Library, 1987), p. 72.

50 Edith Craig was the founder and Director of the Pioneer Players throughout and Norah Lisle Smyth was a member from 1912 to 1914.

51 Anti-suffrage postcard, 'This is the house that man built', reproduced in Tickner, *Spectacle*, p. 51.

52 *Holloway Jingles*, ed. Nicholas A. John (Glasgow Branch of WSPU, n.d. [1912]).

53 Reproduced in Lisa Tickner, *The Spectacle of Women*, p. 219.

54 Three artists produced stencil artwork for the booklet: Ada Ridley, Alice B. Woodward and Paula C. Smith (Tickner 1987: pp. 247–8). A copy is held at the Museum of London, 50.82/1591; and digitised online at https://collections.museumoflondon.org.uk/online/object/718243.html [accessed 13 February 2018]

55 Tickner, *The Spectacle of Women*, pp. 247–8.

56 'Now after even so short experience of the movement as I had known, this "Dream" seemed scarcely an allegory. The words hit out a bare literal description of the pilgrimage of women. It fell on our ears more like an ABC railway guide to our journey than a figurative parable, though its poetic strength was all the greater for that'. Lady Constance Lytton, *Prisons and Prisoners*, 1914 (London: Virago, 1988), p. 157.

57 Wilson Harris analyses the 'complex metaphorical gateway' involving limbo and Anansi; see Wilson Harris, 'History, Fable and Myth in the Caribbean and the Guianas', in *Explorations: A Selection of Talks and Articles 1966–1981*, ed. Hena Maes-Jelinke (Mundelstrup: Dangaroo P, 1981), pp. 147–60; 155. In *The Green Sheaf* and in her Gelukiezanger performances, Smith uses story-telling, meditations on dreams and journeys in Anansi mode as a gateway to another dimension of experience.

5 Maverick Modernists

Sapphic Trajectories from Vernon Lee to D. H. Lawrence

Sondeep Kandola

A century after Ezra Pound's exhortation to 'make it new' and Virginia Woolf's declaration that 'something had fundamentally changed in human nature on 1 December 1910', the relationship of the Modernist movement to its Victorian forebears continues to be interrogated and revised.[1] Jessica Feldman, for example, has challenged the temporal and artistic rupture identified by Woolf, Pound and others as inaugurating the New School by instead recovering artistic continuities between it and its Victorian precursors.[2] Similarly, Vincent Sherry offers a corrective to the originary narrative of high Modernism perpetuated by T. S. Eliot, Ezra Pound and others by highlighting its strategic excision of French and British Decadent writers from its annals in favour of the more palatable Symbolist school because of the perceived threat of emasculation posed by any association with the less than salubrious reputations of the so-called 'Tragic Generation' of the 1890s.[3] By contrast, George Steiner and Susan Sontag have variously argued for the centrality of Victorian queer masculinity in the formation of Modernism's iconoclast agenda.[4] And, in turn, critics such as Shari Benstock and Cassandra Laity have sought to recuperate a parallel tradition of 'Sapphic Modernist' writing to offset not only the manifest androcentrism of the Modernist movement, itself, but also, as seen earlier, one that appears to be shared by some of its modern chroniclers.[5] In this respect, Laity's proposition that 'Sapphic Modernists' (here, identified as Willa Cather, Violet Hunt, Katherine Mansfield, H. D. and Renée Vivien) looked back to Decadent writers such as Swinburne and Wilde to create a 'female' tradition of sexual dissidence that stretched back to Sappho, in part, anticipates Sherry's discussion of the erasure of a palpable Decadent influence from the history of Modernism. Yet, concurrently, Laity is also aware that her observation that 'H. D. and others used the Decadents to fashion a feminist poetics of desire' is equally open to the disapproval of a 'feminist revisionary process' because of its conception that the Decadent effect negatively re-inscribes the very masculine sexual imperatives that Sapphic Modernists sought to evade.[6]

More recently, Laura Doan and Jane Garrity have rerouted 'Sapphic Modernism' and its attendant controversies in favour of a more 'inclusive' and cross-media recovery of a 'Sapphic Modernity', a project which for them is:

> bound up with the circulation of medical and sexological knowledge in the late nineteenth and early twentieth centuries, with the publication of works such as Richard von Krafft-Ebing's *Psychopathia Sexualis* (1886) and Havelock Ellis's *Studies in the Psychology of Sex, vol. II Sexual Inversion* (1897), to name two studies that were most influential in identifying the category of "sexual inversion" in Britain and North America.[7]

The fact that the relationship of the novelist and art historian Vernon Lee and her then lover the poet Mary Robinson was, at one point, seriously considered as a case study for Ellis's pioneering sexological text tantalisingly suggests the existence of a Victorian precursor to the Sapphic Modernity of the twentieth century.[8]

Modernism(s)?

For Modernists such as T. S. Eliot and Virginia Woolf, Vernon Lee was undoubtedly an anachronism. In a cancelled draft version of 'The Fire Sermon' from *The Waste Land* in which Eliot parodied 'The Rape of the Lock', his cultured lady 'Fresca' is 'baptised in a soapy sea / Of Symonds – Walter Pater – Vernon Lee'.[9] In a letter to Violet Dickinson in 1909, Virginia Woolf unkindly described the now semi-deaf Lee as 'a garrulous baby' and later declared herself to be morally outraged by Lee's experimental anti-war plays 'The Ballet of the Nations' (1915) and *Satan the Waster* (1920) for what she described as their 'unpatriotic' pacifism.[10] For the critic Dennis Denisoff, it would appear that Woolf was suffering from a severe case of 'the anxiety of influence' as he identifies the indebtedness of Woolf's *Orlando* (1928) to Lee's story of 1886 'Oke of Okehurst' and Hilary Fraser highlights the Dadaist inflections of *Satan the Waster*.[11] Was Lee, as understood by the Modernists, a literary anachronism or a Modernist foremother? Poignantly, it seems that Lee herself plumped for the former as in 1890, she came to privately regret that old age and infirmity now prevented (in her own words) 'all possibility of personal contact with the generation to which I ought to have belonged'.[12] Notwithstanding Lee's personal pessimism about her seemingly superannuated status, Catherine Maxwell and Patricia Pulham observe that 'We have now begun to appreciate that Vernon Lee's work, far from being irrelevant to modernism, is crucial to its development'.[13]

Strikingly, in its promotion of art in the service of good health, both physical and moral, and its championing of an empathetic (female) homosociality, Lee and her co-researcher and lover Clementina (Kit) Anstruther-Thomson's investigation into the field of 'psychological aesthetics' between 1888 and 1912 appears to anticipate both the counter-Decadent and Sapphist strains of the Modernist movement(s). In this, revisiting Lee and Thomson's project also promises to further assuage Lee's elision from the developmental narrative of Modernism. At the turn of the century, Lee's search for invigorating intellectual activity both in the face of her own bouts of ill health and the cultural degeneration diagnosed as symptomatic of the Victorian *fin de siècle* saw her reject the 'intellectual rebellion and lawlessness' of the Aesthetic School and its Decadent successor in favour of exhorting contemporary artists to produce healthy and morally educative art.[14] And yet, contemporaneously, in the context of the feverish atmosphere of the 1890s, Lee also bravely laid claim to a 'queer comradeship' with the 'outlawed thought' of the literary avant-garde.[15] In pursuit of mental and physical equanimity for herself and others, Lee now reframed Aestheticism's clarion call for 'art for art's sake' as 'Art not for art's sake but art for the sake of life – art as one of the harmonious functions of existence'.[16] In this less than pithy aphorism, Lee suggested that the psychological affect of art could be manipulated to induce physical and mental well-being.

Prone, as Lee was, to sustained bouts of neuralgia and nervous depression from a young age, one of her main struggles in life appears to have been to achieve and maintain physical health and psychological equanimity for herself. Where her older half-brother, the minor poet Eugene Lee-Hamilton, had succumbed to what appears to have been a psychosomatic illness in the 1870s which left him paralysed for over twenty years and which required Lee and her mother to be in constant attendance, it was not until 1894 that she came (in her own words) to 'recognize that on one side [her] family is, acutely neuropathic and hysterical'.[17] Here, despite her sustained pursuit of aesthetic health, Lee's private self-diagnosis unexpectedly appears to internalise the emotive terms with which Cesare Lombroso's *Man of Genius* (1888) and Max Nordau's *Degeneration* (1892) had popularly pathologised the New Schools. Her most sustained bout of neurasthenia appears to have taken place in 1888, directly after the collapse of her relationship with her first love Mary Robinson when she had broken with Lee to become engaged to the eminent French philologist and Orientalist, James Darmesteter, a man crippled by a childhood spinal disease. A disgusted Lee cruelly described her rival as a 'Quasimodo', 'dwarf', 'cripple' and 'humpback' and she and her equally prurient brother spent several months writing to the affianced pair to exhort them to keep the marriage Platonic.[18] The entrance of the expert horsewoman and Judo player Kit Anstruther-Thomson at this juncture as both nurse *and* acolyte proved timely for Lee who later recalled how 'these strange dream-like months of illness and hopelessness, of misery' were offset by the 'enveloping happiness

out of which [Kit's] patience and loving kindness drew me, a new creature'.[19] While the tortured and hysterical state of mind engendered by
the split from Robinson is perhaps best evinced in Lee's highly coloured
1896 fairy tale 'The Virgin of the Seven Daggers', a feverish story based
on her ostensibly recuperative journey to the warmer climes of southern
Spain and Tangiers, the sustained emotional sustenance that Thomson
afforded Lee also appears to have been similarly sublimated into her
work. Although the concept of 'psychological aesthetics' was explicitly
generated out of Lee's desire for mental and physical health, underpin-
ning it all was Lee's wounded obsession with Mary Robinson's reproductive health, the spectre of the 'humpback' fiancé and finally, her own
undoubted attraction to Thomson's 'boyish' beauty.

In Thomson, Lee, who had been reading and researching the works of
William James, Grant Allen, Theodor Lipps and Karl Groos in the com-
paratively new field of psychology for over a decade, found a uniquely
invaluable subject for her nascent research into psychological and attendant physiological responses to art. Squiring her through the galleries of
Western Europe, Lee discovered that Thomson was a 'motor' type who
was acutely sensitive to the changes in her breathing and concomitant
muscular tensions induced in her subject in the presence of all manner of art objects from classical statues, to paintings, Gothic churches
and pieces of Chippendale furniture. Lee devoted months to listening
and watching her subject in order to document in her gallery notebooks
the minute physical sensations that Thomson experienced. Lee and
Thomson first showcased their experiments in psychological aesthetics
in an 1897 article published in the *Contemporary Review* called 'Beauty
and Ugliness'. Although jointly authored, Lee's voice dominated the article, interpreting and analysing Thomson's description of the bodily responses that various art objects elicited in her. The opening of the article
expressed Lee's belief that their model of psychological aesthetics superseded earlier conceptions of how the aesthetic phenomenon affected the
viewer. Thomson's body was a living prescription for good health since
it was in the (almost imperceptible) physical responses that she described
to Lee in front of chosen art objects that Lee founded her belief that
viewing beautiful form was physiologically restorative. As Thomson described it to Lee, looking at a chair affected the movement of the eyes,
changed her breathing pattern and made her subtly mime the position
of the object in her own stance. Physical sensations were divided into
the agreeable and disagreeable, the sensations pertaining to beauty and
ugliness, respectively. Beauty induced tensions of 'lifting up' and 'press-
ing downwards' which effected an 'agreeable arrangement of agreeable
movements in ourselves' that constituted 'a harmonious total condition
of our adjustments'.[20]

For Lee, classical art stood as the epitome of the beautiful and she argued that ideal forms on display in antique sculpture could invigorate the

viewer's experience of their own body. In their extended meditation on the medicinal function of Greek sculpture, they noted that the 'antique statue' had a 'much finer muscular system' than a human being and that the act of 'miming' this perfected form 'gives us the benefit of the finer organism represented'. A series of 'muscular adjustments' was elicited in the 'beholder' where the 'sight of the easy carriage of body' illustrated by the statue gave the viewer 'a sense of increased lightness and strength' in themselves (*BU*, 221–2). Believing that the act of recognising beauty was an empathetic action because in 'looking at the Doric column for instance, and its entablature, we are attributing to the lines and surfaces, to the spatial forms, those dynamic experiences which we should have were we to put our bodies into similar conditions', Lee concluded that the 'projection of our own life into what we see is pleasant or unpleasant ... facilitates or hampers our own vitality' (*BU*, 20). Psychological aesthetics presented itself as more than a dynamic model of aesthetic criticism; rather, beauty, according to the data amassed from Thomson's responses, could, as seen earlier, engender good health as the 'correct' viewing of beautiful form would, by extension, regulate the viewer's nervous system into a state of invigorating physiological equanimity.

The search for what Lee privately called a theory of 'absolute aesthetics'[21] was very much a product of the post-Wildean *fin de siècle* having, as it did, a counter-Decadent remit. Lee 'discard[ed]' her own 'doubtful assumptions concerning association of ideas' and publicly rejected Grant Allen's latest theory of the 'new hedonism', the recourse to 'sexual selection' to account for the aesthetic response (*BU*, 172). The fact that the search for invigorating aesthetic experience was an antidote to hedonism and Decadent ennui was the animating principle of the article is signalled by Lee's declaration that appreciation of aesthetic form 'implie[d] an active participation of the most important organs of animal life' (*BU*, 157). This counter-Decadent note is made even more strident in Lee's assertion that the desire for beauty was 'no unaccountable psychic complexity, but the necessary self-established regulation of processes capable of affording disadvantage and advantage to the organism' (*BU*, 225). And in reaction to Wilde's controversial aphorism that 'All art is quite useless', Lee countered that 'The aesthetic instinct is never so utterly the master as when art is described as the servant of utility'.[22] In light of the 'sickly sensuousness' and 'superlative nauseousness' that 'sound and healthy' people associated with the French and British Decadent movements, Lee and Thomson's alternative prescription for aesthetic health appears to literalise counter-Decadent discourse.[23]

To this day, questions of Lee's lesbianism (sublimated or otherwise) and its attendant impact on the couple's research remain contentious. Christa Zorn has found the application of a single lesbian identity to Lee to be reductive and argues that 'we need to see (Lee's) lesbianism ... as one of the many contingencies that shape her "difference" as a writer and critic'.[24]

And, while Kathy Psomiades has read the project as a sublimation of Lee's lesbianism where '[k]nowing the beloved's bodily sensations' operated as Lee's substitution 'for a carnal knowledge of [Thomson's] body', in turn, Joseph Bristow rejects Psomiades's reading because it 'seeks to disclose ... the astonishing lengths to which Lee could, through her aesthetic practice, sublimate her erotic yearning for another woman'.[25] For Bristow, Psomiades's central misapprehension resides in reading Lee's 'disavowed "lesbian aesthetics" ... her renunciation of same-sex passion' as one that nevertheless paradoxically 'maintains a "sexual style"'.[26] Not only because of the public obloquy that attended events such as the Wilde trials of 1895 and, later, the dancer Maud Allan's 'Cult of the Clitoris' libel action in 1918, but also the fluidity of female homosocial relations in the period *per se*, the precise nature and extent of Lee and Thomson's intimacy will necessarily remain hidden to us. However, it is significant that from its first public appearance in an article for the *Contemporary Review* in 1897 to its final appearance in the valedictory that Lee wrote to Thomson in *Art and Man* (1924) (fragments of Thomson's art criticism that Lee had edited after her death), the project reveals an emboldening of Lee's sense of the socially regenerative power of female homosociality. Where preceding texts by Lee such as her novel *Miss Brown* (1884) in which she envisioned a sexless gender identity for women 'made not for man but for humankind' reveal her commitment to strategically develop non-normative and socially engaged gender roles for women, her decision to accent the same-sex modality of their project for the first time in *Art and Man* is certainly arresting.[27]

Where in the original articles, in using the initials C. A-T, Thomson's body was figured as gender-neutral, Lee's introduction to *Art and Man* explicitly restored the homosocial aspect of their work. Lee, who had devoted her life to aesthetics, made the poignant confession that:

> It was only as a result of intimacy with Kit Anstruther-Thomson that I became aware that, as much as I had written and even much as I had read about works of art, I did not really know them when they were in front of me.... And, becoming aware that, in her sense of seeing, I saw half nothing, I tried to learn a little to see by looking at her way of looking at things.[28]

Here, Lee was explicit about looking upon Thomson looking at art and thus effectively incorporated her body as instrumental to experiencing art clearly for the first time. While this act of submission on Lee's part partially rebalanced the relationship of teacher and acolyte between herself and Thomson that Lee had earlier immortalised in her dialogues *Althea* (1894), Lee was keen to emphasise that it was Thomson who took the lead role in practising and maintaining a socially reformist agenda for the project. On a public level, 'psychological aesthetics' was conceptualised by both practitioners as a form of therapeutic Platonism for the masses; this theory that looking at ideal forms could induce universal physical health would inspire Thomson to perform her Delphic role in front of working-class women in public galleries. Describing Thomson's political leanings as 'socialistic' and 'democratic', Lee recalled how Thomson desired 'to show the galleries to the East End People' and how she had spent the summers of 1892–1893 lecturing at Toynbee Hall and teaching drawing classes for working men in London.[29] For Thomson, Lee declared, 'art could never be in her eyes a mere private pleasure, still less an amusement for leisured folks. She saw it rather as a semi-religious side of life, into which every one, and the disinherited foremost, must be initiated by those who were specially gifted and fortunately circumstanced'.[30] In retrospect, Thomson's agenda was perhaps only Socialistic in that peculiarly obtuse late nineteenth-century mode where the upper-class Thomson played a real-life 'Princess Casamassima' by herding the London proletariat into museums to watch her demonstrations. The image of the 'specially gifted' Thomson leading the 'disinherited' to the sacrament of healthful art is certainly ideologically problematic for us today. Moreover, it is deeply ironic that what had started as a curative project for Lee ended in physical collapse for Thomson. In a confessional mode in *Art and Man*, Lee chastised herself that her own 'preoccupation of rendering our new-fangled notions less startling by an array of already accepted psychological facts and theories ... may have been done at the expense of my collaborator's already strained nerves'. 'Kit', Lee concluded, 'may have felt as if her very personal and living impressions were being deadened under what perhaps struck her as philosophical padding'.[31] Diluted down to fragmentary impressions on art objects in *Art and Man*, Thomson's role as the gallery Messiah continued to be directed and circumscribed by Lee into the 1920s.

Lawrence and (Counter-)Decadence

Notwithstanding Lee's influence (after Denisoff) over Virginia Woolf's *Orlando* and recent critics linking Lee and Lawrence through their attempts to capture the *genius loci* of Italy in their travel writings, Kirsty Martin has placed the evolution of the three writers' fictional and non-fictional works on the subjects of the emotions and empathy in circumstantial relation to each other. For Martin, 'Lee, Woolf and Lawrence are not obvious writers to place together' and she continues that while 'They were ambivalent and sometimes hostile towards each other's work, ... they did not exert direct influence on each other's writing'.[32] In light of the aforementioned examples and the commitment to a counter-Decadent ethos that can be elicited from Lee's research in psychological aesthetics and, as we shall see, from Lawrence's novels *The White Peacock* (1911) and *Women in Love* (1920), Martin's caveat begins to appear tenuous. And, while a counter-Decadent animus drives the work of both writers, it is also striking that, like Lee before him, Lawrence sought to assuage the feeling of national and cultural decline that prevailed at the turn of the twentieth century and beyond by advancing the ideal of a socially regenerative (male) homosociality. Faced with the heightened psychosexual anxieties engendered by national events such as the Wilde trials of 1895, the dancer Maud Allan's notorious libel action in 1918 against M. P. Noel Pemberton-Billing and the censorship of James Joyce and Lawrence's own novels on the grounds of obscenity, both Lee and Lawrence bravely struggled to define, understand and, to a certain degree, exercise these non-normative sexualities for themselves. Tantalisingly, the fact that the influence of Lee and Thomson's groundbreaking work can also be elicited in the pivotal 'Moony' chapter of *Women in Love* suggests (after Steiner et al.) another palpable line of influence from Victorian queer sexualities to male Modernists. Ironically, not only does this association engender a timely reappraisal of the homophobia famously ascribed to Lawrence but also it begs the question to whom exactly the term 'Sapphic Modernists' should be applied.

While Max Nordau conceived of literary Decadence, sexual permissiveness and other "90s manias' in his treatise *Degeneration* as the cause *and* effect of the perceived social and physiological decline of *fin-de-siècle* Europe, the First World War saw Lee and Lawrence invert the terms of this debate. For Lee, who wrote two stylistically innovative and politically controversial anti-war plays in 1915 and 1920 and, for Lawrence, who was the subject of political surveillance during the war years, the Great War was not the natural apotheosis of a rampant culture of permissiveness (Nordau's so-called Dusk of the Nations) but rather that of a worn-out social conservatism and growing political intolerance. In 1915, Lawrence, in responding to the suppression of *The Rainbow,* opined that 'I think there is no future for England: only a decline and fall' and that 'This is the dreadful and unbearable part of it: to have been born into a decadent era, a decline of life, a collapsing civilization'.[33] As masterfully described by Vincent Sherry, the prevalent feeling of social decline that haunted Lawrence can be elicited in the taxonomy of (counter-)Decadence that shapes *Women in Love*, a novel which both frightened its author for being so 'end of the world' and yet also encouraged him that 'The people that can bring forth the new passion, the new idea, this people will endure'.[34]

Glimmerings: *The White Peacock*

Letters from 1908 to 1910, written while Lawrence was crafting both his first collection of poems and his first novel *The White Peacock*, articulate a conflicted response to the turn of the century French Decadent and Symbolist schools and their British confreres. Lawrence described

buying a second-hand copy of the ur-text of French Decadence, Baudelaire's *Les Fleurs du Mal,* as 'a fine capture' and he later teased Louie
Burrows (briefly his fiancée) that he would read Paul Verlaine's poems
to her and anticipated what 'fun' it would be to see how they would
make her 'eyes swing round'.[35] Although he claimed to 'like' Verlaine's
'vague suggestive' poetry more than the 'Plaster cast' poetry of English
contemporaries like A. E. Housman, Lawrence was adamant that he
himself would not practice Verlaine's style because 'Before everything I
like sincerity and a quickening spontaneous emotion' and he could not
bring himself to 'worship music or the "half said thing"' of Symbolist
verse.[36] Simultaneously drawn and repelled by French Decadence and
its Symbolist compeer, ironically, Lawrence's determination to avoid
stylistic opacity resulted in a reaction to the work of British Decadents
Oscar Wilde and Aubrey Beardsley in *The White Peacock* that verges
on the prurient. As we see later, Lawrence's novel, somewhat disingen-
uously, offsets the putatively 'immoral' aspects of Wilde's play *Salome*
and Beardsley's final illustration for it with one particularly unabashed
scene of homoeroticism. In this, Lawrence's first novel appears to evince
a compelling, if contentious, homologue to Cassandra Laity's vision of
Sapphic Modernists' reliance on a male Decadent tradition to forge their
own sexually dissident works.

Depicting middle-class life in rural Nottinghamshire, *The White Peacock* is narrated by the figure of Cyril Beardsall, a character that Lawrence tellingly observed was 'too much *me*', who recounts the ill-fated
love affair of his sister Lettie and the young farmer George Saxton.[37]
The title of the novel refers to the fifty white peacocks that Wilde's lech-
erous King Herod offers Salome for performing 'The Dance of the Seven
Veils' for him in order to forestall her vengeful demands to be presented
the head of John the Baptist (Iokanaan) because he has rejected her sexual advances. Where Kristin Morrison observes that 'The association of
peacocks with Salome's perversity in Wilde's text, and ... the identification of peacocks with Salome herself in Beardsley's illustrations, establish the white-peacock woman as decadent, possessive, and deadly', an
actual, rather than a figurative, peacock reveals a nascent anti-feminism
on Lawrence's part.[38] When Cyril, in the company of the gamekeeper
Annable, sees a peacock befoul a churchyard statue of an angel, the in-
censed Annable decries 'The proud fool! – look at it! Perched on an angel,
too, as if it were a pedestal for vanity. That's the soul of a woman – or it's
the devil. ... A woman to the end, I tell you, all vanity and screech and
defilement'.[39] In Lawrence's novel, like *Salome* and Beardsley's illustrations before it, the peacock exemplifies the insatiability of female desire
and the inherent corruption of the sex.

The novel's references to Wilde's *Salome* are amplified further when
Cyril somehow acquires prints of Aubrey Beardsley's 'Atalanta' and his
tailpiece to Wilde's play which he initially intends to show to Lettie.

Having got hold of the prints in the first place, Cyril's later claims to be 'fascinated and overcome' and 'yet full of stubbornness and resistance' to them appear disingenuous especially in light of the transparently erotic response that George Saxton has to them (*WP*, 178). When he tells Cyril that 'The more I look at these naked lines, the more I want her [Lettie]. It's a sort of fine sharp feeling like these curved lines. I don't know what I'm saying – but do you think she'd have me?' George is clearly picturing Lettie as Beardsley's naked and prone Salome (*WP*, 179). In comparison to Cyril's sensitive bewilderment, George's reduction of Beardsley's art to the level of pornography not only diminishes the high art status of Decadence but also exposes Cyril's apparent naiveté to be self-deceptive, at best.

Cyril's disingenuousness is again in evidence in a later chapter when he and George take a naked swim together after which Cyril allows himself to be towel dried by his friend and luxuriates in the experience of 'the sweetness of the touch of our naked bodies one against the other' (*WP*, 249). The fact that the chapter is entitled 'The Poem of Friendship' signals that for Lawrence, at any rate, the unabashed homoeroticism of the scene was to be understood in terms of a homosocial rather than homosexual bond, one which 'satisfied in some measure the vague, indecipherable yearning of [Cyril's] ... soul', a feeling which tellingly he also presumes to be shared by George (*WP*, 249). Cyril's declaration that their love 'was more perfect than any love I have known since, either for man or woman' (*WP*, 249) certainly was to perplex E. M. Forster who privately read this scene as 'the queerest product of subconsciousness that I have yet struck' and one in which he thought Lawrence had 'not a glimmering from first to last what he's up to'.[40] More recently, Howard Booth has similarly also conferred a degree of sexual naiveté to Lawrence in this scene.[41] And yet, Eve Kosofsky Sedgwick's influential observation that 'For a man to be a man's man is separated only by an invisible, carefully blurred, always-already-crossed line from being "interested in men" inevitably compromises both the putative homosociality with which Lawrence framed this encounter and the unwitting innocence that Forster and Booth respectively impute to him'.[42]

(Wo)Men in Love

Lawrence's biographer, Mark Kinkead-Weekes, argues that in 1913, Lawrence came to accept himself as bisexual.[43] However, by 1915, Lawrence was writing letters that reveal a nascent homophobia which, at the very least, suggests a conflicted sexuality on his part. In April of that year, Lawrence wrote to David Garnett that although he 'never considered Plato very wrong, nor Oscar Wilde', seeing the homosexual John Maynard Keynes in his pyjamas 'has been like a little madness to me ever since' which was carried along with the most dreadful sense of repulsiveness – something like carrion – a vulture gives me the same feeling'.[44] As this letter reveals, Lawrence's apparent acceptance of homosexuality as an abstract concept was undermined by a sense of visceral disgust when physically confronted with the actual homosexuals of his acquaintance. Moreover, the fact that Lawrence remained uncertain about his sexuality is evidenced by the cancelled 1916 prologue to *Women in Love* which was overtly homoerotic in tenor, while, in turn, the finished novel instead avows a deep, if ultimately unachievable, commitment to male homosociality.[45] And, in comparison to Lawrence's oscillating attitude towards the physical act of 'men loving men', his response to 'the woman question' can at best be described as portentous. Here, it is significant that Carolyn Tilghman argues that Lawrence initially supported women's suffrage but that by 1915, his letters disclose a 'strong ambivalence about the new freedoms demanded by women'.[46] A letter of 1917 further reveals that Lawrence's uncertainty about first-wave feminism had intensified to the point of seeing the achievement of women's suffrage as a pyrrhic victory of cataclysmic proportions.[47]

While Lawrence offered apocalyptic predictions about female suffrage contemporaneously, he also considered the 'War [to be] a great and necessary disintegrating autumnal process' out of which love 'the great creative process' would emerge and triumph.[48] Although the Great War is never explicitly mentioned in *Women in Love*, it filters into the narrative as an incessant drive towards discord and destruction at every level of society and one that is marked stylistically by an amplification of the counter-Decadent, anti-feminist and homosocial notes earlier evinced in *The White Peacock*. Where, according to Lawrence, love will forestall the negative effects of war, the emotional vicissitudes experienced both by Ursula and Gudrun Brangwen and their respective lovers in their attempts to achieve emotional fulfilment manifest in this time of war and female suffrage as a desire for mastery over each other. For Birkin, in particular, 'The hot narrow intimacy between man and wife was abhorrent' and he seeks to subjugate Ursula and what he considers to be her woman's 'lust for possession, a greed of self-importance in love'.[49] In turn, it is significant that Ursula considers Birkin to be the embodiment of a 'death eating' '*pervers*[ity]', a Decadent *ex post facto* as suggested by his consistent (self) identification with Baudelaire's *Fleurs du Mal* (*WL*, 319, 177, 400).[50] Indeed, as identified by Vincent Sherry, Lawrence consistently reanimates the ghost of late nineteenth-century Decadence across the novel in order to underline not only modernity's continuities with the Victorian past but also Modernism's debt to its Decadent predecessor.[51] And while Birkin conceives of male homosociality as 'something clearer, more open' than the 'dreadful bondage' of heterosexual marriage, the response to this 'other kind of love' with which Ursula closes the novel ('It's an obstinacy, a theory, a perversity') consigns male homosociality to the ignominious fate which was accorded to the Decadent mode in Modernism's originary narrative (*WL*, 205, 499).

While the cancelled (1916) prologue to *Women in Love* and the novel's extant 'Gladiatorial' chapter which sees Birkin and Crich engage in naked wrestling (the 'physical junction of two bodies clinched into oneness') clearly highlights Lawrence's privileging of male homosociality over heterosexual union, Tilghman notes 'the excision of female homosocial desire and sexuality from Birkin's newly carved sexual terrain' (*WL*, 280–1).[52] Although Lawrence's patent distaste for lesbianism is in evidence in his earlier depiction of Ursula's failed relationship with Winifred in *The Rainbow*, in *Women in Love*, a momentary scene of female homosociality from which the Decadent Birkin is barred both challenges Tilghman's observation and elicits a closer alliance between Lawrence's work and Lee and Thomson's 'absolute aesthetics'. In the pivotal chapter 'Moony', a key scene animates the possibility of a productively healthful act of a woman looking at, not another woman, in this instance, but the figurative feminine (the Moon) as a means of forestalling the onslaughts of cultural Decadence. Ursula comes upon Birkin in the middle of night throwing stones at the reflection of the Moon in a pond and secretly watches him for some time. Birkin keeps throwing stones until the reflection is absolutely obliterated. Decadent tropes abound: the sinister face of the moon, white and deathly, the inviolable moon as a white body, the fragments of its reflections as tattered rose petals (*WL*, 255–7). All these images tangibly resonate to the nexus of moon images present in Wilde's *Salome* as Lawrence focuses on Ursula's overwrought physical response to this visual violation of the Moon that is being enacted through Birkin throwing stones at it. 'Ursula was dazed', Lawrence writes, 'her mind was all gone. She felt she had fallen to the ground and was spilled out, like water on the earth' (*WL*, 257). Her physical agitation recedes only when the reflection of the moon restores itself at the cessation of male violence. The description of this process envisions the very physical act of a woman looking at the feminine Moon as an antidote to the Decadent mode:

> Gradually the fragments [of light] caught together re-united, heaving rocking, dancing, falling back as in panic, but working their way home again persistently, making resemblance of fleeing away when they had advanced, but always flicking nearer, a little closer to the mark, the cluster growing mysteriously larger and brighter, as gleam after gleam fell in with the whole, until a ragged rose, a distorted, frayed moon was shaking upon the waters again, reasserted, renewed trying to recover from its convulsion, to get over the disfigurement and the agitation, to be whole and composed, at peace (*WL*, 257).

Where in Wilde's play, the Young Syrian's description of Salome represents her as 'the shadow of a white rose in a mirror of silver',[53] the 'Moony' scene inverts this Decadent derealisation of the feminine by effecting the material restoration of the moon. Thus, the passage suggests that the act of a woman looking recasts Decadence's sterile account of the Moon (and by extension, femininity) into one of serenity and harmony. Momentarily, Lawrence animates a scene where fellowship between the female viewer and the figurative feminine restores physical equanimity and mental serenity, a process from which, significantly, the Decadent Birkin is banished. A scene of a hieratic female communion through spectatorship is similarly invoked in *Art and Man* by Vernon Lee some four years later. Standing in the Elgin rooms

> bring[s] a sudden feeling [to Lee] – more than a mere recollection – of our expectant wandering among the statues in what, comparatively speaking, had been our distant youth; a sense of the presence of Kit – a goddess among goddesses, poised in intent contemplation before her broken and battered antique sisters.[54]

Poignantly, for Lee the memory of Thomson is 'more than a mere recollection' and it is this presence of the beloved that enacts a palpable 'rupture in the social and cultural fabric', the quintessence of Sapphic Modernism, as identified by Shari Benstock.[55]

In the final instance, uncovering the counter-Decadence and homosociality that unite Lee and Lawrence's work affords a timely reappraisal of both the historical parameters and the constituency of the term Sapphic Modernist. Given both Lee and Thomson's circumspection about their relationship, their commitment to performing 'psychological aesthetics' before working-class audiences *and* the aristocratic hauteur later cultivated by Sapphists such as Radclyffe Hall and Vita Sackville-West, would Lee and Thomson have embraced the Sapphic nomenclature? Moreover, while the couple's commitment to counter-Decadence preempts the high Modernist movement's excision of the 'Tragic Generation', concomitantly the fundamental homosociality of the 'psychological aesthetics' project similarly debars the couple from membership of the androcentric New School. Where Cassandra Laity envisions Sapphic Modernists, such as Willa Cather and Renée Vivien, drawing on a male Decadent tradition to forge their own sexually dissident works, in turn, it is significant that Lawrence's novels *The White Peacock* and *Women in Love* offer a compelling homologue to the intertextual relationship that Laity adduces between Sapphic Modernists and Decadents. And despite Lawrence's patent distaste for lesbianism as evinced in *The Rainbow* and his later short story 'The Fox' and his conflicted response to same-sex relations more generally, it is striking that he chose to use his antipathy towards literary Decadence as a vehicle to articulate his own dissident, albeit conflicted, sexuality. Moreover, the fact that Wilde's *Salome* casts a shadow over *The White Peacock* and *Women in Love* and that the trace of Lee and Thomson's groundbreaking work can be adduced in the pivotal 'Moony' chapter suggests, after Steiner et al., another palpable line of influence from Victorian queer sexualities to male Modernists. Ultimately, it is hoped that this analysis will, at the very least, help stimulate a re-evaluation of what the precise constituency and provenance of Sapphic Modernist writing might actually be.

Notes

1 Virginia Woolf, *Collected Essays*, I (London: Hogarth P, 1966), p. 320.
2 Jessica R. Feldman, *Victorian Modernism: Pragmatism and the Varieties of Aesthetic Experience* (Cambridge, New York et al.: Cambridge UP, 2002), p. 3.
3 Vincent Sherry, *Modernism and the Re-invention of Decadence* (Cambridge and New York: Cambridge UP, 2015), pp. 3–4.
4 Gregory Woods, *Homintern, How Gay Culture Liberated the Modern World* (New Haven, CT and London: Yale UP, 2017), p. 29.
5 Shari Benstock, 'Expatriate Sapphic Modernism: Entering Literary History', in *Lesbian Texts and Contexts: Radical Revisions*, eds. Karla Jay and Joanne Glasgow (New York and London: New York UP, 1990), pp. 183–5; Cassandra Laity, 'H. D. and A. C. Swinburne: Decadence and Sapphic Modernism', in *Lesbian Texts and Contexts*, p. 218.
6 Laity, 'H. D. and Swinburne', pp. 218–9.
7 Laura Doan and Jane Garrity, eds., *Sapphic Modernities: Sexuality, Women and National Culture* (London: Palgrave Macmillan, 2006), p. 3.
8 Phyllis Grosskurth, *John Addington Symonds: A Biography* (London: Longmans, 1964), p. 223n.
9 Catherine Maxwell and Patricia Pulham, eds. and intro., *Vernon Lee: Decadence, Ethics, Aesthetics* (Basingstoke and New York: Palgrave Macmillan, 2006), p. 2.
10 Catherine Maxwell and Patricia Pulham, eds. and intro., *Hauntings and Other Fantastic Tales* (Peterborough, Canada: Broadview P, 2006), p. 19; Maxwell and Pulham, *Vernon Lee*, p. 2.
11 Dennis Denisoff, 'The Forest Beyond the Frame: Picturing Women's Desires in Vernon Lee and Virginia Woolf', in *Women and British Aestheticism*, eds. Talia Schaffer and Kathy Alexis Psomiades (Charlottesville: U of Virginia P, 2000), p. 253; Hilary Fraser, 'Evelyn De Morgan, Vernon Lee, and Assimilation from Without', *Journal of Pre-Raphaelite Studies* 14 (Spring 2005): 75–90, p. 88.
12 Maxwell and Pulham, *Hauntings*, p. 27.
13 Maxwell and Pulham, *Vernon Lee*, p. 2.
14 Vernon Lee, *Gospels of Anarchy and Other Contemporary Studies* (London: T. Fisher Unwin, 1908), p. 14.
15 Lee, *Gospels of Anarchy*, p. 73.
16 Vernon Lee, *Renaissance Fancies* (London: Smith, Elder & Co, 1895), p. 257.
17 Vineta Colby, *Vernon Lee: A Literary Biography* (Charlottesville and London: U of Virginia P, 2003), p. 2.
18 Colby, *Vernon Lee*, p. 125.
19 Colby, *Vernon Lee*, p. 146.
20 Vernon Lee and Clementina Anstruther-Thomson, *Beauty and Ugliness and Other Studies in Psychological Aesthetics* (London: John Lane, 1912), p. 164. Hereafter cited as *BU*.
21 Colby, *Vernon Lee*, p. 154.

22 Oscar Wilde, *The Picture of Dorian Gray*, ed. Joseph Bristow (Oxford: Oxford World Classics, 2006), p. 4; Lee, *Beauty and Ugliness*, p. 178.

23 Hugh Stutfield, 'Tommyrotics', *Blackwoods Edinburgh Magazine* 157.956 (June 1895): 833–45.

24 Christa Zorn, *Vernon Lee: Aesthetics, History and the Victorian Female Intellectual* (Athens: Ohio UP, 2003), p. 23.

25 Kathy Psomiades, '"Still Burning from This Strangling Embrace": Vernon Lee on Desire and Aesthetics', in *Victorian Sexual Dissidence*, ed. Richard Dellamora (Chicago, IL: Chicago UP, 1999), p. 36; Joseph Bristow, 'Vernon Lee's Art of Feeling', *Tulsa Studies in Women's Literature* 25.1 (Spring 2006): 117–39, p. 124.

26 Bristow, 'Art of Feeling', p. 135.

27 Vernon Lee, *Miss Brown: A Novel*, 3 vols. (Edinburgh and London: William Blackwood and Sons, 1884), vol. 2, p. 308.

28 Vernon Lee, 'Introduction', in C. Anstruther-Thomson, *Art and Man: Essays and Fragments*, ed. and intro. Vernon Lee (London: John Lane at the Bodley Head, 1924), pp. 29, 30.

29 Lee recalled how Thomson 'had struck up a friendship with the late Clementina Black, and already in 1888 she was assisting that most courteous and witty of socialists in an agitation against the poisonous manufacture of matches'. Lee, Introduction to *Art and Man*, p. 26.

30 Lee, Introduction to *Art and Man*, p. 27.

31 Lee, Introduction to *Art and Man*, p. 53.

32 Kirsty Martin, *Modernism and the Rhythms of Sympathy: Vernon Lee, Virginia Woolf and D. H. Lawrence* (Oxford: Oxford UP, 2013), p. 10.

33 Qtd in Sherry, *Reinvention of Decadence*, p. 139.

34 David Herbert Lawrence, *The Letters of D. H. Lawrence*, Vol. III, 1916–1921, *The Cambridge Edition of the Letters and Works of D. H. Lawrence*, eds. James T. Boulton and Andrew Robertson (Cambridge et al.: Cambridge UP, 1984), p. 25; 'Foreword', *Women in Love*, eds. David Farmer, Lindeth Vasey, and John Worthen (Cambridge: Cambridge UP, 1987), p. 486.

35 David Herbert Lawrence, *The Letters of D. H. Lawrence*, Vol. I, 1901–1913, *The Cambridge Edition of the Letters and Works of D. H. Lawrence*, ed. James T. Boulton (Cambridge et al.: Cambridge UP, 1979), pp. 179, 61.

36 Lawrence, *The Letters of D. H. Lawrence*, Vol. I, p. 63.

37 John Worthen, *D. H. Lawrence: The Life of an Outsider* (London: Penguin, 2006), p. 63.

38 Qtd in Jack Stewart, *The Vital Art of D. H. Lawrence: Vision and Expression* (Carbondale and Edwardsville: Southern Illinois UP, 1999), p. 12.

39 David Herbert Lawrence, *The White Peacock*, ed. and intro. David Bradshaw (Oxford: Oxford UP, 2000), pp. 166–7. Hereafter cited as *WP*.

40 Qtd in Howard J. Booth, 'D. H. Lawrence and Male Homosexual Desire', *Review of English Studies, New Series* 53.209 (February 2002): 86–107, p. 88.

41 Booth, 'D. H. Lawrence and Male Homosexual Desire', p. 88.

42 Eve Kosofsky Sedgwick, *Between Men: English Literature and Male Homosocial Desire* (New York: Columbia UP, 1985), p. 89.

43 Qtd in Booth, 'Homosexual Desire', p. 87.

44 David Herbert Lawrence, *The Letters of D. H. Lawrence*, Vol. II, 1913–1916, *The Cambridge Edition of the Letters and Works of D. H. Lawrence*, eds. J. Kyztaruk and James Boulton (Cambridge et al.: Cambridge UP, 1981) pp. 320–1.

45 '[A]lthough [Birkin] was always drawn to women ... it was for men that he felt the hot, flushing roused attraction which a man is supposed to feel for the other sex he male physique had a fascination for him, and for the female physique he felt only a fondness, a sort of sacred love, as for a sister', Qtd in David Bradshaw, 'Introduction', in D. H. Lawrence, *Women in Love*, ed. and intro David Bradshaw (Oxford: Oxford UP, 2000), p. xxxiii.

46 Lawrence, *Letters*, I, p. 320; Carolyn Tilghman, 'Unruly Desire, Domestic Authority and Odd Coupling in D. H. Lawrence's *Women in Love*', *Women's Studies* 37.2 (Mar 2008): 89–109, p. 99.

47 Lawrence wrote to Lady Cynthia Asquith that:

> All I can say is that in the tearing asunder of the sexes lies the universal death, in the assuming of the male activities by the female, there takes place the horrid swallowing of her own young, by the woman ... I am sure woman will destroy man. Intrinsically in this country ... I am sure there is some ghastly Clytemnestra victory ahead for the women. Qtd in Tilghman, 'Unruly Desire', p. 99

48 Qtd in Bradshaw, intro. to *Women in Love*, p. xiii.

49 Lawrence, *Women in Love*, pp. 205, 206. Hereafter cited as *WL*.

50 Lawrence, *Women in Love*, pp. 319, 177, 400. Emphasis in the original.

51 See Sherry, *Reinvention of Decadence*, pp. 138–47.

52 Tilghman, 'Unruly Desire', p. 95.

53 Oscar Wilde, *Salome: Tragedy in One Act, Plays 1: The Duchess of Padua, Salomé: Drame en un Acte, Salome: Tragedy in One Act, The Complete Works of Oscar Wilde*, vol. 5, 659–750, ed. Joseph Donohue (Oxford: Oxford UP, 2013), p. 707.

54 Lee, intro to *Art and Man*, p. 33.

55 Benstock, 'Expatriate Sapphic Modernism', p. 186.

6 'Modernistic Shone the Lamplight'

Arthur Symons among the Moderns

Kostas Boyiopoulos

By the time John Betjeman one evening in 1940 penned 'On Seeing an Old Poet in the Café Royal', Arthur Symons, once the firebrand of Decadence and its zeitgeist, was a ghostly figure left behind by the times. Confounding him with Theodore Wratislaw, the lyric portrays Symons as 'Very old and very grand' where 'Modernistic shone the lamplight / There in London's fairyland'.[1] The 'Modernistic' air is oddly at variance with Symons styled as a dignified Victorian sage. Betjeman's observational approach vicariously espouses Symons's own attitude and treatment of the Café Royal almost half a century earlier. A devoted patron, Symons returned to its glitzy premises throughout his life. In 'East and West End Silhouettes', Symons records details of a memorable evening in 1892 which he shared with fellow poets John Davidson and John Barlas. Each of the three 'had written a poem about the Café Royal – something modern, modernity in poetry'.[2] Symons's 'modern' take was a sonnet he entitled 'Ambiguë', which is about a glamorous, alluring demimondaine, a 'Sphinx' who seduces the speaker from a distance with a casual furtive glance. The speaker does not wish the spell broken: 'smile thus / Forever with that air ambiguous'. The emphasis is on upholding appearances: what could lie beneath that 'air' in the sonnet's closing line is 'Her if the snake is in your paradise' (*Memoirs*, 81).

This trotted-out metaphor relating to the Original Sin is a vital clue to the direction Symons steered his poetics in the twentieth century. He carved a rogue trail of a quasi-Romantic self-introspection and erotic mysteriousness clothed in myth, especially of the Judeo-Christian variety of Genesis. This is in juxtaposition with Ezra Pound's generation which, reflecting radical social and technological shifts, sought the angular poetics of clarity and engagement. Although Symons spearheaded modernity in the Nineties, and later was perceived as its guru, after his mental breakdown in Italy and partial recovery in 1908–1910, he became an anchorite, out of touch with the surge of innovative literary developments. He kept producing voluminously on Decadent themes, but his publications during the Interwar period did not make a dip in the literary scene. Elisa Bizzotto points out that a combination of a 'certain dementophobia', a 'modernist aversion to figures even obliquely seen as

Victorian' and 'an actual decline in the quality of Symons's work first published after 1908' tarnished the reputation of his early work and was the reason for a general lack of scholarly interest in him.[3]

The relationship between Symons's late poetry and Modernist developments is subtler and more complex than it first appears. His post-War volumes, *Lesbia and Other Poems* (1920), *Love's Cruelty* (1923) and *Jezebel Mort* (1931), offer creatively distorted perspectives on Modernism as well as insights into the course of his own vision. My chapter suggests that through Biblical mythology, tropes of mythmaking and intense states of subjectivity, Symons's late period offers a poetics which, although deviates from Modernism, curiously, shares some of its hallmarks, inverting, deflecting and rerouting them.

Symons, Modernity and Myth

Symons remained out of touch with Modernist literary developments throughout the interwar years. In his memoir of his mental collapse in Italy, *Confessions: A Study in Pathology* (1930), he divulges: 'I could neither read nor write. I understood nothing of what was going on in the literary world, which was my world'.[4] For practitioners of post-Victorian Decadence, according to Kristin Mahoney, keeping a distance from contemporary developments was an informed, critical stance. With writers such as Vernon Lee and Max Beerbohm in mind, Mahoney argues that 'reinvigorating a past aesthetic operated as a method for subtly communicating distaste for the methods and values of the present'.[5] This idea is appositely applicable to Symons. His self-marginalisation seems to be a conscious strategy of quietly disapproving a Modernist engagement with the world. His published poetry in the 1920s and 1930s, slanted towards sexual archetypes and myths of damnation, has an aura of escapism. It stubbornly follows a disconnected, parallel course from the Modernist preoccupation with the broken psyche and loss of meaning in the aftermath of the Great War. 'To the Dead', 'Song' and 'The Hour' in *Lesbia and Other Poems* seem to be the only instances in which Symons obliquely appears to elegise the War.

Even so, comparative parallels between Symons's generation and Modernist culture abound and were first suggested by Modernist writers themselves. In a perfunctory comment in 1925, Joyce wrote that 'there is a certain resemblance between the group of writers who collected around Pound, I mean W. L., T. S. E., H. D. etc., and the writers of the Yellow Book Row of half a century ago [*sic*] who collected around Arthur Symons'.[6] Joyce's remark reflects a wider self-awareness of Modernism in relation to 1890s culture of eclectic tastes and coteries. On the other hand, Regenia Gagnier notes that Symons demonstrates Modernism's 'worst excesses of elitism, solipsism, and the great divide between high and low culture'.[7] The notion of the coterie forms the basis of Bizotto's examination of the continuities between Symons and Modernism. Focusing on Symons's 'Editorial Note' to his short-lived little magazine project *The Savoy* (1896), Bizotto argues that it 'exudes a radical artistic-cultural elitism that will become essential in modernist poetics, with its stress on high culture, difficulty and learned obscurity'.[8] Symons introduced 'a framework of hostile exclusiveness and close community that prefigures the "minority culture" of the ensuing decades' (33).[9]

After all, Symons's early work and credentials were instrumental in shaping literary Modernism. The unobtrusive dovetailing of his early poetics into individual influences is well documented. He was personally involved in launching the career of James Joyce, helping him break into the publishing world with the Nineties-flavoured poetry volume *Chamber Music* (1907). *The Symbolist Movement in Literature* (1899/1919) was an indispensable document for T. S. Eliot and the latter's discovery of the French Symbolists, especially Jules Laforgue.[10] Eliot's 'mythographic' sense of the 'Unreal City' was indebted to Symons's 'pompous and distressing unrealities of a great city' (*London: A Book of Aspects* [1909]) as Roger Holdsworth astutely has highlighted.[11] Symons's Impressionistic lyrics anticipate Imagism; Hugh Kenner sees especially 'Pastel: Masks and Faces' as a precursor to Pound's 'In a Station of a Metro'.[12] And in his analysis of 'Hymn to Energy' from *The Fool of the World* (1906), Tom Gibbons shows how Symons abandons the defeatist, melancholic aspect of Symbolism for a more aggressive one that predates the Futurists of Filippo Marinetti's manifestoes.[13] Even Katherine Mansfield, in her experimentation with Symbolist techniques, was under Symons's spell.[14] The continuum of scholarly interest in the many parallels and connections between the generation of Eliot and Pound and Symons's early poetry and critical prose sidesteps neatly his post-mental breakdown output.

This sidestepping is abetted by Symons's own gradual withdrawal from literary forefronts, his eremitic and absorbed self-isolation. Still, he does not reject the spirit of modernity but tailors it to his own idiosyncracies. In 'Some Makers of Modern Verse' (1921), Symons abhors what he calls 'bourgeois solemnity', reflected in 'respectable' verse that is produced 'now-a-days', a term for which he reserves a special interpretation that sheds light on his stance as a malingering artist in his late years:

> Only, when I use the word now-a-days, the word itself is as explicit to me at the exact moment when I am writing these lines, as it was in the days of Dowson, as it was in the days of Verlaine. The taint, the plague-spot of bad verse has always been that of the bourgeois. Only, at that time, none of us who were actually artists, were afraid of emotion, were ashamed of frivolity, were aghast at passion. Only, now, certainly, I know not how many verse makers are concerned only with the question that the sentiment as well as the rhyme must be right. (478)

It is unclear whether in his pejorative comment to verse makers Symons castigates the Georgians or other groups of the 1910s. But the over-coded term 'now-a-days', implies a perpetually updated re-enactment of a cultural conflict. The dominant taste of bourgeois orthodoxy, antagonised by tendentious, contumacious voices in the margin, is always present in every period and age. Periods and ages then, in a way, become parallel universes that succeed one another in a spiral of repetitive patterns. In an ambivalent turn of thought, Symons writes: 'who can define the meaning of the word Modernity? Every age has its different form of modernity. Poetry is Eternal' ('Some Makers', 484). Or, as he writes in a sonnet from *Lesbia*,

> will the glass
> Of Memory, that has shown in every Age
> Faces of lovers loving, leave no trace
> Of ours, that on the Stage met face to face?[15]

Essentially, Symons offsets modernity as an idea which, on a foundational level, is constant but acquires specific characteristics when it responds to different cultural pressures. There is a string of fashions that do not wear off when they succeed one another but remain equally modern in the temporal continuum. Yet, by framing modernity in the past, Symons turns it into its antithesis: myth. And the lines quoted above are nothing short of transforming the present into a self-conscious living myth.

By conceiving poetry as a conduit to eternal, intense passion, Symons renders it a means for channelling a primeval energy which transcends the present. He writes that Robert Bridges and George Meredith (whose *Modern Love* is 'like the touch of a corroding acid') are modern but not William Morris whose medievalism, although possesses all the hallmarks of passion, lacks 'intensity' ('Some Makers', 486). Symonsian intensity is concomitant with a certain Dionysian creative madness. In *Confessions*, which Beckson refers to in relation to 'madness and sexuality – the "Dionysian" element in Modernism' (Beckson, 333), Symons records his 'volcanic'[16] creative activity of his mental institution period. The excesses of his trancelike subjectivity in his late poems reflect a state of divine afflatus. Symons emphasises that 'to have drunk of the cup of dreams [like Gerard de Nerval] is to have drunk of the cup of eternal memory' (*Confessions*, 10, 88). His inward visions essentially tap into the fabric and reservoir of myth.

In his studies of myth and Modernism, Michael Bell draws on Nietzsche's *The Birth of Tragedy* (1872) to explain the role of myth for the Modernists. Nietzsche's legacy to the Modernist generation, Bell argues, is that whilst mimetic Realism denies the Dionysian, 'imaginative literature always retains the possibility of reawakening the Dionysian power through the means of myth'.[17] In Bell's distillation of Nietzsche's thought, the pre-Aesthetic 'unity' of being is blocked forever; but it can be substituted by Apollonian 'Aesthetic creation' on the condition that it is 'a created world inhabited with self-consciousness. The aesthetic is the modern equivalent of ancient myth' (69). Bell singles out Yeats, Thomas Mann and Joyce as the authors who best represent this concept.

Just as the Modernists interpreted the post-Darwinian world through multifarious uses of the aesthetics and metaphysics of myth—Joyce's inculturated Odyssean theme, Lawrence's mystical primitivism, Yeats's Irish legend and occultism and Pound's myth syncretism—so is Symons's late poetry steeped in its own branding and appropriation of myth. Symons expatiated on an erudite set of Decadent mythologies, culling from a variety of antique and contemporary sources. The lynchpin of his late period is that of the Original Sin, the Judeo-Christian system of Good and Evil, damnation and redemption, in relation to male sexuality. Symons's poetic stock in *Lesbia, Love's Cruelty* and *Jezebel Mort* in large part revolves around Lilithian and Fall narratives: Satan, Hell, the forbidden fruit, the Tree of knowledge, serpents and demons. A direct offshoot or even a byproduct of Original Sin mythopoeia is the Swinburnian-Paterian figure of the *femme fatale*. The girls of Parisian night haunts that inspire Symons carry 'the seeds of Eve' (Symons, *Memoirs*, 147). A litany of animalistic seductresses, Lamia, Lilith, Salome, Cleopatra, Columbine and especially Faustian Helen of Troy, parades in his verses. His narratives of famous mythical figures in those volumes are often conflated with a mythological treatment of his personal encounters with the woman of the 1890s, the 'Maenad of the Decadence' ('Nini Patte-en-L'Air') (*Lesbia*, 27–8). As Regenia Gagnier aptly concludes, Symons has used woman to craft his 'personal mythos' (115).

But how is Symons's late poetic project situated in relation to Nietzschean 'mythopoeic consciousness' (Bell, 68–9)? In a short, compressed lyric entitled 'Song' (1921), Symons might be commenting on pioneering Modernist techniques whilst providing his perspective on the role of myth:

> Why write in images like Donne?
> There is no Iris in the room
> To scatter roses and perfume
> In the house of John.
>
> All ye that live in Babylon
> Beware of any harlot's tomb
> The dust of the centuries consume
> Under the sway of the sun.[18]

Eliot, of course, championed John Donne in 'The Metaphysical Poets' (1921), where he gives the difference between the 'intellectual' and the 'reflective' poet as that between Donne's School and Tennyson and Browning who 'think' but 'do not feel their thought as immediately as the odour of a rose',[19] a phrase curiously paralleling Symons's 'roses and perfume'. Symons too had written an essay on 'John Donne' (1899), praising his poetic gift but panning his use of unconventional vocabulary and detachment, his 'frightful faculty of seeing through his own illusions'.[20] The two perspectives seem to intersect. Symons apparently disapproves of Donne's Apollonian intellectual conceits, while he is heedful of the Dionysian apocalyptic Babylon, the disruptiveness of the myth of aeonian, primeval sexuality. The poem, however, cannot make a clear-cut choice between the two: its two stanzas dramatise a tension produced when Dionysian myth is filtered through the Apollonian aesthetic.[21] The Original Sin, being the point of no return, embodies that tension, placing Symons in the company of the Moderns, yet distinctly apart.

Original Sin and Subjectivity

The numbing, purposeless violence and nihilistic voids of the First World War funnelled an existential crisis of faith lost. As Thomas Hardy profoundly laments in 'God's Funeral' (1914), we move 'toward our myth's oblivion', and are 'Sadlier than those who wept in Babylon, / Whose Zion was a still abiding hope'.[22] Recuperating the individual through the mythical narrative of humanity's fundamental flaw, Original Sin, was imperative even for Eliot who believed that 'To do away with a sense of sin is to do away with civilisation'.[23] Eliot is in line with T. E. Hulme who argues for the importance of the Original Sin in reflecting the imperfection of man in a post-Enlightenment context.[24] In 1925, Symons admits the pervading presence of sin in his work as 'good and evil' has bewildered his imagination from *Days and Nights* (1889) all the way to *Lesbia* and *Love's Cruelty*, apprehending passion in 'infinite ways as well as entanglements' (*Memoirs*, 141).

Although impervious to home-grown and Continental literary developments after the 1910s, Symons's poetic variations on the Original Sin myth, nevertheless, respond to modernity when refracted through Eliot's critical assessment and juxtaposed with the latter's theory of 'depersonalisation'. In Eliot's 'Tradition and the Individual Talent' (1919), the artist should not emulate the tradition of the past but, true to the pressures of his own culture, transform tradition and ensure its development by a repeated process of expunging personality.[25] Eliot deploys a famous analogy of a chemical reaction to illustrate that in depersonalisation, 'art may be said to approach the condition of science' (108). Symons's Decadent poetics conflicts with Eliot's formula of the effaced personality. Symons's poems are oppressed by the speaking voice. Highly subjective, they are like threadbare diary entries that belie his personality and experiences. In a counter-Modernist move, as it will become evident, Symons does not transform emotion, but elaborates on it by masking it in mythmaking scenarios. Curiously, his practice, too, approximates the condition of science, albeit in a different manner: even though he does not transform personal emotion alchemically, he goldbeats it into an arabesque, calling to mind his famous definition of Decadent style as 'an over-subtilizing refinement upon refinement'.[26] Eliot highlights the transmutation of the poet's emotion into 'a new art emotion'; this is the opposite of a poet who seeks 'for new human emotions to express; and in this search for novelty in the wrong place it discovers the perverse' (111). Symons fits exactly that perversity here Eliot cautions against.

The catalytic role of Judeo-Christian sin in the expression of Symonsian subjectivity as an oppositional variation to Eliotic 'depersonalisation' can be inferred from Eliot's direct critique of Symons's interpretation of Baudelaire, whose preoccupation with sin bears on much of *Lesbia*, *Love's Cruelty* and *Jezebel Mort*.[27] In his review of Symons's *Baudelaire: Prose and Poetry* (1926), entitled 'Baudelaire in Our Time', originally published as 'Poet and Saint ...' (1927), Eliot argues for Symons as an appropriator of the French poet. Eliot parallels different periods which he calls '*literary* generations',[28] an idea that speaks to Symons's conception of 'modernity' in 'Some Makers'. Focusing on Symons's preface, Eliot notes the 'attitude ... of his epoch toward "vice"' and his 'liturgy' of 'sin' ('Baudelaire', 71–2).[29] Despite the kinship he upholds towards the Nineties, Eliot contends that Symons distorts Baudelaire's complexity of vision through a puerile, jejune enthusiasm and turns him into a contemporary of himself (see 74). He likens Symons to a 'sensitive child, who has been taken into a church, and has been entranced with the effigies, and the candles, and the incense' (72). Symons's attitude towards 'a religion of Evil, or Vice, or Sin', for Eliot, 'is no more than the game of children dressing up and playing at being grown-ups' (73).

Eliot understands that it is the appearance of religion (ritualism) and not religion itself that appeals to Symons. By aestheticising religion, Symons enters the territory of myth as a mirror for the poet's self, or an inert background whose transcendental possibilities are muted by its malleable aesthetic appeal. Symons projects his own sensibility on Baudelaire and by doing so he envelops in myth his own Fallen state. In *Charles Baudelaire: A Study* (1920), Symons's comment on the poet reinforces his own aesthetic, scientific approach to sin: 'Fascinated by sin, he is never the dupe of his emotions; he sees sin as the Original Sin; he studies sin as he studies evil, with a stern logic'.[30] In a passage which he overhauls for his 1926 book on Baudelaire, and which Eliot quotes in his subsequent review, Symons describes the French poet's devotion to passions as a 'deliberate science of sensual perversity' (38).

The pseudo-analytical manner by which Symons's personality takes charge and calibrates his verse is noticed almost consistently by the scant reviews of his volumes in the 1920s. Herbert Gorman, Joyce's first biographer, wrote a lukewarm review of *Lesbia* befittingly entitled 'A Revenant of the Nineties' in which Symons 'no longer sighs about his own moods.

The approach is too cerebral now. Whether or not this is better for the future of poetry cannot be settled while we are in the midst of this new mode' (85).[31] Gorman classes Symons tentatively among contemporary modern poets, observing an artificiality of utterance that can also be discerned in Pound's seven cantos (85). Similarly, Ernest de Selincourt sees Symons's poems as occupying the space of 'hell', using 'sin' as a mere foil in order to explore 'ever more curiously the sickly rocking caverns'.[32] Dominating the verse with the poetic voice means that the deceiving appearance of objective treatment can be the cloak of a genuine serpentine scheme.

What the myth of Original Sin, then, sustains for Symons is the sexual act as a *felix culpa*, a Promethean transgression of the *subject* in the face of a meaningless, alien modernity. In an elucidating, posthumously published memoir, 'Sex and Aversion', Symons inverts the Fall by framing it as a positive force, evoking Milton's Satan who in *Paradise Lost* famously implores, 'Evil, be thou my Good' (4.110).[33] He proclaims that 'the infernal fascination of Sex' is his 'chief obsession': it is 'One's own Vitality: that is a centre of Life and Death. It is also the centre of Creation' (*Memoirs*, 138). In essence, he uses inferential language to evoke the conflated Tree of Life and Tree of Good and Evil from Genesis. His approach to the trope of the Fall is non-dogmatic and so reinforces Eliot's assessment of Symons's sinfulness as aesthetic posturing. In a key passage (again taking a cue from Baudelaire), he attests that the Christian Fall is an aesthetic background that epitomises creative afflatus as the conduit of the self. Through his 'Erotic Verses',

> a man's work and a man's existence are mixed together in an inextricable fashion; certainly not to be imaged by the knots of serpents who are literally strangling one another with terrified struggles to escape from Medusa's brain, but by the innate corruption of what is in such cases a mere parody of the Original Sin. (*Memoirs*, 140)

Serpentine imagery, and by virtue of it the poet's self, imbues his creative efforts. In this adroit comparison of Classical and Biblical myths, art is not the product of a force that violently strives to escape the mind, and manifest and crystallise in fixed form in the public space. On the contrary, it is the inward and inborn projection of the mind contaminating itself in meditative introversion, bearing out the inherent nature of Original Sin. The word 'parody' accentuates the Apollonian yet postlapsarian positioning of the self through mythopoeia.

Postlapsarian Self-Contemplation

Indifferent to the developments of free verse and adhering mostly to traditional rhythms in a range of stanzaic patterns, the 1920s volumes' heavy substrate of a synergistic double mythopoeia—biblical and *fin-de-siècle*—offsets Symons's continued crisis of solving the mystery of desire and hence confronting the self. In their Fallen state, his poetic speakers inhabit a psychological, ontological and theological conflation of Hell, responding to the fragmented world through a certain counter-Eliotic cerebral subjectivism.

Many of the poems in *Lesbia*, which the American poet Babette Deutsch described as 'a little odd and unreal clothed in the Satanic flame and scented hair of 1890',[34] have a strong Lilithian element. Lilith was Adam's first wife, created simultaneously. She rebelled and fled to the desert, becoming a succubus, haunting men's dreams and inducing nocturnal emissions. Lilith's dangerous femininity anchors Symonsian self-analysis firmly to a seething Dionysian life force. In the sonnet-like sequence of 'Helen and Faustus', a rich psychological study of 'The Architecture of his Lust' (54), the Faustian narrative fits seamlessly the subject's state of damnation and spectral inaccessibility of the object of desire. Helen is a Lilithian figure representing a primordial transgression: 'that painted Sin / After the old inevitable fashion / When Lilith gave the snake her passion' (52). This poem forms a cluster with 'Helen', bridging the mythological with personal experience, and 'A Song for Helen' and 'Song' (62), slight lyrics that hint at the disaffection of modernity by positing a Nietzschean death-of-God variation in which an eternal mythical icon is subjected to ephemerality and mortality: 'Nothing but love and lust / Left, and our thought' (61).

'The Vampire', the proemic sonnet to *Lesbia*, addresses in a tumescent tone the Lilith-like 'Intolerable woman' who hovers 'over dead men's tombs' and drains their lifeblood until the 'man swoons ecstatically on death' (1). The verse invites the fanciful suggestion that Symons unwittingly co-opts the post-apocalyptic setting of the First World War to Gothic erotic horror and to the shattering force of dark femininity. But despite the devastation induced by the feminine other, the speaker is self-feminised, articulating obliquely an erotic fantasy of helplessness. The overarching irony of *Lesbia* and the subsequent volumes of verse is that the tyranny of the mythic soul-destroying woman turns into a thin disguise for the tyranny of the poet's personality.

In a short lyric entitled 'Lamia', the speaker proffers: 'She is the very Lamia of my soul' (*Lesbia*, 22). Such ambiguous syntax teeters between the mythical demoness as an external agent and a metaphor for self-projection and self-analysis. Lamia is associated with Lilith and midway through the lyric the speaker reveals its figurative use, referring presumably to a lingering lost love:

And she as Lamia veritably trod,
With snake's feet and snake's wings, the ground when God
Planted the Tree of Evil and of Good.
Is she not in the blood that feeds my blood?

Prior to the Fall, the Serpent possessed limbs, as it is evident in the inference of Genesis 3:14. Symons seems to draw from the Zohar according to which Lilith is the female part of another serpent, Leviathan, and who causes the Fall by tempting Eve to eat the fruit of forbidden knowledge and coax her to seduce Adam.[35] Symons retrocedes prelapsarianism to a prior phase of the Genesis myth, or pollutes the innocence of Paradise with Lilith's undercurrent evil (knowing), an idea he schematises also in 'The Adder' (78). In tagging this element of myth to the object of his desire, the speaker of 'Lamia' emphasises the primordial and animistic power of the myth and not just its aetiological aspect. The ever-unsatisfied sexual impulse is inherent in human nature and is not merely the result of the Serpent's deception. The speaker's question is further suggestive of entangled subjectivity: the repetition of the word 'blood' (also a possible parodic allusion to the Sacrament of Holy Communion) collapses the mythological schema into a self-mirroring of the circularity of pure urge.

This self-mirroring is staged in a Pre-Raphaelite triptych entitled 'Stella Maligna' through an apparatus of biblical Creation similitudes. In the first part, 'Stellae Figura', the speaker offers an ekphrastic portrait of a 'serpentine' (36) *femme fatale* in an almost ceremonial accrual of attributes of dangerous femininity. In the second part, 'Laus Stellae', he switches from the third person to the intimacy of the second person, as he compares the unnamed woman's beauty to 'a garden planted / With tropic flowers of poisonous breath'. This is not an innocent, Edenic garden of plenitude, but a mock-biblical inversion of it, not of 'blossoms but the flowers of Death', populated by men's ensnared souls. In this inversion, the Forbidden Fruit's dooming allure is here suffused and amplified in the whole of the garden (female body). In addition, the addressed woman is exalted to a supreme fabulous status as her 'subtle poison mocks' the '[p]ale witchcraft of the earlier world', the lunar activities of Thessalian sorceresses. Her 'subtle poison', itself a perverted variation of the Forbidden Fruit, is served in a '[s]parkling' and 'impearled' cup which, in Symons's characteristic syntactic doubling, 'Once drained, shall drain all reason up' (38). In this re-imagined Fall, with Temptation directed at the male speaker, the purging of the faculty of reason is analogous to the Original Sin's transformational effect.

'Stellae Anima Clamat', the third part of the sequence, casts a light of cerebral subjectivity on the preceding parts as it cleverly imagines occupying the object of desire's self. In reverberant heroic quatrains, Symons gives voice to the unnamed woman and compares her to Lilith who incapacitates her male victims with her 'golden hair' and cogitates recursively, while gazing at herself: 'She sat before her mirror, and she gazed / Deep into eyes that gazed at her again' (39). Symons revisits the Victorian age-old motif of the self-gazing *femme fatale* as he nods to Dante Gabriel Rossetti's Lilith in the sonnet 'Body's Beauty' in which 'Adam's first wife' destroys men with 'her enchanted hair' and is 'subtly of herself contemplative'.[36] Even more so, he alludes to his own *London Nights* (1895), to the mirror-gazing dancer from 'La Mélinite: Moulin Rouge' and the mistress from 'White Heliotrope' ('The mirror that has sucked your face / Into its secret deep of deeps').[37]

Self-referential probing raises memories of a throng of ruined male lovers' ghosts: 'She saw her slain revive, the tombless dead'. Although she had been to men a poisonous '*Rosa mystica*', her *own* ruin is in the lack of mystique in her inability to taste 'love'. In this sense, she literally mirrors her victims but differs from them in that the cause of her undoing is her very nature. She complains to her mirror:

> [...] I have been, yet never plucked, the rose;
> And I have quenched, yet never felt, that thirst
>
> 'Whereby we put on immortality.
>   Is it too late I find it? must the sod
> Press down this body that is all of me,
>   And shall not Love survive it, who is God?

This manner of reimagining the other does not conform to Eliot's 'depersonalisation', though it nods to Keats's negative capability which Symons prized.[38] Symons here achieves something much more radical, yet tangled. In a double gender switch identity, the male poetic voice inhabits the mind and body of the haughty woman of his desire, who, in turn, fantasises herself exhibiting the force of desire that defines the male psyche. Pining for 'thirst', however, is itself a backslid thirsting, placing the Lilith-like woman in the same category of suffering as her male victims. In this double recursion, the poet may appear to but eventually does not escape the confines of the self. Inhabiting the object of desire and empowering her with language that critiques patriarchy ('must the sod / Press down this body'), calling to mind the Jungian *anima*, leads to re-personalisation. Poetry turns the deified feminine into an echo chamber of male selfhood. In a kind of psychological mithridatism, Symons administers analgesic doses of the 'subtle poison' of the enigma of human sexuality through his cerebral poetic memories in order to temper its Dionysian force.

Love's Cruelty continues to intone the Satanic theme in reminiscing moods that range from despondence to melancholia, and from wistfulness to lament. The speaker of this volume's preamble, also titled 'Love's Cruelty', is under the spell of his erotic memory cerebrally, 'heart and brain' (*Love's*, 9). Symons's keynote is the lover's 'Infinite enigma of [her] eyes'. Whilst one of the characteristics of myth is its power of exegesis, meaning and interpretation, its flipside is religious mystery, the obfuscation of meaning. For Symons, erotic mysteriousness and self-analysis are two sides of the same coin. The acknowledgement of mystery implies the search for meaning. The active search for meaning is, of course, a hallmark of the enigmatic arrangement of cultural artefacts and images in Eliot's and Pound's poetry. For Symons, however, it is approached through introspection.

Symons explores this epistemology of the self in 'The Impenetrable', a sonnet bookended and so closed off by the line, 'I am of all men the most Impenetrable'. He ruminates: 'Some say that I am cold as any stone', and 'with mine own Self alone / I go at the wind's wild will where none can tell / The secret of my Soul' (*Love's*, 47). These lines, arguably, could be read in the context of Symons's place in the artistic and intellectual world of the 1910s. His seclusion from the radical literary experiments mushrooming in Britain and Europe, as well as from the mainstream literature of the time, owes to the fact that his contemporaries could not appreciate or *penetrate* his personal psychodrama of desire unfolding within the poetic self. His post-Nineties poetic vision, although not radical, follows an unpredictable and so equally cryptic 'wind's wild will'. Christian sinfulness and redemption come into play and although the speaker 'adore[s]' the miracle of Jesus before 'God's throne', in the volta and the sestet,

> Backward the gates are thrown
> Of Hell where Satan in His supreme pride
> Gazes into the mirror of mine eyes,
> The clouded mirror of my Destinies,
> In whose deep depths the untroubled ghosts abide.
> Some say that I have fathomed mine own Hell.
> I am of all men the most Impenetrable.

The image of ghosts entrapped in a djinn-like fashion in the eyes' mirrors is the one that resonates often in Symons's work. In 'Stellae Anima Clamat', the mirror-gazing woman sees the 'sad ghosts her mournful memory raised' (*Lesbia*, 39). In 'The Impenetrable', Symons turns around the perspective: the entrapped ghosts in his eyes stand for the mistresses of his past; this is a gender-inverse trope that casts the male speaker into the mythical *femme fatale* Symons is obsessed with in his work. The male speaker here with the emphatically tautological 'deep depths' of his eyes is as inscrutable as the 'infinite enigma' of the woman's eyes in the proemic lyric to *Love's Cruelty* itself. He resembles the transgendered blind seer Tiresias in *The Waste Land*, or the feminised and sexually violated Leopold Bloom in the dream sequence of 'Circe' in *Ulysses*. But whilst Tiresias is a diagnostic agent of meaning in a heartless and standardised fragmented modern world, and the reconceived Bloom lifts the veil to expose the human psyche through sexual shame, Symons's gender role transversal turns the poetic speaker into a myth. Ironically, one wonders whether the self's impenetrability automatically melts away when it is articulated with such an unmistakable subjectivity.

Similarly, in 'The Wanderer's Lament', exemplifying a postlapsarian waste land, Symons asserts the impenetrability of selfhood while deconstructing the myth of love in its paradoxical 'eternal change': 'I follow after changeless love, and find / Nothing but change' (49). The futility of love and even its Prufrockian, ritualistic monotony is the result of a hypertrophied, opaque self-awareness that blunts connection with the other. The world is consumed by the self, governed by a lack of reciprocity: she 'shows me mine own image in her eyes, / And in mine own eyes [...] her own desire beholding her', asseverating about the tyranny of the self, 'I am mine own rival' (50).

Symons's mythmaking of his past and his subsequent obsession with the contours of the self persist in ever-expanding angles and variations in *Jezebel Mort*. Jezebel is a Baalite witch and royal consort who perishes in a disgraceful death (1 Kings 16:31; 2 Kings 9:35–36). In the context of an aged Symons's work, she is suggestive of the tension between myth and the thinning of its aura. Symons's last volume of verse, published when he was sixty-six years old, at over two hundred pages long, is a loose mishmash of sonnets, ballads addressing female figures in intimate settings, dialogues, city vignettes and nature sketches. This is a volume of uneven quality, dishing out poems kept in the drawer alongside new compositions. According to Beckson, in *Jezebel Mort*, Symons's 'capacity for poetic expression is greatly impaired' (321). Symons, however, thought very highly of the volume and in 1932, he wrote to Joyce to enquire news about the publication of *The Joyce Book* to which he supplied an 'Epilogue', informing him of *Jezebel Mort* that it contains some of his 'best and most abnormal and passionate poems. And there are certain traces of Baudelaire'.[39]

The volume's dominant mood is that of religious iconoclasm, demonic and Fallen sexuality, as in suggestively titled pieces such as 'Incantation', 'Lilith', 'Satan' and 'Baudelaire in Hell' (1920). Narratives of and imaginative speculations on the Fall proliferate: 'The Pit of Hell' (1921), a long poem in quintains is a tortuous exploration on the existential drama of the self at the mercy of the infernal Woman. 'Visions and Vanities' (1919) is a Flaubertian bestiary of Chimera, the Sphinx, the Queen of Sheba and Ammonaria, forming an imposing creation narrative to account for the sterile force of 'Desire' (100). 'A Vision' (1927), resembling a stream of consciousness with its scant punctuation, meditates extravagantly on the Original Sin: 'to have lost Immortality in a Kiss / Is to have fallen into utmost Hell'.[40] 'Satan and the Serpent' (1927) is a proper retelling of Eve's Fall from Genesis, but one that narrows down the meaning of Original Sin to the cerebral awareness of sensuality: in the Serpent's argument, the biting of the fruit means that Eve will acquire an Apollonian self-awareness and 'shall see / All that lacks for the lure of [her] Love' (231). The poem invites comparison with but is set apart from Paul Valéry's 'Ébauche d'un serpent' (1941) in which, in

Eliot's words, 'personal emotion, personal experience, is extended and completed in something impersonal'.[41]

Elsewhere, in Symons's tactics of introspection, myth is circumscribed as the intrusion of a transfiguring ancientness in the abject present. In 'A Vision of Serpents' (1923), 'in the scented darkness' of the speaker's room, his 'mirror', 'Like sacred incense from some ancient tomb / Flung Images of wonderful delight' (188). Those images from myth bestirred to life are not exactly Yeats's 'masterful images'[42] that reflect the creative struggles of the self-conscious mind. Their potency lies in their spectral, tentative nature. Once the speaker attempts to snatch a tress of the conjured female figure, a naked 'strange vision of unseen loveliness', he is sabotaged by 'the Serpents of the Night' who are momentarily 'freed from their eternal weariness' (188). This formulation mirrors the speaker's own happy disruption of his weary life, a mirroring corroborated by a line in 'Le Strige' in which the Notre Dame gargoyle-demon's 'Infinite Weariness' is 'as infinite as our Sin' (34). 'A Vision of Serpents' can be twinned with 'The Harlot' (1926) where, in an equally private setting, the harlot's 'mirror wakens from an ancient Tomb' (201) transfiguring the lowly surroundings and exalting her to a cosmic, living myth 'That even Corruption covets on her Bed'. In 'Hallucination' (1929), the prostitute of a dingy brothel is transfigured to 'a Flower of Evil' and is compared to 'Pagan Heathens in their Period / Who gave themselves abnormally to the Devil' (212). Eliot's accusation of Symons's misconstruing of Baudelaire's sinfulness is blatant in these lines.

A third of *Jezebel Mort* is a section entitled 'Setebos', comprising poems mostly written in the 1920s, inspired by his cats, Setebos and Zambo. These cats do not possess the anthropomorphic playfulness of Eliot's *Old Possum's Book of Practical Cats* (1939).[43] Similar to Symons's animalistic *femmes fatales*, and especially the sinuous snake, the cat is the 'Eternal Sphinx' (124), amalgamating divine mystique with primeval energy. In many of these poems, Symons describes the mundane routine of his cats in an elevated context of Judeo-Christian sinfulness, damnation and redemption, casting them as both serpentine and Christlike. These cats are perpetuators of the Original Sin narrative, for 'The SERPENT must have taught them the love of SINNING' (133). The 'Setebos' section rivals Modernist attitudes as a more exaggerated variation of ancient, primitive myth intruding in the drab present. Yet, contrasting Eliot's and Hulme's advocacy of Original Sin in an age of progress, Symons neutralises Sin as an acknowledgement of human imperfection by defiantly twisting it into a celebration of vice, proclaiming the 'infallibility' of his 'Impenitence' (*Jezebel*, 178). Perhaps, through a rebellious disposition towards his Methodist upbringing, Symons expresses a kind of sincerity born out of his aesthetic treatment of the Original Sin myth.

**

Reflecting on his evening in Café Royal in 1892 with Barlas and Davidson, which resulted in the composition of 'something modern' (the sonnet 'Ambiguë'), alluded to in the introduction to this essay, Symons writes 'Ballad of the Café Royal' (1921). Here, he enumerates the animalistic 'Goddesses' who 'ply their Trade', concluding that 'No Priest shall serve these Pagan Deities' and their 'obscene meaning' (*Jezebel*, 209–10). Although their brazen sexuality strips them of their mythic aura, they are already immortalised and clad in the mystical world of Symons's memory and art. The processes by which this paradox is manifested in a sense encapsulate Symons's eccentric modernity. Symons's late work expresses his own way of espying the Dionysian: by appropriating a postlapsarian standpoint. His mythologisation of sensuality becomes a parable of the post-Romantic inward gaze, of the Decadent introspective self crashing on a new war-ridden reality in which the fragmented psyche cannot be mended. The reason for this development is Symons's 1890s Decadent worldview as a template that pre-empts the future. As he says of one of his mysterious sensual cats,

> His feverish activity
> Keeps me in safe captivity
> And in his eyes Futurity
> Flames like some Sunset on the Sea. ('Lines', *Jezebel*, 147)

Just as the Dionysian intrudes and is filtered in the present, the period of the Decadent Nineties tears its way through Modernism by circumscribing and encoding its own defiant persistence and isolationism in the first half of the twentieth century. 'Futurity' does not bring about Eliotic alchemical transformation; instead, Symons's poetics of Decadent subjectivity in its temporal protraction is a further growth, elaboration and decay, 'like some Sunset on the Sea'. Therein lies its peculiar modernity.

Notes

1 John Betjeman, *John Betjeman's Early Poems*, compiled by the Earl of Birkenhead, 1958 (Oxford and New York: Clio P, 1986), p. 58.

2 Arthur Symons, *The Memoirs of Arthur Symons: Life and Art in the 1890s*, ed. Karl Beckson (University Park: Pennsylvania State UP, 1977), p. 81.

3 Elisa Bizzotto, 'Re-Editing Arthur Symons, Decadent-Modernist Literary Ghost', in *Reconnecting Aestheticism and Modernism: Continuities, Revisions, Speculations*, eds. Bénédicte Coste, Catherine Delyfer, and Christine Reynier (New York: Routledge, 2016), pp. 31–44, p. 31.

4 Arthur Symons, *Confessions: A Study in Pathology* (New York: Foundation P, 1930), p. 32.

5 Kristin Mahoney, *The Literature and Politics of Post-Victorian Decadence* (Cambridge: Cambridge UP, 2015), p. 3.

6 James Joyce, *Letters of James Joyce*, ed. Stuart Gilbert (London: Faber and Faber, 1957), p. 226.

7 Regenia Gagnier, 'Art, Elitism, and Gender: The Last of the Aesthetes', *Review* 12 (1990): 107–17, p. 115.

8 Elisa Bizzotto, 'Re-Editing Arthur Symons, Decadent-Modernist Literary Ghost', in *Reconnecting Aestheticism and Modernism: Continuities, Revisions, Speculations*, eds. Bénédicte Coste, Catherine Delyfer, and Christine Reynier (New York: Routledge, 2016), pp. 31–44, p. 33.

9 See also Karl Beckson, *Arthur Symons: A Life* (Oxford: Clarendon P, 1987), p. 195.

10 See Thomas Stearns Eliot, *Inventions of the March Hare: Poems 1909–1917*, ed. Christopher Ricks (London: Faber and Faber, 1996), pp. 395–6.

11 Roger Holdsworth, 'Introduction', in Arthur Symons, *Selected Writings*, ed. R. Holdsworth, 1974 (New York: Routledge, 2003), p. 13. See also Beckson, p. 242.

12 See Hugh Kenner, *The Pound Era* (Berkeley: U of California P, 1971), pp. 183–4.

13 See Tom Gibbons, 'The Shape of Things to Come: Arthur Symons and the Futurists', *Journal of Modern Literature* 5.3 (1976): 515–21.

14 See Sydney Janet Kaplan, *Katherine Mansfield and the Origins of Modernist Fiction* (Ithaca, NY: Cornell UP, 1991), pp. 48, 62, 64.

15 Arthur Symons, *Lesbia and Other Poems* (New York: E. P. Dutton, 1920), p. 21.

16 Arthur Symons, *Confessions: A Study in Pathology* (New York: Foundation P, 1930), p. 47.

17 Michael Bell, 'An Analytic Note on Myth in Modernism: The Case of T. S. Eliot', in *Religion and Myth in T. S. Eliot's Poetry*, eds. Scott Freer and Michael Bell (Newcastle upon Tyne: Cambridge Scholars, 2016), pp. 65–76, 68.

18 Arthur Symons, *Love's Cruelty* (London: Martin Secker, 1923), p. 73.

19 Thomas Stearns Eliot, 'The Metaphysical Poets', *The Complete Prose of T. S. Eliot: The Critical Edition: Volume 2: The Perfect Critic, 1919–1926*, eds. Anthony Cuda and Ronald Schuchard (Baltimore, MD: Johns Hopkins UP, 2014), p. 380.

20 Arthur Symons, *Figures of Several Centuries* (New York: E. P. Dutton, 1916), p. 101.

21 The John and Iris of the poem also allude to painter Augustus John, friend of Symons, and to popular model and poetess Iris Tree, to whom Symons might have been attracted in the 1920s.

22 Thomas Hardy, *The Collected Poems of Thomas Hardy*, ed. and intro. Michael Irwin (2002; Hertfordshire: Wordsworth, 2006), p. 298.

23 Eliot's letter to Eleanor Hinkley (13 September 1939), qtd by Nevill Coghill, in his introduction to *The Family Reunion* (London: Faber and Faber, 1969), p. 44.

24 See Thomas Ernest Hulme, *Speculations*, ed. Herbert Read (London: Routledge and Keegan Paul, 1936), pp. 46–82.

25 Eliot, 'Tradition and the Individual Talent', *Perfect Critic*, p. 108.

26 Arthur Symons, 'The Decadent Movement in Literature', *Harper's New Monthly Magazine* 87 (1893): 858–67, p. 858.

27 See also Lhombreaud, pp. 280, 293–4.

28 Thomas Stearns Eliot, 'Baudelaire in Our Time', *The Complete Prose of T. S. Eliot: The Critical Edition: Volume 3: Literature, Politics, Belief, 1927–1929*, eds. Frances Dickey, Jennifer Formichelli, and Ronald Schuchard (Baltimore, MD: Johns Hopkins UP, 2015), p. 71.

29 In addition, Virginia Woolf protests that Symons's prose reflects a '[p]rofound religious gravity' ('Mr Symons's Essays', 623).

30 Arthur Symons, *Charles Baudelaire: A Study* (London: Elkin Matthews, 1920), p. 31.
31 Herbert S. Gorman, *The Procession of Masks* (Boston, MA: B. J. Brimmer, 1923), p. 82.
32 Ernest de Selincourt, 'A Poet for Our Sins', *The Times Literary Supplement* 1137 (1 November 1923): 722.
33 John Milton, *Paradise Lost*, ed. Christopher Ricks (London: Penguin, 1989), p. 81.
34 Babette Deutsch, 'Poets and Prefaces', *The Dial* 70 (January 1921): 92.
35 See Rosemary Ellen Guiley, *The Encyclopaedia of Demons and Demonology* (New York: Facts on File, 2009), p. 147.
36 Dante Gabriel Rossetti, *Collected Poetry and Prose*, ed. Jerome McGann (New Haven and London: Yale UP, 2003), p. 161.
37 Arthur Symons, *London Nights* (London: Leonard Smithers, 1895), pp. 24, 49.
38 See Symons, *Memoirs*, p. 143.
39 Qtd in Karl Beckson and John M. Munro, 'Letters from Arthur Symons to James Joyce: 1904–1932', *James Joyce Quarterly* 4.2 (Winter 1967): 91–101, p. 100.
40 Arthur Symons, *Jezebel Mort and Other Poems* (London: William Heinemann, 1931), p. 126.
41 Thomas Stearns Eliot, 'A Brief Introduction to the Method of Paul Valéry', in Paul Valéry, *Le Serpent*, trans. Mark Wardle (London: The Criterion, 1924), pp. 7–15, p. 14.
42 'The Circus Animals' Desertion'. William Butler Yeats, *Selected Poems*, ed. and intro. Timothy Webb (London: Penguin, 2000), p. 224.
43 See also Beckson, p. 321.

7 Richard Le Gallienne

A Jongleur Strayed into the Modern World

Margaret D. Stetz

In their 'Introduction' to *Reconnecting Aestheticism and Modernism* (2017), a collection of essays dedicated to proving that there were more 'continuities between the two movements … than discontinuities', the volume's editors acknowledge that they must confront, in order to resist, the 'traditional narrative of the history of aestheticism and modernism'.[1] They assert that this simplistic narrative, which posits the existence of a 'radical break' between the philosophies and practices at the end of the nineteenth century and the new modes that dominated the first half of the next century, especially in the transatlantic literary world, has been wrongly imposed by scholars on a nuanced and complex reality.[2] While this may be so, it is nonetheless also true that such an account was never a mere invention of academic critics. The opening decades of the twentieth century saw not only the surviving proponents of Aestheticism (which, of course, had once been reviled as a revolutionary movement), but the adherents of a range of more conventional literary styles, engaged in open warfare with a new group of writers who affiliated themselves with Modernist principles. The resulting combat was, on both sides, bloody and, in the case of poets such as Richard Le Gallienne (1866–1947), who straddled the divide between the fin de siècle and the age of Modernism, often deeply personal.

One year after the publication of its first issue in 1914, *BLAST*, the short-lived attempt by Wyndham Lewis (1882–1957) to use an avant-garde British magazine of the arts as an assault weapon had already fizzled out. This did not mean, however, that the fireballs it had launched and encouraged other Modernist-friendly periodicals to aim at Old Guard artistic norms and styles had ended. As Andrzej Gasiorek notes, *BLAST* 'had Aestheticism firmly in its sights',[3] along with everything else that it identified as allegedly feminine or effeminate, and it went after its targets with the aggressive 'spirit of knock-about comedy'.[4] Far from being over with the paper's demise, these sorts of attacks spread widely and, over the next decade, struck with undiminished fury in the realm of literature in particular. Indeed, nothing appeared off limits, especially in critical reviews. Any newly published work that still displayed appreciation of less radical ways of writing—let alone allegiance to fin-de-siècle ideals of *l'art pour l'art* and Beauty (with a capital 'B')—could become a target, and so could any individual author.

Sometimes, the harsh salvos were tempered by faint praise. Such was the case when John Gould Fletcher's 'Once More the Georgians', a review of the volume *Georgian Poetry, 1916–1917*, appeared in the September 1918 issue of *Poetry: A Magazine of Verse*. *Poetry* was, of course, the Chicago-based periodical founded in 1912 by Harriet Monroe (1860–1936), who quickly made it the American home of Modernist poetry. It was perhaps unsurprising that this critique by Fletcher (1886–1950), who was himself a transatlantic figure and a poet, would display the same tensions that had surfaced already in British literary circles, and that it would reflect what Dominic Hibberd has called 'the split' between the Georgians and the Modernists—a feud simmering since as early as 1912 in the short-lived magazine, *Poetry Review* (1912–1915), which grew out of Harold Monro's Poetry Bookshop in London.[5] The Georgians were, in a sense, 'new' writers, and thus they differed from the earlier generation of poets who had become inseparable from the taint of Victorianism; yet, Fletcher made it clear that despite their attempts 'to discover a new note', their verse was not new enough.[6] It was, albeit occasionally leavened by a 'grim honesty' when treating matters related to the First World War, too often guilty of 'jingly metre, and subject-matter which is simply nothing but the apotheosis of picture post-card prettiness' (Fletcher, 336, 334). Claiming to 'know what these Georgian poets are aiming at', he accused them of having achieved instead little beyond 'the jejune, the banal, the vaporous, the jingling', and of having represented 'a world of unrealities, of abstractions, of exhausted platitudes' (335, 337). Worse yet (and here was perhaps the most damning charge of all), some of the poetry in this collection read, according to Fletcher, like 'an etiolated echo of Oscar Wilde' (333). As Wilde was still considered the epitome not merely of literary Aestheticism, but of Decadence and so-called perversion—a charge once more levelled at him publicly in a British courtroom during the notorious libel suit of 1918 that was brought against Noel Pemberton Billing by the dancer Maud Allan, over her performance as Salomé[7]—such an association was certainly meant to wound.

Not all writers who bore the impress of the late Victorian period and remained active at the time of the First World War were prepared either to sit back when accused of producing 'exhausted platitudes' or to cede the literary field to Modernist upstarts. They were, on the contrary, ready to hit back, and they did so using both the press and publishers on both sides of the Atlantic. Among these was the prolific American editor, novelist and poet Carolyn Wells (1862–1942), who had come to public attention in 1896 as a contributor to the *Lark*, the 'little magazine' founded by Gelett Burgess in 1895 and influenced by the sly, satirical side of British Decadence and art as embodied by Aubrey Beardsley. Despite this early affiliation, Carolyn Wells subsequently showed little allegiance to any movement and, in numerous examples of literary humour throughout the first decade of the twentieth century, had poked fun at verse by the Great Victorians, such as Tennyson, and by late Victorians alike. Nonetheless, in one work after another published shortly before and during the 1920s, she proved unsparing in her efforts to push back against the tide of Modernism, in particular, through ridicule.[8] For *Harper's Monthly Magazine* in July 1917, for instance, she imagined how various nineteenth-century British poets, had they lived until the present day, might have been compelled to give up their own distinctive voices and write in the approved Modernist style instead. Thus, her 'Bob' Browning assured the Pre-Raphaelite poet, 'Dan' Rossetti, that it would be no problem at all to emulate the new mode, once he caught the trick of it: 'And the subjects must be concrete – that's the idea, concrete. No more sunset and evening star of Freedom on a mountain height, but stick to tomato-cans or a bent hairpin or a little dog who doesn't feel very well. And keep him concrete'.[9] Objecting not only to a lack of artistry, but to what struck her as vulgarity and an obsession with shock for its own sake, Wells went on to make her dissatisfactions with Modernist modes plain, too, in a subsequent sarcasm-laden poem, published in the *Bookman* of June 1919, under the title of 'On First Reading the "New" Poetry':

> I put it off long as I might – and then
> I put it off again – and yet again,
> 'For', – said I, musing, – ''tis not easy lore, –
> I must jack up my slipshod soul before
> I strive to reach the heights they stoop to brush
> With their great wings of genius. I must lush
> My soul in laving fountains. I must use
> All aids to listen to the modern muse.' ...
> Leveling my head,
> Expectantly I sat me down and read.
> Read? Nay, devoured! Drew in, gulped down, absorbed,–
> As gasping, panting, open-mouthed, sound-orbed,
> I galloped on! Just pausing here and there
> To note a new bad word or novel swear, –
> Then, – something seemed upsetting in the talk –
> I hurriedly went out and took a walk
> * * *
> That first mad reading I shall ne'er forget;
> The second? Well, – that hasn't happened yet![10]

An even more vocal and vociferous opponent of the 'new', whether in poetry or prose, was the Liverpool-born Richard Le Gallienne, who had begun life as a disciple of Oscar Wilde, and whose attacks upon Modernism and statements in defence of late-Victorian aesthetic notions were rarely leavened by humour, except of the most bitter and biting sort. In private, he railed against what he saw as the destroyers of Beauty and idealism in literature, complaining as late as 1931—a time when the Moderns had largely won the battle—in a letter to J. (James) Donald Adams (1891–1968), the editor of the Book Review section of the *New York Times,*

> And speaking of 'modernity', I don't suppose you've seen the latest abhorrence in the form of the 'intelligentsia' magazines, 'The New Review', edited by Samuel Putnam. ...I cannot but feel that censorship is justified when such stuff can be put forth in all the pomp of luxurious format. It is the absolute limit, not merely of eroto-mania, but of *dirto*-mania; just reveling, like filthy little boys, in shouting out as many dirty words as possible for their own sake: the very quintessence of Joyce-ism....[11]

Earlier, while the outcome of the contention between the Modernists and the anti-modern camp was by no means a settled matter, Le Gallienne had been, if anything, even more outspoken, using his own published books of verse as platforms from which to hurl thunderbolts. Both his targets and his intentions were clear at the end of his 1922 collection, *A Jongleur Strayed: Verses on Love and Other Matters Sacred and Profane*, which was published by Doubleday, Page, in the U.S. and written during the roughly twenty years of his residence there. The final poem, 'To a Contemner of the Past', stood out typographically, moreover, as it was the only one in the volume to be printed entirely in italics, signalling its importance to Le Gallienne as an artistic credo and a rebuke:

> YOU that would break with the Past,
> Why with so rude a gesture take your leave?
> None hinders, go your way; but wherefore cast
> Contempt and boorish scorn
> Upon the womb from which even you were born?
> Begone in peace! Forbear to flout and grieve,
> Vulgar iconoclast,
> Those of a faith you cannot comprehend
> To whom the Past is as a lovely friend....
> O base and trivial tongue
> That dares to mock this solemn heritage,
> And foul this sacred page!
> Sorry the future that hath you for sire!...
> From out our sanctuaries
> Begone – and gladly gone![12]

Le Gallienne's use of anachronistic diction to link his work self-consciously with the English of the Elizabethans and other predecessor poets served as a deliberate affront to the *BLAST*ers (who had also turned italics into an instrument of aggression).

A Jongleur Strayed seemed designed from the outset as, so to speak, a counterblast, especially given its 'Introduction'—a delicate appreciation of Le Gallienne by the comic writer and artist Oliver Herford (1863–1935), who was closely associated with Carolyn Wells as both a friend and a frequent illustrator of her work, and who was, like Le Gallienne himself, a transplanted Englishman living in New York. Herford paid homage to Le Gallienne for what was by then a nearly forty-year-long career, remembering him in the early 1890s as the apostle of Aestheticism and as an habitué of Oscar Wilde's circle: 'One Spring day in London, long before the invention of freak verse and Freudism [*sic*], I was standing in front of the Café Royal in Regent Street when there emerged from its portals the most famous young writer of the day, the Poet about whose latest work "The Book Bills of Narcissus" [1891] all literary London was then talking'.[13] Herford's tribute took a fanciful turn, as he constructed an elaborate metaphor around the cab that he had seen spiriting the 'Poet' away, describing *A Jongleur Strayed* itself as like a 'golden' coach—'built on the authentic lines of the best workmanship, made to last for generations, maybe for ever'.[14] (As a few readers in 1922 might have remembered, this image itself constituted an approving backwards glance to the year 1896 and to Le Gallienne's essay 'The Boom in Yellow' from his volume *Prose Fancies, Second Series*, where he had written that 'Amber is yellow … and so were stage-coaches and many dashing things of the old time'.[15]) But the real point of this seemingly innocent paean became clear at its conclusion, as Herford rained abuse down upon the generation of Modernists who had failed to acknowledge Le Gallienne's supremacy: 'Before this Master Coach of Poesy the rattle-jointed Tin Lizzie of Free Verse and the painted jazz wagon of Futurism and the cheap imitation of the Chinese palanquin must turn aside, they have no right of way, these literary road-lice on the garlanded Via Laurea'.[16]

Both Herford and, even more, Le Gallienne threw down a gauntlet, albeit a 'golden' one—its colour perhaps also a reminder of the *Yellow Book* (1894–1897), the Aesthetic magazine with which this 'Poet' had been so closely affiliated through his professional and personal connections to its publisher, John Lane of the Bodley Head. It was, therefore, scarcely surprising that an American reviewer who admired the Modernist project would take up their challenge. In the *Nation* of 15 November 1922, the poet and Columbia University professor of English, Mark Van Doren (1894–1972), could hardly have been more scathing or more dismissive both of Herford's metaphor and of Le Gallienne's right to occupy a 'golden' vehicle of any sort:

> Mr. Le Gallienne stepped into this coach years ago, not because it was gold – it wasn't and isn't – but because it was rolling down Easy Street. And still he rolls there, smiling proudly at a population which doubtless smiles back but which contains not one true poet, not

one true lover of the potent, honest word. Those fellows are off on side streets, working very hard at tough material, perhaps beneath a Ford in the dust. Mr. Le Gallienne among his cushions is living evidence of how fatal it is to play safe and dodge the questions which modern life puts to an artist.[17]

Such vitriol on Van Doren's part was only to be expected. By 1922, to be on the side of 'modern life' meant, particularly in the U.S., to value the 'tough' and 'potent' world of 'fellows' working 'in the dust', while rejecting whatever hinted at an effete and unmanly Aestheticism. With his well-known image from the 1890s as a long-haired, velvet-coat-and-floppy-tie-wearing aesthete still largely intact, Richard Le Gallienne was the very embodiment of an errant and suspect form of masculinity, tied both to dissident sexualities and to elitism in social and political terms (although his background, as the son of a British brewery manager named 'Gallienne', without any 'Le', was actually lower-middle-class). Well aware that to demonstrate an unabashed allegiance to Aestheticism in the new century defined him not merely as unfashionable, but as contemptible in the eyes of some, Richard Le Gallienne nonetheless remained a loyal and devoted admirer of Walter Pater. In an article titled 'On Rereading Walter Pater', he had continued to affirm in print the importance of Pater's ideas as answers to what Van Doren would call 'the questions' of 'modern life'. To write rhapsodically, as he did for the February 1912 issue of the *North American Review*, that Pater was 'an artist' of 'rare insight and magic' and of 'deep humanity as well as esthetic[sic] beauty', while also praising him as 'the teacher of a way of life at once ennobling and exquisite',[18] was calculated to alienate a generation of Modernists who had renounced Pater and, in some cases, had openly denounced the kind of impressionistic writing that he had pioneered.

Yet if Le Gallienne seemed, in essays such as this, to plant himself firmly in the past by declaring Walter Pater 'among the great teachers and artists of our time',[19] and thus to be standing stubbornly on the other side of a historical divide from those who defined both 'our time' and its needs quite differently, the truth was more complicated. What Le Gallienne preached and what he actually practised as a poet did not always align. In the poems that he had been writing since the start of the twentieth century, and in the volumes of poetry that he published during the same period when he and the first waves of Modernists were at war, Le Gallienne often showed that he was by no means a figure cut off from the concerns of the present. The reputedly unbridgeable gulf between a vision of life and of art as reaching towards the 'ennobling and exquisite' and an aesthetic committed to embracing what, in Mark Van Doren's words, was 'potent' and 'tough' proved one that, despite his own hostile rhetoric about literary Modernism, Le Gallienne himself repeatedly bridged.

This willingness to engage in acts of bridging was never clearer than in, appropriately, Le Gallienne's 'Brooklyn Bridge at Dawn', a poem first published in the February 1905 issue of *Metropolitan Magazine* after he had largely abandoned London for New York. Despite his geographical relocation, Le Gallienne had by no means relinquished earlier British literary forms and traditions, even when approaching an American urban subject like 'Brooklyn Bridge at Dawn'; neither had he, on the other hand, let this inheritance go untouched or unchanged or by the new cultural landscapes he encountered:

> Out of the cleansing night of stars and tides,
>   Building itself anew in the slow dawn,
>   The long sea-city rises: night is gone,
> Day is not yet; still merciful, she hides
> Her summoning brow, and still the night-car glides
>   Empty of faces; the night-watchmen yawn
>   One to the other, and shiver and pass on,
> Nor yet a soul over the great bridge rides.
>
> Frail as a gossamer, a thing of air,
>   A bow of shadow o'er the river flung,
>   Its sleepy masts and lonely lapping flood;
> Who, seeing thus the bridge a-slumber there,
>   Would dream such softness, like a picture hung,
> Is wrought of human thunder, iron and blood?[20]

What would have struck readers first in Le Gallienne's poem was its obvious debt to, and deliberate evocation of, perhaps the most famous of all 'bridge' sonnets, William Wordsworth's 'Composed upon Westminster Bridge, 3 September 1802'. Like Wordsworth's poem, 'Brooklyn Bridge at Dawn' was set at early morning. Like Wordsworth's, too, it was not about the rush of humanity crossing a bridge, but about absence and emptiness—not about the tension between the natural world and artificial urban constructions, but about their harmony, united by the power of the poet's vision. Though writing a century and an ocean apart, both speakers regarded the respective bridges with a sense of marvel and wonder.

Unlike Wordsworth's, however, Le Gallienne's sonnet concludes with a rhetorical question that focuses on one aspect of that wonder—on the contrast between the visual illusion of 'softness' and fragility, produced by the effects of light and shadow, and the massive solidity and energy that the bridge actually embodies. Also unlike Wordsworth, Le Gallienne ends his sonnet with a word that abruptly carries the poem into a different sphere, out of the dream world into the real, as he reminds readers of the human toll—of the 'blood'—that the making of such a structure exacted. In his 2005 study, The *Brooklyn Bridge, A Cultural History*, Richard Haw refers to Le Gallienne's sonnet as having demonstrated an approach to the bridge that is 'the essence of romanticism'.[21] Yet, that final word, 'blood', to which the poem gives extra emphasis with the insertion of its sole exclamation point immediately afterwards, changes both the context and the register dramatically. It invokes what Richard Le Gallienne would have learned, albeit at second hand, as a new resident of New York—the history of the deaths of over two dozen workers during the building of the Brooklyn Bridge, by the time of its completion in 1883. The presence of 'blood'—and the unanswered question as to whose blood this might be—forces the reader as well as the poet to shift suddenly, and without preparation, away from Romantic idealisation, particularly as it follows a stark reminder of what industrial works entail—i.e. not air, but 'iron' as their material. But even before this jarring transition, there are allusions within the dreamlike setting to such quotidian, unglamorised facts of modernity and urban life as the public transit system, with the mention of the 'night-car' of the trolley continuing mechanically to traverse the scene, whether carrying passengers or not.

While Richard Le Gallienne's 'Brooklyn Bridge at Dawn' quite literally *spanned* English literary history and contemporary U.S. urban sights/sites when it was published in an American periodical in 1905, its role as a bridge between eras and styles of writing increased exponentially with its next appearance in print, in *The Book of New York Verse*. That anthology, issued in 1917 by G. P. Putnam's Sons, was the brainchild of a native New Yorker, Hamilton Fish Armstrong. Born in 1893 and, in his youth, a poet himself, Armstrong would go on to fame as a commentator on politics and a specialist in international relations, later editing the journal *Foreign Affairs* for several decades before his death in 1973. At the moment when he created *The Book of New York Verse*, he was an idealistic twenty-four year old and a recent graduate of Princeton University, yearning to accomplish two goals. The first was to bring together from three different centuries the voices of poets—native-born or not, regardless of the clashing styles and aesthetics they represented—to celebrate the city he had loved since birth. His second purpose was to remind readers in the U.S., which had just entered the First World War, that they could not live in isolation, nor should they refuse to identify with the fates of European nations and cultures. Their duty was both to cherish their own local history and to see beyond the land they inhabited, using their love of literature to build bridges across the Atlantic to the so-called Old World, in particular, in order to aid their allies in Europe by joining the fighting forces abroad. All three of his own New-York-based poetic contributions to the volume offered, in fact, propagandistic arguments in favour of Americans going (as the contemporary song title put it) 'Over There'.

To say that Armstrong had an ambitious agenda for what was, after all, a mere anthology would be an understatement. The fact that he knew he was launching his project at a time when divisions, chronological or otherwise, were omnipresent—including, but not exclusively, those to be found in the literary world—was obvious from the start of the volume's 'Introduction'. Its opening read, 'The last generation would likely enough have looked upon a book in honour of New York as a vain undertaking for almost unworthy ends', for the 'affection which many of us feel for the city, the affection which day by day it is becoming more the fashion to cultivate, would have met with slight comprehension and considerable ridicule fifty years ago'.[22] Certainly, even among Armstrong's contemporaries, what he described as a feeling that 'the city daily grows more extraordinary, more thrilling'[23] was not universally shared. It was an especially unpopular sentiment among members of the privileged classes to which he belonged by birth, as a descendant of Peter Stuyvesant (1610–1672) and of the distinguished New York politician Hamilton Fish (1808–1893). At that moment in 1917, many of his peers felt as threatened by the waves of working-class European immigrants that had been entering through Ellis Island, and they shrank in horror from the polyglottal populations now claiming space alongside them in the urban streets.

Perhaps Armstrong found it easy to rise above these conflicts during the assembling of *The Book of New York Verse* and, while celebrating both old and new modes, to stay aloof as well from literary contentions between the anti-Modernist and Modernist poetic schools, because he knew that a greater battle lay ahead for him. His 'Introduction' to the volume, dated 1 September 1917, ended with this disclaimer, 'At the moment New York and its libraries are far away. That this was the case during the correction of much of the proof must be my excuse if revision has not been as minute as would have been possible in less topsy-turvy times'.[24] He was, in fact, at that very moment attending Officers' Training Camp in Fort Meyer, Virginia, and preparing to ship off with the 22nd Infantry, although he was soon to be appointed instead as Military Attaché to the Serbian War Mission. Readying himself for action far from the literary scene, he could afford to ignore whatever objections might arise during the period of his anthology's reception and thus prepare the sort of hybrid collection that suited his own tastes—one that, in turn, showcased the hybridity of poems such as Le Gallienne's 'Brooklyn Bridge at Dawn'.

Making no distinction between older poetical styles and newer ones in the treatment of New-York-related subjects, *The Book of New York Verse* was, like the city it hymned, a site of diverse perspectives, encompassing sometimes stark differences, where readers could find both a backwards-glancing lyricism and a forward-looking radicalism, as they encountered Sara Teasdale (1884–1933) and Ezra Pound (1885–1972) side by side. Throughout its 447 pages, where literary selections were interspersed with seemingly random illustrations ranging from a fashion plate of 1806, showing early nineteenth-century urban dress styles, to Henri de Ville's image of the Woolworth Tower in 1915, there were paeans both to the natural landscapes of New York and to its industries and crowded cityscapes. Between the opening and closing poems—each one by Walt Whitman, and each titled 'Mannahatta', forming, as it were, the architectural pillars at opposite ends of the volume—there were works that reflected nostalgia for New York's pastoral and orderly past, such as Charles Coleman Stoddard's 'When Broadway Was a Country Road', alongside others that revelled in the speed and the din of modern public transportation, such as Chester Firkins's 'On a Subway Express'.

Armstrong positioned Le Gallienne's 'Brooklyn Bridge at Dawn' in a way calculated to set off perfectly the poem's own bridge-like character. Immediately preceding it was 'Brooklyn Bridge Towers' (a title that was itself a nice linguistic play, with its final word both a noun and a verb) from *Poems of Men and Events* (1899) by the journalist and novelist George Alfred Townsend (1841–1914), who chose to anthropomorphise and mythologise the iconic structure in a traditional paean. In Townsend's hands, the Brooklyn Bridge's enormous supporting towers became two of the Greek poet Hesiod's Cyclops brothers, Brontés and Argés, serving as heroic guardian spirits of the city. These two immortal giants engaged in a dialogue about their need always to stand tall and unyielding, while bound together by the hair (i.e. actually by the steel cable wires) of one of them, which he had thrown across to his sibling.[25]

Immediately following Le Gallienne's poem, in contrast, was a work by Don Marquis (1878–1937)—now remembered chiefly for his humorous verse about a cockroach ('Archy') and a cat ('Mehitabel') in New York's *Evening Sun* newspaper—titled 'The Towers of Manhattan'. Marquis's poem, which was making its debut in 1917 in *The Book of New York Verse*, both commented upon and amplified Le Gallienne's concluding point about the presence of 'blood' in New York's seemingly beautiful industrial constructions, due to the ruthlessness of the builders:

> For they wrought in the sordid humor
> Of greed, and the lust of power;
> They wrought in the heat of the bitter
> Battle for gold;
> And some of them ground men's lives to mortar,
> Taking the conqueror's toll,
> From the veins of the driven millions;
> Of curses and tears they builded,
> Cruelty and crime and sorrow –...[26]

Such placement by Armstrong of Le Gallienne's 1905 poem, when sandwiched between Townsend's and Marquis's works, made literal its role in straddling styles and eras and underlined its movement, at the end, towards modernity and realism. At least, one contemporary reviewer appeared to appreciate Armstrong's aims, both here and throughout the volume, noting approvingly that 'No rigid classification has been attempted, but the poems that build up chords of remembrances follow one another in effective sequence, and the arrangement of the poetry of new New York is for the most part artistic'.[27]

To focus on 'Brooklyn Bridge at Dawn' does not imply, however, that this was Le Gallienne's sole effort at gesturing towards modernity, literary or otherwise. In 1920, for example, as though inspired by *The Book of New York Verse* and in self-conscious dialogue with Don Marquis's 'The Towers of Manhattan', he returned to the subject of the disjuncture between his own impulse to aestheticise early twentieth-century urban life and his awareness of what such sights had extracted from those tasked with constructing them. 'The Human Sacrifice: A New York Picture', for his volume *The Junk-Man and Other Poems* (1920), not only showed Le Gallienne grappling with this tension, but using a distinctly Modernist form—colloquial, immediate, concrete and imagistic—to do so.

The poem begins with its speaker positioned inside a New York skyscraper, as another one rises in front of him:

> High at a window on the nineteenth floor,
>   We talked, my friend and I. Across the
>   way,
> The iron frame of one new building more
> Grew as we watched it, with incessant scream
> Of hoisting engines, iron chirp and drone...[28]

Soon, the men notice that one of the 'rivet-drivers' is perched precariously on a metal beam:

> Straddling a narrow rib of the gaunt frame,
> Tossed rivets white and molten – like a game –
> Pitcher and catcher; cigarette on lip,
> A battered bucket – if his hand should slip! – ... (203)

At this point, the speaker's friend invites him to consider the ethics of what he has been observing with seeming equanimity, as a mere spectacle:

>   My friend said: 'Do you know
> For each such building men must lose their lives?
> It is as sure, almost as sure, as though
> When the contractor figures out the cost,
> So many tons of pressure floor by floor,
> He wrote – So many lives of workmen lost. ...' (203)

Moved by what he had, quite literally, lost sight of in his contemplation of the scene, the speaker now imparts a vision of the modern urban landscape as a graveyard, with its proudest architectural achievements rising up out of corpses:

These haughty towers on bones of broken men,
Climb to the sky, and glitter in the sun;
Beneath the ball-room floors dead workmen lie,
Light feet above their nameless ashes glide ... (205)

The poem closes with a series of disjointed scenes that flash by quickly, to create a kind of shorthand form of narrative that readers must fill in and connect for themselves. Le Gallienne's concluding image is of the concrete detritus of modern life: a cigarette butt left on the pavement. The poem's final phrase, moreover, which follows an ellipsis, exists in a perpetual present and gives a rawness and immediacy to the image of a workingman's death:

A foot that slipped, a long despairing cry,
A hurrying ambulance with icy clang,
A muffling sheet, through which the warm blood
    drips –
Ah! that young voice that from the girder
    sang...
This cigarette still smoking from his lips! (205)

If this was poetry still connected to roots in the fin de siècle, then it was certainly not linked merely to Paterian ideals, but haunted also by the grim proto-modernity of Oscar Wilde's final poem, 'The Ballad of Reading Gaol' (1898), which was itself, according to Nicholas Frankel, 'a hybrid production, the work of 'a romantic artist ... working on realistic material', as Arthur Symons once put it'.[29] Le Gallienne, moreover, had already explored further this topic of the violence being done to the bodies of men in the contemporary world in a slim volume, *The Silk-Hat Soldier and Other Poems*. Published in 1915 and thus in the midst of the First World War, it tied him directly to the creations of the new generation of the soldier-poets.

Ironically, though, it was *A Jongleur Strayed*, the 1922 volume that contained both Oliver Herford's harsh critique of the followers of Modernism in his 'Introduction' and Richard Le Gallienne's own excoriation of them in '*To a Contemner of the Past*', that also offered one of Le Gallienne's most experimental poems about the present moment. 'The Overworked Ghost' was derisive in tone, gimlet-eyed and filled with fragments of unornamented, everyday speech, much like some of the Modernist works that Le Gallienne mocked for their lack of interest in achieving Beauty. In this attack on the post-war fad for spiritualism—a transatlantic obsession driven, in large part, by the grief of those who had lost loved ones in the War and were desperate to contact the dead— Le Gallienne presented a remorselessly satirical scenario. The speaker, who is newly a ghost, cannot enjoy his eternal sleep, because he is constantly being summoned by a series of meddlesome amateur mediums:

> But scarcely had I laid me down,
>> When comes a voice: 'Is that you, Joe?
> I'm calling you from Williamstown!
>> Knock once for "yes," and twice for "no."'
> Then, hornet-mad, I knocked back two –
>> The table shook, I banged it so –
> 'Not Joe!' they said, 'Then tell us who?
>
> We're waiting – is there no one here,
>> No friend, you have a message for?'
> But I pretended not to hear.
>> 'Perhaps he fell in the great war?'
> 'Perhaps he's German?' someone said;
>> 'How goes it on the other shore?'
> 'That's no way to address the dead!'...[30]

Unlike its more complex predecessor poem in the nineteenth century, Robert Browning's 'Mr. Sludge, the Medium' (from *Dramatis Personae*, 1864), Le Gallienne's 'The Overworked Ghost' had no aim but to demolish its modern-day subject, while using up-to-date diction and ending with a very current reference: '"Rest!" – don't believe it! Well, good-by! / That's Patience Worth there on the phone!'[31] ('Patience Worth' was, as most readers knew in 1922 when *A Jongleur Strayed* appeared, a seventeenth-century spirit brought back from the land of the dead by Pearl Curran, an American woman, and thus allegedly the true author of the many volumes of automatic writing that Curran produced.[32]) Clearly, Le Gallienne was not so wedded to riding in, to use Oliver Herford's phrase, the golden Coach of Poesy that he was unwilling occasionally to commandeer a bus and drive it headlong through a designated target in the modern world.

'Few poets have been so ardent in the worship of beauty, and few so severely reproved for lingering in Arcadia'.[33] So wrote Benjamin Griffith Brawley (1862–1939)—an African American poet, literary historian and professor at Morehouse College—in a 1918 essay about Richard Le Gallienne for the *Sewanee Review*. At that very moment, Le Gallienne was indeed being 'severely reproved' by a variety of voices including, as Brawley reported, that of the American critic Paul Elmer More (1864–1937), a Christian philosopher and close friend of T. S. Eliot. Wherever Le Gallienne turned in the aftermath of the First World War, it seemed that either Modernist poets or their allies were waiting for him with a dismissive and slighting judgement. Attempting in 1918 to sum up Le Gallienne's career to that point, Brawley was certainly correct in saying, 'All around him beckoned the beautiful, and to all he gave the deepest appreciation', thus deliberately invoking, at the end of that sentence, a word designed to bind Le Gallienne tightly to the Paterian tradition.[34] Brawley was, however, less accurate when declaring, 'Few modern poets have lived so aloof from the forces of industrialism' or when implying that Le Gallienne was not only opposed to the modern age of 'athleticism and brawn', but entirely remote from it.[35] Richard Le Gallienne's literary tastes did indeed remain static—fixed permanently in the decades of the 1880s and 1890s, which had seen the flourishing of Aestheticism but his literary talent was more mobile, and it moved in a surprising variety of directions. As he demonstrated on more than one occasion in his poetry from the early twentieth century, he was capable of leaping over barriers in terms of subject matter, of crossing boundaries in terms of style and even, quite unexpectedly, of building bridges.

Notes

1 Bénédicte Coste, Catherine Delyfer, and Christine Reynier, 'Introduction', in *Reconnecting Aestheticism and Modernism: Continuities, Revisions, Speculations*, eds., Bénédicte Coste, Catherine Delyfer, and Christine Reynier (New York and London: Routledge, 2017), p. 5.

2 Coste, Delyfer, and Reynier, 'Introduction', in *Reconnecting Aestheticism and Modernism*, p. 2.

3 Andrzej Gasiorek, 'The "Little Magazine" as Weapon: *BLAST* (1914–15)', *The Oxford Critical and Cultural History of Modernist Magazines. Vol I, Britain and Ireland 1880–1955*, eds. Peter Brooker and Andrew Thacker (Oxford: Oxford UP, 2009), p. 294.

4 Gasiorek, 'The "Little Magazine" as Weapon', p. 297.

5 Dominic Hibberd, 'The New Poetry, Georgians and Others', in *The Oxford Critical and Cultural History of Modernist Magazines. Vol I*, p. 186.

6 John Gould Fletcher, 'Once More the Georgians', *Poetry* 12.6 (September 1918): 332–7, 332.

7 For more about Wilde's meaning for the British public in 1918, see Judith Walkowitz, 'The "Vision of Salome": Cosmopolitanism and Erotic Dancing in Central London, 1908–1918', *American Historical Review* 108.2 (April 2003): 337–76; and also Philip Hoare, *Oscar Wilde's Last Stand: Decadence, Conspiracy, and the Most Outrageous Trial of the Century* (New York: Arcade, 1998).

8 See Margaret D. Stetz, '"To amuse intelligently and cleverly": Carolyn Wells and Literary Parody', *Transgressive Humor of American Women Writers*, ed. Sabrina Fuchs Abrams (Basingstoke: Palgrave Macmillan, 2017), pp. 17–36.

9 Carolyn Wells, 'The Re-Echo Club', *Harper's Monthly Magazine* (July 1917), p. 297.

10 Carolyn Wells. 'On First Reading the "New" Poetry', *Bookman* (June 1919), p. 458.

11 Richard Le Gallienne, qtd. in Richard Whittington-Egan and Geoffrey Smerdon, *The Quest of the Golden Boy: The Life and Letters of Richard Le Gallienne* (London: Unicorn P, 1960), p. 513.

12 Richard Le Gallienne, 'To a Contemner of the Past', *A Jongleur Strayed: Verses on Love and Other Matters Sacred and Profane* (New York: Doubleday, Page, 1922), pp. 173–4.

13 Oliver Herford, 'Introduction', in *A Jongleur Strayed: Verses on Love and Other Matters Sacred and Profane*, by Richard Le Gallienne (New York: Doubleday, Page, 1922), p. xv.

14 Herford, 'Introduction', p. xvii.

15 Richard Le Gallienne, 'The Boom in Yellow', *Prose Fancies, Second Series* (Chicago, IL: Herbert S. Stone and London: John Lane, 1896), p. 88.

16 Herford, 'Introduction', p. xvii.

17 Mark Van Doren, 'In Line', *Nation* 115.2993 (15 November 1922): 530.

18 Richard Le Gallienne. 'On Re-Reading Walter Pater', *North American Review* (February 1912): 214.

19 Le Gallienne. 'On Re-Reading Walter Pater', p. 224.

20 Richard Le Gallienne, 'Brooklyn Bridge at Dawn', *Metropolitan Magazine* (February 1905): 526–7.

21 Richard Haw, *The Brooklyn Bridge: A Cultural History* (New Brunswick, NJ: Rutgers UP, 2005), p. 177.

22 Hamilton Fish Armstrong, 'Introduction', in *The Book of New York Verse*, ed. Hamilton Fish Armstrong (New York: G. P. Putnam's Sons, 1917), p. iii.

23 Armstrong, 'Introduction', p. iii.

24 Armstrong, 'Introduction', p. v.

25 George Alfred Townsend, 'Brooklyn Bridge Towers', in *The Book of New York Verse*, pp. 256–8.

26 Don Marquis, 'The Towers of Manhattan', in *The Book of New York Verse*, p. 261.

27 [Anon.], 'With the Authors and Publishers', *New York Times Book Review* (6 January 1918), p. 66.

28 Richard Le Gallienne, 'The Human Sacrifice: A New York Picture', *The Junk-Man and Other Poems* (New York: Doubleday, Page, 1920), p. 202.

29 Nicholas Frankel, *Oscar Wilde: The Unrepentant Years* (Cambridge, MA: Harvard UP, 2017), p. 182.

30 Richard Le Gallienne, 'The Overworked Ghost', *A Jongleur Strayed: Verses on Love and Other Matters Sacred and Profane* (New York: Doubleday, Page, 1922), pp. 158–9.

31 Le Gallienne, 'The Overworked Ghost', p. 161.

32 'Patience Worth: Author from the Great Beyond', *Smithsonian Magazine* (September 2010). https://www.smithsonianmag.com/arts-culture/patience-worth-author-from-the-great-beyond-54333749/.

33 Benjamin Brawley, 'Richard Le Gallienne and the Tradition of Beauty', *Sewanee Review* (January 1918), p. 47.

34 Brawley, 'Richard Le Gallienne and the Tradition of Beauty', p. 47.

35 Brawley, 'Richard Le Gallienne and the Tradition of Beauty', p. 47.

Part III

Double Voices

Central and Peripheral
Transactions

8 'If I'm Not Very Careful, Something of This Kind May Happen to Me!'

The Preordained Role of the Reader in M. R. James's Ghost Stories

Luke Seaber

The ghost stories of M. R. James (1862–1936) are commonly recognised as being amongst the finest ever written. They have terrified generations of readers, listeners and viewers since he first began telling them as oral narratives given on Christmas Eve to his intimate friends in Cambridge.[1] However, although their importance in the horror tradition is unquestioned, the critical response to them has been limited, with James's reticence to be considered anything other than a teller of tales, for his tales to be considered as anything other than 'the bagatelle of an idle hour',[2] as Julia Briggs puts it in her important study of the English ghost story, *Night Visitors*, is all too often taken at face value. Indeed, Clive Bloom has claimed that James's stories are particularly effective in producing horror in the reader *because* they have nothing behind the horror: 'Much went into the creation of these tales, but they refuse to be read as sexual, psychological or social allegories'.[3] There have been important studies of James that do view him as a writer worth analysing in detail and depth, but these have tended either to remain firmly focused on him as a genre writer (as in *Night Visitors*) or have looked at single themes in his work—homosexual panic[4] or Victorian science and the role of the unconscious mind,[5] for instance. Although the latter approaches are interesting, they do not make any particularly wide-ranging claims for James: the themes in question are also to be found in many other more canonical writers of the period. I wish here to argue that not only are there other levels to James's stories that he is as careful not to impose upon the reader as he is to do no more than hint at the horrors his characters experience, but also that these hidden levels are of an innovative importance that deserves to give him a place amongst the more obvious experimenters considered canonically Modernist. Umberto Eco wrote that in writing *Lector in fabula* (1979), many of the theories expounded in which are central to the reading of James's works offered here, he was faced with the choice of talking either about the pleasure given by a text or about why a text can give pleasure.[6] Equally, the aim of this chapter is not to discuss the horror James's stories can instil in a reader, but rather why they are so able to do this.

James's first ghost story both in composition and insofar as it opens his first collection, *Ghost Stories of an Antiquary* (1904), was 'Canon Alberic's Scrap-book', and may thus be considered the reader's introduction to the world of James's ghosts and narrative strategies. In it, a Cambridge don, whom the author calls Dennistoun, is on a holiday in the Pyrenees with two friends whom he leaves behind at Toulouse to go to visit the cathedral at Saint-Bertrand-de-Comminges. Once there, he pays the sacristan to guide him round the church, where the two men hear what seems to be strange laughter in the empty cathedral. The sacristan then suggests that Dennistoun might be interested in an old book that he has at home. The book offered to him is the scrapbook of a seventeenth-century canon, Alberic de Mauléon, who raided the Chapter library of its best manuscript pages. The book also contains a map of part of the cathedral with a Latin text in Canon Alberic's hand from which Dennistoun understands that the canon has hunted for treasure and an illustration of a demon brought before a king. The demon frightens the Englishman, who nonetheless buys the scrapbook at an exceedingly low price, even though he insists that the sacristan accept more. That evening, whilst he leafs through the treasures contained in the scrapbook, he begins to feel nervous and has the sensation that something is behind him; he then sees an object on the table where the book is resting: it is the terrifying hand of the demon. The story finishes with various observations on the death of Alberic de Mauléon, adding that the original of the illustration has been burnt and only a photographic reproduction remains.

At first sight, everything seems to fit into the usual plan of one of James's stories: we have a terrible and not fully explained experience undergone by an English scholar whom a passion for knowledge puts at risk of supernatural forces. Typical Jamesian narrative details are also present: the detailed description of a real place and a full scholarly apparatus of footnotes and Latin texts.

Things are not that simple, however. At this early point in his narrative career, James's sure-handedness in his form is less obvious. Dennistoun is portrayed as having the habit of inveterately talking to himself, and whilst on the one hand this in itself merely places him more firmly in the large class of relatively lonely Jamesian protagonists,[7] the narrative use made of it is in contrast to what would become the author's chief technique in the stories to follow. The whole grisly denouement of the sight of the demon's hand is conveyed not through third-person narration but through Dennistoun's own thoughts on what he is seeing: 'A penwiper? No, no such thing in the house. A rat? No, too black. A large spider? I trust to goodness not—no. Good God! a hand like the hand in the picture!'[8] This inclusion of the protagonist's own description of the monster assailing him, a description unmediated by hindsight or reflection, risks becoming rapidly absurd, as Simon MacCulloch has pointed out.[9] Its use here, in James's earliest story, weakens the horror in a way that is rare in the stories that will follow.

There is another way in which 'Canon Alberic's Scrap-book' differs, I believe, from what would become the classic James ghost story, and it lies at the heart of the reading that I am proposing here. This is related to something James said regarding J. S. Le Fanu: 'And again the unexplained hints which are dropped are of the most telling kind. The reader is never allowed to know the full theory which underlies any of his ghost stories [...]. Only you feel that he has a complete explanation to give if he would only vouchsafe it'.[10] This is also a very good description of James's technique, and would at first sight also appear to be the case here: the demon's nature is only hinted at, as are the details of Alberic's eventual death; the exact nature of the sacristan's experiences is never explained, and it is never made clear whether the laughter in the tower comes from a true ghost—of Alberic, one presumes—or instead another incarnation of the demon. Nor is the curious fact that the sacristan insists on an absurdly low price for the scrapbook ever explained, although Helen Grant has made a valiant attempt to do so by appealing to the motif of Stevenson's 'bottle imp',[11] but James quite simply does not provide the reader with enough information to allow a firm conclusion to be reached.

I believe that the situation in which Grant finds herself bespeaks James's status here as an author still unsure of his material and his technique. As we shall see, in later tales, unexplained details fall reasonably neatly into two categories: those that can be explained through reference to various fields of erudition—folklore and biblical apocrypha, for example—with which James was familiar; and those that cannot, but that nonetheless have a degree of consistency within the tale that leads the reader to feel, like James when he read Le Fanu, that there *is* a full explanation somewhere, known to the author but never revealed to the reader. We can see that James only partially achieves this in his first published story. His huge knowledge of biblical apocrypha does indeed go towards laying down clues as to the identity of the demon that has tormented the sacristan (identified by Helen Grant as a certain Ornias found in the apocryphal *Testament of Solomon*, a text that James knew well);[12] however, the implications of the scrapbook's low price peter out despite their seeming importance. They are detailed enough, and the odd behaviour of the sacristan and his daughter is stressed enough, for it to be fair for the reader to presume that they have a certain role in the text. Following up the clues, however, leads us to no firm conclusions, and the amount of inconclusive things we can find out is too great to leave us believing that there is a true explanation known to the narrator. This simultaneous overabundance and insufficiency of information is a weakness that James very soon moved beyond, and in the multitude of later stories where hints at unspoken things are given, the quantity of information is nearly always such as to lead the reader either to their own discovery of the truth or to have faith in James's knowledge of it.

As an example of this, we may turn to 'Count Magnus'. The story is presented as having been put together by the narrator from the papers of a Mr Wraxall, who had been travelling in Sweden in 1863 with an eye to writing up his journey for publication. This book was to include 'episodes from the history of some of the great Swedish families' (*CGS*, 64), and so Wraxall, who fits nicely the mould of the Jamesian protagonist, goes to an ancient manor house in Västergötland in a place referred to as Råbäck (although this is not its name). He becomes interested in the mausoleum of the first of the de la Gardie family, to whom the manor house belongs, Count Magnus, a man with a reputation for cruelty and about whom stories still circulate, one of which relates that he 'had been on the Black Pilgrimage, and had brought something or someone back with him' (*CGS*, 67). The landlord of the inn tells Wraxall of an episode occurring on his grandfather's day, when two men who were hunting in the woods that had belonged to Count Magnus were found after a terrible scream followed by a terrible laugh had been heard: one man was driven out of his wits and the other had had the flesh sucked off the bones of his face. It is the day after hearing this that Wraxall finally gains entrance to the mausoleum, where he finds the Count's sarcophagus, which has strange carvings on it of what appears to be a hunting scene, where a man runs from a dwarfish figure, the only part of which is not cowled being a tentacle, and the whole scene is watched by a cloaked and hatted figure on a hill who would appear to be enjoying the spectacle. Wraxall also notes that one of the three padlocks closing the sarcophagus is broken. On two occasions following, he finds himself muttering his wish to meet the Count: each time is accompanied by a breaking padlock, and when the third padlock breaks, the sarcophagus lid too begins to open. Wraxall leaves for England, yet on his canal-boat journey through Sweden is plagued by a conviction that there are two extra passengers, one short and one tall and both cloaked so as to be unidentifiable. As he flees to the village of Belchamp St Paul after his disembarkation at Harwich, Wraxall sees the two figures waiting at a crossroads. At the village, he locks himself in his room. Here there ends the material from Wraxall's notes, and the narrator informs us that his body was found soon after in a state that caused seven of the coroner's jury to faint. The papers were left in the house, which was eventually inherited by the narrator, thus explaining how the story came to light.

'Count Magnus' has inspired some of the finest antiquarian research on James's sources. Rosemary Pardoe has argued convincingly that the use of the names de la Gardie and Magnus indicates that James based details of the character of the Count not so much upon Count Magnus Gabriel de la Gardie (1622–1686), but rather on his father, Count Jacob

Pontusson de la Gardie (1583–1652), with possible details added from his grandfather, Pontus de la Gardie (1520–1585).[13] Equally, Rosemary Pardoe and Jane Nicholls have collected an impressive amount of information not only on Magnus's supposed Black Pilgrimage, which from the fragments written by Count Magnus entitled 'Liber nigræ peregrinationis' that Wraxall finds would appear to have been to the Biblical city of Chorazin, but also on that city itself: they reach no conclusion, however, over whether or not the Black Pilgrimage is pure Jamesian invention or not.[14] A key question still remains about the use of 'black': Pardoe and Nicholls discuss whether, besides the traditional negative implications of the colour,[15] it might be related to the black basalt out of which Chorazin was built or its use as a term in alchemy, given that Count Magnus's text is found amongst (genuine) works of alchemy, but no firm conclusion is reached. A source that they do not discuss is the one that is more important for another James story set in Sweden, 'Number 13', which shows us that James was familiar with the pact with the devil written by the Swedish professor of theology Daniel Salthenius when young (an artefact which exists in the real world and is preserved in Uppsala).[16] Article Four is 'That I now receive from you the Black Book',[17] which mysterious volume was the supposed repository of mysterious knowledge shared by the devil and experts in the supernatural.[18] This reference to the colour gives us a possible source for James's use of it 'Count Magnus'—'Black Book' could easily be a shorthand for a book detailing a Black Pilgrimage—especially given another Article in Salthenius's contract:

> 2. You shall grant me particular success in the world with gentlemen and ladies of high station, as well as success in hunting and fishing, so that I never return empty-handed.[19]

Salthenius (who was less than fifteen when he wrote it, whence, as Lindow rightly notes, 'the somewhat puerile tone of the contract and its demands')[20] petitions the Devil for success in hunting, and there is a good reason to believe that Magnus was a keen huntsman. Only one scene on his sarcophagus portrays the cloaked and hatted figure as which he appears when recalled to the world: he is overseeing a hunt, where the prey is human and the pursuer the squat demon that we may presume returned with him from the Black Pilgrimage. Equally, the two men who were killed or driven mad in the forest in the innkeeper's grandfather's time had decided to go hunting in the Count's woods; the case may be made that they were punished more precisely for poaching than trespassing. Furthermore, if we take Magnus's chief interest, as it were, to be hunting, we can explain one of the more mysterious aspects of Mr Wraxall's death. Why did Count Magnus and his demon track him from Sweden to England and yet not kill him until Belchamp St Paul? The explanation, I think, lies in the fact that when Wraxall reaches his lodging there, he stops fleeing and concludes 'What can he do but lock his door and cry to God?' (*CGS*, 74). Wraxall is killed when he stops running, but we cannot ascribe this to his being caught up by his pursuers—his time on the boat with them would be more than sufficient for them to carry out their aims, and when he sees them from his fly at the crossroads, they are already ahead of him and waiting. It is also significant that once he stops running and goes to ground, as it were, he, for the first time, experiences some respite, having twenty-four hours of peace from those following him. Surely, the easiest way to explain this given what we know of Magnus, and bearing in mind Salthenius's request for hunting prowess, is to posit that Magnus will prolong the chase for as long as it is entertaining. Once the prey stops running, some time is given to see if the pursuit will start again; once it does not, the order for the *coup de grâce* is given, as the huntsman's enjoyment is over.

We owe our knowledge of James's knowledge of Salthenius's pact with the devil to 'Number 13'. The story tells of the narrator's cousin, Anderson, who visits Viborg to examine archives relating to church history. He takes Room 12 in the Golden Lion, noting the absence of any Room 13 between his room and Room 14 on the list of rooms, which he puts down to superstitious triskaidekaphobia, especially when he sees the door to Room 13 on his first night in the hotel. His research in the Rigsarkiv leads him to the correspondence of the last Roman Catholic incumbent of the see, in which there is a discussion of one Mag. Nicolas Francken,[21] who is accused of witchcraft and is a tenant in a house belonging to the bishop. That night, he sees the shadow of the occupant of Room 13 cast against a dull red light on the wall opposite his window. As during the previous evening, he notes how much smaller his room looks at night. The next morning, he notes to his surprise that there is no door marked 13, and the landlord confirms the absence of Room 13. The next night, he is disturbed by the bizarre singing and dancing in the room next to his, which must of course be Room 14: the occupant of Room 14, Jensen, then comes to complain about the noise that Anderson is making. Back out in the corridor, Anderson, the landlord and Jensen gather outside Room 13—which has reappeared—and an arm is seen to come out of the door and flail at Jensen. Servants are called to break down the door; this vanishes, and Rooms 12 and 14 reassume their usual proportions. The floor space where Room 13 may be presumed to exist is taken up: all that is found is a manuscript in an unknown script. The story ends with the narrator being chidden by his cousin for laughing over Salthenius's pact with the devil: the suggestion is that Francken had made just such a pact and was in some way being punished for it.

What makes 'Number 13' such a fascinating work is the degree to which it plays with the reader's expectations. The very title itself sets up expectations in the reader that will not be met in the expected way:

a ghost story named 'Number 13' suggests, surely, some sort of plot dealing with the unluckiness of that number—a haunted room, perhaps. This is suggested by the landlord's words to Anderson, talking of the triskaidekaphobia prevalent amongst Danish commercial travellers: 'Quantities of stories they have among them of men that have slept in a Number 13 and never been the same again, or lost their best customers, or—one thing and another' (*CGS*, 55). This is the sort of story that the title and the opening paragraphs prepare us for. James subverts the reader's expectations, though. The fact that the room that appears is numbered 13 can only be a coincidence: we may presume that the house belonging to Bishop Friis in which Francken lived has become the Golden Lion, but the fact that the phantom room takes up part of both Rooms 12 and 14 means that the dividing walls of the hotel are an addition postdating Francken's residence in a space that would not have been any sort of thirteenth room at the time. The unlucky associations of the number 13 here are purely by the by.

Another false expectation is set up in the description given of Anderson's room, which contains a cast-iron stove, 'on the side of which was a representation of Abraham sacrificing Isaac, and the inscription, "1 Bog Mose, Cap. 22" above' (*CGS*, 49). 'Number 13' is James's fifth story: we may presume that by this point, he was aware not only of readers' responses to ghost stories in general but also to his ghost stories in particular. Knowledge of 'Canon Alberic's Scrap-book' alone would have alerted readers or listeners to this story to the possibility that foreign-language phrases could be important, as could the least of details about iconography, folklore, the Bible and so on. Here, we have both combined: the Danish for 'First Book of Moses' (which is to say Genesis) and the representation of Abraham's attempted sacrifice of Isaac. James here is laying a false trail for his audience: leaving them searching for a significance in the Biblical scene that cannot be found.

It is worthwhile to open a parenthesis here about the identity of the narrator in James's stories. Given their oral origins, it would be reasonable to identify him with James himself. Nonetheless, the narrator's presence in many of the stories is not limited to narration: he also plays a part on occasions in the stories, and the end of 'Room 13' is an excellent example of this. I therefore think it overly simplistic to consider the narrator merely a stand-in for the author, as it were, especially in those stories, like this one, where there arise questions involving the narrative that make no sense if a one-to-one identification of author with narrator is practised. Whilst it is fair to speak of James himself laying a false trail in the detail of the stove, it makes no sense for the narrator who is retelling his cousin's experience to do so.

Towards the end of the story, the narrator almost admits that the story is a game of unfulfilled expectations, in a passage that has often been noted as an example of James's playing with his public's expectations.

When the floorboards are taken up, the narrator notes: 'You will naturally suppose that a skeleton—say that of Mag. Nicolas Francken—was discovered. That was not so' (*CGS*, 61). What is found is the indecipherable text mentioned earlier. However, while the lack of a skeleton and the explanation to the strange phenomena that this would afford is an obvious refusal to meet expectations, the fact that the text found is *also* an example of this has hitherto been overlooked. The final sentence of the paragraph detailing the discoveries under the floor of the phantom Room 13 runs as follows: 'Both Anderson and Jensen (who proved to be something of a palæographer) were much excited by this discovery, which promised to afford the key to these extraordinary phenomena' (*CGS*, 61). This hope is never realised. The text remains untranslated. Nor should it be thought that this is merely in order to mock Jensen's abilities: the narrator compares Jensen and Anderson's failure to his in reading a text written on the flyleaves of a book he owns. In other words, *there is no explanation given of the events in 'Room 13'*. As noted earlier, there is the suggestion that the text found was a pact with the devil like that written by Salthenius, but it is a suggestion made only by apposition, as it were. Indeed, the very identification of the figure in Room 13 with Francken is supposition. After all, what do we actually know about the figure? The descriptions given are vague: 'He seemed to be a tall thin man—or was it by any chance a woman?—at least, it was someone who covered his or her head with some kind of drapery before going to bed' (*CGS*, 53); the arm that grabs at Jansen 'was clad in ragged, yellowish linen, and the bare skin, where it could be seen, had long grey hair upon it' (*CGS*, 59). How long is that hair? For all we know, the figure in Room 13 could be a demon of the type encountered in 'Canon Alberic's Scrap-book', summoned up by Francken. The reader quite simply does not know—and nor, for that matter, does Anderson. The story concludes: 'That same afternoon [Anderson] told me what you have read; but he refused to draw any inferences from it, and to assent to any that I drew for him' (*CGS*, 62). The narrator alone draws inferences, and in doing so, and in presenting the material as he presents it, lures the reader into making the same inferences.

The narrative form (the very fact that this is a ghost story) makes these inferences appear to be an explanation of events, but they only explain them insofar as they convince, and conviction is no proof of accuracy. 'Room 13' undermines simple forms of reading, tricking the reader into believing that a coherent closure has been narrated of events, whereas the reality is that no such thing has taken place.

I believe that the reason James plays these games of meaning, inserting these narrative uncertainties or these allusions that may lead the reader to further, extratextual, uncertainties brings us back to James's goal of frightening his readers (it should be repeated: I am arguing for innovation in technique; the goal of inculcating fear in one's readers is anything but innovative in itself). In order to see exactly what James is doing, in this reading of his stories, it is instructive to turn to another work that marked an important innovation in the field of horror: *Scream* (1996). This, written by Kevin Williamson and directed by Wes Craven, has been explored as a postmodern and even hyperpostmodern text, insofar as it, like its sequels, takes 'the previously subtle and covert intertextual reference [found in earlier slasher films] and transform[s] it into an overt, discursive act'.[22] The characters in *Scream* are deeply familiar with the type of film in which they unknowingly and unfortunately find themselves, with perhaps the most famous example—certainly the most openly self-reflexive—being that in which Randy elaborates 'the rules' to a group of friends at a party:

> There are certain rules that one must abide by in order to successfully survive a horror movie. For instance: 1. You can never have sex. Big no-no. Sex always equals death. 2. Never drink or do drugs. It's an extension of number one. And 3. Never, ever, ever, under any circumstances, say "I'll be right back".[23]

This is intertextual, just as we might say that James's references to other, less popular and more obscure texts, are intertextual. In one sense, the *practical* influence of this intertextuality can also extend extratextually: it is possible that within the text of the film, Randy or any of his listeners decides to remain an abstemious virgin in order not to risk being murdered; it is possible (which is not to say that it is in any way likely) that viewers of the film also decide to refrain from drugs and sex in order not to run any risk of being brutally murdered. This practical influence can only work, however, in suggesting ways to be safe. A slasher film, even so cunning a one as *Scream*, is unable to oblige its viewers to lose their virginity or take drugs whilst it is being watched; it cannot have built into its narrative structures mechanisms for reproducing textual realities extratextually at the moment of the text's consumption; it cannot make its viewers put themselves at risk of sharing the fate of the characters that they are watching.

It is in this that the great originality of James lies. His work *is* able to make the leap into the extratextual; his readers may in a certain sense become characters in a potential M. R. James ghost story. It is easy to illustrate how this works: most of this chapter has in fact been an example of it. The majority of James's characters to whom unpleasant things happen make the mistake of conducting academic or antiquarian research: *this is exactly the situation of many of James's readers.* By performing the sort of research that I have carried out earlier, or that which Patrick J. Murphy carries out in his excellent book *Medieval Studies and the Ghost Stories of M. R. James*,[24] or much of that carried out over the years in the two incarnations of *Ghosts & Scholars* by the redoubtable Rosemary Pardoe and others,[25] we reproduce outside of the text what is happening within it. In his preface to *More Ghost Stories of an Antiquary* (1911),

James suggests that one, or perhaps the chief, aim of his ghost stories is to 'put the reader into the position of saying to himself, "If I'm not very careful, something of this kind may happen to me!"' (*CGS*, 406). This has become something of a cliché in studies on James, insofar as it appears in numerous titles and introductory passages (as indeed it does here), but what has been missed is that by reading a James story, one has already stopped being careful; one has already begun that process of reading that is the actual beginning of research and the potential beginning of doom.

Who are these 'readers' of James, about whom I have so glibly been talking? Is it fair (or useful) to presume that the actual readers of James's ghost stories—other than those academic readers of the type alluded to above—behave as I am suggesting James's texts cause their Model Readers to behave? Umberto Eco summarised a rule of texts by saying that the addressee's competence is not necessarily that of the sender:[26] presuming that the actual readers of his texts share the philological, antiquarian, ecclesiological and so on learning and leanings of the actual author may appear to be theoretically naïve, asserting things about actual readers properly only to Model Readers. However, the particular details of the genesis and critical reception of James's texts allow us, I think, to conflate these categories in a justifiable way. James's stories were primarily written to be read, and his original audience ('original' both in the sense that they were the first people to hear all of his early stories and in the sense that they were the first of these primary audiences, later stories sometimes having different original addressees) were very much academics in the same or similar mould to the author. In other words, the Model Readers assumed by James's texts coincide, insofar as theoretical potentialities can coincide with historical actualities, with the original actual readers, and James was aware of this, although of course not in these terms. Equally, the critical history of James shows actual readers unconsciously giving in to James's texts and becoming Model Readers of the type that I posit here.

In an important passage in *Lector in fabula*, Eco talks of texts' relationships to the 'real' world of the reader and the world(s) it itself contains:

> The text, as it were, 'knows' that its Model Reader will make erroneous predictions (and will help him or her to make them), but the text as a whole is not a possible world: it is a portion of the real world and is at most *a machine for generating possible worlds*—that of the fabula, those of the characters in the fabula and those of the reader's predictions.[27]

James's texts, however, are not so much interested in their readers' predictions of how the various fabulae will develop as making possible a contagion of the reader's world by that of those fabulae.

The ways to the various terrible ends suffered by James's characters are many, and each chooses his own within the narrative universe; these are the 'possible worlds' of which Eco writes. James's great innovation is in allowing his readers too to choose their own paths to potentially the same terrible ends outside the narrative universe. He extends the possible worlds out from the possible world(s) within the text into the real world, where they come into being and lurk in wait, traps for careless and careful readers alike if they follow the academic or antiquarian road that leads to them, the road on which James has set their feet and started them on their journey.

Eco has spoken of the difference between 'open' and 'closed' fabulae; simplistically, the difference between a work that leads its readers along a set path, where only one of the reader's various possible hypotheses over future events is 'correct' (Figure 8.1),

Figure 8.1

and one that allows various possibilities to branch off, and makes no affirmations about the fabula's final state, with a Model Reader cooperative enough to construct their fabulae on their own (Figure 8.2).[28]

Figure 8.2

I would suggest that the typical model for a James story of the type that we have been discussing can (heuristically, at least; this is not the place to enter into discussion of the 'true' narratological nature of the stories) be considered a third type (Figure 8.3),

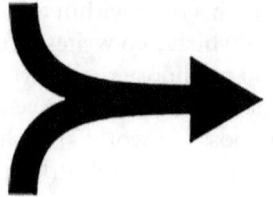

Figure 8.3

where the end result is imposed by the fabula, but the path taken to reach it is not: researchers into antiquarian matters must always move towards a terrible fate, both textually and extratextually, but the route taken within the text is not the same as that taken outside of it, and the extratextual reader has the luxury of always, we hope, stopping before the horrific textual endpoint is reached extratextually.

It is in this power of contaminating the world outside his stories with the world within them, of anticipating his readers' responses to his texts and playing with them, both as a child plays with other children and as a cat plays with a mouse,[29] that makes him an innovator and postmodernist *avant la lettre* in a way his popular and critical reception has tended hitherto to overlook. M. R. James's understanding of how to foresee and control readers' actions in the world outside his texts makes him not just, as he has long been recognised, 'one of the few really creative masters in his darksome province',[30] as Lovecraft put it, but also an unrecognised creative master for literature in the twentieth century and beyond.

Notes

1 Darryl Jones's introduction to the 2011 edition of James's collected ghost stories, the edition referred to here, gives a good idea of what these story sessions were like. Montague Rhodes James, *Collected Ghost Stories* (Oxford: Oxford UP, 2011), pp. ix–x.
2 Julia Briggs, *Night Visitors: The Rise and Fall of the English Ghost Story* (London: Faber and Faber, 1977), p. 125.
3 Clive Bloom, 'M. R. James and His Fiction', in *Creepers: British Horror and Fantasy in the Twentieth Century*, ed. Clive Bloom (London: Pluto P, 1993), pp. 64–71, 70.
4 Mike Pincombe, 'Homosexual Panic and the English Ghost Story: M. R. James and Others', in *Warnings to the Curious: A Sheaf of Criticism on M. R. James*, eds. S. T. Joshi and Rosemary Pardoe (New York: Hippocampus P, 2007), pp. 184–96.
5 Brian Cowlishaw, '"A Warning to the Curious": Victorian Science and the Awful Unconscious in M. R. James's Ghost Stories', in *Warnings to the Curious: A Sheaf of Criticism on M.R. James*.

6 Umberto Eco, *Lector in fabula: La cooperazione interpretativa nei testi narrativi* (Milan: Bompiani, 1998), p. 11.

7 See Simon MacCulloch, 'The Toad in the Study: M. R. James, H. P. Lovecraft, and Forbidden Knowledge', in *Warnings to the Curious: A Sheaf of Criticism on M.R. James*, eds. S. T. Joshi and Rosemary Pardoe (New York: Hippocampus P, 2007), pp. 76–112, 99–100.

8 Montague Rhodes James, *Collected Ghost Stories*, ed. Darryl Jones (Oxford: Oxford UP, 2011), p. 11. Hereafter cited as *CGS*.

9 MacCulloch, 'The Toad in the Study', p. 99.

10 Montague Rhodes James, 'M. R. James on J. S. Le Fanu', *Ghosts & Scholars* 7 (1985): 24–7; 27.

11 Helen Grant, 'The Nature of the Beast: The Demonology of "Canon Alberic's Scrap-book"', in *Warnings to the Curious: A Sheaf of Criticism on M. R. James*, pp. 235–7.

12 Grant, The Nature of the Beast, pp. 230–4.

13 Rosemary Pardoe, 'Who Was Count Magnus?: Notes towards an Identification', in *Warnings to the Curious*.

14 Rosemary Pardoe and Jane Nicholls, 'The Black Pilgrimage', *Ghosts & Scholars* 26 (1998): 48–54.

15 Pardoe and Nicholls, 'The Black Pilgrimage', p. 51.

16 John Lindow, *Swedish Legends and Folktales* (Berkeley: U of California P, 1978), pp. 45–6.

17 Lindow, *Swedish Legends and Folktales*, p. 45.

18 Lindow, *Swedish Legends and Folktales*, pp. 10, p. 47.

19 Lindow, *Swedish Legends and Folktales*, p. 45.

20 Lindow, *Swedish Legends and Folktales*, p. 46.

21 'Mag.' is the abbreviation of 'Magister', the equivalent to a doctor's degree in philosophy up to 1824 in Denmark.

22 Valerie Wee, 'The Scream Trilogy, "Hyperpostmodernism", and the Late Nineties Teen Slasher Film', *Journal of Film and Video* 57.3 (2005): 44–61, 47.
This article gives an extremely useful reading of the film and its sequels in terms of intertextuality and self-reflexivity that it is instructive to read alongside the explorations of James's technique given here.

23 Kevin Williamson, *Scream* (N.p.: Miramax Books and New York: Hyperion, 1997), pp. 127–8.

24 A splendid example—one of many—is the groundbreaking research into the manuscript of '"Oh, Whistle, and I'll Come to You, My Lad"'. Patrick J. Murphy, *Medieval Studies and the Ghost Stories of M.R. James* (University Park: Pennsylvania State UP, 2017), pp. 45–51. Murphy also very tellingly notes that James 'leads us to read like an antiquary. I am not the first to be led down this path ...' (Murphy, 186).

25 The examples are legion. Limiting ourselves just to works already cited here: Grant, 'The Nature of the Beast'; Pardoe, 'Who Was Count Magnus?'; Pardoe and Nicholls, 'The Black Pilgrimage'.

26 Eco, *Lector in fabula*, p. 53 ('la competenza del destinatario non è necessariamente quella dell'emittente'. My translation).

27 Eco, *Lector in fabula*, p. 173. ('Il testo, per così dire, "sa" che il suo Lettore Modello sbaglierà previsione (e lo aiuta a formulare previsioni sbagliate), ma il testo nel suo complesso non è un mondo possibile: esso è una porzione del mondo reale ed è al massimo *una macchina per produrre mondi possibili*: quello della fabula, quelli dei personaggi della fabula e quelli delle previsioni del lettore. My translation).

28 Eco, *Lector in fabula*, pp. 120–1, figures simplified from which, with arrows added to show direction.
29 See Sean McCorristine, 'Academia, Avocation and Ludicity in the Supernatural Fiction of M. R. James', *Limina* 13 (2007): 54–65, especially 57–60, on lucidity in James's stories.
30 Howard Phillips Lovecraft, 'Supernatural Horror in Literature', in *Warnings to the Curious*, p. 52.

9 'A Large Mouth Shown to a Dentist'

G. K. Chesterton's Surgical Parodying of T. S. Eliot

Michael Shallcross

In his 1959 study, *The Centre of Hilarity*, Michael Mason finds G. K. Chesterton and T. S. Eliot to be such self-evident opposites that it would be 'almost ludicrous to compare them', since Chesterton had represented the 'popular bowels' of British culture, while Eliot stood for its 'clerkly head'.[1] More recently, Lee Oser has reemphasised this projection of disparity: 'Chesterton is comical, democratic, and orthodox. Eliot is ironic, aristocratic, and a priest of art'.[2] In the binary terms of this narrative, Eliot and his fellow exponents of 'high Modernism' formed an aesthetically radical, though culturally elitist vanguard, while Chesterton led a culturally democratic, if aesthetically retrograde counter-insurgence. Although Chesterton won the occasional contemporary skirmish in this contest of values, Eliot ultimately won the war, as Modernism gradually became entrenched in the academic canon as the preeminent aesthetic movement of the early twentieth century. By the mid-1920s, Eliot was already emerging as perhaps the ultimate Modernist insider, while Chesterton's determined projection of anti-Modernism increasingly rendered him a semi-occluded cultural presence, heckling from the margins.

As Andreas Huyssen has observed, Modernism 'constituted itself through a conscious strategy of exclusion, an anxiety of contamination by its other: an increasingly consuming and engulfing mass culture'.[3] Chesterton, the staunch populist, came to stand as an exemplar of this rejected other, as illustrated by Eliot's 'Observations' in an article for the *Egoist* in May 1918: 'I have seen the forces of death with Mr. Chesterton at their head upon a white horse. Mr. Pound, Mr. Joyce, and Mr. Lewis write living English; one does not realize the awfulness of death until one meets with the living language'.[4] The mock-apocalyptic quality of Eliot's bifurcating vision bears a certain resemblance to the discriminatory drive of parody, in which rival discourses are ridiculed through a process of investing implicitly dead language with a ludicrous new vitality. However, Elizabeth Sewell argues that the parodist's techniques of textual infiltration also speak to an unresolved tension between 'close emotional kinship (a kinship that itself involves a compelling pull toward sameness and a death of subjectivity) before ultimate self-assertion (a pull toward difference)'.[5] Consequently, as Simon Dentith observes,

'parody has always been liable to oscillate into and out of the critical attitude', in a manner that complicates the very factionalism that the form
is conceived to bolster.[6]

Just such an oscillation is perceptible in Chesterton's parodic treatment of the themes and stylistics of Eliot's early work, from *Prufrock and
Other Observations* (1917) to *The Waste Land* (1922), in 'To a Modern
Poet', an apparently throwaway skit published in *G. K.'s Weekly* on 31
May 1925. Chesterton's parody stages a struggle for cultural authority
in a manner that finally betrays a deeper existential affinity, through a
combination of combative nonsense rhetoric, motivated by a tacit fear
of identification, and more subtly emollient gestures, suggestive of an
underlying sympathetic understanding. The bulk of the parody sets out
to expose the ontological scepticism and pessimism that Chesterton perceives to underpin Eliot's handling of the world of objects, as revealed by
the unorthodox similes to which the poet turns, which the more stolid
parodist finds somewhat bemusing:

> [...] I am very unobservant.
> I cannot say
> I ever noticed that the pillar-box
> was like a baby
> skinned alive and screaming.
>
> I have not
> a Poet's
> Eye
> Which can see Beauty
> everywhere.
> Now you mention it,
> Of course, the sky
> is like a large mouth
> shown to a dentist,
> and I never noticed
> a little thing
> like that.
>
> But I can't help wishing
> You got more fun out of it;
> you seem to have taken
> quite a dislike
> to things.[7]

The lines, 'Of course, the sky / is like a large mouth / shown to a dentist', comically skew the terms of Eliot's bravura simile of introduction
to the poetic world, from 'The Love Song of J. Alfred Prufrock' (1915),

in which 'the evening is spread out against the sky / Like a patient ether-
ized upon a table', to emphasise the deprecation implicit within the original image.[8] Chesterton sets out to tie Eliot's unorthodox vocabulary to
an apparently cultivated posture of aversion to the material world that
renders the poet an unlikely locus of regenerative energies. As Chesterton complains in his autobiography, via a further anthropomorphic
nonsense image perhaps inspired by Eliot's vision of the 'dry grass singing' in *The Waste Land*, 'I have read modern poems obviously meant to
make grass seem something merely scrubby and prickly and repugnant,
like an unshaven chin'.[9] Eliot's wan observations stand in sharp contrast
with the 'passionate sense of the *value* of *things*' (second emphasis mine)
that Chesterton avowed in his youthful correspondence with his fiancée,
Frances, in 1899, and which he expressed through a comparable category mistake in reference to the evening sky: 'If there was such a thing
as *blue*-hot iron, it would describe the sky tonight'.[10] While the vitiated
'Love Song' of Eliot's title conveys a trapdoor irony comparable to that
of Oscar Wilde's mock-paean to being earnest, Chesterton's galvanising
love letter articulates an unqualified existential reverence.

The titular link to Wilde is instructive. Eliot's implicit authorial
stance in 'Prufrock'—that of the urbane Laforguean man of the world,
who observes 'the essential mediocrity of life [...] from a lunar perspective'—is articulated through a combination of the temperamental
detachment and textual derangement that Chesterton associated with
Decadence, a movement that he considered to have 'outraged sanity'
without even 'attain[ing] exuberance'.[11] In a palimpsestic enterprise,
Chesterton's skit not only carries the ghost of Eliot's text within it, but
also exposes the apparently innovative 'observations' of the poet to be
a pastiche of his immediate precursors, even as the parodist archly concedes himself to be 'very unobservant' (CN, 50). This produces a kind of
intertextual geological survey, comparable to the White Knight's song
in Lewis Carroll's *Through the Looking-Glass, and What Alice Found
There* (1871), which Susan Stewart describes as a 'language event [...]
caught in a historical regress. What the song "really is" becomes only
one of its possible aspects through its history of use'.[12] This correspondence situates Chesterton in a position of interpretive mastery over his
antagonist: '"the tune *isn't* his own invention", [Alice] said to herself',
as the White Knight declaims his proto-Prufrockian song of an absurd
'aged man'.[13]

One of Eliot's purposes in assembling the elusive retinue of Laforguean
disguises that characterised his early verse was to evade the potential
charge of earnest adherence to Decadence. Lyndall Gordon detects a
'wilfully defeatist identity' in the work that immediately postdates Eliot's
reading of Arthur Symons' study of the late nineteenth-century continental avant-garde, *The Symbolist Movement in Literature* (1899), while the
temperamental and stylistic influence of Symons' own poetry upon Eliot

has been convincingly mapped by Roger Holdsworth.[14] Although often arresting, Symons' verse is prone to a complacent, sentimental pessimism, which skirts the kind of unintentional self-parody later mocked by Max Beerbohm in 'Enoch Soames' (1916), his tale of a second-rate Decadent poet whose tepid volume of 'Negations' meets with universal indifference.[15] Registering this potential site of attack, Eliot took the precaution of sloughing off his *Weltschmerz* onto a series of archly scrutinised avatars. The fallibility of these evasive strategies is not only illustrated by Chesterton's parody, but also by Beerbohm's glancing satires of Eliot, which identify *both* inscrutable irony *and* anaemic pessimism as the salient features of his verse. Alluding to Eliot's feline fogs, Beerbohm glosses 'Prufrock' as an exercise in 'ironically analysing an empty sardine tin', while elsewhere reimagining *The Waste Land* as a morose music-hall sketch: 'Wot's the good o' trying to earn a living nowadays? ... Wot's the good of ennyfink? Why, nuffink!'[16] Eliot's associate and rival, Wyndham Lewis, later crystallised the duality at hand: the young Eliot was 'a very attractive young Prufrock indeed [...] *moqueur* to the marrow [...] But still a Prufrock!'[17]

In 1926, John Middleton Murry argued that despite Eliot's much-vaunted literary 'classicism', he was really 'an unregenerate and incomplete romantic [...] his professions and his reality remain utterly divorced'.[18] Likewise, once Lewis no longer held any commercial stake in conveying group unanimity with his fellow 'Men of 1914'—Eliot, James Joyce and Ezra Pound—he took to situating Eliot as 'the last of [a] line of romantics' stretching from Baudelaire to Wilde, while referring darkly to Pound's equally 'romantic tendencies' in *Time and Western Man* (1927).[19] In *Blasting and Bombardiering* (1937), Lewis implies that a sort of repentant Romantics' support group had been established between the collaborative pair: Pound's 'very powerful influence' upon the young Eliot was responsible for lifting him 'out of his lunar alley-ways and *fin de siècle* nocturnes'.[20] Eliot later protested that it was Pound whose Romantic tendencies had required purgation, recalling that Pound's pre-war verse had 'seemed to me rather fancy, old-fashioned, romantic stuff, cloak-and-dagger kind of stuff'.[21] Of course, 'cloak-and-dagger' not only evokes ingenuous, swashbuckling play, but also a more unscrupulous air of double-dealing.

Chesterton's image of the sky as a 'large mouth / shown to a dentist' is suggestive of the surreptitious process of classical re-education that Eliot and Pound had undertaken in the wake of their exposure to the idiosyncratically classical precepts of T. E. Hulme's criticism and Lewis's art. The simile conjures an association with the aesthetic surgeon correcting the unwieldy profusion of nature, editing down the existential grotesque to the elegant restrictions of the classical, in accordance with Lewis's vision of the hairdresser, in *BLAST* (1914), as an artist pursuing a similar agenda to his own: 'attack[ing] Mother Nature for a small fee […] correcting the grotesque anachronisms of our physique'.[22] Lewis later explained that his debut novel, *Tarr* (1918), had been 'clipped […] to the bone of all fleshy verbiage', an image anticipated by another of Eliot's early criticisms of Chesterton in the *Egoist* ('Professional, Or ...' April 1918), in which we are informed that the latter's critical writing is 'fleshed and boned in irrelevance'.[23]

If the increasingly pared-down verse of Eliot and Pound came to stand as an aesthetic corollary of their espousal of classicism, 'To a Modern Poet' not only summons forth a personally embarrassing return of repressed Romanticism, but also acts as a publicly damaging subversion of the commercial game plan that the principle of sparseness increasingly came to serve within the cultural entrenchment of Modernism. Chesterton's 'large mouth', in the literary form of a 'mechanical dribble' of 'irrelevance', had been the focus of high-Modernist critical fire from Lewis's polemical article, 'Futurism and the Flesh' (1914), to Eliot's 'Professional, Or ...'[24] Pinpointing Chesterton's ostensible surplus production served to advertise a binary divide between the enigmatic brevity of the new school and an old guard characterised by exhausting verbosity. Ironically enough, in Lewis's later novel, *The Childermass* (1928), the Chestertonian figure of the Bailiff is made to voice a similar complaint about Joyce: '"God thought fit to furnish him with an out-size gab but not enough wisdom to discount it for what it's worth"'.[25] Pound and Eliot were determined to make no such mistake. Pound's paradigmatic Imagist artefact, 'In a Station of the Metro' (1913), was famously clipped down from 'a thirty-line poem' to just fourteen words.[26] In a letter sent by Pound to Eliot's father in 1915, he avers that 'man succeeds either by the scarceness or the abundance of copy'.[27] Taking note, Eliot explained to an ex-teacher that 'I write very little, and I should not become more powerful by increasing my output. [… The] only thing that matters is that [the poems] should be perfect in their kind, so that each should be an event'.[28]

In George Eliot's work of pseudonymous cultural criticism, *Impressions of Theophrastus Such* (1879), the 'cracked mirror' of the burlesque humourist is censured for its alleged role in 'debasing the moral currency' of society.[29] To consider this phraseology in fiscal, rather than ethical, terms, debasement occurs when scarcity is reduced, so that the commercial value of any item becomes defined to a large extent by the limitation of its availability and/or accessibility. With 'To a Modern Poet', Chesterton threatens to debase Eliot's cultural currency through an act of literal appreciation, by producing a burlesque addendum to his slender oeuvre, conceived to render the apparently impenetrable poet's ideas accessible to a popular audience. By amassing new similes in a travesty of Eliot's voice, Chesterton divests him of the agency to prevent surplus production, exacting an apposite revenge upon the persecutors of his prolixity by imaginatively ransacking the mouth of the celebrated poet and claiming to discover a hinterland of tooth decay behind the scrupulously brushed exterior.

Gary Saul Morson's view of parody turns upon a comparable fiscal analogy, here implicitly invested with a constructive ethical value: 'Parody implies currency' because it 'discredits what others might credit [...] reveals as counterfeit what others might take for true coin'.[30] In an article on 'Parody in Our Times' (*Illustrated London News*, 2 May 1925), published just a few weeks before 'To a Modern Poet', Chesterton contends that the methods of Modernist art make this interpretive challenge especially taxing: one is 'hardly able to distinguish a modern Vorticist picture from an imitation of it by some contemporary caricaturist'.[31] With 'To a Modern Poet', Chesterton tests this premise in textual terms. As Hugh Kenner notes, Eliot's writing has consistently inspired an obscure 'conviction that it means more than it seems to'.[32] One thinks of Chesterton's critique, elsewhere, of the cultural 'mystagogue', who 'succeeds because he gets himself misunderstood', a counterintuitively commercial methodology that rests upon manipulating the insecurities of a snobbish audience.[33] The narrator of Beerbohm's 'Enoch Soames' corroborates this principle when he records his consecutive responses to the poet's verses: 'suppose Enoch Soames was a fool! Up cropped a rival hypothesis: suppose *I* was!'[34]

Bradford Morrow's account of *BLAST* conveys a remarkably similar reception dynamic: Lewis sets out to breed the 'paranoia that comes when one hears a brilliant joke which is truly funny but is not comprehensible, and which may or may not be about oneself', a methodology that 'troubled [his] audience'.[35] Likewise, Rafey Habib finds the 'ultimate level of irony' in 'Prufrock' to reside in Eliot's 'laughing at the increasingly puzzled reader', a stratagem later exemplified by the notes to *The Waste Land*, which came to be viewed by the poet's interpreters as the microcosmic exemplar of his scholarly austerity, but which he subsequently debunked as a miasmic 'wild goose chase' of 'bogus scholarship'.[36] Indeed, when Eliot's endnotes direct the reader to a chapter of *The Golden Bough* (1890) in which Sir James Frazer describes the Sibylline Books as 'that convenient farrago of nonsense', it seems that we are dealing, at least in part, with the 'explanatory note [that is] only mock-explanatory', a cryptic form of buffoonery that Noel Malcolm places in 'the tradition of academic self-parody'.[37]

Malcolm goes on to observe that 'the self-parodic routines of nonsense poetry are characteristic products of enclosed, self-conscious institutions such as clubs'.[38] Likewise, in a multilayered, dog-whistle approach to reception management, Eliot bluffs the common reader into a conviction that he is in charge of a highly exclusive club, into which all but the most erudite of initiates are denied membership, while covering his back by subtly informing more sophisticated readers that he has merely been playing an elaborate practical joke all along. In this light, there is a distinct prescience to Chesterton's analysis of elitist culture in 'The Queer Feet' (1910), a *Father Brown* story that turns upon a theft committed in an exclusive gentlemen's club. Rather than the complacent aristocrats or the harried underlings of the story, Eliot's cultural position most closely resembles the intermediary role occupied by the club's proprietor, Mr Lever, whose apparent self-effacement masks a subtle manipulation of the system to his greatest advantage, by establishing a club that 'paid, not by attracting people, but actually by turning people away'.[39] As the Chestertonian narrator explains, '[i]n the heart of a plutocracy trades-men become cunning enough to be more fastidious than their customers. They positively create difficulties so that their wealthy and weary clients may spend money and diplomacy in overcoming them'.[40] While Lever's commercial strategy prefigures those forms of Modernism that special-ised in setting up a textual difficulty to be overcome by the leisured liter-ary consumer, his exceptionally 'fastidious' persona offers a foretaste of Eliot's later public reputation as a highly particular assessor of aesthetic relevance, possessing a critical sensibility that resembled, in John Gross's words, 'a kind of sieve: the finer it is, the more it rejects'.[41]

This elaborate confidence trick, in the fullest sense of the phrase, can be understood to derive from Eliot's own fear of ridicule: he once in-formed Virginia Woolf that 'humiliation' was his greatest fear.[42] This anxiety was compounded by his status as a US émigré in the heavily codi-fied society of literary London. Upon arriving in Britain in 1914, he wrote to his friend, Conrad Aiken, of the urgency of perfecting his innate gift for mimicry: 'I must learn to talk English'.[43] He went on to actively court Bloomsbury, earning its patronage and mockery in equal measure: while the Hogarth Press published *The Waste Land* and Woolf venerated his verse, Clive Bell later claimed that he and Woolf considered Eliot 'a sort of "family joke"'.[44] Although Eliot's troubled youthful verse, 'Humour-esque' (1910), had been inspired by the petty social world of Boston, the poem's waspish 'spectres' accusing one another of provincialism—'"Why don't you people get some class?"'—are not so far removed from Peter Kaye's account of the snobbish milieu of Bloomsbury, in which 'unspo-ken rules govern speech and action and the inhibitions, deceptions, and masks of civility reign'.[45] Uncertain of his aptitude for decoding the rules of the social games into which he was thrust, Eliot withdrew into a non-sense game in which he could make up the rules himself, while setting about persuading 'the right people' that his was the only game in town.[46]

The strategy paid off. Between Eliot's earliest criticisms of Chesterton in the *Egoist* and the parodic response of 'To a Modern Poet' fell the shadow of *The Waste Land*, a momentous cultural event that augured a seismic shift in power relations, leaving Eliot in the ascendancy and Chesterton's influence in decline. Given Chesterton's complaint that the estranging devices of the 'mystagogue' erected socially disenabling bar-riers to mutual comprehension, it is unsurprising that Eliot's newly es-tablished cultural dominance should have proved unsettling to him, not least since the poet's commercial strategy entailed a concerted projection of animosity towards Chesterton himself. The alacrity with which Eliot, Lewis, and Pound latched on to the public image of Chesterton as a propitious straw man to pummel was wedded to their view of the cultural agon as a detached nonsense game that necessitated the treatment of 'people [as] things', to borrow from Sewell's account of Carroll's *Wonderland*.[47] In this light, compare Chesterton's address to Eliot—'you seem to have taken / quite a dislike / to things'—with his defensive reply to a correspondent to the *Nation* several years earlier: 'you seem to have taken quite a dislike to me'; a verbatim facsimile, save for the replacement of 'me' with 'things'.[48] The passage of 'To a Modern Poet' in which Chesterton sets out to convey Eliot's deprecatory attitude towards 'things' is immediately preceded by a reproachful first-person address in which the identity of the Eliotic antagonist becomes confounded with that of the sometime Vorticists, Lewis and Pound:

> I did not give you
> a green pain
> or even
> a grey powder.
> It is rather you, so winged, so vortical,
> Who give me a pain. (*CN*, 50)

Here, Chesterton presents his private feelings as an effaced narrative, trampled by the greater publicity power of the culturally ascendant targets, while the 'green pain' hints at a return of the migraines that Maisie Ward reports him to have suffered during his youthful grappling with the scepticism of the Decadent followers of the green carnation.[49] Eliot's radical fracturing of space in 'Prufrock' into a chaotic 'bric-a-brac' of body parts and material detritus was ideally primed to trigger the anxieties over ontological unravelling that had pursued Chesterton from the *corps morcelé* of Professor de Worms in *The Man Who Was Thursday* (1908)—'whenever the man moved a leg or arm might fall off'—to the shattered horizon-line of *William Blake* (1910): 'I have always a nervous fear that the sea-line will snap suddenly'.[50] Chesterton's earliest verse collection, *Greybeards at Play* (1900), had articulated a visionary apprehension of a scenario in which 'Art [...] snapt / The Covenant of Things'; Eliot's emergence as a purveyor of ontologically deranging imagery, packaged in a culturally alienating manner, brought this fear comprehensively back to the fore (*CN*, 16).

Accordingly, Chesterton seems to have conceived the linguistic and ocular derangement of Modernism as a potential psychic pollutant, a view that Eliot was happy to encourage during the period in which he was straining to identify himself as a protean constituent of a band of aesthetic revolutionaries, bent upon achieving the audacious category mistake of killing John Bull with Art, as Lewis put it.[51] In Chesterton's picaresque satire, *The Ball and the Cross* (1909), MacIan explains to a magistrate that he cannot tolerate the 'blazing scepticism' of his adversary, Turnbull, because if he were to accept this position '"I should burst like a bubble and be gone. I could not live in that imbecile universe. Shall I not fight for my own existence?"'[52] This existential duel-to-the-death finds an echo in the apocalyptic confrontation of living and dead *littérateurs* envisioned by Eliot, as well as the judicial setting of Lewis's *The Childermass*, in which a disciple of the 'classical' figure, Hyperides, gestures angrily towards the Chestertonian Bailiff: '"Who is to be *real –* this hyperbolic puppet or we?"'[53] In an article in the *Egoist*, Dora Marsden makes a similar complaint about Chesterton: his increasingly Manichean cultural outlook 'has nothing to do with which world is the better: it is solely a matter of which is becoming the more real. [...] Those whom he loves not he leaves without even a world to live in'.[54]

Something of this partisanship is discernible in an editorial for *G. K.'s Weekly* (4 April 1925), published two months before 'To a Modern Poet', in which Chesterton guardedly defends the rather alarming conclusion of his contributor, Bernard Gilbert, that Joyce should be killed for having written *Ulysses* (1922), noting that his columnist has at least 'the moral courage to say "let us burn this masterpiece"'.[55] Gilbert advocates Joyce's murder for much the same reason cited by MacIan in his clash with Turnbull, while mirroring Pound's equably expressed wish, elsewhere, that Chesterton should have 'never been born': 'I enjoy [Joyce's] art [...] as I enjoy [the] striped liveliness of a hornet. We kill the hornet, without malice [...] as a danger to our being'.[56] Conrad Aiken compared Eliot to a different insect, nicknaming him 'Tsetse': a fly that passes on infection with its bite.[57] While the moniker was intended to evoke Eliot's acerbic wit, the poet's apparently limitless capacity to infect his audience with the dark mood of his verse inspired Chesterton to take up the forceps of the parodist. By performing selective surgery upon the mouth of the modern poet, Chesterton accumulates ammunition to counter the psychological challenge that his worldview presents. By pulling Eliot's leg, Chesterton is also pulling his teeth.

Nonetheless, Chesterton's wary backward step from the fascinating cultural antagonist not only fosters psychological reassurance, but also critical perspective. In a later article, 'On Sense and Sound' (collected in *All I Survey*), Chesterton sets out to draw Eliot's sting via an allusion to Vorticism that reimagines those involved as harmless convalescents: although 'Mr. T. S. Eliot's wildest verses [...] mak[e] the head go round', they finally suggest 'a cosy life in the hollow heart of a cyclone or a whirlpool'.[58] Chesterton's astute pinpointing of Eliot's urge to withdraw from life is lent a more visceral satirical edge in the concluding lines of 'To a Modern Poet', which archly acknowledge Eliot's status as the spearhead of 'the New Movement / The Emetic Ecstasy' (*CN*, 51). By situating the poet's mouth as a repellent site of abjection, this sardonic pay-off suggests that

Chesterton's cheek was not always so entirely scrubbed free of Rabelaisian toilet humour as Pound had implied in *BLAST*, when scoffing at the freshly 'glisten[ing ...] cheek of a Chesterton'.[59] While the pun on 'movement' activates a carnivalesque transference of abstract intellectualism to indecorous corporeality, it also illustrates a genuine critical insight into its subject: the young Eliot had written to Aiken of his appreciation of any literature able to 'provoke [a] strong nausea with life'.[60] Julia Kristeva argues that the urge to vomit is a quintessential expression of abjection, because in the very act of revolt against the condition, the subject simultaneously projects forth abject matter from within.[61] In conjoining this visceral gesture to a state of 'ecstacy', Chesterton implies that Eliot derives a curiously masochistic pleasure from the act of vomiting out his sense of existential abjection.

This euphoric expulsion has interesting implications for an understanding of Eliot's elitism, as well as Chesterton's opinion that 'Modernism is [...] a form of snobbishness'.[62] In a letter sent to Eleanor Hinkley in 1914, Eliot confessed himself 'a thorough snob', a disposition corroborated by Lytton Strachey's report that around 1918, Eliot was wont to imitate Dostoevsky's Raskolnikov, declaring the citizenry of London to be 'divided [...] into "supermen", "termites" and "wireworms"'.[63] This snobbery later found expression in Eliot's portrayal of the 'young man carbuncular', in *The Waste Land*:

> A small house agent's clerk, with one bold stare,
> One of the low on whom assurance sits
> As a silk hat on a Bradford millionaire.[64]

Here, Eliot's distaste at 'the low' seems tinged with tacit envy of the 'bold [...] assurance', a dynamic that accords with Chesterton's analysis of the 'internal insecurity' that motivates 'The Snob' (*Daily News* 4 April 1908).[65] Chesterton's journalistic essay on snobbery prefigures his invocation of 'ecstacy' in 'To a Modern Poet' in a synaesthetic context that also anticipates the skit's speculation that the poet might suffer from a 'green pain': 'The snob's delight is to rise high and have all the time the secret joy, the purple ecstacy of feeling low'.[66]

Chesterton's impatience with such attitudes derived from the painful process through which he had overcome the 'sterile isolation' of his own adolescent solipsism and, with it, the influence of his closest youthful friend, E. C. Bentley, who later found fame as the inventor of the 'clerihew' nonsense form.[67] Eliot's lines on the house agent's clerk are remarkably similar to comments recorded in Bentley's diaries of the 1890s regarding those who inhabit the 'lowest of the business classes, just where clerkdom begins. [...] Imagine their lives among themselves – the psychological dirt of it'.[68] Elsewhere in the diaries, Bentley gazes out upon Hampstead Heath and finds only an infestation of 'swarming heaps of people – the ignorant almost entirely. [...] Almost all of them were young unmarried people, in couples and parties, giving a frightful promise of more swarming heaps of the ignorant to come. It is a sombre thing to watch the People enjoying itself'.[69] In diametric contrast, it is on Hampstead Heath that the narrator of Chesterton's first *Father Brown* story, 'The Blue Cross', experiences an adulatory vision of 'the sublime vulgarity of man'.[70] In 'The Philosophy of Sight-seeing' (collected in *Alarms and Discursions*), Chesterton notes that 'I know nothing so vulgar as that contempt for vulgarity which sneers at the clerks on a Bank Holiday or the Cockneys on Margate Sands'.[71]

Bentley's reflections on 'the People' came just a day after a dinner party held to celebrate the inauguration of the new *Speaker*, a periodical on which he subsequently worked with Chesterton. After the event, Bentley recorded his self-disgust in contemplating the auspicious figures seated around him, not least his 'successful rival' at Oxford, Hilaire Belloc: 'Very annoying evening [...] I had to go in morning clothes, which made me very angry [...] These men are far above me. They can do things I daren't contemplate. [...] My mind beside Belloc's, for example, would look a mean and disgusting thing'.[72] As this episode suggests, Bentley's diaries are frequently proto-Prufrockian in their adumbration of a lengthy catalogue of social anxieties. Prufrock's interminable prevarications are anticipated by the 'things I daren't contemplate', while Bentley's fear of his mind being exposed as a 'disgusting thing' accords with Prufrock's apprehension of the external display of his 'nerves in patterns on a screen'.[73]

Wim Tigges argues that for Edward Lear, 'nonsense was a method of self-defence, an escape to hide his feelings, his despair, his sense of failure'.[74] Bentley's son, Nicolas, considered his father's failure to secure a first class degree at Oxford as a pivotal moment in his life: a 'failure [...] of self-confidence rather than of intellect', which was 'probably a fundamental clue to his character, to the hesitancy, the aloofness, as it seemed to some, the withdrawal from any approach to intimacy, which kept him on the sidelines throughout his life'.[75] In his diaries, Bentley discusses the 'feeling of black despair and self-contempt' engendered by his self-perceived 'failure as an Oxford man'.[76] A month after receiving his classification, he notes that '[t]he world is becoming very real and threatening now'.[77] Again, Prufrock offers an apt accompaniment: 'in short, I was afraid'.[78] As with Eliot's fear of humiliation, Bentley's accounts suggest that the 'rigid flippancy' that Chesterton impatiently ascribed to his friend should be understood as a defence mechanism, the recourse to arch inscrutability characteristic of the individual who feels unequal to the demands of improvised repartee, and who shrinks from anticipated social failure into pre-emptive withdrawal.[79]

The temperamental similarities of Eliot and Bentley help to account for the confluence of affinity and antipathy that brought Chesterton into later textual dialogue with Eliot. 'To a Modern Poet' hits its target because the parodist understands that of which he speaks: Eliot's snobbery echoes Chesterton's own youthful correspondence with Bentley, in which he had imitated his friend's distaste for the 'plebeian excursionist'.[80] Equally, Eliot's negotiation of existential disquiet is pre-empted by the divergent ways in which Bentley and Chesterton responded to a threatening universe: Bentley with withdrawal, Chesterton with carnivalesque buffoonery. If Chesterton occasionally seems insufficiently mindful of the potentially oppressive nature of his hearty adherence of 'uproarious materialism' to acutely sensitive individuals, it is essential to recognise that he developed this philosophy as an urgent remedy for his own neuroses, which led him to seek refuge in the comforts of communality.[81]

With 'To a Modern Poet', Chesterton sets out to combat the sense of *déjà vu* produced by Eliot's new brand of nonsense by raiding a store of imagery borrowed not only from the poet, but also from his own creative explorations of themes of verbal production and digestive consumption. In this way, Chesterton mediates his disquiet by joining in genially with Eliot's verbal derangement of language, while exploring burlesque variations on Eliot's ontologically destabilising visions of digestive consumption. For example, Chesterton's 'large mouth' gambit not only alludes to the anthropomorphic opening of 'Prufrock', but also the cavernous 'oval O cropped out with teeth' that Eliot would later affix to 'Sweeney Erect' (1920), as well as the more gruesome vision of a '[d]ead mountain mouth of carious teeth that cannot spit', in *The Waste Land*, in which a welter of abject phraseology—dead, carious, teeth, spit—is applied to a vision of the landscape as an enormous mouth.[82] Eliot's imagery brings to mind Dixon Scott's account of the object-world of *Father Brown*, 'waxing horribly, like a face in a fever', while 'struggling to express something too monstrous for speech'.[83] In 'A Nightmare', a sketch composed in 1907, Chesterton depicts a philosopher of ontological pessimism named Professor Pyffer, who articulates his creed merely by yawning. An acolyte of the Professor glosses the moral at hand: '"In that yawn [...] he has swallowed all the stars"'.[84]

Disproportionately enlarged mouths and inexplicable screams are a recurring feature of Chesterton's discussions of *fin-de-siècle* pessimism, from the 'absent-minded scream' that he ascribes to Bentley in the dedicatory preface to *Greybeards at Play*, to 'the shrieks of Schopenhauer' invoked in *Orthodoxy* (1908).[85] 'To a Modern Poet' revisits this nightmare-world with its supposition that Eliot might perceive a 'pillar-box' to resemble 'a baby / skinned alive and screaming', an image that turns upon a visceral removal of physical defences against external threats, and which conjures a considerably more disturbing vision than anything found in Eliot's poetry. As Freud observes of the 'emotional ambivalence' of taboo, 'the obsessional act' of the neurotic subject works 'ostensibly

[as] a protection against the prohibited act; but [is] *actually* [...] a repetition of it'.[86] In a correspondence with Maud Ellmann's analysis of *The Waste Land*, Chesterton's parody not only 'surreptitiously repeats the horror that it tries to expiate', but substantially amplifies it.[87]

In Lewis's account of the 'screaming voice' of his cartoonish Tyro-figures the mouth is conceived as 'the gate of the organism'; the Bailiff in *The Childermass* also recognises that '"[t]he mouth's important"', and wields an 'electric torch [...] to illuminate his mouth when he was saying "Ah!"'.[88] When the Bailiff discusses the passage of souls through the afterlife in carnivalesque terms—'"[a]s we have compared this process with that of the human digestion, it will cause no surprise that they reach the anus symbolized by the circular gate"'—one is reminded of another large mouth to which Chesterton draws attention, that of the fairy-tale 'ogre, *edax rerum*, who devours all without distinction'.[89] Mikhail Bakhtin argues that images of exaggerated mouths manifest a fear of mortality, while simultaneously serving to manage that anxiety through comic mediation: although the 'gaping mouth is related to the image of swallowing, [the] most ancient symbol of death and destruction [...] exaggeration of the mouth is the fundamental traditional method of rendering external comic features'.[90] To borrow a further formulation from Lewis, such images are 'screamingly funny'.[91]

Lewis's conjoining of the apparent semantic contraries of fear and amusement complements the ambivalent dynamic of 'To a Modern Poet' in a wider sense. Much as Robert Phiddian argues that 'the potential volatility of parodic language' may complicate the satirist's attempt to achieve a straightforwardly adversarial or instructional effect, Chesterton's *appreciation* of Eliot's corpus, discussed earlier in terms of mischievous surplus production, also rebounds upon the parodist, revealing identification even as it strains to establish difference.[92] As Chesterton argues in an early essay on Tolstoy, the typical writer 'teaches far more by his [...] costumes, his idiom and technique – all the part of his work, in short, of which he is probably unconscious, than by the elaborate and pompous moral dicta which he fondly imagines to be his opinions'.[93] Equally, the parodist might claim to be exposing and debunking the fallacious premises of the *urtext*, but it is just as valid to say that if divested of the author's putative satirical intent—as signalled by the self-distancing sarcasm of Chesterton's '[o]f course, the sky is like ... ' (my emphasis)—what the parodist has produced is an imitative appreciation of the terms of the original, reframed in a comic modality. Thus, the 'of course' becomes an astonished exclamation of recognition, rather than an urbane foreclosure of possibility.

Read in this way, a sense arises that Chesterton is joining in ebulliently with a game in which the challenge is to juggle the poet's referents to produce different kinds of nonsense based upon the same set of structural rules. The result is something akin to Alice's bursting in on the

Mad Hatter's exclusive tea party: 'The table was a large one, but the three were all crowded together at one corner of it. "No room! No room!" they cried out when they saw Alice coming. "There's plenty of room!" said Alice indignantly, and she sat down in a large arm-chair at one end of the table'.[94] This gesture of confrontational amity is brought out further by the appearance of a pivotal 'but' in Chesterton's skit. While his parody begins with a cross between an unimpressed shrug and an attempt to start a fight—'Well, / What / about it?'—Chesterton's later remark, 'But I can't help wishing / You got more fun out of it' suggests that he has talked himself down, the equivocation allowing the curious concession that if Eliot could take pleasure in the concept of a pillar box resembling an excoriated baby, the literary offence might not be so great (*CN*, 50–1).

As this implies, for Chesterton ontological scepticism is a venial sin, when compared to ontological pessimism. After all, the writer who locates the opening of 'The Blue Cross' '[b]etween the silver ribbon of morning and the green glittering ribbon of sea' is clearly not averse to producing the occasional category mistake for aesthetic effect.[95] Likewise, when the narrator of Chesterton's picaresque satire, *The Flying Inn* (1914), writes, '[w]hite morning lay about the grey stony streets like spilt milk', this is not a barbed parody, but a sympathetic anticipation of the semantically deranging feline imagery of Eliot's early work.[96] Chesterton's protestation, elsewhere, that his 'reaction to' the Modernist avant-garde is 'not that of the ordinary reactionary' proves warranted: rather than making the more stolid, conventional complaint of the time—that Eliot draws upon burlesque material that is inappropriate to serious poetry—Chesterton implies that in admirably widening the subject-potentialities of the form, the poet seems merely to indefinitely expand the range of phenomena to be deprecated.[97]

Linda Hutcheon argues that parody is finally 'less an aggressive than a conciliatory rhetorical strategy'.[98] Equally, Chesterton affirmed that the skilled parodist must be adept at combining the 'sympathetic and analytical': insofar as 'real parody [is] inseparable from admiration [...] Mere derision, mere contempt, never produced or could produce parody'.[99] By framing his charges against Eliot in terms of a 'wish' that the game could be more 'fun', Chesterton puts these theoretical precepts into practice, positing the parodist's role as that of 'a sympathetic dentist', as his agent of moral satire, Innocent Smith, is described in *Manalive* (1912).[100] In this sense, the cultural exchange at hand comes to hinge upon two distinct versions of good manners. Much as Chesterton had imagined the mystagogue enquiring nonsensically, '"[y]ou don't see anything wrong in drinking a Benedictine on Thursday? ... No, of course *you* wouldn't"', Eliot's foundational commercial methods had conflated poetry with etiquette, that alienating form of good manners through which elite groups set out to differentiate themselves from the aspirant classes by instigating a perpetual, baffling game of catch-up.[101]

As Chesterton had sought to emphasise in 'The Queer Feet', etiquette is a travesty of meaningful civility, divorced from any connection to a generative geniality. In contrast, Chesterton advances the principle of politeness as a strategy for binding the social body. In 'Spelling Reform and Hidden Meanings' (*Illustrated London News*, 29 September 1906), he develops an analogy between 'polite' and 'police', on the basis that each term derives from '*polis*', or 'body of citizens': 'the word "polite" and the word "police" have the same origin and meaning [...] Politeness is not really [...] a thing merely suave and deprecating. Politeness is an armed guard, stern and splendid and vigilant, watching over all the ways of men; in other words, politeness is a policeman'.[102] In 'To a Modern Poet', politeness polices the parodic self, in a manner calculated to draw together the cultural *polis*. Chesterton's courteous reluctance to overstate his case enables his critique of Eliot's dislike of things to reach its target, both with the third-party reader, who might otherwise grow suspicious of the partiality of the terms, and with the directly addressed poet—references to 'you' and 'I' recur throughout the skit, in an echo of the conversational familiarity of the opening line of 'Prufrock'—who may be placated by these concessions into receptivity to the argument.

In this way, public controversy becomes conjoined to personal entreaty. Three years after the publication of 'To a Modern Poet', Chesterton and Eliot entered into a correspondence inspired by a further act of public parodying on Chesterton's part. In 'An Apology for Buffoons' (*London Mercury*, June 1928), Chesterton had gently mocked the occasional haughtiness of Eliot's critical tone, causing the latter to fire off an ill-tempered dispatch, in which he complains of Chesterton's slight misquotation of the line from 'Preludes' (1915) that refers to the 'smell of steaks in passageways': 'as a humble versifier [...] I *prefer* my verse to be quoted correctly, if at all'.[103] Eliot's accusation that Chesterton is guilty of the heresy of paraphrase might seem a little over the top under the circumstances; one wonders whether the more wilful distortions of 'To a Modern Poet' may have contributed to the intemperance of his response. In the same missive, Eliot avers that 'snob is not the right corrective' where he is concerned, to which Chesterton replies, three days later, with a 'who, me?' protestation: 'I cannot imagine that I ever said anything about you or any particular person being a snob; for it was quite out of my thoughts'.[104] Chesterton goes on to conjure a caricature of himself as a clapped-out member of the old guard, indulging in his own particular brand of nonsense: 'I am so very sorry if my nonsense in the Mercury had any general air of hostility [...] I meant it to be quite amiable; like the tremulous badinage of the Oldest Inhabitant in the bar parlour, when he has been guyed by the brighter lads of the village'.[105]

Thereafter, Chesterton's mollifying tone drew a more moderate response from Eliot that implies a new sense of identification, mirroring Chesterton's self-deprecation while empathising with his famous incapacity to render quotations accurately: 'I [...] made twelve distinct mistakes in well-known passages of Shakespeare'.[106] In a subsequent letter, Eliot claims that his initial complaint had merely been 'a pretext' through which to establish communication, since 'I did not like to be judged by anyone of your importance at second hand'.[107] A further dispatch from Chesterton includes the speculation that he might 'someday write an even longer and even more rambling article in the *Mercury* called "An Apology to T. S. Eliot"'.[108] Seven years later, he made good on this promise with the preface to *The Well and the Shallows* (1935), in which an expression of regret over ever 'having misquoted' the poet was capped with the proclamation, 'I should be proud to dedicate this book to T. S. Eliot'.[109]

With the permanent closure of Chesterton's surgical practice a year later, Eliot composed an obituary for the *Tablet*, recording his 'sense of personal loss' at the news, and attesting to Chesterton's enduring 'claim on our loyalty'.[110] If a rare moment of truce had been achieved in the culture wars of the early twentieth century, the foregoing account demonstrates that this was not as counterintuitive a convergence as critics have often supposed. Perhaps, after all, comparison of Chesterton and Eliot really is as 'ludicrous' as commentators have claimed: the Latin, *lūdere*, means to play, and Chesterton's playful parodic mischief had been pivotal in drawing the sometime adversaries into productive dialogue.[111] As Chesterton argued, '[p]arody does not consist merely of contrast; at its best it rather consists of a superficial contrast covering a substantial congruity'.[112] His ventriloquistic flirtation, in 'To a Modern Poet', with a mind superficially contrastive, yet substantially congruent, to his own, closely resembles the technique that Eliot considered the key to successful criticism: 'the reason why some criticism is good [...] is that the critic assumes, in a way, the personality of the author whom he criticises, and through this personality is able to speak with his own voice'.[113] Or, one might equally say, with his large mouth.

Notes

1 Michael Mason, *The Centre of Hilarity: A Play upon Ideas about Laughter and the Absurd* (London: Sheed and Ward, 1959), pp. 13–15.

2 Lee Oser, *The Return of Christian Humanism: Chesterton, Eliot, Tolkien, and the Romance of History* (Columbia: Missouri UP, 2007), p. 39.

3 Qtd in Charles Ferrell, *Modernist Writing and Reactionary Politics* (Cambridge: Cambridge UP, 2001), pp. 3–4.

4 Thomas Stearns Eliot, 'Observations,' *Egoist* (May 1918): 69–70, 69.

5 Elizabeth Sewell, *The Field of Nonsense* (London: Chatto and Windus, 1952), pp. 276–7.

6 Simon Dentith, *Parody* (London: Routledge, 2000), p. 185.

7 Gilbert Keith Chesterton, *Collected Nonsense and Light Verse*, ed. Marie Smith (London: Methuen, 1989), pp. 50–1. Hereafter cited as *CN*.

8 Thomas Stearns Eliot, *The Poems of T. S. Eliot,* 2 vols., eds. Jim McCue and Christopher Ricks (London: Faber and Faber, 2015), Vol. 1, p. 5.

9 Thomas Stearns Eliot, *The Poems of T. S. Eliot*, p. 69; Gilbert Keith Chesterton, *Autobiography* (London: Hutchinson, 1936), p. 338.

10 Qtd in Maisie Ward, *Gilbert Keith Chesterton* (London: Sheed and Ward, 1945), p. 101/98.

11 M. A. R. Habib, *The Early T. S. Eliot and Western Philosophy* (Cambridge: Cambridge UP, 2008), p. 35; Gilbert Keith Chesterton, *The Defendant* (London: J. M. Dent, 1940), p. 127.

12 Susan Stewart, *Nonsense: Aspects of Intertextuality in Folklore and Literature* (Baltimore, MD: John Hopkins UP, 1989), pp. 116–17.

13 Lewis Carroll, *The Annotated Alice*, ed. Martin Gardner (Harmondsworth: Penguin, 1970), p. 307.

14 Lyndall Gordon, *Eliot's Early Years* (Oxford: Oxford UP, 1988). p. 29; see Roger Holdsworth, 'Introduction', in Arthur Symons, *Selected Writings*, ed. Roger Holdsworth (Manchester: Carcanet, 2003), pp. 13–18.

15 Max Beerbohm, *Seven Men and Two Others* (London: Prion, 2001), p. 13.

16 Qtd in Jacobus Gerhardus Riewald, *Max Beerbohm's Mischievous Wit: A Literary Entertainment* (Assen: Van Gorcum, 2000), p. 188; John Felstiner, *The Lies of Art: Max Beerbohm's Parody and Caricature* (London: Victor Gollancz, 1973), p. 65.

17 Wyndham Lewis, *Blasting and Bombardiering: An Autobiography, 1914–1926* (London: John Calder, 1982), p. 283.

18 John Middleton Murry, 'The "Classical" Revival', *Adelphi*, February 1926, in *T. S. Eliot: The Contemporary Reviews*, ed. Jewel Spears Brooker (Cambridge: Cambridge UP, 2004), pp. 132–6, p. 135.

19 Lewis, *Blasting*, p. 249; Wyndham Lewis, *Men Without Art* (New York: Russell & Russell, 1964), p. 81; Wyndham Lewis, *Time and Western Man* (London: Chatto and Windus, 1927), p. 55.

20 Lewis, *Blasting*, p. 285.

21 Qtd in Lyndall Gordon, *T. S. Eliot: An Imperfect Life* (New York: W. W. Norton, 2000), p. 30.

22 Wyndham Lewis, ed., *BLAST* 1 (Santa Rosa, CA: Black Sparrow P, 1989), p. 25.

23 Lewis, *Rude*, p. 129 (XXXX); Thomas Stearns Eliot, 'Professional, or...', *Egoist* (April 1918): 61.

24 Wyndham Lewis, *Creature of Habit and Creatures of Change: Essays on Art, Literature & Society 1914–1956* (Santa Rosa, CA: Black Sparrow P, 1989), p. 35.

25 Wyndham Lewis, *The Childermass* (London: John Calder, 1965), p. 173.

26 Ezra Pound, *Gaudier-Brzeska: A Memoir* (London: John Lane, 1916), p. 103.

27 Thomas Stearns Eliot, *The Letters of T. S. Eliot: Volume 1, 1898–1922*, ed. Valerie Eliot (San Diego, CA: Harcourt Brace Jovanovich, 1989), p. 103.

28 Eliot, *Letters*, vol. 1, p. 285.

29 George Eliot, *Impressions of Theophrastus Such: Essays and Leaves from a Notebook* (Edinburgh: William Blackwood, 1901), p. 95.

30 Gary Saul Morson, 'Parody, History, and Metaparody', *Rethinking Bakhtin: Extensions and Challenges*, eds. Gary Saul Morson and Caryl Emerson (Evanston, IL: Northwestern UP, 1989), pp. 63–86, 73.

31 Gilbert Keith Chesterton, *The Collected Works of G.K. Chesterton*, 37 vols. to date, eds. George J. Marlin, Richard P. Rabatin, and John L. Swan, gen. (San Francisco, CA: Ignatius, 1986), vol. 33, p. 546.

32 Hugh Kenner, *The Invisible Poet: T. S. Eliot* (London: Methuen, 1965), p. 4.

33 Chesterton, *Collected Works*, vol. 28, p. 32.
34 Beerbohm, *Seven*, p. 10.
35 Bradford Morrow, 'Blueprint to the Vortex' *BLAST* 1 (Santa Rosa, CA: Black Sparrow P, 1989), p. viii.
36 Habib, *Early*, p. 78; Thomas Stearns Eliot, *On Poetry and Poets* (London: Faber, 1969), pp. 109–10.
37 Qtd in Habib, *Early*, p. 233; Malcolm, *Origins*, p. 16/21.
38 Noel Malcolm, *The Origins of English Nonsense* (London: Fontana P, 1997), p. 22.
39 Gilbert Keith Chesterton, *The Complete Father Brown Stories*, ed. Michael Hurley (London: Penguin, 2012), p. 36.
40 Chesterton, *The Complete Father Brown Stories*, p. 36.
41 John Gross, *The Rise and Fall of the Man of Letters: English Literary Life since 1800* (London: Penguin, 1991), p. 250.
42 Qtd in Peter Ackroyd, *T. S. Eliot* (London: Abacus, 1985), p. 84.
43 Eliot, *Letters*, vol. 1, p. 58.
44 Qtd in Mark Hussey, 'Bloomsbury', in *T. S. Eliot in Context*, ed. Jason Harding (Cambridge: Cambridge UP, 2011), pp. 231–40, 235.
45 Eliot, *Poems*, vol. 1, p. 237; Peter Kaye, *Dostoevsky and English Modernism 1900–1930* (Cambridge: Cambridge UP, 1999), p. 67.
46 Richard Aldington qtd in Ackroyd, *T. S. Eliot*, p. 89.
47 Sewell, *Field*, p. 141.
48 Qtd in Julia Stapleton, *Christianity, Patriotism, and Nationhood: The England of G. K. Chesterton* (Plymouth: Lexington, 2009), p. 116.
49 See Ward, *Gilbert*, p. 45.
50 Maud Ellmann, *The Poetics of Impersonality: T. S. Eliot and Ezra Pound* (Cambridge, MA: Harvard UP, 1987), p. 78; Chesterton, *Collected Works*, 6:523; Chesterton, *William Blake*, 47.
51 See Lewis, *Creatures*, p. 40.
52 Chesterton, *Collected Works*, vol. 7, p. 222/61.
53 Lewis, *Childermass*, p. 55/320.
54 Dora Marsden, 'Views and Comments', *Egoist* 1 (November 1915), p. 168.
55 Gilbert Keith Chesterton, Editorial, *G. K.'s Weekly* 4 April 1925, in *G. K.'s Weekly: A Sampler*, ed. Lyle W. Dorsett (Chicago, IL: Loyola UP, 1986), p. 75.
56 Ezra Pound, 'The Revolt of Intelligence IV', *New Age* 1 (January 1920), pp. 139–40, 139; Bernard Gilbert, 'The Tragedy of James Joyce', *G. K.'s Weekly* (4 April 1925), in *G. K.'s Weekly: A Sampler*, ed. Lyle W. Dorsett (Chicago, IL: Loyola UP, 1986), p. 83.
57 Qtd in Ackroyd, *T. S. Eliot*, p. 46.
58 Gilbert Keith Chesterton, *All I Survey* (London: Methuen, 1934), p. 84. Although Eliot was not directly associated with Vorticism, selections from his poetry were published in the second issue of *BLAST*.
59 Lewis, *BLAST* 1, p. 49.
60 Eliot, *Letters*, vol. 1, pp. 145–6.
61 Julia Kristeva, *Powers of Horror: An Essay on Abjection* (New York: Columbia UP, 1982), p. 3.
62 Gilbert Keith Chesterton, *All Things Considered* (New York: John Lane, 1909), p. 4.
63 Eliot, *Letters*, vol. 1, p. 61; qtd in Ackroyd, *T. S. Eliot*, p. 96.
64 Eliot, *Poems*, vol. 1, p. 63.
65 Gilbert Keith Chesterton, *G. K. Chesterton at the Daily News: Literature, Liberalism and Revolution, 1901–1913*, 8 vols, ed. Julia Stapleton (London: Pickering & Chatto, 2012), vol. 5, p. 49.

66 Gilbert Keith Chesterton, *G. K. Chesterton at the Daily News*, p. 49.

67 Chesterton, *Autobiography*, p. 92.

68 19 Mar. 1900, Bod MS Eng.misc.e.869. Bentley's diaries are housed at the Bodleian Library, U of Oxford, and Catalogued as Bod MSS.Eng. misc.e.861–870. 'Diaries of E. C. Bentley, 1894–1905'.

69 16 July 1899, Bod MS Eng.misc.e.869.

70 Chesterton, *Complete Father Brown*, p. 13.

71 Gilbert Keith Chesterton, *Alarms and Discursions* (Gloucester: Dodo P, 2008), p. 33. For an incisive analysis of Chesterton's satirical response to Eliot in the context of holiday-making, see Luke Seaber's article, 'The Meaning of Margate: G. K. Chesterton and T. S. Eliot', *English* 59.225 (2010): 194–211.

72 25 October 1894, Bod MS Eng.misc.e.862; 15 July 1899, Bod MS Eng. misc.e.869.

73 Eliot, *Poems*, vol. 1, p. 8.

74 Wim Tigges, 'An Anatomy of Nonsense', *Explorations in the Field of Nonsense*, ed. Wim Tigges (Amsterdam: Rodopi, 1987), p. 43.

75 Nicolas Bentley, *A Version of the Truth* (London: Andre Deutsch, 1960), p. 23.

76 21 July 1898, Bod MS Eng.misc.e.867; 4 November 1898, Bod MS Eng. misc.e.869.

77 17 August 1898, MS.Eng.misc.e.867.

78 Eliot, *Poems*, vol. 1, p. 8.

79 Chesterton, *Autobiography*, p. 77.

80 BL MS Add. 73191 fol. 11. Letter sent from Chesterton to Bentley. Manuscript held in the British Library, London. Indexed in *The British Library Catalogue of Additions to the Manuscripts: The G. K. Chesterton Papers*. ed. Richard Albert Christophers (London: British Library, 2001).

81 Chesterton, *Collected Works*, vol. 4, p. 95.

82 Eliot, *Poems*, vol. 1, p. 36; vol. 1, p. 68.

83 Dixon Scott, 'The Guilt of Mr. Chesterton', *Manchester Guardian* (July 1911), *G. K. Chesterton: The Critical Judgments 1900–1937*, ed. Denis J. Conlon (Antwerp: Antwerp UP, 1976), pp. 265–8, 267.

84 Gilbert Keith Chesterton, *The Coloured Lands* (Paulton: Purnell, 1938), p. 230.

85 Gilbert Keith Chesterton, *Orthodoxy* (Mineola, NY: Dover, 2004), p. 64.

86 Sigmund Freud, *Totem and Taboo: Some Points of Agreement between the Mental Lives of Savages and Neurotics*, trans. James Strachey (London: Routledge & Kegan Paul, 1961), pp. 18–50.

87 Ellmann, *Poetics*, p. 95.

88 Wyndham Lewis, ed., *The Tyro: A Review of the Arts of Painting Sculpture and Design* 1 (1921), p. 2; Lewis, *Childermass*, 272–9.

89 Lewis, *Childermass*, p. 138; Gilbert Keith Chesterton, *Fancies versus Fads* (London: Methuen, 1923), p. 120.

90 Mikhail Bakhtin, *Rabelais and His World*, trans. Helene Iswolsky (Bloomington: Indiana UP, 1984), p. 325.

91 Lewis, *Men*, p. 112.

92 Robert Phiddian, 'Are Parody and Deconstruction Secretly the Same Thing?', *New Literary History* 28.4 (1997): 673–96, p. 684.

93 Gilbert Keith Chesterton, *Twelve Types* (London: Arthur L. Humphreys, 1902), p. 147.

94 Carroll, *Annotated*, p. 93.

95 Chesterton, *Complete Father Brown*, p. 3.

96 Gilbert Keith Chesterton, *The Flying Inn* (Harmondsworth: Penguin, 1958), p. 167.

97 Chesterton, *Collected Works*, vol. 34, p. 606.

98 Linda Hutcheon, *A Theory of Parody: The Teachings of Twentieth-Century Art Forms* (Urbana: Illinois UP, 2000), p. xiv.

99 Gilbert Keith Chesterton, *Varied Types* (New York: Dodd, Mead, 1903), 181–4.

100 Gilbert Keith Chesterton, *Manalive* (Stilwell, OK: Digireads.com, 2008), p. 55.

101 Chesterton, *Collected Works*, vol. 28, p. 35.

102 Chesterton, *Collected Works*, vol. 27, pp. 292–3.

103 Eliot, *Poems*, vol. 1, p. 15; Eliot, *Letters*, vol. 4, p. 198.

104 Thomas Stearns Eliot, *The Letters of T. S. Eliot: Volume 4, 1928–1929*, eds. Valerie Eliot and John Haffenden (London: Faber, 2013), p. 201, n. 1.

105 Eliot, *Letters*, vol. 4, p. 201.

106 Eliot, *Letters*, vol. 4, p. 202.

107 Eliot, *Letters*, vol. 4, p. 283.

108 Eliot, *Letters*, vol. 4, p. 493, n. 3.

109 Chesterton, *Collected Works*, vol. 3, p. 340.

110 Thomas Stearns Eliot, 'Obituary of G. K. Chesterton', *Tablet* (20 June 1936), in *G. K. Chesterton: The Critical Judgments 1900–1937*, ed. Denis J. Conlon, (Antwerp: Antwerp UP, 1976), pp. 531–2.

111 Robert K Barnhart, ed., *Chambers Dictionary of Etymology* (London: Chambers Harrap, 2011), p. 613.

112 Gilbert Keith Chesterton, *The Common Man*, ed. Dorothy Collins (London: Sheed and Ward, 1950), p. 54.

113 Thomas Stearns Eliot, *The Use of Poetry and the Use of Criticism: Studies in the Relation of Criticism to Poetry in England* (London: Faber, 1969), p. 112.

10 Modernist or Realist?

The Double Vision of E. M. Forster

Kate Symondson

Critics have long debated whether E. M. Forster's writing qualifies him as a Modernist author. *The Cambridge Companion to Forster* attests to this. In her chapter on 'Forster and the Novel', Elizabeth Langland hesitates to label him a Modernist. Forster, she writes, not only employs a 'narrative technique more characteristic of high Victorianism than of modernism', 'his work presents none of the stylistic resistance and technical virtuosity characteristic of his notable contemporaries such as James Joyce and Virginia Woolf'. Langland concludes that, 'at best', Forster 'claims a precarious stake in the twentieth-century canon'.[1] Conversely, though, in the same volume of essays, Jane Goldman writes that 'if we are to make sense of women in Forster's fiction, then, we must acknowledge that Forster is a modernist writer'. To quote her reasons, it is 'the elements of textual self-consciousness, metanarrative, poetic or lyric discourse, and myth' that qualify Forster as a Modernist writer.[2] Peter Childs' chapter on *A Passage to India* sanctions this association of Forster with Modernism with the assertion that Forster ought to be placed as a 'modernist writer in his later work'.[3] In the chapter titled 'Forster and Modernism', however, Randall Stevenson declares that Forster was 'scarcely a modernist'.[4] He continues: 'even when he did employ tactics modernism developed, it was often in ways more familiar from the nineteenth century than the twentieth'.[5] Outside of the Cambridge companion, Michael Levenson admits that Forster 'continues to occupy an ambiguous position in the history of modern fiction'.[6] And in his book *Forster's Modernism*, David Medalie speaks of 'the reluctant modernism of E. M. Forster', figuring him, as Levenson does, as an author caught between two traditions of writing: nineteenth-century Realism and twentieth-century Modernism.[7]

Virginia Woolf's 1927 essay on 'The Novels of E. M. Forster' deems the 'double vision' to be the 'failure' of his writing. Woolf identifies a conflict between Forster's dual presentation of a concrete and an intangible aspect. She writes,

> It is the soul that matters; and the soul, as we have seen, is caged in a solid villa of red brick somewhere in the suburbs of London. It seems, then, that if his books are to succeed in their mission his

reality must at certain points become irradiated; his bricks must be lit up; we must see the whole building saturated with light. We have at once to believe in the complete reality of the soul.[8]

The 'solid villa of red brick' is pitted against the 'soul'. In Forster, the visible, concrete world requires its opposite—something unseen, metaphysical—to convey reality. Woolf terms the two facets of this double vision: 'the real' and 'the symbolical'. In the transition between 'realism' and 'symbolism', Woolf protests that 'the object which has been so uncompromisingly solid'—the 'villa of red brick', for instance—'becomes, or should become' (she qualifies), 'luminously transparent'.[9] Forster 'fails however, because he has recorded too much and too literally. He has given us an almost photographic picture on one side of the page; on the other he asks us to see the same view transformed and radiant with eternal fires'.

The photographic or 'real' aspect is equivalent to the nineteenth-century Realist tradition. The 'solid villa of red brick' summons the characteristic red brick of Victorian edifices to mind, and evokes the concrete exactitude of the Realist aesthetic. The transformed, or transfigured, view—the eternal fires, the irradiated bricks, the soul—casts out from the tangible aspect towards an ambiguous 'something beyond'. The 'symbolic' aspect (as Woolf names it) seeks to communicate 'something more' than the solid, Realist aspect, and is, in this sense, more akin to Modernist experimentation. 'The conjunction of these two realities', Woolf declares, 'seems to cast doubt upon them both'. And it is this 'double vision'—this apparent straddling of two traditions—which prompts Woolf to ascribe the word 'failure' to Forster's writing. Moments of Modernist experimentation unsettle the traditions the writing is grounded in.

Woolf's essay is an example of an approach that leads to the undervaluing of an author's individual aesthetic. In the critical endeavour to determine whether Forster is in the Mr Bennett or the Mrs Brown camp, whether Realist adherent or Modernist pioneer, his writing emerges as the awkward product of both: an aesthetic in its adolescence, a segue between genres. I argue that this pigeon-holing is detrimental to our understanding of Forster's writing, and demonstrate that his so-called 'double vision' is as significant and calculated a response to the conditions of early twentieth-century modernity as any other canonical, established Modernist experiments.

This Disordered Planet

In his 1925 essay 'Anonymity: An Enquiry', Forster differentiates between the two functions that words perform: 'they give information or they create an atmosphere'.[10] At one end of the spectrum lies 'pure information'. This 'creates no atmosphere', it is perfunctory and factual.

At the other end of the spectrum lies lyric poetry which, in its lack of pragmatic function, is pure atmosphere. The novel lies somewhere in between. It is both information and atmosphere. It is a compromise between the two functions of words. Forster claims that literature can speak of reality in a way that facts cannot. 'Fiction', he writes, 'is truer than history, because it goes beyond the evidence, and each of us knows from his own experience that there is something beyond the evidence'.[11] It is the atmosphere of the novel which allows it to speak of that which history, fact and the purely informative function of words cannot. Atmosphere, he writes, 'is the power that words have to raise our emotions or quicken our blood'. But more than that:

> It is also something else, and to define that other thing would be to explain the secret of the universe. This "something else" in words is indefinable. It is their power to create not only atmosphere, but a world, which, while it lasts, seems more real and solid than this daily existence of pickpockets and trams.[12]

In Woolf's essay, nineteenth-century Realism is concentrated in the solid villa of red brick. Here, the 'pickpockets and trams' are synecdochic for the Victorian tradition. Dickensian London burgeons from these evocative minutiae. The indefinable 'something else'—the atmosphere, the 'something beyond'—likewise corresponds to Woolf's identification of the 'symbolic' aspect of Forster's writing: the 'eternal fires', the transfigured object, the 'soul'. Both authors, both essays, figure the novel in binary terms: information and atmosphere, the real and the symbolic. Woolf criticises the 'double vision' of Forster's writing, whilst Forster defines his vision of literature using remarkably similar terms.

For Woolf, Forster's 'double vision' is an aesthetic issue. What she overlooks, however, is the philosophy underneath the surface. Where Woolf unhesitatingly attributes the 'real' to these photographically rendered objects of the visible world—the pickpockets and trams, the red brick villa—for Forster, it is the words that evoke atmosphere—that 'go beyond'—that are, he says, 'more real and solid' than the mainstays of Victorian Realism. In 'Anonymity', Forster states that 'information is relative'. Literature, on the other hand, is 'absolute'.[13] The impact of scientific discovery upon metaphysics is the key to understanding Forster's dualistic vision.

We know that the significant discoveries of physics in the late nineteenth and early twentieth centuries undermined the notion of absolute truth. Certainly, this continues to be important for understanding the relativity and subjectivity that characterises much of the Modernist vision. For Forster, too, science had rendered the visible world unstable, chaotic, relative. But when critics (Woolf included) consider the dualism that pervades his writing, little, if anything, is said of how this connects to Forster's ontology.

Writing of the condition of modernity, Forster regrets that 'the heavens and the earth have become terribly alike since Einstein'. Forster continues:

> No longer can we find a reassuring contrast to chaos in the night sky and look up with George Meredith to the stars, the army of unalterable law, or listen for the music of the spheres. Order is not there.[14]

As relativity came to dominate physics and monism swept through philosophy, Forster mourned the loss of the absolute order associated with the 'other' realm in dualism. 'Order', he wrote, 'in daily life and in history, order in the social and political category, is unattainable under our present psychology'. It *is*, however, attainable in the novel. Art, he asserted, is 'valuable because it has to do with order'. It 'creates little worlds of its own, possessing internal harmony in the bosom of this disordered planet'. The 'double vision' that Woolf perceives to be the failure of Forster's literature, and that other critics have regarded as an awkward straddling of two literary traditions, can be reinterpreted as the reinstatement of the dualism that modern thinking had declared was no longer (ontologically) tenable. The marriage of order and chaos that had been lost from his world is fundamental to Forster's vision of art.

Schlegels versus Wilcoxes

This dualistic model is evident in all of his novels, most prominently, perhaps, in *Howards End*.[15] *Howards End* is a novel composed of binaries. The story pivots on the conflict and negotiation between opposing realms and ideologies. Familiar tensions—between the public life and the private; social convention and personal relations; fact and imagination; the unseen and the tangible—are explored here, alongside other paired opposites: between England and the continent; the pastoral and the urban; the halcyon day and modern progress. Broadly speaking, the Wilcoxes and Schlegels represent the warring realms. Paramount to both the thematics and the aesthetics of the novel is the navigation between these separate realms, and the connection and compromise between disparate elements of the narrative.

The Schlegels place personal relations at the centre of their world, whereas the Wilcoxes are more concerned with subscribing to the codes of conduct which structure public life. Margaret Schlegel describes these two realms, explaining to her sister that,

> The truth is that there is a great outer life that you and I have never touched – a life in which telegrams and anger count. Personal relations, that we think supreme, are not supreme there. There love means marriage settlements; death, death duties. [...] But here's my

difficulty. This outer life, though obviously horrid, often seems the real one – there's grit in it. [...] Do personal relations lead to sloppiness in the end?[16]

It is no stretch to connect the telegrams and anger of the Wilcox world with Woolf's pickpockets and trams and the red brick villa. They occupy the realm of facts and information; their world is concrete. Whilst the world of the Wilcoxes is firmly presented in these markedly realist terms, that of the Schlegels is suffused with an abstract quality. The Wilcox world is populated with trains, boats, trams, fortresses and various other bastions of commerce, civilisation and empire. All that imposes structure and order in the novel is Wilcoxian. Hard, specific detail—trams, telegrams—paint a sort of Dickensian realism, whilst the intertwining ideologies attributed to the outer life—the codes of conduct, civilisation, commerce—weave the structures of a social fabric akin to George Eliot's type of realism. Margaret's suspicion that this outer life is 'the real one' associates the Wilcoxian world with what Woolf called the 'almost photographic' aspect of Forster's writing.

By contrast, the Schlegels and their values are described in markedly less concrete terms. They are often discussed in the abstract. Their Germanic heritage, for instance, helps separate them from the typically 'English' qualities that characterise the Wilcoxes. 'The Continent', it is explained, 'is interested in ideas. Its literature and art have what one might call the kink of the unseen about them'. The narrator continues: 'There is more liberty of action in England, but for liberty of thought go to bureaucratic Prussia. People will there discuss with humility vital questions that we here think ourselves too good to touch with tongs' (87). The English are pragmatists, and the Prussians dwell upon abstractions. The Schlegels are preoccupied with 'infinity' and the 'unseen'. In contrast to the stiff-upper-lipped outer life, the metaphysical mental flights of the sisters are expressive of personal relationships and the private self. The public aspect and its limiting structures are devoid of any metaphysical, abstract quality.

Central to *Howards End* is the attempt to locate the 'real', and to find a compromise between these apparently irreconcilable aspects: the Wilcoxes and the Schlegels, information and atmosphere. In some ways, Forster is also debating how to most truthfully represent reality in art; whether in the Realist tradition of exactitude, mimicry, solidity, or whether in an aesthetic that challenges and thwarts the rules and regulations of conventional structures of representation. Margaret articulates the resolution of the novel's central crisis. She maintains that both realms are requisite for speaking of reality. For Margaret, 'the businessman who assumes that this life is everything and the mystic who asserts that it is nothing, fail, on this side and that, to hit the truth' (195). In other words, choosing one side over the other will always fall short of the 'real'. Her Aunt Juley's suggestion that truth might lie 'about halfway between' is likewise dismissed. Margaret contends:

> Truth, being alive, was not halfway between anything. It was only to be found by continuous excursions into either realm, and, though proportion is the final secret, to espouse it at the outset is to ensure sterility. (196)

A vision of reality—of the 'real'—is most truthfully communicated, for Forster, by a marriage of opposites: information and atmosphere, Wilcoxes and Schlegels.

This kinetic compromise characterises the 'double vision' of Forster's writing.

A Strategy for Ordering the Chaos

In his prefatory note to the 1947 edition of *A Passage to India* (the novel deemed to be his most Modernist), Forster wrote that 'if anyone cares to inquire what my main purpose was, an answer can be found in the subjoined introduction by Peter Burra'. According to Forster, Burra 'saw exactly what I was trying to do'.[17] First published in 1934, Burra's essay deftly grasps the dualism of Forster's fiction. Unlike Woolf, Burra doesn't see Forster's aesthetic as a compromise between a past and an emergent literary tradition. Rather, the double vision of Forster's aesthetic springs from a double vision of reality. Burra recognises the relationship between Forster's writing and philosophical concepts of dualism.

Echoing Forster's own view, Burra declares that 'real life is chaotic and formless', and the task of the artist is to 'select what seems to him its most significant parts, and to arrange the chaos into some sort of an order'. The 'more "like" life a work of art is, the more nonsensical' that work appears to be. It has been the attempt of modern authors, Burra writes, to 'dispel the illusion of life's tidiness'. In order to approach Truth in art, the artist can only convey 'the vital spirit of very life' by 'cutting away as much as possible'. This urge towards abstraction is, observes Burra, an 'increasing tendency' in art. Of all art forms, however, the novel 'is the least abstract', 'the one which has pretended most of all that life is a neat, well-patterned affair'.[18] Citing Forster's regret that the novel depends on this artificial ordering—the need to 'tell a story'—Burra asks why, then, did he not adopt a more abstract form of art? Why not abandon the ordered trappings of Realism, and surrender to the abstractions of Modernism? Why oscillate interminably between the real and the symbolic, the concrete and the abstract?

Forster's double vision restores something of the order that is absent from the chaotic formlessness instated (he believes) by modern philosophy (monism) and physics (relativity), whilst alluding to "something beyond", that ineffable essence that constitutes the 'real'. In this way, Forster can be seen to be adopting a dualistic model akin to the dualism that had hitherto characterised western philosophy and theology, before the likes of Einstein had rendered the heavens and earth so terribly alike.[19]

Looked at this way, the double vision of Forster's writing is not simply the product of a stubborn loyalty to Realism and tentative foray into Modernist experimentalism. It evidences Forster's concern with the situation and definition of the 'real', both in terms of life and literature. Literature becomes, for Forster, a means of dealing with the disruptions of modernity: a strategy for ordering the chaos of existence and a reinstatement of the dualistic model that modern physics and philosophy had otherwise done away with.

Public versus Private

The happy ending of Forster's homosexual love story depends entirely upon the novel's double vision. Some (though not many) critics have written about the dualism of *Maurice*.[20] In 'Romance and Reality: The Dualistic Style of E. M. Forster's *Maurice*', Joyce Hotchkiss writes that 'the novel's main thematic concern is the conflict between two modes of coping with life – the imaginative, poetic, or romantic mode, on the one hand, and the prosaic, realistic or practical mode, on the other'.[21] Hotchkiss distinguishes between two styles: 'plain', which is used for 'realistic description' and 'elevated', used 'to suggest a dimension to experience beyond the commonplace'.[22] Whilst I agree with this dualistic distinction and Hotchkiss's identification of these two styles, her article doesn't explore the connection of this stylistic dualism with that of traditional philosophy. Rather, like Woolf's article, the discussion is confined to style, and fails to relate the dualistic quality of Forster's aesthetic as a crucial means of realising his particular vision. It was crucial to Forster that *Maurice* achieves something that he could not in his own lifetime, namely an openly gay relationship. In this novel, then, the dualistic model that Forster adopts elsewhere in his writing triumphs as a means of overcoming societal barriers.

In some ways, Maurice is the embodiment of the Schlegels and the Wilcoxes combined. The 'plain' aspect (as Hotchkiss calls it) is the Wilcoxian societal world of 'pickpockets and trams', 'telegrams and anger'. The 'elevated' expresses the inner world and the "true" self. Maurice is narrated at a critical point between these apparently irreconcilable aspects, caught between his public and private self. The subject matter and imagery engineers and maintains this dualism throughout. The narrative pivots on an oppositional language, of light versus dark, reality versus fantasy, concrete versus abstract. The dualism that had, until the latter half of the nineteenth century, been broadly accepted as defining reality is adopted by Forster in *Maurice* as a model for speaking of the unspeakable, for articulating and overcoming the impossibility of homosexuality within the context of Edwardian society.

From the fore, darkness creeps into the imagery of the novel, an unknown threat to the familiar. Although we are initially told that, as a boy, Maurice was 'afraid of the dark', it becomes evident that, actually, it is twilight that perturbs him.[23] It is the shade between the oppositional states of light and dark that represents the tension of the novel. In his room at night, Maurice is afraid of the half-light he has to endure, first cast by the candle, then the streetlight:

> The trouble was the looking-glass. He did not mind seeing his face in it, nor casting a shadow on the ceiling, but he did mind seeing his shadow on the ceiling reflected in the glass. He would arrange the candle so as to avoid the combination, and then dare himself to put it back and be gripped with fear. He knew what it was, it reminded him of nothing horrible. But he was afraid. (23)

Seeing himself reflected as a shadow—as the ambiguous midpoint between light and dark—is the visual expression of Maurice's conflict of private and public self. In this moment of fear, in the shadowy darkness, Maurice remembers George—the recently departed garden boy—and whispers his name. This invocation and his yielding to the sorrow of George's absence allows him to overcome 'the spectral' (24). Twilight elicits desires that Maurice has yet to articulate. 'He knew what it was', but its lack of materiality in the visible world is both intriguing and frightening. When Maurice whispers 'George', the inarticulate is given a name. Although the sense of the inexplicable prevails—'who was George? Nobody'—the sheer fact of having ascribed some-*thing* to the shadow allows Maurice to overcome its intimidation. Articulation, however vague or inscrutable, is what is sought after.

This incident is the first of many shadowy vignettes that recur throughout the novel. Crepuscular situations are the points at which Maurice ventures towards a greater sense of clarity. Early on, we are assured by the narrative that:

> Where all is obscure and unrealised the best similitude is a dream. Maurice had two dreams at school; they will interpret him. (25)

The dreams represent Maurice's 'secret life' (26). They are the hazy adumbration of that which cannot otherwise be spoken of. The second dream is the more mysterious of the two, and it proves to be of greater significance in the course of the novel.

> The second dream is more difficult to convey. Nothing happened. He scarcely saw a face, scarcely heard a voice say, 'That is your friend', and then it was over, having filled him with beauty and taught him tenderness. (26)

The dream is akin to the quality of twilight. It is 'scarcely' tangible, and its apparency is achieved more through effect—of 'beauty' and of 'tenderness'—than it is through any visible manifestation. The narrative continues along these shadowy lines, explaining that,

> Maurice forbore to define his dream any further. He had dragged it as far into life as it would come. He would never meet that man nor hear that voice again, yet they became more real than anything he knew, and would actually [...]. (26)

Maurice's dream is broken by the interruption of a teacher's voice, calling him to attention, 'Hall! Dreaming again!'. Maurice and the reader are abruptly recalled from metaphysical contemplation, 'dragged' back into the frame of the visible world. The contrast between Maurice's abstract contemplation and the barked orders of the teacher is a stark reminder of the two realms. Although the dream defies definition and has no manifestation in the visible world, it is 'more real than anything he knew'. These recurrent dream vignettes—the crepuscular episodes that happen at the border of the imagination and 'life'—are associated with a discourse often used to speak of an ontological abstract, metaphysical realm. The fact that the dreams are closer to the 'real' than the tangible elevates them as something more 'true', more fundamental to existence.

At critical points, Maurice's condition is communicated in terms that figure him in relation to the two conflicting spheres. During his visit to the newly married Clive, a tortured Maurice acknowledges that 'there was now a complete break between his public and private actions'. In the same passage, we are also told that 'as twilight fell, he entered a new circle of torment' (148). Maurice is caught between his public and private self. Just as twilight figures a liminality between light and dark, Maurice is a shade between his public façade and private self.

After being with Alec for the first time, however, Maurice gradually shifts towards the darkness of the private realm. The familiar, visible dimension becomes alien to him, 'each human being seemed new, and terrified him: he spoke to a race whose nature and numbers were unknown, and whose very food tasted poisonous' (175). The language speaks of falling edifices, 'he had disturbed his life to its foundations, and couldn't tell what would crumble' (176). The structures that sustain the public give way in the face of the unfathomability that he has confronted and embraced. The public realm of code and conduct is so anathema to the realm of Maurice's true, homosexual desires that if one is to be fully realised, the other must disintegrate. Darkness is only embraced in the destruction of light. When Clive leaves Maurice's house and Maurice's life 'for ever', this permanent departure is signified by Clive's transition from one realm to another:

> He left the darkness within for that without: [...] the mist enveloped him. It was so late that the lamps had been extinguished in the sub-urban roads, and total night without compromise weighed on him, as on his friend. He too suffered and exclaimed, "What an ending!" but he was promised a dawn. (115)

Leaving the 'darkness within' amounts to saying that Clive lets go of any homosexual desire. Although he exits into 'total night', he, unlike Maurice, is 'promised a dawn'. As Clive sets out to lead a life of convention, we are told that the 'love of a woman would rise as certainly as the sun, scorching up immaturity and ushering the full human day'. His homosexual impulse is euphemistically reduced to a dark period of immaturity; it is irradiated out by the light associated with the public life that Clive chooses.

Speaking the Unspeakable

Forster narrates the developments and tensions of the novel in this dualistic discourse—light and dark, public and private, tangible and intangible—as a means of structuring a reality where the illicit, unspeakable love between two men is achievable. The dream of the desired friend becomes a reality through a complicated process of merging and exchanging the characteristics of the separate spheres. The scarcely perceptible dream—where the desire for the friend finds its first articulation—is firmly situated in the metaphysical realm. Though it feels 'more real' than anything else Maurice has ever known, it is confined to representing Maurice's 'secret life', and is screened off from the 'broad daylight' of the visible world. The coming together of Clive and Maurice is facilitated by a dream. An 'image' of Maurice visits Clive in his sleep, and, 'in the first glimmer of dawn', causes Clive to call 'Maurice-' 'out of dreams' (62–3, 71). 'His friend had called him', and Maurice answered, whispering Clive's name as he climbs the mullion to meet him. 'They kissed, scarcely wishing it. Then Maurice vanished as he had come, through the window' (71). Here, the metaphysical and the tangible converge. Clive's dream re-enacts the scene where Maurice whispers for 'George' in the half-light of his bedroom. The fact that 'they kissed, scarcely wishing it' immediately recalls

Maurice's 'scarcely' perceptible dream. In this instance, however, the metaphysical and the tangible collide. The dream allows the desires of the metaphysical realm to be embodied in the tangible.

There is a sense that in the twilight, these two spheres have, to an extent, found a situation where they can coexist. Significantly, however, this dream is realised in the context of 'the first glimmer of dawn'. It is twilight that Maurice cannot endure, and, as the disintegration of their relationship evidences, the convergence and compromise between the two spheres are unsustainable. Clive chooses the side of the light, and Maurice is left in a crepuscular limbo, caught between 'his public and private actions'. This relationship was never consummated, which is symptomatic of a crucial connection not made, a prevailing irreconcilability of two beings, two spheres. But Maurice's relationship with Alec is different. It is in the development of this relationship that the character of the spheres is settled, the muddle between them is resolved and Forster's reason for narrating in these dualistic terms is realised.

Alec and Maurice connect in the realm of total darkness. Outside at Penge, the two men enjoy an innocuous exchange, and we are told that 'they harmonised in the darkness'. Inside, however, Maurice encounters Clive's wife, and the outward social form is resumed: 'her face clicked into position as he entered, so did his own'. The contrast between the artifice of the public sphere and his natural desires is at its most heightened here. Following these two polar exchanges, Maurice looks out of his window into the darkness, saying, 'Ah for darkness – not the darkness of a house which coops up a man among furniture, but the darkness where he can be free!' (71). He craves 'big spaces where passion clasped peace, spaces no science could reach, but they existed forever, full of woods some of them, and arched with majestic sky and a friend...' (166). Maurice's desire for a friend is articulated in terms of the outside, of the beyond. In yet another revisualisation of the dream, Maurice wakes himself up 'when he sprang up and flung wide the curtains with a cry of "Come!"' (166). Opening the curtains is like opening the portal to the other sphere. Alec emerges from this outer, dark realm in a scene that distinctly recollects both the time that Maurice came to Clive and the scarcely perceptible dream. Just as Maurice came (and vanished) through the window when he answered Clive's call, so does Alec in response to Maurice's subconscious summoning. Alec also echoes Maurice from the previous scene, telling Maurice (as he had Clive), 'I know'. Rather than name the figure emerging through the window, the narrative refers to him as someone Maurice 'scarcely knew', connecting him to the scarcely seen or heard figure from Maurice's dream.

The reverberation of the earlier scenes in this one invites direct comparison between the dream of the friend and the realisation of that friend. Maurice asks Alec whether he has ever dreamt he had a friend,

'Someone to last your whole life and you his. I suppose such a thing can't really happen outside sleep', he concludes (167). But for Forster, 'a happy ending was imperative'. Though his own society—at the time of writing—would not legally or socially allow for such a union, he was 'determined that in fiction at least? two men should fall in love and remain in it for the ever and ever that fiction allows' (218). The initial presentation of Maurice's desire for a friend as a dream pits it against the world of appearances, conveying it—as Maurice suspects—as something unrealisable in 'reality'. The recurrent interweaving of the dream in the context of Maurice's actual experience, however, eventually recognises it as the very essence of reality. Forster uses the dualistic model to achieve his 'happy ending'. In the terminal note, he writes that Alec 'must loom out of nothing until he is everything' (220). This is precisely what the navigation between the two realms achieves. In a final act of exchange, the dream is realised as essentially real, and the world of appearances, as artifice. What first seemed equatable to 'nothing' in the terms of the apparent world, becomes, in the last passages of the novel, 'everything'.

Maurice's union with his 'longed-for friend' is only realisable through the totality of darkness. The imagery of the final pages of the novel abandons the twilight that characterises the earlier narrative, speaking only in terms of the irreconcilability of light and dark. Darkness becomes the only realm in which Maurice can find sense and order. Muddled by his situation with Alec, the two 'strode raging through the last glimmering of the sordid day; night, ever one on her quality, came finally, and Maurice recovered his self-control and could look at the new material that passion had gained for him' (197). Paradoxically, darkness gives Maurice clarity of vision, and, as 'ever one', it promises unity. For Forster's happy ending to be achieved, Maurice knows that:

> They must live outside class, without relations or money; they must work and stick to each other till death. But England belonged to them. That, besides companionship, was their reward. Her air and sky were theirs, not the timorous millions' who own stuffy little boxes, but never their own souls. (208–9)

Maurice and Alec must live in the other realm, 'outside' of the confines and conventions of the public sphere, outside of the 'redbrick house(s)'. But their exile is not narrated in negative terms. All the qualities that have gathered in association with the dark aspect throughout the story converge in the imagery of the final pages, celebrating darkness as essential and light as superficial. Earlier on, Maurice tells us that 'if the will can overleap class, civilisation as we have made it will go to pieces' (181). This, it seems, is the case here. A limitlessness is ascribed to the "place" Maurice and Alec disappear into. The indefinability of the darkness, the expanses of the air and the sky, endless companionship and freedom outside of convention all maintain the metaphysical quality of dream, despite having now been fulfilled.

In the final scene, Maurice becomes darkness itself. He comes to Clive when 'the hour was extremely late, and the night dark' (211). He remains outside, invisible, just a voice speaking from the unfathomable black of night as though the scarcely seen or heard voice from his dream. Clive detects Maurice as a 'core of blackness in the surrounding gloom', and 'felt that his friend' had become 'essential night' (211–2). Next to Maurice's absolute, essential quality, Clive's preoccupation with civilisation, codes of conduct and 'Cambridge men ... pillars of society' seem arbitrary (213). As Maurice disappears into darkness forever, Clive's last words to him—'Dinner-jacket's enough, as you know'—work as shorthand for the class and code that Maurice chooses to live outside of. Whilst Maurice's acceptance of the realm of darkness leaves him with the feeling that the 'universe had been put in its place', as Clive turns back into his house and the light, it is with the thought that he must 'correct his proofs', and 'devise some method of concealing the truth from Anne' (209, 215). By situating Maurice's illicit, unspeakable desire in the metaphysical, unfathomable realm, Forster acknowledges it as a truth underlying artifice, and a reality 'more real' than any concrete edifice. The dualism of *Maurice* not only articulates the irreconcilability of Edwardian society and homosexuality, it exposes the superficiality of social convention, and sanctifies the love between two men as essential.

In 'A Book that Influenced Me', Forster wrote that 'I like that idea of fantasy, of muddling up the actual and the impossible until the reader isn't sure which is which, and I have sometimes tried to do this when writing myself'.[24] The two realms of *Maurice* are a double vision of the actual and the impossible, of realism and fantasy. As the conclusion of the novel demonstrates, however, 'the daily existence of pickpockets and trams' is insufficient for truly speaking of reality. The dinner-jacketed world of drawing rooms and decorum becomes equatable with Forster's view of history and facts as insufficient for speaking of the essence of life. The fantastical, metaphysical aspect, however, is demonstrative of the capability of literature for 'true' representation. Unfettered by the constraints of convention, it 'goes beyond' and, in doing so, realises the very thing which, in the actual realm, was considered impossible. As Wendy Moffat articulates, '[w]hat was art for, if not to show a new way forward?'[25] Forster's yoking together of the actual and the fantastical, the tangible and the metaphysical, demonstrates that, in art at least, the impossible is attainable.

Notes

1 Elizabeth Langland, 'Forster and the Novel', in *The Cambridge Companion to E. M. Forster*, ed. David Bradbury (Cambridge: Cambridge UP, 2007), p. 92. Hereafter *CCF*.

2 Jane Goldman, 'Forster and Women', *CCF*, pp. 120–37, p. 129.

3 Peter Childs, 'A Passage to India', *CCF*, p. 202.

4 Randall Stevenson, 'Forster and Modernism', CCF, p. 209.

5 Stevenson, 'Forster and Modernism', *CCF*, p. 220.

6 Levenson, *Modernism and the Fate of Individuality: Character and Novelistic Form from Conrad to Woolf* (Cambridge: Cambridge UP, 1991, repr. 1995), p. 78.

7 David Medalie, *Forster's Modernism* (Hampshire: Palgrave, 2002), p. 1.

8 Virginia Woolf, 'The Novels of E. M. Forster' (1927), in *The Death of the Moth* (London: Hogarth P, 1942), pp. 104–2 (pp. 107–8).

9 Woolf, 'The Novels of E. M. Forster', *CCF*, 108.

10 Edward Morgan Forster, 'Anonymity: An Enquiry' (1925), in *Two Cheers for Democracy*, 1951 (Middlesex: Penguin, 1965, repr. 1970), pp. 85–96 (p. 85). Hereafter *TCD*.

11 Forster, 'Anonymity: An Enquiry', *CCF*, pp. 69–70.

12 Forster, 'Anonymity: An Enquiry', *CCF*, p. 89.

13 Forster, 'Anonymity: An Enquiry', *CCF*, pp. 89–90.

14 Forster, 'Art for Art's Sake', *TCD*, pp. 96–103, p. 99.

15 The prevalence of opposites in *Howards End* has rarely gone unnoticed in the critical response. As David Bradshaw, in '*Howards End*', in *The Cambridge Companion to E. M. Forster*, ed. David Bradshaw, *CCF*, pp. 151–72, observed, 'questions of "contrast" dominate *Howards End*, the criticism it has generated and the challenges it presents. [...] The cleavage between the *Weltanschauung* of the Schlegels and the Wilcoxian worldview is something about which every critic of the novel has something to say' (p. 153). John Sayre Martin, in *E. M. Forster: The Endless Journey* (Cambridge: Cambridge UP, 1976), asserts that this 'novel's world is composed of contraries – of antithetical places and people, embodying antithetical values' (p. 110). For Martin (and various others), however, the dualistic framework is to the detriment of certain aspects of this novel. Of the Wilcoxes, for instance, Martin argues that it is their antithetical conception that renders them 'types rather than individuals, and types, it must be said, that would tax the credulity of a child and the sympathy of a saint' (p. 114). These reductive criticisms of Forster's dualist frame suggest a need to re-evaluate the prevalence and importance of a 'double vision' in his writing.

16 Forster, *Howards* End, 1910, ed. Oliver Stallybrass (London: Penguin, 1989), p. 41.

17 Forster, Prefatory Note to the 1957 Everyman Edition of *Passage*, Appendix I, in *A Passage to India* (1924) ed. Oliver Stallybrass, introd. Pankaj Mishra (London: Penguin, 2005), p. 307.

18 Peter Burra, Introduction to the 1942 Everyman Edition, Appendix II, in *Passage*, (first publ. as 'The Novels of E. M. Forster', in *The Nineteenth Century and After*, 1934), pp. 309–26, p. 310.

19 Forster's dualism might correspond (in character, at least) to a conventional philosophical or theological dualism, but it is important to isolate his double vision and mysticism from any religious association. He did not subscribe to any theology, describing himself in an interview as a 'non-believer'; in 'Call Me An Unbeliever: Interview With E. M. Forster', The Statesman, Calcutta, 23rd September 1968, cited in G. K. Das, E. M. Forster's India (n. p.: Macmillan, 1977), pp. 118–9. Various critics have observed that, as Frederick Crews puts it, Forster was one who had a 'theological preoccupation without a theology to satisfy it', cited in Judith Scherer Herz, The Short Narratives of E. M. Forster (New York: St. Martin's P, 1988), p. 44.

Likewise, Trilling argued that 'Forster is not a mystic in any precise sense of the word. Yet there is an element in his work that does give the appearance of mysticism' (p. 44). His persistent mysticism and invocation of the unseen point to a 'theological preoccupation', but these abstractions are, I shall demonstrate, devices and expressions of other aesthetic and philosophical concerns, and ought not be read as religious.

20 Critics of Maurice have, in the main, been distracted by the homosexual theme of the novel. It has been difficult for many to read it as anything other than, as Christopher Gillie describes it in *A Preface to Forster* (Essex: Longman, 1983), 'a myth to console' Forster (p. 127). Gillie refuses, in fact, to regard its literary or aesthetic achievements at all, declaring that, 'as a contribution to his reputation, *Maurice* was not worth publication'. Its only use, he says, is to help us better understand why, in the other novels, his portrayal of heterosexual relationships is often a failure (p. 128). Gillie is so preoccupied with Forster's handling of the taboo, the other elements of the text pale into insignificance. For others, all aspects of the text are appropriated in their quest to define Maurice as a pioneer of queer literature. There have been many, Francis King for one, that have avoided any full discussion of this novel thinking it to be 'the least satisfactory of all Forster's novels', in *E. M. Forster and his World* (London: Thames & Hudson, 1978), p. 113. Likewise, John Sayre Martin describes this novel as 'the narrowest and least resonant of Forster's six novels' (p. 128), declaring 'its construction' to be 'weak' (p. 136). For these critics, it might be said that their issues with Maurice derive from its apparent rejection of Edwardian realism, and its triumphing of (and dependence upon) fantasy. In this vein, a review in the *Guardian* (by Julian Mitchell, 'Fairy Tale', 7 October 1971) warned that 'the academics who depend so much on Forster for "value" will have a terrible time [...] justifying an ending which in any other context would be called woman's magazine. The failure to connect fantasy to recognisable life seriously mars the other novels: here it's utterly destructive', in *The Critical Heritage*, ed. Philip Gardner, *E. M. Forster: The Critical Heritage* (London: Routledge & Kegan Paul, 1973), p. 439. With a fresh analysis of the role dualism plays in realising the novel's overriding concerns, we can appreciate the aesthetic construct of Maurice in a more positive light. As Howard J. Booth suggested in '*Maurice*' in *CCF* (pp. 173–87), Maurice ought no longer be thought of as 'unsophisticated' (p. 173) because 'Even when it appears otherwise, Maurice is not simple and straightforward' (p. 185).

21 Joyce Hotchkiss, 'Romance and Reality: The Dualistic Style of E. M. Forster's *Maurice*', in *The Journal of Narrative Technique* 3.4 (1974): 163–75; 163.

22 Hotchkiss, 'Romance and Reality', p. 164.

23 Forster, *Maurice*, introd. Philip Nicholas Furbank (London: Penguin, 1972), p. 17. '[T]otal darkness he could bear' (p. 23).

24 Forster, 'A Book that Influenced Me', in *Two Cheers*, pp. 222–6, 226.

25 Wendy Moffat, *E. M. Forster: A New Life* (London: Bloomsbury, 2010), p. 114.

11 The Amateur Modernist

C. L. R. James in Bloomsbury

Saikat Majumdar

Most of us would agree today that Modernism as a literary movement and English literature as an academic subject were cohering roughly around the same time, at least in England. Several social theorists of literary pedagogy, including Chris Baldick and Terry Eagleton, have pointed out the ideological nature of this pedagogical enterprise and the institutionalisation of English literature as an academic discipline.[1] This enterprise, they have reminded us, is traceable to the Arnoldian recipe of civilising the savages, and of soothing and becalming the disrupted social fabric of the nation, especially of seething class wars within.

Matthew Arnold, who significantly used the term 'culture' as a translation of the German *bildung* (more commonly translated as education or training), was a staunch champion of the idea of formative training, of contact with good literary models in particular, in the hope that a new trained body of teachers could be brought 'into intellectual sympathy with the educated of the upper classes'.[2] Arnold's bold claim on behalf of the civilising force of literary studies laid the ideological ground for the institutionalisation of the discipline, but larger social and educational developments eventually made this institutionalisation possible. Of these developments, Baldick lists three as most important:

> first, the specific needs of the British empire expressed in the regulations for admission to the Indian Civil Service; second, the various movements for adult education including Mechanics Institutes, Working Men's Colleges, and extension lecturing; third, within this general movement, the specific provisions made for women's education.[3]

If English was to be a 'civilizing subject', its civilising impact was to play the most crucial role in the education of women, the working classes and in the business of empire, in the training of its civil servants as well as of colonised subjects. 'Arnold's conceptions of the humanizing and socially healing power of literary culture', writes Baldick, 'had in fact quickly taken root where Homer was unavailable: among women, artisans, Indians, and their respective teachers'.[4]

Gauri Viswanathan has helped us better understand the export edition of this philosophy that has intriguingly predated the domestic version, going back to the Victorian heyday of the British Empire.[5] The landmark moments of this history have included the East India Company report of 1855, which outlined plans under the 1853 India Act to open up the most prestigious and lucrative administrative posts in the empire to competitive examinations, for which English literature was to become an important subject. And as Baldick reminds us, Thomas Babington Macaulay's invocation of the civilising powers of British literature is now legend: 'that literature before the light of which impious and cruel superstitions are fast taking flight on the banks of the Ganges ... And, wherever British literature spreads, may it be attended by British virtue and British freedom'.[6]

This early project of imperial curricular intervention is now well established in the history of the discipline. Today, in an age of heightened disciplinary professionalisation that also experiences deep anxieties about the future of the humanities, it feels ironical to remember that the very first attempts to professionalise English studies had important ideological motivations and equally far-reaching ideological consequences. If the literary amateur signified an older world of aristocratic male privilege, professionalisation, while conferring on literary-critical discourse a clear disciplinary identity and distinct institutional status, was also a pedagogic gesture towards attaining social cohesion in an increasingly unstable world, nowhere more so than in late Victorian England. This was done most clearly in the form of providing an accessible and ideologically appropriate subject to new social groups—women, the working class and colonised peoples—that needed to be trained and educated in a professional way. English literary study was felt to possess not only adequate intellectual value but also the correct ideological capital to be designed as a disciplinary condition of professionalisation for subjects key to imperial administration.

Viswanathan's work to reveal the symbiotic relation between the institutionalisation of English studies and the British imperial project in India has opened up new frontiers in intellectual history. She has reminded us that 'English literature appeared as a subject in the curriculum of the colonies long before it was institutionalized in the home country'.[7] It was in fact as early as the 1820s, when the classics dominated the curriculum in England, and English literature had already become a curricular subject in British India. If the institutionalisation of English literature was, in turn, to become a condition of *bildung* of professional subjects, it had a twofold goal: to train and qualify British civil servants for service in India and to educate a class of native Indians in English culture and values so that they became effectively English in their taste and sensibilities while Indian in flesh, a class of men who would be the intermediary between the British rulers and the native masses. English literature was to occupy the central place in this education. The professionalisation of English as a curricular discipline, in other words, got under way with definite goals of social and imperial cohesion in view.

***

Has the trajectory of professionalisation dismissed the amateur for good in the longer history of English-language literary thought and practice? What about the humanities on the whole? Is the humanist thinker decisively a professional or does she continue to be an amateur? If philosophy, literature, music and the visual arts are 'soft' subjects, naturally moored in our daily hopes and fears, pain and pleasure, our quotidian language and emotions, our private, social and communal relationships, how badly do they need the 'hardness' of academic discipline? In early twentieth-century England, specifically in Leavisite Cambridge that formed the academic-critical backdrop of literary Modernism, English literary studies fought and finally overpowered this very scepticism in order to entrench itself as an academic discipline. But that did very little to seal the amateur-versus-professional debate. In his book *The Modernist Novel and the Decline of Empire*, John Marx has persuasively argued that the writing of fiction was sharpened into a state of deeply professionalised artistry in the hands of self-conscious practitioners of the form such as Joseph Conrad.[8] The interiority, self-consciousness and the Romantic immersion in the conception and the practice of literature as a high art that followed the Enlightenment and Romanticism, in many ways, reached a high point of culmination with literary Modernism. What I would like to reveal in this essay, however, is that the thought and practice of high Modernism were still significantly haunted by a sense of amateur play, and that much of the energy behind this play came from its colonial peripheries, from forces that our collection has aptly titled 'unsettling presences'.

Within the institutional terrain of English studies, however, the historic assumption of academic identity has, quite naturally, arrived with attempts to dismiss the nagging question about the professional-amateur status of the literary thinker, but it has never done so with definitive success. The literary, or for that matter, the humanist, amateur has never quite withered away. Unlike merely recreational—and perhaps just a little ridiculous—figures such as the amateur engineer or the amateur scientist, when we talk about literature, history or even philosophy, the amateur even becomes an empowered figure of sorts, occasionally cheating the fully credentialed academic specialist of her authority.

Indeed, I would say that it is happy news that well beyond the institutionalisation of a humanistic curriculum in the Anglophone world, the amateur critic of literature, culture and social phenomena remains a striking figure. It is not surprising that such a figure is at its most provocative in its startling defection from the programme of institutionalisation of the humanities as part of the ideology of late colonial Britain. My particular interest here is the intellectual self-fashioning of the provincial autodidact who hails from a background where the curricularisation of English literature—and, in a wider sense, of the European humanistic tradition—formed part of the administrative strategy of colonialism, also reaching to a point of culmination, through Victorian England to the period of high Modernism. In such a context, autodidacticism signifies—above and beyond the idiosyncratic imagination of the individual subject—a peripheral position in relation to the mainstream narrative of professional and intellectual development that this administrative strategy sought to design. I seek, therefore, to foreground the amateur intellectual who springs from the kind of autodidactic *bildung* that has something in common with the literary self-tutelage of the English working class as chronicled by Jonathan Rose.[9]

Rose tells the vibrant story of working-class autodidactism in his book *The Intellectual Lives of the British Working Classes*. This history of autodidactic engagement with English literature is especially illuminating here, not only because it focuses on the very period of the beginning and full development of the professionalisation of literary study—from the early nineteenth to the mid-twentieth centuries—but because its autodidactic subject is the British industrial working class of this period, whose education was a significant goal for the institutionalisation of English literary studies in England. Rose reminds us that a passionate, self-driven study of English literature thrived within the industrial working class even as English continued to be entrenched as an academic discipline within the universities and literary Modernism came to be fully formed as a movement. As Stefan Collini, one of England's most noted theorists and champions of intellectual life beyond the academy, points out, at the heart of Rose's ambitious attempt at the history of working-class reading lies deeply moving individual stories: 'weavers propping books up on their looms, miners disputing the merits of their favourite poets while digging coal deep underground, office boys reading far into the night to sustain themselves through the tedium of another day in the counting-house'.[10]

If, however, an autodidact is someone who consumes knowledge, howsoever arbitrary on non-institutional the manner of consumption is, he or she is not necessarily an intellectual, by which I mean someone who does not only consume knowledge but also produces it. Rose's account is pertinent to the question as to whether the Anglophone literary intellectual can thrive as an amateur after the academic institutionalisation of literary study—not only due to the historical overlap between the narrative he chronicles and the professionalisation of English studies, but perhaps even more pertinently, between the conceptual and practical overlaps between the autodidact and the amateur. The autodidact, one might say, is an amateur learner, especially after the field of learning in question has become institutionalised as an academic discipline. Rose's work does not help to answer the question whether the literary intellectual can credibly remain an amateur after the institutionalisation of academic literary studies, but it pushes us to examine more closely the relation between the amateur intellectual and the autodidact. This connection is an important one if we are to explore the existence of the amateur intellectual following the period of this very institutionalisation. Is the amateur intellectual also necessarily an autodidact? Or is the amateur, as Marjorie Garber has speculated, actually a professional advanced enough in their professionalism to be able to artfully conceal it?[11] In other words, is the amateurism of the amateur literary intellectual a result of a lack of access to the privileges of professional discourse, or of an advanced immersion into it? Is the amateur intellectual, in the end, a figure of privilege—as the seventeenth-century virtuoso was— or a socially and intellectually marginalised figure—as the autodidactic member of the British working class as described by Jonathan Rose? This becomes a crucial question when we examine the amateur interlocutor of—and interloper into—literary Modernism from the colonial periphery of the British Empire.

If, in order to give solidity and shape to critical discourse, John Crowe Ransom called for a sustained mobilisation of individual intellectuals at the heyday of American Modernism—'the collective and sustained effort of learned persons'—what kind of intellectual intervention is possible from the private, perhaps idiosyncratic recesses of the sensibility shaped by autodidacticism?[12] To ask this question, of course, is not to forget what Stefan Collini has reminded us—that 'no so-called "autodidact" was ever literally, self-educated'; but rather to explore the work of figures whose personal engagement with literary and humanistic discourses not only happened predominantly outside institutional contexts, but which strikingly conflicted, indeed, was in direct opposition with the disciplinary paradigms of the time and place as that the institutional background of high Modernism sought to enact.

* * *

The colonial and postcolonial writer shaped by such an autodidactic *bildung* offers a powerful model of the literary public intellectual whose flawed or deviant relation with curricular education significantly shapes their wide, often provocative appeal. These are writers who grew up in the light—and perhaps more appropriately, the shadow—of the humanistic tradition of European modernity, with English literature occupying a central position within the colonial curriculum, upheld by the ideological enterprise of the British Empire. As the twentieth century rolls in, the culture, practice and ideologies of high

Modernism become a powerful magnet of influences for many of these writers, but one also besets with a phalanx of contradictions. It is not in the least surprising that their engagement with these traditions—first of European modernity and then of literary high Modernism—which shaped many of them to a great extent, strikingly disrupts the narrative of professionalisation this pedagogy sought to design to satisfy the administrative needs of Empire.

It becomes all the more intriguing, therefore, how the personal trajectory of the development and maturation of the Anglophone literary writer as a 'public' commentator in colonial and postcolonial cultures simultaneously allegorises a complex narrative of colonial modernity. This narrative is often rooted in autobiography, the story of one's *bildung*, which articulates itself in a wide and complex range of prose—personal essay, memoir, novels, autobiographical fiction, criticism, lectures and forms of prose that break the barriers between genres, and, from time to time, reveal the fissures between the discursive genres inherited from European modernity and those shaped by local traditions. It is a personal narrative that often also contains a troubled yearning for modernity, both temporal and spatial, which idiosyncratically refracts the national longing for modernity, and often, the complex regional entanglement with such modernities bequeathed by colonialism and its afterlife. But at the same time, the fractured manner of their education variously indicates the imperfect and incomplete nature of this modernity, the irregular consequences of its pedagogic enterprise—sometimes, the poor and uneven quality of provincial educational institutions—and in the end, the strange impact of the humanistic legacy of colonialism on the idiosyncratic sensibility of imaginative individuals. The amateurism of their intellectual identity is therefore partly rooted in the flawed realisation of the colonial pedagogic enterprise.

Viewed this way, the colonial literary intellectual emerges as an amateur figure who subverts the professionalising impulse of imperial education in spirit even as she affirms it—often rather patchily—in letter. Such intellectuals, evident across the length of the global British Empire, are interpellated in the humanistic, especially the literary culture that the British Empire put forward as an administrative ideology. At the same time, they emerge as flawed amateurs rather than rigorous scholars whose playful amateurism, indeed, scholarly failings endear themselves to wide readership. Their amateur status is shaped by an intriguing flirtation with the literary culture of the imperial metropolis which undercuts their interpellation into it. Such amateurism, I would argue, became a natural mode for the public intellectual struggling with colonial education and its ideological pressure points. At the same time, the personal trajectory of the development and maturation of the Anglophone literary writer as a 'public' commentator in colonial and postcolonial cultures allegorises paradox-driven stories of colonial modernity.

In this reading, the growth and development of the colonial literary intellectual engage with the structure and trajectory of the *Bildungs-roman*, and of the negotiation of the personal with the social that is usually understood to define its narrative arc. Especially relevant is Franco Moretti's understanding of the *Bildungsroman* as the symbolic form of modernity, and the more recent work by Pheng Cheah, Joseph Slaughter and Jed Esty on the *Bildungsroman* as the narrative genre where not only the contested relation of the private and the public, but also that of Western and colonial modernity is uneasily enacted.[13] A full understanding of the critical intervention made by colonial literary intellectuals, I argue, cannot be achieved without carefully attending to the manner in which such figures negotiate a private, fiercely idiosyncratic world, often located on the remote outpost of empire, with a wider public world of colonial modernity usually situated in the imperial centre. The most striking embodiment of this modernity is literary Modernism, at once cool, fashionable and imperial.

In this version of the *Bildungsroman*, the colonial youth migrates to the hip urban district of Modernism from the provincial backwaters of empire. The long and arduous trek, the youthful hunger for a wider world and the autodidactic scavenging through dusty bookshops and abandoned bookshelves are shared sensual features that point to a pattern of development common to these narratives. This intellectual migrant is often something of an autodidact, a peripheral figure with an insatiable, and often under-satiated appetite for 'English' literature who sometimes evokes the English working-class autodidact as described variously by Jonathan Rose and Stefan Collini. Mapping the structure of the *Bildungsroman* onto the genealogy of the colonial literary intellectual, I would argue that the yearning for growth and fulfilment articulated in this *bildung* mirrors a colonised or newly decolonised nation's yearning for metropolitan modernity, and the eventually disruptive fate of that yearning. As I have argued elsewhere, the amateurism becomes the epistemological articulation of the arrival of metropolitan modernity in the colony in an incomplete and fragmented form.[14] The milieu created by this fragmented arrival of modernity nourishes the growth of a form of knowledge that appears inadequate, flawed and variously deviant from the institutional paradigms of learning put in place by the colonial system of education. While irregular scholarship enables the wide and provocative appeal of these writers and intellectuals later in their careers, it also marks them as the products of the ideologically rifted systems of colonial and as I have shown in another instance, postcolonial education.[15]

***

The Caribbean islands offer a vantage point from which to observe Modernist literary aspirations that sprouted in the colony and the narratives of migration, such aspirations eventually came to shape. The longing for colonial modernity as a viable space for the literary is germane, for instance, to the *bildung* of a writer such as V. S. Naipaul, in his actual journey to Oxford to study English literature as in his abstract aspiration from an early age: 'I wished to be a writer. But together with the wish there had come the knowledge that the literature that had given me the wish came from another world, far away from our own'.[16]

But it is in the life and work of Naipaul's Trinidadian predecessor, C. L. R. James, that we see a poignant aspiration for metropolitan modernity that ends up in a delicately fractured relationship with the ethos and practice of high Modernism. James is arguably the greatest twentieth-century Caribbean literary intellectual to command a wide public audience. Much of James's appeal comes from an idiosyncratic blend of the amateur and the professional, the serious and the playful, the intellectual and the physical. Would we have the James we do without the heady partnership of cricket and English literature? It is impossible to believe that we would.

'In reality', James writes, 'My life up to ten laid the powder for a war that lasted without respite for eight years, and intermittently for some time afterwards – a war between English Puritanism, English literature and cricket, and the realism of West Indian life'.[17] His growing sensibility, while deeply interpellated by British culture as ideologically planned by imperialism, was a constant seesaw between disciplinary structure and eclectic amateurism, as between the tireless but random novel-reading habits of his mother and the more pedagogically structured educational methods of his teacher father, both of which left their mark on James.

The arc of James's intellectual development clearly marks him out as an ideological product of the British empire, and yet this development is marked by an odd flirtation with the systematic structure of colonial pedagogy, perhaps most notably in his absorption in the aesthetics of cricket, indeed, of his elevation of the sport above literature as a force of culture in nineteenth-century England. There is something of the enlightened amateur, and something powerfully plebeian, in the cultural critic who can thus equate sports with literature. Literary criticism, James insists unsurprisingly, *must* be for a popular audience. This is evident not only in his provocative argument for a popular tradition that continues all the way from classical Greek playwrights to popular twentieth-century filmmakers, but most significantly, through his spirited but eclectic engagement with the literary culture of Bloomsbury.

Two essays from James's *Letters from London*, 'The Bloomsbury Atmosphere' and 'Bloomsbury Again', together describe about ninety-six frenetic hours spent by James in Bloomsbury in 1932. It is one of the most arresting narrative accounts of the physical environs of the epicentre of literary Modernism, its idiosyncratic networks, artistic vibrancy and a seamlessly bohemian lifestyle. How does that describe that description? It is impossible to do so. James himself lays out the impossibility of attempting it himself, right at the outset: 'I shall best describe it by not trying to describe it at all, but by merely setting down faithfully the events of three or four days, just as they happened'.[18]

Truly, he spent these four days in a euphoric state of play. It started with a lecture by Edith Sitwell at the Student Movement House, where James crossed swords with Sitwell in the earnest spirit of banter. He followed it with a whole night of conversation with his new London friends and reading the poems of Rabindranath Tagore. Returning home, he barely had a couple of hours of fitful rest between six and eight before another friend showed up at his doorstep, read aloud Sitwell's poetry and talked about and sang a Handel aria. After he left, James walked around Oxford Street, spent some time in Bumpus's bookshop, came back home to rest for an hour and then went out again to meet friends with whom he read Chekhov's *Three Sisters*. He came back home that night at the surprisingly early hour of midnight. The following morning, he spent some time in bed reading the newspapers and literary periodicals, and then spent the rest of the morning talking and arguing with friends in cafes and common rooms in the neighbourhood, before just about making it in time to the Society of International Studies for a lecture he was scheduled to give there. About the end of the evening, he writes: 'You might think that was enough for one day. You simply do not know Bloomsbury' (*LFL*, 44). After the lecture, they went to a café around midnight, where they spent an hour before going to supper at the home of someone whom he had never met before. After a delightful meal with a fascinating set of people, James went home around four in the morning. He spent the next morning browsing books at the Times Book Club and went home for lunch. 'I was by myself and lunch again was a hopeless failure' (*LFL*, 48). At half past two, a couple came to see him and he spent the rest of the afternoon and evening with them, returning home after one. The stimulants quickly went from tea to beer and whisky, and by the time they were done with Mussolini, Wagner, Rossini, Verdi, Thackerey and Shakespeare, they had also done short work of fifty cigarettes between the three of them. In fact, the evening was punctuated merely because they had run out of provisions. 'At ten o'clock the beer and the cigarettes were finished and it was time to do something. A typical Bloomsbury problem' (*LFL*, 50).

But this frenetic, high-energy narration leads up to a whimpering anticlimax. At the end of it, all he writes: 'Let no one who wishes to write believe that all I have described is life. In one important sense it is not life at all. It is a highly artificial form of living and I would not be surprised if a great deal of what modern work suffers from is not to be traced to that very cause' (*LFL*, 52). After quoting a poignant stanza from Wordsworth's 'The Solitary Reaper', he continues: 'Wordsworth did not learn to write like that by running about in Bloomsbury or any other literary quarter talking about books and art and music. These things come from deeper down' (*LFL*, 53).

What, then, was James was doing for these four days running about in Bloomsbury? He was, I would suggest, playing the role of the amateur Modernist. Freshly arrived from the colonial outpost, he was playing to perfection the role of the canny monger of cultural gossip. Sharply, he guessed who Edith Sitwell meant when she spoke about the young American writer who was a far finer novelist than D. H. Lawrence, or who the big and bustling young composer bruised by Lytton Strachey's putdown at a party (Constant Lambert). He was so good at it that he startled Sitwell to the point that she eagerly wished to make his introduction. Anna Grimshaw aptly calls it 'the encounter between the doyenne of English literary life and the colonial, newly arrived from an island which most of the English had difficulty in locating'.[19]

The island was Trinidad, where the carriers of literary news and gossip, in the form of the newspapers the *Times*, the *Daily Herald*, the *New Statesman* and the *TLS* arrived 'all in a bunch two weeks at a time', unlike in London, where 'you get them as they come and take them in your stride' (*LFL*, 43). Still, notwithstanding the delay, the imperial network of culture ensured the formation of the imagined community of cultural consumers across the grids of Empire. This is clear from James's mastery, not only of English literature but also of the news of the literary establishments of the imperial metropolis. In the long run, this mastery was shaped by the colonial education and its ideological afterlife he describes so evocatively in *Beyond a Boundary*, though perhaps, as Nadia Ellis convincingly argues, the conversation about Lawrence and Faulkner marks the beginning of a turning away from the cultural capital of British literature to a 'capacious Americanism'.[20] And yet what we get when this young Trinidadian arrives in London is not so much passionate engagement with its literary culture sustained over years but a brief period of flirtation, as if some sort of a playful high. The whole point of that engagement, we realise at the end, is a critique of the lifestyle fetishised by the metropolitan literary establishment.

We owe much of our notion of the hip art district, the bohemian artist, the cosmopolitan social network of cafes, art galleries and bookshops to Western Modernism. I don't think it is coincidental that this critique of the canonised idea of 'the artistic life' comes from a writer from colonial Trinidad who merely steps into this role for a little while as an amateur. 'These things come from deeper down'. James writes: 'You get into contact with them by emotional relationships with people and with things and by communion with your own soul'.[21] All that the immersion into milieus like Bloomsbury can give you is form and technique, which is secondary in importance. Art comes not from the frenetic excitement of the surface, but from the unglamorous calm that lies deeper down, perhaps entwined into the marginal moments of the everyday bereft of aesthetic self-consciousness. It is a critique which I believe can also be recognised more obliquely in certain canonised Modernists who also migrated from the colonial periphery to the fashionable hubs of metropolitan literary culture, such as James Joyce and Katherine Mansfield. There is, I think, a touch of the duality of labour and action described memorably by Hannah Arendt. On the one hand, there is the private labour of everyday, primal sustenance, and on the other, the world of action, lit up by the glamor of public life: 'With words and deeds we insert ourselves into the human world'.[22] The bustle of Bloomsbury can make us forget that the true source of action is far more deeply rooted in the quotidian world of primal sustenance than in the fashionable milieus of artistic life valorised by metropolitan literary culture. The former world, James reminds us, is 'the basis of life and great writing and of great art in any part of the world'. Playing the amateur Modernist in Bloomsbury for four days, the young writer from Trinidad offers us this anticlimactic caveat.

***

James's spectral entry into the milieu and lifestyle of high Modernism also offers another caveat—one that is uniquely and ironically suited to this sly and sharp colonial interloper into Bloomsbury. It reminds us that great art is provincial, and this is a reminder that is especially overdue in today's world. In its ironic final twist, James's story forbids us from tempering that with the softer, politically neutered word, 'regional'. It is a reminder to today's artists, intellectuals and scholars that 'Cosmopolitan', much like the glossy magazine that carries its name, and the shiny airplane lounges it adorns, has dominated well-meaning conversations about culture for as long as we can remember, donning ambassadorial goodwill and gaining academic momentum. It has become to culture what multiculturalism has become to affairs of the state and the free market. It is so much nicer to be cosmopolitan, no? To be provincial is not only be narrow and mean-spirited, but also, almost certainly to be reactionary in the bargain, a religious nut perhaps, backward and excluded from the intergalactic flight of modernity, the artistic and intellectual culmination of which was attained by the cosmopolitan aspirations of Bloomsbury.

James's take on Bloomsbury, I would argue, ironises the dominant narratives about cosmopolitanism, and reminds us that these narratives entail a curious transfer of values—in terms of rhetoric, a pathetic fallacy. Where the weeping night ends up containing the tears of the suffering lover—the weeping human being who trades her identity with that of the night incapable of shedding human tears. Cosmopolitanism, we come to realise, is what we expect of the sensibility that engages with the art object, the reader/viewer/listener. It is the magical, sylphlike spirit that can contain multiple aliennesses at the same time, that can step beyond mere markers of alienness such as headgear or vegetarianism and genuinely engage with the alien values that uphold them, indeed, that which have no visible markers at all. There exists no particular burden on the work of art that it be cosmopolitan, human perhaps, but not cosmopolitan in any sense of the term. Its artistic power hangs on its ability to embed itself as deeply as it can within its cultural milieu, not leave it behind in gay abandon and adorn the moving, vacuumed space of transnational flights. Asking a work of art to be cosmopolitan is essentially the same as asking it to be moral, for cosmopolitanism is the goodwill of the nations, the moral impulse of its embassies. In a world where embassies often sponsor the dissemination, indeed, the creation of artwork rapidly commandeered by global capitalism; culture, that can lay the curious claim to cosmopolitanism, has, behind it, the fatally effective combination of national goodwill and global marketability joined together.

How did this happen? This great historic pathetic fallacy that James points out with rich irony? The version of cosmopolitanism that circulates in the realm of culture today is essentially a creation of Western modernity. Arguably, there are other forms of cosmopolitanism, but that is a discussion for another day. If the European Enlightenment of the eighteenth century gave us the modern notion of aesthetic, its sense of interiority and artistic originality, it was the intense flowering of this modernity, aesthetic modernism of the late nineteenth and early twentieth centuries that turned cosmopolitanism the most desired whorl of not only the art object, but of the life of the artist as well. Urban bohemiana, cafes and art galleries, the hip art-district, artistic and intellectual migrancy—in most cases to live and soak in the atmosphere of the Left Bank, Bloomsbury or Greenwich Village—owe their birth to the emerging cityscape of nineteenth-century Europe, especially Paris. Much of what we take for granted about artistic life goes back to aesthetic modernism—that to create art, you must leave the dull backwater where you were born, move to the hip art district in the hip-happening city where on and around December 1910, human nature changed (or a couple of other cities like it, across the Channel and the Pond). And once you are there, you must lead an angst-ridden, hard-drinking, chain-smoking life and trade sexual partners as often as you shed your goth-hipster outfit. And this is where the world gathers, the world that matters anyway and fine art emerges, winged by the blithe spirit of the cosmopolitan. James Joyce and Katharine Mansfield trekked this path of artistic migration from their provincial hometowns, as did T. S. Eliot and Ezra Pound; Gertrude Stein not only did it herself but became a sponsor of all who aspired to do so; Virginia Woolf, of course, was already there and deepened the definition of the cosmopolitan through the fantastic assemblage of minds at Bloomsbury.

But once they reached the heart of the cosmopolis—London-Paris-Trieste-Zurich—what did they write about? The contrast between 'homegrown' American Modernists like Wallace Stevens and William Carlos Williams and the expats like Pound and Eliot is easily obvious, and there are the celebrated international locales of Joseph Conrad and E. M. Forster, but isn't some of the best Modernist literature set in the same provincial locations its exponents supposedly fled from? Joyce's Dublin, D. H. Lawrence's Nottinghamshire mining country, William Faulkner's rural American south—their celebration in literary Modernism seems to mock the very cosmopolitan aspirations with which the movement is overwhelmingly identified. The dull idyll of New Zealand countryside vies with London society and Paris cafes in Katherine Mansfield's fiction, and while quotidian rhythms of Stevens's Hartford may not have the paralysing deadness of colonial Dublin or the illiterate savagery of the Lawrentian mining country, all of these locations can safely be called provincial a long way from the artistic, political and economic centres of the Western world, if not always in terms of physical distance, certainly in the yardstick of culture.

Modernism's seductive import of provincialism to the metropolis has deepened the delusion. The organic and visceral power of the provincial has fallen farther and farther out of artistic and intellectual memories. Once a visitor and an outsider to the throbbing epicentre of high Modernism, the colonial interloper, C. L. R. James, jiggles our memory by playing to perfection the artfully trivial role of the amateur modernist.

Notes

1 Chris Baldick, *The Social Mission of English Criticism, 1848–1932* (Oxford: Clarendon P, 1983) and Terry Eagleton, 'The Rise of English', in *Literary Theory: An Introduction* (Minneapolis: U of Minnesota P, 1996).
2 Baldick, *The Social Mission of English Criticism*, p. 34.
3 Baldick, *The Social Mission of English Criticism*, p. 61.
4 Baldick, *The Social Mission of English Criticism*, p. 72.
5 Gauri Viswanathan, *Masks of Conquest: Literary Study and British Rule in India* (New York: Columbia UP, 1989).
6 Baldick, *The Social Mission of English Criticism*, p. 72.
7 Viswanathan, *Masks of Conquest: Literary Study and British Rule in India* (New York: Columbia UP, 1989), p. 3.
8 John Marx, *The Modernist Novel and the Decline of Empire* (Cambridge: Cambridge UP, 2005), pp. 25–58.
9 Jonathan Rose, *The Intellectual Lives of the British Working Classes* (New Haven, CT: Yale UP, 2001).
10 Stefan Collini, *Common Reading: Critics, Historians, Publics* (Oxford: Oxford UP, 2008), p. 249.
11 Marjorie Garber, *Academic Instincts* (Princeton, NJ: Princeton UP, 2001), p. 47.
12 John Crowe Ransom, 'Criticism, Inc.', in *Selected Essays of John Crowe Ransom*, eds. Thomas Daniel Young and John Hindle (Baton Rouge: Louisiana State UP, 1984), p. 94.

13 Franco Moretti, *The Way of The World: The Bildungsroman in Modern European Culture* (London: Verso, 1987; Pheng Cheah, *Spectral Nationalism: Passages of Freedom from Kant to Postcolonial Literatures of Liberation* (New York: Columbia UP, 2003); Jed Esty, *Unseasonable Youth: Modernism, Colonialism, and the Fiction of Development* (New York: Oxford UP, 2012).

14 Saikat Majumdar, 'The Provincial Polymath: The Curious Cosmopolitanism of Nirad C. Chaudhuri', *PMLA* 130.2 (2015): 269–83.

15 Saikat Majumdar, 'The Critic as Amateur', *NLH: New Literary History* 48.1 (Winter 2017): 1–25.

16 Vidiadhar Surajprasad Naipaul, *Reading and Writing: A Personal Account* (New York: NYRB Books, 2000), pp. 9–10.

17 Cyril Lionel Robert James, *Beyond a Boundary* (New York: Pantheon Books, 1983), p. 30.

18 Cyril Lionel Robert James, *Letters from London: Seven Essays by C. L. R. James* (Port of Spain, Trinidad & Tobago: Prospect P, 2003), p. 19. Hereafter cited as *LFL*.

19 *The C. L. R. James Reader*, ed. Anna Grimshaw (Oxford: Blackwell, 1992).

20 Nadia Ellis, 'Prefiguring Resistant Modernism: CLR James, Edith Sitwell, and a Blooming Americanism', Paper presented at the Modernist Studies Association Annual Conference, Brighton, August 29–September 1, 2013.

21 James, *Letters from London*, p. 53.

22 Hannah Arendt, *The Human Condition* (Chicago, IL: U of Chicago P, 1998), pp. 176–7.

Part IV

Popular Voices

Questions of Realism, Politics and Modernity

12 The Iconoclasm of H. G. Wells and the Modernist Canon

Carey Snyder

In 1928, editor Freda Kirchwey published a letter in the *Nation* lauding H. G. Wells for opening new worlds to 'a whole generation of cocky, iconoclastic young men and women' like herself.[1] Among those rebellious youth were certainly George Orwell and Storm Jameson, who likewise praise Wells as an inspiring, revolutionary figure. Orwell writes of the joy of discovering 'this wonderful man ... who knew that the future was not going to be what respectable people imagined', and Jameson affirms, he 'formed a whole generation [...], overwhelming us with his ideas, some absurd, all explosively liberating'.[2] The image of Wells as a modern iconoclast may be surprising to scholars more accustomed to viewing him through Virginia Woolf's eyes as a retrograde Realist.[3] The familiar version of Wells-the-Edwardian-relic—the antithesis of high Modernism—thus obscures a competing version of this writer as revolutionary, iconoclastic and quintessentially modern.

Wells's exclusion from the high Modernist canon derives not only from his significant aesthetic differences from authors such as Woolf and Henry James, but also from his indisputable popularity, which his highbrow contemporaries regarded as incompatible with serious artistic aspirations. In her oft-cited essay, 'Modern Fiction', for example, Woolf's derision of Wells, along with Arnold Bennett and John Galsworthy, gains force because theirs is 'the form of fiction most in vogue'.[4] Similarly, Henry James's well-known debate with Wells over whether the novel should serve primarily as an aesthetic object (James) or a vehicle for ideas (Wells) finds fuel in James's resentment that the reading public is so 'abjectly gathered' around the younger writer.[5] James was partly envious—in a letter he confessed that reading *The First Men in the Moon* (1901) made him 'sigh' to collaborate with Wells—but also implicitly viewed Wells's popularity as unseemly.[6] A. R. Orage, editor of the radical weekly *The New Age*, likewise found fault with Wells's supposedly crass commercialism: in a 1913 column, Orage chastises 'Mr. Wells, the author of "The Wheels of Chance" and "Mr. Polly"' for 'condescend[ing] from those real heights of literature to contributing ignorant clap-trap – doing stunts, in fact, – for the Daily Mail'.[7] The fact that Wells would stoop to contribute to *The Daily Mail,* one of Great Britain's first mass-circulation newspapers, signals his descent into the vulgar arena of mass culture.[8] As Anna Vaninskaya notes, it 'was not just what' writers like Wells and Bennett said 'but how they said it, where (the *Illustrated London News* or [... *The Daily Mail*]), and to whom, that branded them and banished them from the highbrow literary canon'.[9]

The reluctance to include Wells in the Modernist canon persists, inasmuch as Modernism continues to be coupled with notions of formal experimentation, even as scholars have been forcefully trying to uncouple the two for at least two decades in order to create a more capacious field of study.[10] Robert Casserio argued as early as 1992, 'Our limited awareness of H. G. Wells's fiction [...] and our exclusion of Wells from the modernist canon, is a liability for any theory of the novel and a potential embarrassment for literary history'.[11] Some have attempted to retrofit Wells's writing into an expanded definition of modernism, while others have conceived of alternative categories to describe the writer, such as 'political middlebrow' or 'misfit modern'.[12] Many, however, would still agree with Bonnie Kime Scott's 1990 observation that 'Though engaged in a modern world ... Wells does not strike us as modernist in philosophy or style'.[13] I echo Casserio's call for renewed attention to Wells— particularly to his social realism, which remains in the shadow of his better-known science fiction—though I am less concerned with getting Wells into the Modernist canon than with recapturing a more nuanced appreciation of his place in a broader field of early twentieth-century literature and culture.

Wells himself did not clamour to get into the highbrow canon, expressing ambivalence about literary hierarchies. He famously downplayed his literary stature by claiming to be foremost a journalist and conceding in a self-mocking obituary that most of his fiction was topical and therefore ephemeral.[14] In 1912, he rejected an invitation to become a fellow in the Academic Committee of the Royal Society of Literature, writing to Henry James that he 'would rather be outside the Academic Committee with Hall Caine, than in it with you and [Edmund] Gosse and Gilbert Murray and Shaw'.[15] Gosse was a translator of Ibsen and lecturer at Trinity College; Murray, a renowned classical scholar; Joseph Conrad and Thomas Hardy were also fellows. With this remark, then, Wells rejects the literary establishment, aligning himself instead with the phenomenally popular romance novelist and playwright Hall Caine, who managed to combine staggering sales with socially and politically conscious writing, much as Wells aimed to do.

Wells's bestselling novel *Ann Veronica* offers an entry point for thinking about this author's Janus-faced reputation, viewed alternately as crudely popular and as an icon of modernity—where the 'popular' and the 'modern' seem to be opposing terms, a view this chapter joins recent scholarship in complicating. The novel has lurked on the periphery of the period's literature, going in and out of print, persistently getting rediscovered, while maintaining a hold on the popular imagination: in 1949, *Ann Veronica* was made into a play; in the 1950s and 1960s, a series of made-for-television movies in the US and the UK; and in 1969, a musical; as recently as 2017, the BBC aired a radio dramatisation of the book.[16] By contrasting the novel's reception in the advanced and middlebrow press, this chapter uses *Ann Veronica* as a case study to illuminate these competing versions of Wells that still circulate in critical and popular discourses.

Ann Veronica represents Wells's take on a New Woman novel, a loose genre of the *fin de siècle* typically centring on a young female character's quest for social, political and/or economic equality. Wells reviewed two notable novels of this type, Thomas Hardy's *Jude the Obscure* (first serialised in 1894) and Grant Allen's *The Woman Who Did* (1895), praising the former for its astute social criticism and criticising the latter for failing to breathe life into its heroine, while going on to allude to Allen's novel within his own as a shorthand reference to the New Woman.[17] Like her fictional prototypes, Ann Veronica transgresses restrictive gender roles—running away from her sheltered suburban home, studying biology in London and participating in a suffragette raid on the House of Commons that lands her in jail. Wells conjoins this New Woman plot with a 'Modern Romance' (the novel's subtitle), as Ann Veronica unapologetically pursues her married tutor and the two elope in a protest against bourgeois values. The novel ends in an apparent capitulation to social and narrative convention, with the lovers properly married (Capes having obtained a divorce) and Ann Veronica getting pregnant—an ending that has fuelled a debate over whether the novel is feminist or anti-feminist, modern or retrograde.[18]

The fact that the romance lightly veiled Wells's own adulterous affairs contributed to an aura of scandal surrounding the novel when it was originally published, which, in turn, promoted sales and helped cement the novel's reputation as boldly modern.[19] Wells's previous publisher, Macmillan (whom he described as 'solid and sound and sane' but 'out of touch with the contemporary movement in literature')[20], shied away from it, but it was fittingly taken up by Unwin—a major publisher of sometimes scandalous New Woman fiction in the *fin de siècle*. According to Clare Gill, by 1900, Unwin was 'characterized as much by commercialism, popularity and profit as it was by experimentalism, innovation, and risk'; thus, Unwin's reputation, teetering between the popular and the avant-garde, mirrored the author's own ambiguous status.[21]

Mainstream periodicals both praised and condemned the work for what were deemed its strikingly 'modern' themes. The *Daily News* remarked on Wells's 'singular faculty for envisaging the vast complex of modern society' and the popular *T. P.'s Weekly* worried that this 'dangerous' book would encourage the 'modern daughter [....] to run amuck [...] in the name of self-fulfillment'.[22] The conservative *Spectator*, owned and edited by Social Purity leader John St Loe Strachey, deemed it a

'Poisonous Book', and urged libraries to ban it.[23] Although, as the *Spectator* acknowledged, there was 'not a coarse word in it',[24] the scandal surrounding the novel prefigured, on a smaller scale, later scandals that would become a hallmark of Modernist reception: even D. H. Lawrence remarked that he did not want his 1912 novel *The Trespasser* to be 'talked about in an *Ann Veronica* fashion'.[25] Wells attributed the outcry to his heroine's 'frankness of desire and sexual enterprise, hitherto unknown in English popular fiction', and while Wells exaggerates in deeming such behaviour unprecedented in British fiction, many of the novel's detractors from the popular press clearly found it disturbingly modern in its depiction of a young woman's sexual agency.[26] Indeed, David Bradshaw has recently argued that *Ann Veronica* 'demands to be included' in the modernist canon because of its 'groundbreaking candor' and the censorship controversy that surrounded it.[27]

The aforementioned *New Age*, a socialist review of politics, literature and art, gave the novel a mixed reception. With an average circulation of around 3,000, the review was read by influential political and literary figures along with other readers who wanted to stay current on political events and new intellectual and artistic developments. A. R. Orage, editor from 1907 to 1922, was legendary for orchestrating controversy by pitting opposing voices against each other; in keeping with this editorial platform, the *New Age* not only promoted, but also parodied, an eclectic mix of emerging high Modernists like Ezra Pound alongside traditional Realists like Wells.[28] Wells had been a frequent contributor to the *New Age* since Orage took over the helm and his novel *Tono Bungay* (1909) had been favourably reviewed; however, the journal's mixed response to *Ann Veronica* was emblematic of its shifting attitude towards the author. On the one hand, the *New Age* positioned Wells as a daring, modern writer by highlighting the censorship campaign against *Ann Veronica* both in Arnold Bennett's 'Books and Persons' column—in which Bennett calls the novel 'utterly decent' and 'utterly honest' (24 February 1910; 398)—and in a front-page anti-censorship cartoon featuring Wells's novel atop a pile of burning books, including other supposedly scandalous titles by Hardy, Shaw and James (3 February 1910). On the other hand, *New Age* core contributor and biting satirist Beatrice Hastings panned the novel (anonymously) and she and Katherine Mansfield targeted it in one of a series of witty parodies aimed at stodgy Edwardian realists.[29] As I have argued elsewhere, the parody suggests that the novel not only is stylistically retrograde but also has retrograde gender politics, in spite of its feminist pretenses.[30]

The *New Age*'s ambivalent view of Wells as alternately iconoclastic and reactionary or anti-feminist is echoed in Dora Marsden's *Freewoman* (1911–1912). A radical little magazine dedicated to broadening the discussion of feminism beyond a narrow focus on women's suffrage, the *Freewoman* published frank debates about sexuality and changing gender roles.[31] In 1912, Wells figured prominently in a *Freewoman* debate over the Endowment of Motherhood, a controversial proposal for state-funded maternity pay.[32] The *Freewoman* announced its deep interest in this topic by issuing a questionnaire entitled 'Woman: Endowed or Free'—a title that tips Marsden's hand as staunchly opposed to the endowment for encouraging women's economic dependence on the paternalistic state.[33] Wells's spirited defence of the proposal, entitled 'Mr. Wells to the Attack: Freewomen and Endowment', was the leader in the 7 March 1912 issue; followed by his letter, 'Women Endowed', which leads off the 21 March issue. Marsden's choice to headline the celebrity author in this debate capitalised on his reputation as a controversially progressive thinker, even as she rejected his views as disadvantageous to women. However, not all readers saw Wells in this light. One correspondent, E. B. Watson, deemed Wells a 'moss-grown reactionary' unable to credibly see a woman's point of view, citing *Ann Veronica* as a case in point: she calls Wells's protagonist 'a tissue of absurdities and inconsistencies', who, having 'triumphantly gone off in the teeth of the world with the man of her choice, [...] hasn't even the courage of her act', given that she waits until she is lawfully married to have a child.[34]

Rebecca West likewise questions Wells's supposedly advanced views in a *Freewoman* review of his novel *Marriage* (1912). Ridiculing Wells's foray into New Woman fiction, West writes that 'the sex obsession that lay clotted on *Ann Veronica* [...] like cold white sauce was merely Old Maids' mania, the reaction towards the flesh of a mind too long absorbed in airships'.[35] West's skewering of Wells as modern fiction's 'Old Maid' and Watson's quip that Ann Veronica 'hasn't even the courage of her act' counter a then-prevailing image of the author as a radical proponent of free love. Wells controversially advocated for greater sexual freedom in works such as his 1906 *In the Days of the Comet*, a socialist utopia where jealousy and proprietary love do not exist, and *Ann Veronica* continued Wells's assault on conventional notions of chastity and propriety, as it charts its protagonist's sexual awakening and her active pursuit of a married man. Young feminists (like Amber Reeves, the historical model for Ann Veronica) found Wells's writings about free love emancipatory, and, to an extent, put his ideas into practice in their own unconventional lives.[36] In her 1916 book, *Towards a Sane Feminism,* Wilma Meikle calls Wells and Shaw 'apostles of feminism', recollecting how even before the war, young suffragettes were 'earnestly convinced' by these writers 'that there was something certainly wonderful and possibly glorious about this mystery called sex and that it was their business to discover it'.[37] It was precisely this fear that the novel could corrupt "British daughters" that led Strachey and other moralists to urge libraries to ban *Ann Veronica*.[38] The novel's publication thus fed competing versions of Wells, as at once an outmoded realist and a daring modern author, an apostle of free love and the Old Maid of literature.

While the reception of *Ann Veronica* was somewhat ambivalent in the advanced press, Wells's name and work continued to function as a signifier of the modern in the middlebrow press in the decades after its first publication. First used in the 1920s, the term middlebrow was often pejoratively employed by self-designated highbrows, as in Virginia Woolf's characterisation of middlebrow readers as 'betwixt and between', irresolute in their taste and intellectual application.[39] Middlebrow works were (and still are) assumed to be 'of limited intellectual or cultural value; demanding or involving only a moderate degree of intellectual application, typically as a result of not deviating from convention' (OED). Such aesthetic distinctions work to enforce class hierarchies, as Pierre Bourdieu has influentially theorised, such that in the modern period, the middlebrow reader was assumed to belong to the 'anthematized lower-middle classes', with deficient taste but aspirations for cultural capital.[40] Wells's lower-middle-class origins—together with his lack of obvious stylistic innovation—have contributed to his classification as middlebrow.[41] However, what interests me here is not Wells's potential positioning as a middlebrow writer, but rather the way that *within* what can be termed middlebrow venues and literature, *Ann Veronica*, and Wells more generally, emblematised the modern, or even the highbrow.

One middlebrow venue which associated Wells with modernity was *John O'London's Weekly*. According to Patrick Collier, Wells was 'ubiquitous' in the magazine, appealing to its aspirational readers as a seemingly accessible figure, an 'avatar of the writer as tradesman'.[42] Even as he loomed large as a literary celebrity, Collier explains, Wells was presented as a figure readers could identify with and emulate. They were encouraged to do so in a series of ads for Corona typewriter, including one with the following copy: 'With Corona's help, Wells wrote the story of the human race. [...] You too can hasten your success'.[43] While touting the famous Wells as a 'man of the people', Collier argues, such ads simultaneously 'align him with the definitive characteristics of modernity: speed, mechanical reproduction, the modern literary marketplace itself'.[44] Wells was aligned with modernity not only in British middlebrow magazines like *John O'London's Weekly*, but in middlebrow venues across the Atlantic as well.

In 1917, the American publisher Boni and Liveright reprinted *Ann Veronica* as part of the Modern Library series, which popularised high Modernist writers like Joyce, Stein and Woolf, as well as middlebrow writers like Pearl Buck and Dashiell Hammett. Lise Jaillant has argued persuasively that the series eroded the distinction between these categories by presenting an eclectic list of titles as equally 'modern' and meritorious: Wilde and Wells were presented as aesthetic peers, as were Hammett and Hemingway. Jaillant notes that the series' dust jacket for *Ann Veronica* 'targeted sophisticated readers with modern ideas': the blurb asserted that Wells wrote the book 'when he was still an unqualified radical, pure and simple... Ann Veronica is ... a thorough feminist, espousing the cause of women's emancipation and fighting for the equal rights of the sexes',[45] thus aligning Wells's protagonist with the women's suffrage battle still being waged. *Ann Veronica* was one of the Modern Library's biggest sellers from 1926 to 1933, but its popularity did not prevent it from being a staple on university syllabi in the period.[46] In 1931, the series added *Tono-Bungay*, Wells's 1909 satire of advertising, to its list. Within Modern Library bindings, then, Wells's novels were presented as cutting-edge modern fiction.

Dorothy Whipple's 1930 novel, *High Wages*, also positions Wells at the forefront of modernity. One of six Whipple novels reprinted in the past decade by Persephone Press, *High Wages* was an instant commercial success, helping to establish the English author's popularity throughout the 1930s and 1940s;[47] Whipple's subsequent classification as a 'light' writer is conveyed by Virago founder Carmen Callil's characterisation of the 'Whipple line, below which we would not sink' as the lower limit for quality writing for her press.[48] As the 'Furrowed Middlebrow' notes in his blog entry on this novel, somewhat ironically, Whipple associates a taste for 'light fiction' (such as her own) with 'lower class or less intellectual characters in her novel. Meanwhile, her main character – with whom her readers would have identified so strongly – is rather highbrow'.[49] Whipple's heroine lays 'claim to the highbrow by assuming an easy familiarity with its key texts and attitudes', as Nicole Humble has argued to be the case with much middlebrow fiction.[50] Wells functions as one such highbrow reference in Whipple's novel, in notable contrast to his position in Woolf's cultural economy.

Set in a small town outside of Manchester in 1912, *High Wages* centres on the protagonist Jane Carter's rise from shop girl to small business entrepreneur: unlike her conservative boss who clings to outmoded business practices while cheating Jane out of her commissions, Jane profits from her foresight in anticipating the market's broad shift to ready-made fashion after the war. Having obtained a loan to open a small dress shop, Jane achieves her dream of self-sufficiency, selling 'new clothes for new women'.[51] Whipple prefigures her heroine's capacity for advanced ideas and newly defined roles by alluding early in the narrative to Wells's *Ann Veronica*—apt reading matter for a fictional new woman in 1912, when the novel is set, and still a popular icon for emancipated womanhood in 1930, when it was published. Suggestively, Jane stashes the book behind a shelf to read when there are no customers on the floor, presumably not only because she is a wage-employee and does not want to be caught idling away her employer's time, but also because scandal clings to the novel in Jane's milieu. Jane's intellectual friend Wilifred Thompson, a clerk at the local lending library, has introduced her to the fiction of Wells, along with that of Bennett and Swinburne. The cultural clout these names are meant to carry is made clear in contrast to the more common fare of other library patrons, such as the historical adventures of G. A. Henty and the melodramatic romances of Charles Garvice, both wildly popular, prolific authors whose fiction was formulaic.[52] Part of the newly educated lower middle class, Wilifred devours more challenging authors, while going through the motions of supplying this degraded fare: 'his body left the [unspecified highbrow] book, but his mind was still with it as he took the slip and mounted the steps for a G. A. Henty or a Charles Garvice' (39).[53] Jane, who most frequently quotes the popular women's weekly, *Home Chat*, willingly accepts Wilifred's tutelage, reading copiously across the cultural spectrum.

The narrator describes how Wells has transformed Jane's life: 'Her horizons had widened and extended incredibly. H. G. Wells was like a wind blowing through her mind. She felt strong and exhilarated after reading him. It didn't matter whether she agreed with him or not. She wasn't sure that he ever pointed out any road that she could follow. It didn't matter. He made her want to get up and fight and go on...' (54). *Ann Veronica* becomes a trumpet call for the upwardly mobile heroine, who ultimately outdoes Wells's protagonist by achieving the modern goal of female economic independence. Horizon-widening, exhilarating, rousing, empowering... This is a far cry from Woolf's association of Wells's fiction with dreary details better left to Government officials.[54] For Whipple and her heroine, Wells signifies the new and emancipatory.

This viewpoint is echoed by the letters and diaries of two lower-middle-class women in London, Ruth Slate (1884–1953) and Eva Slawson (1882–1917), whose writings have been collected and contextualised by Tierl Thompson in *The Diaries and Letters of Two Working Women: 1897–1917*.[55] Slate and Slawson, a clerk and a typist, respectively, were close friends and correspondents from 1903 to 1916, and their writings reveal the way their wide-ranging reading helped shape their feminist consciousness and inspire their participation in the women's movement. Wells formed part of that reading, serving as a catalyst for revolt, as Slate relates to Slawson in a letter of 1 January, 1912: 'I wanted to read you wild, splendid passages from Wells – how he stirs the rebel in one! I have just lived in the closing chapters of *The New Machiavelli*. You must read it one day – when you feel quite calm and strong and able to master the slumbering volcanos'.[56] Wells's 1911 novel *The New Machiavelli*, focusing on a promising politician's adulterous affair, continues *Ann Veronica*'s probing of conservative British sexual mores. Slawson deems it in her diary a 'brilliant but shallow book', while concurring with Slate's view of Wells as a revolutionary figure: 'I am essentially constructive, but I have enough of the rebel in me to enable me to appreciate and value the bold, reckless souls who destroy the fictitious peace of society. They disturb us, annoy, irritate and shock us; they are the volcanos of social life, the preventatives of smug self-satisfaction!'[57] For these real-life New Women, as for the shop girl in Whipple's *High Wages*, Wells's social realism embodies the spirit of modern revolt.

Wells speculated that publishing *Ann Veronica* helped turn him into a symbol of defiance 'against the authoritative, the dull, the presumptuously established, against all that is hateful and hostile to youth and to-morrow'.[58] Original readers like Slawson and Slate, along with writers like Whipple, Orwell and Jameson, agree with this image of Wells as an iconoclastic figure, even as canonical Modernist writers like Woolf, West and Mansfield cast the popular writer as retrograde. Wells continues to teeter between iconoclast and traditionalist in both academic scholarship and the popular imagination: one of the latest editions of *Ann Veronica*, published in 2010 by Weidenfeld & Nicolson, features a catchy, faux-newsprint slipcover, with a close-up photograph of a lock and key—referencing the novel's themes of entrapment and liberation. The inside blurb invites the reader to 'Discover a new side of H. G. Wells' in reading *Ann Veronica*, which it glosses as the story of a 'feisty, reckless and fiercely independent' woman who is 'ahead of her time'. Tracing the author's reception across the decades after the novel's publication recovers a fuller sense of Wells's place in literary history, as a figure perceived not just as Woolf and West fashioned him, as a member of the stodgy old guard, but as rousing, disturbing and potentially revolutionary.

Notes

1 Kirchwey recalls at the age of sixteen reading Wells's 1909 novel of female rebellion, *Ann Veronica*, on a train to the Adirondacks. When the middle-aged man beside her asked if her father allowed her to read 'that sort of book', Kirchwey replied flippantly, 'I read them first ... and then decide whether to allow him to'. 'A Private Letter to H. G. Wells.' *Nation* 28 November 1928; p. 576.

2 Orwell, 'Wells, Hitler and the World State' (1941), p. 143, and Jameson, *Journey from the North* (1925), II: 25. In his essay, Orwell sternly faults Wells for not taking Hitler's threat seriously, but goes on to ask, 'is it not a sort of parricide for a person of my age (thirty-eight) to find fault with H. G. Wells? Thinking people who were born about the beginning of this century are in some sense Wells' own creation' (p. 143).

3 In her well-known manifesto, 'Modern Fiction' (1925), Woolf writes that Wells assaults us with a 'plethora of his ideas and facts', 'taking upon his shoulders work that ought to have been discharged by Government officials'. *The Norton Anthology of English Literature: The Twentieth Century*, 7th edn. (New York: Norton, 2000), p. 2149.

4 In 'Modern Fiction', Woolf faults Wells, Bennett and Galsworthy for focusing on external details rather than the inner life and for remaining 'in thrall' to outmoded narrative conventions (p. 2149). In a diary entry, Woolf confirms her resentment of Wells's popularity: in his hour of personal reckoning, Woolf imagines, Wells must recognise that many of his books are mere 'trash'; she claims that he is 'entirely without poetry', but concedes that he probably 'has the greatest circulation in the whole world', *The Diaries of Virginia Woolf*, Vol. 53.

5 Henry James, 'The Younger Generation', *Times Literary Supplement* (2 April 1914), pp. 133–4.

6 23 September 1902. Letter reprinted in Leon Edel and Gordn N. Ray, eds., *Henry James and H. G. Wells: A Record of their Friendship, their Debate on the Art of Fiction, and their Quarrel* (Urbana: U of Illinois P, 1958), pp. 79–80.

7 R. H. C. [Alfred Richard Orage], 'Readers and Writers', *New Age* 13.7 (12 June 1913): 178.

8 Wells maintained a regular relationship with the *Daily Mail*, publishing a series of articles on Utopia in 1905; on marriage and the family in 1909–1910; on labor unrest in 1912; and on 'War and Common Sense' in 1913. In 1918, he would become involved in propaganda-distribution sponsored by the *Daily Mail* until he became disgusted by Northcliffe's hounding of German-born Britons.

9 Anna Vaninskaya, 'The Political Middlebrow from Chesterton to Orwell', in *The Masculine Middlebrow, 1880–1950: What Mr. Miniver Read*, ed. K. Macdonald (Basingstoke: Palgrave Macmillan, 2011), pp. 162–76.

10 See, for instance, *High and Low Moderns: Literature and Culture, 1889–1939* (Oxford: Oxford UP, 1996). Editors Maria DiBattista and Lucy McDiarmid argue that the presumption that there was what Andreas Huyssen influentially termed the 'great divide' between high and low cultures in the modern moment obscures the important ways in which writers regularly crossed that divide: they object that the 'more accessible (i.e. popular as well as easily readable), morally transparent, often socialist "low" modernists—Shaw, Wells and Galsworthy, among others—are treated as if they wrote for different audiences and moved through different worlds than "high" modernists' (p. 4). More recently, scholars have taken two primary approaches to dislodging narrow definitions of the field—either expanding the term Modernism to be more capacious (as in Kristen Bluemel's *Intermodernism: Literary Culture in Mid-Twentieth-Century Britain* (2009) or acknowledging a plurality of kinds of writing within the period, with 'high modernism' simply being one among many, as in Ann Ardis's *Modernism and Cultural Conflict 1880–1922* (2003).

11 Caserio, 'The Novel a Novel Experiment in Sentiment: The Anticanonical Example of H. G. Wells', in *Decolonizing Tradition* (Urbana: U of Illinois P, 1992), p. 88.

12 'Political Middlebrow' is Vaninskaya's label; 'misfit modern' comes from Rob Hawkes's *Ford Madox Ford and the Misfit Moderns: Edwardian Fiction and the First World War* (2012). Among those who argue that Wells is more formally experimental than he appears at first glance are Christiane Gannon's 'H. G. Wells and the Aestheticized Individual: Critiquing the Bildungsroman in the *Bulpington of Blup*.' *Modern Philology* 112.3 (February 2015): 503–21 and William Kupinse's 'Wasted Value: The Serial Logic of H. G. Well's *Tono-Bungay*', *Novel: A Forum on Fiction* 33.1 (1999): 51–72.

13 Bonnie Kime Scott, 'Uncle Wells on Women: A Revisionary Reading of the Social Romances', *H. G. Wells under Revision*, eds. Patrick Parrinder and Christopher Rolfe (Susquehanna UP; Associated UPs, 1990), pp. 108–20.

14 Wells, 'My Auto-Obituary', in *H. G. Wells: Interviews and Recollections*, ed. J. R. Hammond (Totowa, NJ: Barnes and Noble, 1980), pp. 117–19, 117.

15 Leon Edel and Gordon Ray, eds., *Henry James and H. G. Wells, a Record of Their Friendship* (Urbana: U of Illinois P, 1958), p. 163.

16 There were two BBC television versions, the first in 1952 with Margaret Lockwood, the second in 1964 with Rosemary Nicols; there was also a US version with Joan Greenwood that aired on NBC in 1957. The musical,

adapted from the novel by H. G.'s son, Frank Wells, and the playwright Ronald Gow, ran for forty-four performances at the Cambridge Theater in London in 1969. It drains Wells's novel of its emancipatory potential, trivialising issues of gender equality by playing up Wells's comical portrayal of suffragettes and emphasising the novel's romantic resolution.

17 Mr Stanley invokes Allen's novel to rail against his daughter's advanced ideas: 'There was a time when girls didn't get these extravagant ideas. [...] These sham ideals and advanced notions, Woman who Dids' (p. 66).

18 Those arguing that the ending undercuts the novel's feminism include Bonnie Kime Scott (1990) and Jane Eldridge Miller (1994); in contrast, Sylvia Hardy (1994) and John Allet (1993) argue that the novel's ambivalent ending itself highlights the challenges of reconciling independence and marriage, in a self-reflexive, potentially feminist, way. See also Nathalie Saudo-Welby (2011), who argues that the novel is Modernist in its employment of multiple voices.

19 The plot conjoins two of Wells's affairs, the first with his student Amy Catherine Robbins, known as 'Jane', whom he married after divorcing his first wife Isabel; the second with Amber Reeves, a student at Cambridge. See Snyder, introduction to the Broadview edition of *Ann Veronica* (2016), pp. 15–18.

20 Patricia Anderson and Jonathan Rose, eds, *British literary publishing houses, 1820–1880* (Detroit: Gale Research, 1991), p. 189.

21 Clare Gill, 'Olive Schreiner, T. Fisher Unwin And The Rise Of The Short Fiction Collection In Britain', *English Literature in Transition, 1880–1920*, 55.3 (2012): 315–38; 324.

22 R. A. Scott-James, review in *Daily News*, 4 October 1909, 3; John O'London, *T. P.'s Weekly* (22 October 1909): 537–8. The latter has been described as 'a popular literary journal, priced at one penny and designed, in the words of its prospectus, "to bring to many thousands a love of letters"' (Alvin Sullivan, ed., *British Literary Magazines: The Victorian and Edwardian Age, 1837–1913*, Vol. 3, 417 (Westport, CT: Greenwood P, 1983).

23 [John St Loe Strachey], 'A Poisonous Book,' *Spectator* (20 November 1909): 34. Strachey took over the periodical in 1898, and doubled its circulation to 20,000, considerably higher than the 3,000 or less figure associated with little magazines, but considerably less than mass-circulation periodicals like the *Daily Mail*. In grouping this magazine with 'mainstream' publications, I have in mind its social conservatism and broad reach: the *Daily Mail* remarked on its 'influence upon the men who have the power to influence others' under Strachey's editorship (7 April 1899).

24 John St Loe Strachey, 'A Poisonous Book', p. 34.

25 Michael Draper, *H. G. Wells* (Basingstoke: Macmillan, 1987), p. 4. For excerpts from these reviews see Appendix A of the Broadview Press edition of *Ann Veronica*.

26 Wells, *Experiment in Autobiography* (New York: Macmillan, 1934), p. 395. Fictional precedents would include the protagonists of much New Woman fiction, including the heroine of 'Cross Line' by George Egerton, the pseudonym of Mary Chavelita Dunne, and Herminia Barton of Allen's already mentioned *The Woman Who Did*.

27 Bradshaw, 'Bootmakers and Watchmakers: Wells, Bennett, Galsworthy, Woolf, and Modernist Fiction', in *A History of the Modern Novel*, ed. Gregory Castle (Cambridge: Cambridge UP, 2015), pp. 137–52; p. 140.

28 For more on the magazine's readership and its relationship to Modernism, see Ardis, Ann L. 'The Dialogics of Modernism(S) in the New Age', *Modernism/modernity*, 14.3 (September 2007), pp. 407–34.

29 For Hastings's unsigned review of *Ann Veronica*, see *New Age* (14 October 1909), p. 447; for the parodies, see K. M. and B. H., 'A P.S.A.,' *New Age* (25 May 1911), p. 95. My justification for attributing the review to Hastings is offered in Snyder, 'Katherine Mansfield and the New Age School of Satire', *Journal of Modern Periodical Studies* 1.2 (2010): 125–58.

30 See Snyder, 'Katherine Mansfield and the New Age School of Satire', for more discussion of these parodies as well as more context about the shifting attitude towards Wells in this periodical.

31 For more on the *Freewoman*, see Jean-Michel Rabaté's 'Gender and Modernism' in *Oxford Critical and Cultural History of Modernist Magazines, 1: Britain and Ireland 1880–1955*, eds. Peter Brooker and Andrew Thacker (Oxford: Oxford UP, 2009), pp. 269–89.

32 For more on the Endowment of Motherhood controversy, see Lucy Delap's chapter on this topic in her book, *The Feminist Avant-Garde: Transatlantic Encounters of the Early Twentieth Century* (Cambridge: Cambridge UP, 2007), pp. 180–216.

33 Dora Marsden, *Freewoman*, 29 February 1912, pp. 281–3.

34 E. Bruce Watson, *Freewoman*, 4 April 1912, p. 397.

35 Rebecca West, *Freewoman*, 19 September 1912, p. 346.

36 For background on Amber Reeves's relationship with Wells, see my introduction to the Broadview edition of *Ann Veronica* (2016), pp. 16–17.

37 Wilma Meikle, *Towards a Sane Feminism* (London: G. Richards Ltd., 1916), p. 21.

38 On the banning of *Ann Veronica*, see Nicola Wilson, 'Circulating Morals (1900–1915)', *Prudes on the Prowl: Fiction and Obscenity in England, 1850 to the Present Day*, eds. David Bradshaw and Rachel Potter (Oxford: Oxford UP, 2013), pp. 52–70.

39 'Middlebrow,' *The Death of the Moth and Other Essays* (San Diego, CA: Harcourt, Brace and Company, 1942), pp. 176–86.

40 Pierre Bourdieu, *Distinction: A Social Critique of the Judgement of Taste* (Cambridge, MA: Harvard UP, 1987). The characterisation of middlebrow readers as belonging to the 'anthematized lower-middle classes' comes from Erica Brown and Mary Grover's introduction to *Middlebrow Literary Cultures: The Battle of the Brows, 1920–1960* (Palgrave: New York, 2012).

41 Mary Grover asserts that F. R. Leavis 'successfully helped to undermine the cultural value put on H. G. Wells and Arnold Benett … [who] often dealt with the anxieties of the lower middle class and appealed to large numbers of lower middle-class readers' (*The Ordeal of Warwick Deeping: Middlebrow Authorship and Cultural Embarrassment* (Madison, NJ: Fairleigh Dickinson UP, 2009), p. 32.

42 Patrick Collier, 'John O'London's Weekly and the Modern Author,' in *Transatlantic Print Culture, 1880–1940: Emerging Media, Emerging Modernisms*, eds. Ann Ardis and Patrick Collier (Basingstoke: Palgrave, 2008), p. 98.

43 Collier, 'John O'London's Weekly and the Modern Author', p. 106.

44 Collier, 'John O'London's Weekly and the Modern Author', p. 108.

45 Lise Jaillant, *Modernism, Middlebrow and the Literary Canon: The Modern Library Series, 1917–1955* (London: Pikering & Chatto, 2014), p. 26.

46 Jaillant, *Modernism, Middlebrow and the Literary Canon*, p. 33.

47 Several of her books were Book Society choices and two (*They were Sisters* and *They Knew Mr. Knight*) were made into films. See Nicola Beauman, 'Whipple, Dorothy (1893–1966)', *Oxford Dictionary of National Biography* (Oxford: Oxford UP, 2004); online edition, May 2008 [www.oxforddnb.com/view/article/56957, accessed 7 November 2015].

48 Carmen Callil, 'The Stories of Our Lives', *The Guardian* (25 April 2008).
49 Furrowed Middlebrow, Blog: 'Off the Beaten Page: Lesser-Known British Women Writers 1910–1960', 'Dorothy Whipple, High Wages (1930)'. http://furrowedmiddlebrow.blogspot.com/2014/01/dorothy-whipple-high-wages-1930.html.
50 Nicole Humble, *The Feminine Middlebrow Novel, 1920s to 1950s: Class, Domesticity, and Bohemianism* (Oxford: Oxford UP, 2001), p. 29.
51 Jane Brockett, Introduction to Persephone edition of *High Wages*, p. xi.
52 On Henty, see Deirdre McMahon, '"Quick, Ethel, Your Rifle!": Portable Britishness And Flexible Gender Roles In G. A. Henty's Books For Boys', *Studies In The Novel* 42.1–2 (2010): 154–72. On Garvice's formulaic romances, see Laura Sewell Matter, 'Pursuing The Great Bad Novelist', *Georgia Review* (Fall 2007).
53 Although the specific book in question is not named in this scene, his literary preferences are made clear by the books he lends Jane, already mentioned.
54 Woolf, 'Modern Fiction', p. 2149.
55 London: the Women's P, 1987.
56 Ruth Slate to Eva Slawson, *The Diaries and Letters of Two Working Women: 1897–1917*, ed. Tierl Thompson (London: Woman's P, 1987), pp. 158–9.
57 Thompson, ed., *The Diaries and Letters of Two Working Women*, p. 177.
58 Qtd in MacKenzie, Norman and Jeanne. *H. G. Wells: A Biography* (New York: Simon and Schuster, 1973), p. 259.

13 Writing for a New Age

Arnold Bennett and the Avant-Garde

Anthony Patterson

In reference to an exhibition entitled *Manet and the Post-Impressionists*, organised by Roger Fry for the Grafton Galleries in London, Arnold Bennett wrote:

> The exhibition of the so-called "Neo-Impressionists", over which the culture of London is now laughing, has an interest which is perhaps not confined to the art of painting. For me, personally, it has a slight, vague repercussion upon literature. The attitude of the culture of London towards it is of course merely humiliating to any Englishman who has made an effort to cure himself of insularity. It is one more proof that the negligent disdain of Continental artists for English artistic opinion is fairly well founded.[1]

Bennett was responding to the vilification of Fry's exhibition in many sections of the national press.[2] As J. B. Bullen notes, the work of many artists displayed in the exhibition 'posed a threat not just to artistic technique [...] but they seemed to undermine the very ontology which had formed the basis of English art for so many years'.[3] In short, Fry's exhibition was an affront to 'English Realism and English idealism'.[4] Bennett's comments pick up on the parochial limitations of the English critical response in his reference to the derisory response of 'the culture of London', and in how humiliating it was 'to any Englishman who has made an effort to cure himself of insularity'. Bennett here clearly promotes continental avant-garde art against the negligent disdain of 'English artistic opinion'. He also notes continental art's 'slight vague repercussion upon literature'—the article in which these comments appear was entitled 'Neo-Impressionism and Literature'—aligning avant-garde painting to that of literature.

I begin with Bennett's defence of the avant-garde of Fry's exhibition because the same exhibition provoked Virginia Woolf some thirteen years later to famously proclaim in *Mr. Bennett and Mrs. Brown*: 'On or about December 1910, human character changed'.[5] This was, of course, the very essay in which Woolf criticised Bennett for producing an Edwardian Realism whose conventions were no longer of artistic utility to the younger generation of experimental Georgians. Woolf's attack and the ensuing literary feud between Woolf and Bennett have been well documented,[6] but suffice to say the view of Bennett as a champion of the avant-garde appears at odds with the role Woolf assigned to him as a writer tied to a material Realism that could no longer sufficiently respond to the changes she saw heralded by the somewhat arbitrarily, if playfully, chosen year of 1910. As Robert Squillace illustrates, the discourse of Woolf and more broadly of Modernists was 'fundamentally constituted as a discourse of discontinuity' and one in which there could be little continuity between Bennett's fiction and the experimental writing of Modernist writers such as Woolf.[7] This chapter will argue that Bennett's appreciative aesthetic understanding of the avant-garde saw much less discontinuity between the pre-war era, especially as it related to those continental writers that Bennett both defended and promoted, and that of the experimental writers of the 1920s. As such, Bennett's response to the avant-garde locates him as something of an unsettling presence in a still vivid Modernist discourse, a discourse that still all too frequently renders Bennett as a superannuated Realist stranded on the wrong side of the trajectory of literary history.

Bennett, The Bank Clerkly Englishman

Woolf was not alone in seeing Bennett, the novelist and literary critic, as an oppositional figure to the aesthetic values and practices of avant-garde writing. Ezra Pound's character Nixon in *Hugh Selwyn Mauberley*, based on Bennett, is a mediocre artist keener to produce wealth from his craft than genuine art from which there is no profit: 'In the cream gilded cabin of his steam yacht / Mr. Nixon advised me kindly, to advance with fewer / Dangers of delay'. In the fourth stanza, Nixon boasts: 'I never mentioned a man but with the view / Of selling my own works / The tip's a good one, as for literature / It gives no man a sinecure'.[8] Pound aligns Bennett's 'mercenary' materialist fiction with his conspicuous materialist consumption. As Pound's Nixon demonstrates, Modernist resentment turned on Bennett's popular success and the wealth he accrued in part by writing popular genre fiction. Resentment lies, though, not only in the sullied association of art and commerce, as Nixon is, after all the most 'bank clerkly Englishman', but in Bennett's influential position as a significant shaper of literary taste, of his formidable power to influence contemporary readers and as Pound's poem implies to 'butter up' reviewers for his own financial gain and not to 'kick against the pricks'.[9]

Indeed, Bennett became something of a straw man for the Modernist movement. Besides the attacks by Woolf and Pound, a broad range of avant-garde writers assailed him in similar vein. As Chris Baldick comments, younger writers never forgave Bennett for the yacht.[10] Wyndham Lewis portrayed Bennett as Samuel Shodbutt who signified 'the dream of a literary emperor [...] by a mid-Victorian haberdasher'.[11] In *Uncle Bennett* published shortly after Bennett's death, Rebecca West dismissively refers to Bennett as a 'first-rate solicitor's clerk';[12] Modernist writers such as T. S. Eliot and D. H. Lawrence also attacked Bennett, the former describing him as having the aspect of a 'wholesale grocer', the latter referring to him 'as a pig in clover'.[13] Whatever Eliot thought of him, it did not stop him from seeking Bennett's advice about playwriting or Lawrence from asking him for work, and Bennett responding to both with amiable generosity.[14]

Bennett's consistent belief in bridging the gulf between the minority culture of the avant-garde and a mass readership also placed him at considerable distance from the more elitist strands of Modernist writing, and plausibly made him more susceptible to criticism as middlebrow, as Virginia Woolf would later denominate those of Bennett's ilk. As early as 1901 in *Fame and Fiction*, Bennett considers the gulf between the cultural elite and the mass-reading public and finds the former culpable. He writes:

> There must be another explanation of the phenomenon, and when this explanation is discovered some real progress will have been made towards that democratisation of art which it is surely the duty of the minority to undertake, and to undertake in a religious spirit.
>
> The missionary does not make converts by a process of jeers; he minimises the difference between himself and the heathen, assumes a brotherhood, and sympathetically leads forward from one point of view to another.[15]

Such anti-elitism sat uncomfortably with those that 'jeered' at the culture of the masses. Bennett's belief, however, in John Bayley's view to 'narrow the abyss' between these two cultures[16] clearly did not preclude his own appreciation of the avant-garde as can be seen in his comments on Post-impressionism, but merely provoked him to criticise those who valued such art for being unwilling to explicate it.[17] Whether it was Bennett's anti-elitism, his conspicuous consumption or his indubitable power as a leading contemporary literary commentator to make or break writers, or, indeed, his relatively humble and provincial origins, Bennett the man, critic and writer seemed to epitomise much that was anathema to the Modernist project.

Bennett's positioning on the wrong side of literary history, both as an adversary of Modernism and as a stolid producer of an outmoded if commercially successful Realism—the commercialism and the Realism which avant-garde writers must dispense with—as adumbrated by writers such as Woolf and Pound, has been revised considerably, most notably in John Bayley's polemic in which a progressively thinking Bennett is perceived as a hero, his democratic optimism and confidence in the mass-reading public providing a positive contrast to the elitist proto-fascist tendencies of Modernist practitioners such as Wyndham Lewis. Other scholars have also challenged the estimation of Bennett's fiction beyond the lens of Modernist disapproval and to a degree-relocated Bennett within broader trends and practices of Modernism. John Shapcott sees Bennett as linking Victorian textual values to Modernism, while Robert Squillace views Bennett's fiction as making 'the passage from the assumptions of the Edwardians – an older modernity which (as Squillace reminds us) was hardly the stodgy obstruction modernist critics styled it – to the modernist subversion of those assumptions'.[18] This chapter further intervenes in this broader reconsideration of Bennett's relationship to Modernism in particular and the avant-garde more generally but with a specific focus on Bennett's non-fictional writing, first by focusing on Bennett's championing of continental writing, in a sense comparable to his defence of Post-impressionism with which this chapter began, and then by exploring his complex response to the Modernist fiction of the 1920s. The chapter focuses on two of Bennett's columns, both entitled 'Books and Persons', the first for A. R. Orage's *New Age* from 1908 until 1911 under the pseudonym of Jacob Tonson and the second under his own name in Beaverbrook's *Evening Standard* from 1926 until his death in 1931. His *New Age* column demonstrates how Bennett positioned himself as an enthusiastic and influential explicator of, and frequently a proselytiser for, new literary styles and developments; his *Evening Standard* column displays Bennett's largely positive response to the avant-garde writing of the 1920s. Whatever reservations he may have harboured about individual writers, Bennett was invariably more magnanimous to Modernist writers than they were to either Bennett's books or, indeed, his person. Olga Bloomfield has claimed that Bennett achieved 'a rapport with his readers from all levels of society which enabled him to move their perspective into the modern age'.[19] This chapter explores the extent to which Bennett can be said to have encouraged his readers to move their perspective into the modern age as it relates to the reception of avant-garde art.

The Defence of Absolute Realism

Indeed, little more could provide Bennett with greater credentials as a champion of the avant-garde than writing a column for William Orage's *New Age*, a journal that aimed to be cutting edge, cosmopolitan and, distinct from many later Modernist journals if not hugely more successful, popular. Bennett's column, or causerie as he called it, was very much in keeping with the tone of the journal, which elsewhere in its pages discussed contemporary philosophers such as Bergson and Nietzsche, promoted modern art and introduced psychoanalysis to the British public. Bennett's column was very much part of the progressive nature of Orage's *New Age*. Bennett's contribution to this opening up to contemporary literary European culture made, in Frank Swinnerton's opinion, 'London talk so excitedly about Bennett's brilliant causeries about books'.[20] The column reveals Bennett as a progressive critic dismissive of the narrow intellectual and moral confines associated with the provincial and the Victorian so as to encourage more adventurous writing which might incorporate the aesthetic values he recognised in the fiction of foreign writers, especially from France and Russia.

This was the avant-garde that Bennett championed in the *New Age* between 1908 and 1911: the often poorly translated or still untranslated continental writers he deemed superior to their British counterparts. If Woolf's criticism of Bennett was partly deployed as a means of promulgating her own novelistic approach, then Bennett too defined his literary aesthetics in the *New Age* by promoting foreign fiction and contrasting it favourably with British fiction which he criticised for its lack of nerve, its limiting Realist perspective and, in general, its slavish compliance with worn novelistic conventions. Although with notable exceptions such as the fiction of George Moore and Thomas Hardy, British novels were distinctly inferior in responding to the demands of a new age, a not dissimilar criticism that Woolf advances in attacking Bennett. A crystallisation of Bennett's attitude can be seen in his comments on, perhaps, the two towering figures of mid-Victorian fiction: Dickens and Thackeray. Comparing Thackeray to Snowdon and Dickens to Ben Nevis, Bennett comments: 'The Himalayas are not English'.[21] Such writers, though, were symptomatic of a more general malaise. In a column on George Meredith, Bennett makes the claim that 'Between Fielding and Meredith no entirely honest novel was written by anybody in England'. The reason he explains was due to 'the fear of the public, the lust of popularity, feminine prudery, sentimentalism, Victorian niceness'.[22]

If the Himalayas were not English, in literary terms, their lower peaks were in France and their highest in Russia. Woolf's argument in *Mr. Bennett and Mrs. Brown* for a greater presentment of 'life itself' is, perhaps ironically, an apt description of what Bennett believed he encountered in Russian fiction and which he found lacking in its English counterpart. Russian Realists, in Bennett's opinion, have, 'no qualms about disgusting you with nature, for they are not themselves disgusted by it'.[23] Dostoevsky might have 'grave faults' but 'his writing' in Bennett's opinion 'reaches the highest and most terrible pathos that the novelist's art has ever reached'.[24] Bennett, in fact, successfully campaigned for a complete English translation of Dostoevsky's writing.[25] Foreign literature of the calibre of Maupassant, Dostoevsky, Turgenev or Chekhov was, in Bennett's opinion, broader in theme, richer in aesthetic style and more ambitious in scope than British literature. In reference to Chekhov, Bennett writes: 'We have no writer, and we have never had one, nor has France, who could mold the material of life, without distorting it, into such complex forms to such an end of beauty'. Bennett sees in Chekhov's writing, an 'absolute realism': 'His climaxes are never strained; nothing is ever idealized, sentimentalized, etherealized; no part of the truth is left out, no part is exaggerated'.[26]

In the same causerie, Bennett writes: 'The progress of every art is an apparent progress from conventionality to realism. The basis of convention remains, but as the art develops it finds more and more subtle methods fitting life to the convention or the convention to life – whichever you please'.[27] Woolf's later attack on Bennett also bears resemblance to Bennett's assault on British fiction, at least in the sense that Woolf too argues for an apparent progress from the old tired conventions of Edwardian Realism to the struggle to find new conventions so as to represent lived experience more realistically. Indeed, Bennett in his praise of the fiction of writers such as Chekhov and Dostoevsky and his disparagement of contemporary English fiction produces a dividing practice every bit as sharp, and in many ways as unjust, as Woolf's separation between Georgians and Edwardians. Both Bennett and Woolf position themselves as forward-thinking, and on the side of the new against the tired, parochial conventions of the old. Bennett, as much as Woolf, felt himself to be writing for a new and radically different age, an age in which it was necessary to break free from the shackles of the Victorian novel in comparable ways that Woolf thought the Georgians must discard the conventions of Edwardian Realism. In thirteen years, however, Bennett, the apostle of the cutting edge became, for Woolf, a primary example of the failure of the old. Bennett in Woolf's essay is cast in a not dissimilar role as Thackeray is in Bennett's criticism.

To an extent, both writers might be perceived to be deploying similar tactics and for similar reasons, both representing a younger generation making claims for their art at the expense of the old, and in demarcating the superior value of emergent modes of literary expression at the expense of outworn dominant conventions. Such an explanation could be considered reductive, however, in the sense, at least, that it would ignore the extent to which Bennett continued to critically appreciate, understand, value and promote avant-garde writing in the 1920s and also the extent to which he consistently fought a rearguard action against a prevalent British cultural insularity. Thus to a considerable degree, and though Bennett was aware of the seismic shift of avant-garde experimentation in the 1920s, such experimentation forms a greater continuum, in terms of Bennett's critical view, with earlier literary innovations than the Modernist 'discourse of discontinuity' might suggest.

One element of British cultural insularity against which Bennett fought, often tenaciously, was the moral censure, and occasional censorship, from which avant-garde writers frequently suffered.[28] From Bennett's defence of George Moore in 1901 to his rebuttal of the morally censorious response to Norah James's *The Sleeveless Errand* (1929),

Bennett was both an inveterate defender of what he deemed 'serious fiction' and a vituperative attacker of those who wished to maintain the moral standards of Victorian household reading. The restrictions of censorship on experimental art and writing have been well documented, and Modernism's strategic struggle to challenge them has been well researched.[29] Suffice to stay Bennett's influence on the reading public, what Bloomfield called moving the perspective of the reading public into the modern age, must be considered in relation to Bennett's generally staunch defence of the novelist's right to explore aspects of experience which many thought should be prohibited from fiction.

Writing two years before his death, Bennett was keenly aware that many censorial restrictions remained:

> Now the public does several things which are inconvenient for the novelist. In the first place, it establishes taboos. There are various enthralling things of which it dislikes to mention. Some taboos have been lifted within the last ten years; and today the novelist actually enjoys about fifty per cent of the freedom of talkers around the dinner table. Nevertheless we are still victims of powerful taboos.[30]

As arguably the leading commentator on literary matters in England for the first third of the twentieth century, Bennett might be given some credit for his role in shifting some of the taboos under which writers laboured. The steadfastness of Bennett's stance is evident in both 'Books and Persons' columns. In 1910, he defined what he believed was a distinctly English phenomenon: 'I have lived too long in foreign parts not to see the fineness of England. But in matters of hypocrisy there is really something very wrong with this island, and the atmosphere of this island is thick enough to choke all artists dead'.[31] Comparing the public display of 'celebrated living harlots all over the place', Bennett continues, 'But if you desire to read a masterpiece of social fiction, some mirror of crass stupidity in a circulating library will try to save you from yourself'.[32] Eighteen years later, the problem persisted. In 1928, with reference to the banning of Isadora Duncan's autobiography, Bennett could write that some 'libraries are under the delusion that the nineteenth century had not yet come to an end' as they were offering moral guidance which, in Bennett's opinion, 'ninety-five per cent of subscribers did not wish'. Indeed in the last year of his life, in an article entitled, 'Shocking People: An Author's Duty to Go on Doing It', Bennett wrote that for him, literary vulgarity consisted in insincerity and exaggeration, 'neither of which are discovered in acknowledged masterpieces. Both of them are plenteous in books which made a row in the world – and which are soon forgotten'.[33] Literary vulgarity, as defined by Bennett, cannot but fail to explore truthfully and frankly the world which the more realistic and honest writer inhabits. For all of his professional life, Bennett saw literary censorship as an impediment to serious explorations of life which he perceived in the aesthetic refashioning of writers whose broader subject matter could cause moral offence.

Bennett and the Modernists

James Joyce's *Ulysses* (1922) provides an interesting example of both Bennett's attitude to the avant-garde writing of the 1920s and more specifically towards the generally perceived obscenity of the novel. Bennett acknowledges that the book is not pornographic but that it is obscene; in fact, more obscene than many pornographic novels, but unlike the majority of Britons who he believes would wish it to be censored, Bennett argues: 'For myself I think that in the main it is not justified by results obtained; but I must plainly add, at the risk of opprobrium, that in the finest passages it is in my opinion justified'.[34] Bennett, however, remained adamant that the book, great though it was, could not be placed on general sale to the public. Writing about Norah James's suppressed *Sleeveless Errand*, a novel which Bennett admired, Bennett expands on his view regarding the censorship of Joyce's novel:

> Am I in favour of a censorship? Of course I am. No country can exist without one. I was asked the other day whether I would permit in Britain the unrestricted circulation of one of the most wonderful and original of modern novels, James Joyce's *Ulysses*. My plain reply was that I would not. It simply would not do. A censorship there must be. But I maintain that any form of censorship does some harm, and that our present censorship does immensely more harm than good.[35]

Perhaps the key phrase here is 'unrestricted circulation'. Bennett does not call for a blanket ban of the novel but recognises in the climate in which he lives, Joyce's 'obscene' novel needs some form of distributive regulation even if it is 'the most wonderful and original of modern novels'. A response to a letter in the *Evening Standard* complaining of Bennett's interest in Joyce, perhaps somewhat further clarifies his position:

> I understand Mr Jones's attitude ... I have no desire to compel him to read books which offend him; but I do not appreciate his desire to prevent me from reading books which, though they may in places offend me, in other places give me great and not ignoble pleasure. There is not one decent public; there are forty decent publics. The tastes of all those publics can be satisfied, if common sense and reasonable compromise in distribution are brought into play. (342)

While Bennett may acknowledge that a large-scale distribution of the novel should not be granted, he also implies that for those interested, a restricted circulation should be allowed. Bennett's considered comments should be contextualised by the general moral opprobrium cast upon Joyce's novel by other influential critics such as James Douglas who could not see beyond its obscenity and condemned it deploying the same kind of bombastic rhetoric of disgust that Bennett had contested all his professional life.[36] Bennett's reservations about the novel should also be contextualised by avant-garde writers themselves: Virginia Woolf also expressed concerns over its obscenity and its ability to invoke boredom, and D. H. Lawrence accused Joyce of writing a dirty book.[37]

Bennett's considered opinion of the novel's aesthetic worth can be gleamed from his review of *Ulysses* for *The Bookman* in 1922.[38] He begins by discussing *A Portrait of the Artist as a Young Man*, a novel recommended to him by H. G. Wells who, according to Bennett, admired it extremely. Bennett concedes that the novel was 'great stuff' but concludes that 'in accessible thickets of my mind I heard a voice saying: "On the whole the book has bored you"'. Discussing *Ulysses*, Bennett is critical of the difficulty of Joyce's work for the reader: 'I must animadvert upon his damnable lack of manners. For he gives absolutely no help to the reader'. In Bennett's opinion, Joyce breaks the bond between writer and reader: '*Ulysses* would have been a better book and a much better appreciated book, if the author had extended to his public the common courtesies of literature'. Thus, Joyce's Modernist style, the lack of explanatory external detailing and the difficulty of the novel for the reader are tantamount, in Bennett's opinion, to literary bad manners. While Bennett acknowledges that Joyce 'is trying to reproduce the thoughts of the personage, and his verbal method can be justified', he criticises him for a lack of selectivity. He also complains that Joyce lacks 'poetical sense', and from the point of view of perspective, having 'a colossal down on humanity'. Such a view of Joyce could be construed as being commensurate with Woolf's estimation of Bennett as a Realist of an older school blind to the nature of avant-garde experiment; however, Bennett continues his review by claiming,

> Withal, James Joyce is a very astonishing phenomenon in letters. He is sometimes dazzlingly original. If he does not see life whole he sees it piercingly. His ingenuity is marvelous. He has wit. He has a prodigious humor. He is afraid of naught. And had heaven in its wisdom thought fit not to deprive him of that basic sagacity and that moral self-dominion which alone enable an artist to assemble and control and fully utilize his powers, he would have stood a chance of being one of the greatest novelists that ever lived.[39]

Although Bennett perhaps sees the obvious flaws that might be expected of an 'Edwardian' Realist, he still clearly recognises the greatness of Joyce as a writer. His claim that Molly Bloom's soliloquy surpasses not only Rabelais at his finest, but 'any work of literature' surely demonstrates the inaccuracy of Robert H. Deming's contention that Bennett 'presented the middlebrow point of view'.[40] Bennett summarises his view of *Ulysses* thus: 'My blame may have seemed extravagant, and my praise may seem extravagant; but that is how I feel about James Joyce'. As Catherine Turner has correctly noted, Bennett's mixed views created a degree of both confusion and curiosity about Joyce's novel.[41] However, the least that can be said about Bennett's review is that his 'extravagant praise', including his claim that Molly Bloom's soliloquy surpasses 'any work of literature', surely demonstrates Bennett's perceptive understanding of not only Joyce's craft as a novelist but also how open he was as a critic to avant-garde experimentation.

If anything, later considerations of the novel show Bennett's increasing admiration and his clear acknowledgement of the significance of Joyce's immense contribution to literature. In 1928, while noting that Joyce was exasperating and 'capable of unsurpassed tedium' (161), he also claims that Joyce 'has done things as good as anybody ever did. Proust at his best is not better than James Joyce at his best. He is an originator. His influence is considerable. And will be' (161). These comments come in a review of A. C. Ward's *Twentieth Century Literature: The Age of Interrogation* (1928) in which Bennett attacks Ward for giving 'only a few lines to the immense portent of James Joyce'. Significantly, Bennett recognises not only Joyce as avant-garde in that he 'is a novelist who brought new methods into the composition of a novel' but Joyce's positive contribution to the development of the novel. Ward's dismissal of Joyce, Bennett claims, 'militates against literary evolution in Britain' (162). Bennett's appraisal of Joyce here is comparable to his comments on Post-impressionist art in that in both, he attacks critics for a shortsightedness that retards the development of art. In a later column in 1929, Joyce is placed in the company of other writers including D. H. Lawrence, R. H. Mottram and Aldous Huxley—although Joyce is deemed as the 'biggest of these'—as an example of how the novel has dramatically improved in the preceding thirty years. The novel has been 'galvanised by the very important experiments' of' these writers who have 'all brought something new into it'. Specifically in terms of *Ulysses*, although the novel is 'eccentric' and 'obscene', 'it did something that had never been done before. Its influence has far exceeded its circulation, and is everywhere perceptible' (229). Bennett also notes Joyce's potential influence on his own writing: 'I never write fiction without thinking of Joyce's discoveries'. Here seems to be a clear acknowledgement of the kind of significance of the 'Georgians' that Woolf herself claimed in her critical essay on Bennett declaring 'we are trembling on the verge of one of the great ages of English literature'.[42] Joyce is fully acknowledged, by Bennett, to have not only broken with the past but in doing so has positively galvanised the novel and significantly improved it.

However, Bennett's view of Joyce's avant-garde writing had limits as his reaction to *Finnegans Wake* demonstrates. In 1929, while still praising *Ulysses* as 'a work distinguished by much greatness and still more originality' (292), Bennett confesses to a degree of exasperation and not 'having the least idea of what the story is about' (293). While Bennett is impressed 'by the man's learning, ingenuity, and astounding capacity for multiple allusiveness' ultimately the section of *Finnegans Wake* which Bennett read as a *Work in Progress* is 'the oddest novel ever written' (293). Unlike *Ulysses*, it will have no imitators and demonstrates that 'Joyce has been wasting his time (and other people's) and his genius'. Although, prophetically he claims, 'that anyone who is prepared to make the reading of James Joyce's new, incomplete book a life's career, and who has the lexicographical skill to construct a James Joyce encyclopaedic diction might conceivably derive emotional benefit from *Work in Progress*, and might procure the same benefit for at most a dozen other bizarre human beings' (293). In reference to Anna Livia Plurabelle, Bennett sees 'the wild caprice of a wonderful creative artist who has lost his way' (307). Bennett was not alone in his befuddlement as the critical response to the novel demonstrates. Wyndham Lewis, Ezra Pound and even enthusiastic sympathisers of Joyce such as his publisher Harriet Weaver had strong misgivings about the novel.[43] *Finnegans Wake* aside, Bennett's estimation of Joyce as late as 1930 was high: Bennett upheld Joyce as 'the most powerful influence on modern fiction' (342).

Arnold Bennett was equally enthusiastic about D. H. Lawrence. Lawrence was viewed as an original stylist (41) and one of two novelists—the other in Bennett's opinion was R. H. Mottram—who 'continually disclose genuine originality, the two real British geniuses of the new age' (212). Again in 1929, Bennett lauds Lawrence as a genius: 'Unequal, wayward, obsessed, but a genius. He has enlarged the scope of the novel' (229). Bennett referred to him as 'the strongest novelist writing today' (164). Although he criticised Lawrence for occasional 'morbidity', he could write of 'The Woman Who Rode Away': 'There are whole pages together where every sentence gives new light on human nature and, reading them, you know that you are face to face with a rough demonic giant' (164). A month after Lawrence's death in March 1930, Bennett confesses to being 'a tremendous admirer' (364) and defended Lawrence against those who deemed he was obsessed with sex:

> The fact is that at his best he was no more obsessed with sex than any other normal human being. But he wrote more frankly and cleanly about it than most. He tried to fish up sex from the mud into which it had been sunk for several hypocritical and timid English generations past. (364)

Bennett felt that Lawrence lacked 'the power to discipline and control his faculties', but ultimately that 'no finer work had been done in our time than Lawrence's finest' (364). One can possibly see that in many respects, Lawrence's early fiction had resonances with Bennett's own, plausibly more so than with Joyce, in their concentration on exploring lower-class characters in an unfashionable midlands setting. As Ruth Robbins has noted that although both are very different novelists, they share similar 'concerns with form and theme'.[44] However, Bennett's appreciation of Lawrence for broadening the scope of the novel and with Joyce for improving the quality of novel-writing in the first third of the twentieth century shows an acute appreciation of the quality of both writers; however, much of their writerly strategies differed from his own.

His literary nemesis, Virginia Woolf, did not fair quite so well. Bennett is scathing, for example, of *Orlando* (1928). If the first chapter is 'goodish', 'the second chapter shows a startling decline and fall-off. Fanciful embroidery, wordy, and naught else!' (211), but still he can generously write that 'Mrs Woolf has accomplished some of the most beautiful writing of the modern age' (211). Indeed overcoming his 'notorious grave reservations concerning Virginia Woolf' (59), he praises *To the Lighthouse*, for its originality and its characterisation of Mrs Ramsey noting, plausibly with a degree of grudging irony considering that at the crux of their literary feud was the ability to describe character that she 'almost amounts to a complete person' (59).

Beyond the experimental writing of British authors, Bennett gave high praise to Faulkner's *The Sound and the Fury*, which, although exasperating, demonstrated that 'he evidently has great and original talent' (334); and to Hemingway's *Farewell to Arms*: Hemingway's dialogue 'is masterly at reproductive Realism. Short sentences, page after page, admirably marshalled and grouped. Its detachment is perfect' (322). As regards European avant-garde writing, he views Kafka's *The Castle* as 'a very remarkable novel' for 'its technical accomplishment' and 'conscious artistry' (363). It is complex, 'and full of subtle implications, different from all other novels' (363). Bennett has some reservations about Proust's *Remembrance of Things Past* and wonders whether it is a 'masterpiece in its entirety', but 'the novel contains within its vast borders several small masterpieces' (87). Bennett also expresses some reservations about Stefan Zweig's *Conflicts: Three Tales*, but also acknowledges that 'it has sparks of divine fire'

Thus then, it can be said that Bennett, with some reservation, held much experimental writing of the 1920s in high esteem. Bennett clearly acknowledges the value of the innovative craft of writers such as Lawrence and Joyce. While often critical of what he sees as the difficulty for the reader of the works of, say, Joyce or Faulkner, he can strenuously defend the avant-garde from those who objected to it on moral or aesthetic grounds. In fact, a strong argument can be made that unlike

Woolf's acute separation between Edwardians and Georgians, Bennett, in his criticism, sees less a neat demarcation between his own aesthetics and that of later writers, than a continuation, if not altogether seamless, between the originality of those continental writers he defended when he was writing for the *New Age* and of the later novelistic experimentation of the 1920s. The writing of the younger generation was not judged by a new aesthetics, but by a similar Realist aesthetics that had earlier formed Bennett's literary views. It is indeed their veracity and ability to represent lived experience which links say Chekhov's 'absolute realism' to Lawrence's ability to give 'new light on human nature'. What is perhaps most remarkable about Bennett's articles for the *Evening Standard* is not the consistency of his aesthetic approbation but the catholicity evident in his aesthetic appreciation of both writers such as R. H. Mottram and avant-garde writers such as Joyce who he could see were pushing the boundaries of literary experimentation well beyond Bennett's own novelistic innovations, even if scholars such as Squillace have noted that these were much greater than many gave him credit for.

To return to the column of 1910 on Neoimpressionism that began this chapter. Bennett supposes that some writer might do in literature what the Postimpressionists have done in art. Although he imagines this happening to a younger person than himself, he claims it is conceivable that he would be

> [...] disgusted with nearly the whole of modern fiction, and I might have to begin again [...]. Supposing a young writer turned up and forced me, and some of my contemporaries – us who fancy ourselves a bit – to admit that we had been concerning ourselves unduly with inessentials, that we had been worrying ourselves to achieve infantile realisms. Well, that day would be a great and a disturbing day – for us. (284)

This bears a remarkable similarity to Woolf's later criticism of Bennett in 'Mr Bennett and Mrs Brown'. However, given Bennett's critical response to the avant-garde, even if we take his comments in 1909 as an accurate prediction of what Woolf deemed to have happened, it should be noted how unperturbed Bennett was by later avant-garde experimentation given the considerable extent to which he embraced it. Equally self-deprecating as his comments about writing an 'infantile Realism', Bennett in his *Evening Standard* 'Books and Persons' column declared himself 'a low brow', writing 'on behalf of the great trade union of average intelligent persons'. Placing himself as an advocate of the democratisation of art, his columns show him to be an astute and generous critic of the avant-garde, and at times a significantly important proselytiser for literary experimentation and innovation throughout his all too brief professional life.

Notes

1 *New Age*, 8 December 1910.
2 The extent to which Fry's exhibition was derided can be seen in the harshness of the reviews it received in the press. Charles Harrison notes some of the words that were applied to Fry's exhibition: 'horror', 'madness', 'infection', 'sickness of the soul', 'putrescence', 'pornography', 'anarchy' and 'evil', Charles Harrison, *English Art and Modernism, 1900–1939*, 2nd edn. (New Haven, CT: Yale UP, 1994), p. 47.
3 J. B. Bullen, *Continental Crosscurrents: British Criticism and European Art, 1810–1910* (Oxford: Oxford UP, 2005), p. 1.
4 Bullen, *Continental Crosscurrents, p. 1*.
5 Virginia Woolf, *Mr. Bennett and Mrs. Brown* (London: Hogarth P, 1924), p. 2.
6 The first notable critical evaluation was arguably by Samuel Hynes. See Samuel Hynes, 'The Whole Contention between Mr. Bennett and Mrs. Woolf', *Novel: A Forum on Fiction* 1.1 (Autumn, 1967): 34–44. The most recent, to my knowledge, in 2015. See Randi Saloman, 'Mr Bennett and Mrs Brown: A Reassessment', *An Arnold Bennett Companion* (Stoke: Churnett Valley, 2015), pp. 173–92.
7 Robert Squillace, *Modernism, Modernity and Arnold Bennett* (Lewisburg: Bucknell UP, 1997), p. 17.
8 Ezra Pound, *New Selected Poems and Translations*, ed. Richard Sieburth (New York: New Directions, 2010), p. 115.
9 Pound, *New Selected Poems and Translations*, p. 115.
10 Chris Baldick, *The Modern Movement, 1910–1940* (Oxford: Oxford UP, 2004), p. 44.
11 Qtd in Margaret Drabble, *Arnold Bennett: A Biography* (1974, Boston, MA: G. K. Hall, 1986), p. 290.
12 Qtd in Bonnie Kime Scott, *Refiguring Modernism: Vol.1 The Women of 1928* (Bloomington: Indiana UP, 1995), p. 30.
13 Drabble, *Arnold Bennett*, p. 235.
14 Benjamin Madden, 'Arnold Bennett and the Making of Sweeney Agonistes', *Notes and queries* 58.1 (2011): 106.
15 Arnold Bennett, *Fame and Fiction: An Enquiry into Certain Popularities* (London: Richards, 1901), p. 5.
16 John Bayley, *The Intellectuals And The Masses: Pride and Prejudice Among the Literary Intelligensia, 1880–1939* (London: Faber, 2002), p. 163.
17 Bennett fictionalises this gulf in 'The Death of Simon Fuge' (1907) in which a representation of metropolitan culture, Loring, ventures into the Five Towns to have his sense of cultural elitism challenged by the good sense of the locals who dispel his sense of aesthetic superiority. See Anthony Patterson, 'Democratizing Art: Realism in Arnold Bennett's Short Stories', in *Arnold Bennett Companion Volume II*, ed. John Shapcott (Staffordshire: Churnet Valley, 2017), pp. 157–71.
18 John Shapcott, 'Introduction', *The Pretty Lady* (1918, Leek: Churnet Valley Books, 2009), p. iii; Robert Squillace, *Modernism, Modernity and Arnold Bennett* (MA, Associated UP, 1997), p. 18.
19 Olga Bloomfield, *Arnold Bennett* (Boston, MA: Twayne, 1984), p. 136.
20 Frank Swinnerton, *Arnold Bennett* (London: British Council, 1950), p. 21.
21 *Evening Standard*, 28 July 1927.
22 *New Age*, 27 May 1909.
23 *New Age*, 27 May 1909.
24 *New Age*, 31 March 1910.

25 Indeed, Dostoevsky, in his role in European Literature and his position in terms of his own avant-garde status, became a significant figure in the ongoing dispute between Woolf and Bennett. See Peter Kaye, *Dostoevsky and Modernism* (Cambridge: Cambridge UP, 2004), pp. 74–7.

26 *New Age*, 18 May 1909.

27 *New Age*, 18 May 1909.

28 A fuller discussion of Bennett's defence of literature against censorship can be found in Anthony Patterson, 'Books, Persons and Censorship: Arnold Bennett's Defence of the Sacred Cause of Literature', in *An Arnold Bennett Companion*, ed. John Shapcott (Stoke: Churnett Valley Books, 2015), pp. 57–72.

29 See Adam Parkes, *The Theatre of Censorship* (Oxford and New York: Oxford UP, 1996); Celia Marshik, *British Modernism and Censorship* (Oxford and New York: Cambridge UP, 2006); Alison Pease, *Modernism, Mass Culture, and the Aesthetics of Obscenity* (Cambridge: Cambridge UP, 2000); and Anthony Patterson, *Mrs Grundy's Enemies: Censorship, Realist Fiction and the Politics of Sexual Representation* (Oxford: Peter Lang, 2013).

30 Arnold Bennett, 'Books and Persons', *Evening Standard* (22 August, 1929).

31 Bennett, *New Age*, 13 January, 1910.

32 Bennett, *New Age*, 13 January, 1910.

33 Arnold Bennett, *The Evening Standard Years: Books and Persons 1926–1931*, ed. Andrew Mylett (London: Archon, 1974), p. 161. Hereafter cited parenthetically as *EVS*.

34 Arnold Bennett, 'James Joyce's *Ulysses*', *The Bookman* (London: Hodder and Stoughton, 1922), pp. 337–9; 339.

35 See John Shapcott's comments on Bennett's defence of Norah James, John Shapcott, 'Aesthetics for Everyman: Arnold Bennett's *Evening Standard* Columns', in *Middlebrow Literary Culture: The Battle of the Brows*, eds. Mary Grover and Erica Brown (New York: Palgrave Macmillan, 2011), pp. 82–97; 93–4. (see *EVS*, 7 March 1929).

36 Douglas wrote: 'All the secret sewers of vice are canalised in [*Ulysses's*] flood of unimaginable thoughts, images, and pornographic words. And its unclean lunacies are larded with appalling and revolting blasphemies directed against the Christian religion and against the holy name of Christ [...]'. Qtd in David Bradshaw, 'James Douglas: The Sanitary Inspector of Literature', in *Prudes on the Prowl: Fiction and Obscenity in England, 1850 to the Present Day*, eds. David Bradshaw and Rachel Potter (Oxford: Oxford UP, 2013), pp. 90–110; 97–8.

37 Margaret Drabble, *Arnold Bennett: A Biography* (1974; Boston, MA: G. K. Hall, 1986), p. 289.

38 Bennett, *The Bookman*, p. 570.

39 Bennett, *The Bookman*, p. 570.

40 Robert H. Deming, ed., 'Introduction', in *James Joyce: The Critical Heritage Vol. 1. 1907–1927* (London: Routledge, 1970), p. 20.

41 Catherine Turner, *Marketing Modernism between the Two World Wars* (Boston: U of Massachusetts, 2003), p. 185.

42 Woolf, *Mr. Bennett and Mrs. Brown*, p. 24.

43 See Lee Spinks, *James Joyce: A Critical Guide* (Edinburgh: Edinburgh UP, 2009), pp. 169–73.

44 Ruth Robbins, 'Long Shadow: Victorian Themes and Forms in the Edwardian Provincial Novel – Arnold Bennett and D. H. Lawrence', *Victoriographies*, 1.1 (April 2011), pp. 1–13, p. 1.

14 *Parade's End* and the Modernist Legacy of Nineteenth-Century Literary Toryism

Koenraad Claes

The 2012 screen adaptation of Ford Madox Ford's *Parade's End* (1924–1928) was one of the BBC's most-watched series of that year, and was generally received with much acclaim in the press. Most reviewers praised scriptwriter Tom Stoppard for his translation of this hefty and complex Modernist text to the format of a period drama, and those who did not appreciate the adaptation usually acknowledged that the shortcomings they found were caused by difficulties already present in the source material. In an op-ed of 3 September 2012 for the *Guardian* website, historian David Priestland voiced a more fundamental objection, asking why the BBC had 'given us such a Tory version of this novel'.[1] Priestland claimed that Stoppard's script, aided by an overly sympathetic performance by lead actor Benedict Cumberbatch, had portrayed main character Christopher Tietjens more positively than he is characterised by Ford. Stoppard and Cumberbatch's Tietjens would conform to a newly popular, *Downton Abbey*-ish type of 'Gentle Tory', whereas Ford would not have intended him to be likeable at all, let alone for his moral and political creeds to be perceived as attractive. Priestland overstated the ideological critique implicit in Ford's characterisation of Tietjens, but it is true that there is a large dose of satire in the four books that has puzzled readers since their first publication and that can be easily misread as an outright dismissal of Tory worldviews. This essay will argue that such ambiguity was an inherent aspect of major nineteenth-century novels by Sir Walter Scott, Benjamin Disraeli and Mrs. Humphry Ward that explicitly work out conservative ideologies in ages of socio-political transition, and that by borrowing narrative structures and stock characters from these ideologically conservative novelists, Ford delivers a politically revisionist and narratively Modernist pastiche of nineteenth-century Toryism and literary conventions for his own age. These intertextual references suggest that instead of it being a refutation of Tory doctrines, *Parade's End*'s links to conservative discourses may actually run deeper than is apparent at first glance.

The complex issue of the political beliefs represented in the novel has already been thoroughly explored in earlier studies.[2] The state of the art in academic criticism on the novel is that *Parade's End* does not ultimately denigrate Tietjens's Tory ideals, which actually resemble those of the author: wary of collectivism but devoted to solidarity between the classes, patriotic but not jingoist, essentialist in gender ideology but at least by intent non-misogynist. Ford was a critical, but, according to himself, also 'always a sentimental Tory'.[3] His novel would rather portray these as being put to the test of the hostile conditions of the early twentieth century, namely an Edwardian Period made up of mouldering vestiges of Victorian culture (esp. in the first volume *Some Do Not...*) and the devastating crisis of the First World War (*No More Parades* and *A Man Could Stand Up–*), with the fourth and final volume (*Last Post*) suggesting how Tietjens could function in post-War society by updating his enduring principles within the new institutional framework.

As Ford insisted in his critical writings, one of those institutions, and not the least important one at that, was the novel. Like many of his contemporaries, he thereby presents the War as an epochal event that finally marks the true end of the nineteenth century in which he had started his career. He inventively does this through a conspicuous deployment of supposedly obsolete literary conventions associated with preceding generations of British 'nuvvelists'.[4] His novel's thematic preoccupation with the political legacy of a bygone era is thereby reinforced by its adoption of those formal tropes and themes that Modernist experimental fiction was attempting to render obsolete.

A 'Last Post' for the Scottian Historical Novel?

> No more respect... For the Equator! For the Metric system. For Sir Walter Scott! (Valentine, in *A Man Could Stand Up–*)[5]

It is commonly accepted that *Parade's End* is to be considered the fulfilment of Ford's self-declared 'one unflinching aim [...] to register [his] own times in terms of [his] own time'.[6] As he put it in the autobiographical *It Was the Nightingale* (1933), with these books, he 'wanted the Novelist to appear in his really proud position as historian of his own time'.[7] Ford's most recent biographer Max Saunders confirms that *Parade's End* is 'a historical novel of Ford's own times',[8] but nuances this idea by pointing out that 'Ford's attitude to literary form is [...] dual: he's so formal he can't do without the conventions of romance, the historical novel, impressionism; but too aware of their falsities to use them single-mindedly'.[9] Adopting basic narratological jargon, we could say that in this and other works of historical fiction by Ford, a Modernist discourse, involving the narration and focalisation of events, calls into question a nineteenth-century story, or the events in causal and chronological sequence. That story can be traced back to the basic plot popularised by an author whose 'constituted Authority and consecrated Experience', according to Valentine in the third volume, might no longer hold sway after 'this crack across the table of History': Sir Walter Scott (*AMCSU*, 17–18).

In *Parade's End*, the fragmented social reality of the War years is formally represented by means of the scattered ordering of the narrated events, such disruptions in discourse time being the novel's main hermeneutic hurdle, along with a problematisation of narratorial reliability and of focalisation. Hereby, this novel's narrative formally represents Tietjens's war traumas and the gradual collapse of the ever unstable social value system that he has constructed as the mainstay of his life. In each separate volume and throughout the novel as a whole, there is a tendency to increase the density of these Modernist narrative devices as the story progresses, following the structural plan of the *progression d'effet* developed by Ford and his close collaborator Joseph Conrad whereby the engagement with the psychological states of the characters intensifies as the narratives progress. At the onset, we are guided by a heterodiegetic and extradiegetic narrator, who is omnisciently detached from the sentiments and observations of the characters, and free to give ironic yet reliable accounts of the narrated events. For the most part, the first volume *Some Do Not...* (1924) is thereby allowed to be a conventional comedy of manners for the Edwardian period. From the second half of this book, however, as the War edges closer, this narrative reliability is regularly compromised by means of an ever denser use of internal focalisation, whereby the earlier occasional passages of free indirect speech give way to streams of consciousness that can last for several pages. Particularly in the trench scenes in the middle volumes, *No More Parades* (1925) and *A Man Could Stand Up–* (1926), overarching narration often disappears altogether, and the final book, *Last Post* (1928), features extended interior monologues reflecting on the post-War lives of the figuratively and/or literally shell-shocked characters amongst the ruins of society. This change in style corresponds to the gradual social alienation of the characters, representing their estrangement from the invalidated social context that before gave meaning to their lives.

This seems to be in agreement with Marina MacKay's recent summary of the relationship of Modernist fiction to that of the preceding era, being 'a rejection of the novel's traditional endorsements of the individual will to power triumphing over intractable reality, and a rejection of the moral assurances and shapely plots typically associated with nineteenth-century realism'.[10] While this is true for the thematic and formal focuses of *Parade's End*, the story of *Parade's End*, abstracted from this discursive problematisation, does stay close to that of older novels, except for the notable difference that the standard nineteenth-century plot is turned on its head. While Romantic- and Victorian-era narratives progress from an experience of fragmentation to one of completion, the characters of *Parade's End* start off with an ironic but genuine belief in social consistency that gradually disintegrates, leaving open the inevitable question whether they will manage to build a new world after the end of the narrative. The novel's inverted but otherwise faithfully copied nineteenth-century conventions are literary relics of a bygone age, that just like Tietjens, the embodied 'Last of England',[11] represent passing cultural standards that have been toppled, but not yet replaced with new ones. This tension suits a novel that is above all an account of historical transition. Conrad may have spoken too soon when he praised Ford's earlier novel series *The Fifth Queen* (1906–1908) equivocally as 'the Swan Song of Historical Romance'.[12] Writing about this earlier cycle, Seamus O'Malley has recently argued that 'what ultimately separates Ford from Scott and the nineteenth-century historical novel, and marks one defining element of a modernist historical novel' is Ford's highlighting of the 'reconstructed nature of any history'.[13] In the later historical novel *Parade's End*, the reader is tasked with piecing together from the fragments of events a plot which turns out to be not that different from older historical and realist novels, even if these would be dismissed by Ford as artistically superseded 'Nuvvles' in his critical writing.

Arguably, the most influential outline for the standard plot of the pre-Modernist novel was provided by Georg Lukács in his *Theory of the Novel* (1920), nearly contemporaneous with *Parade's End*, and according to Massimo Fussilo articulating best the 'critical myth' on the genre's early history that was prevalent throughout interbellum European Modernism.[14]

> The inner form of the novel has been understood as the process of the problematic individual's journeying towards himself, the road from dull captivity within a merely present reality—a reality that is heterogeneous in itself and meaningless to the individual—towards clear self-recognition.[15]

When the setting for this quest is a moment in the (remote or recent) past represented as a time of transition between distinct social realities, we speak of a historical novel, a subgenre that, more than by any other author, was popularised across Europe and the Americas by Walter Scott. After his conversion to Marxism, Lukács would claim that the conventions of plotting and the selection of his protagonists of this vastly influential Tory author would be based on Scott's unease at the decline of the feudal order in favour of rising capitalism. As Scott's themes and formal innovations were disseminated, his ideological slant of a 'narrow conservatism' that correctly identified but ultimately did not seek to resolve social ills would have become the implicit message intrinsic to the historical novel in general.[16] In novels like *Waverley* (1814), Tory heroes find their place in a transitional civilisation that is moving away from the standards and institutions with which they initially identified, and so doing help society regain an equilibrium that mitigates the threat of disruptive political heterodoxies. The hero's gradual acceptance of the imperfection and imperfectability of society, key concepts of the political creed of Scott and other early nineteenth-century Tory authors, would also, according to Terry Eagleton, soon become the implicit theme behind all conventional novels of the nineteenth century, and the teleology of their plots.[17] By inverting the plot of such older novels and refusing to end his story in a state of stability, Ford rejects the complacency of much nineteenth-century fiction that was in his own time also regretted by politically progressive commentators. Nevertheless, his choice to move from a state of perceived completion to one of fragmentation at the end of the novel suggests that the loss of the 'parade' of consensus is at least problematic, and far from a finished desirable alternative to society as it had been before.

The formal distinctions between Ford's Modernist historical novels and their nineteenth-century predecessors that were suggested by O'Malley certainly hold water, but should not be overstated. It is important to acknowledge that the historical novel has always been an intrinsically self-conscious subgenre to begin with, already from the publication of the first examples by pioneering authors such as Maria Edgeworth, Jane Porter and, above all, 'the Author of *Waverley*'. The historical novel being an account of a period in the past, and therefore available for evaluation, is inevitably relativistic. Scott has his narrators and fictional editors constantly emphasise the anachronism of the elements that he borrows from earlier eras in comparison to his own times, and so doing he too indirectly furnishes a 'historical novel of [his] own times', as discussed earlier. For reasons of affect as well as instruction, historical novelists need to make readers appreciate the differences between the time of writing and the time in which the story is set, and that involves a process of relating to or distancing from topical issues. The choices behind the selection and representation of historical events to fictionalise, and characters to feature, therefore, have to be situated in an implicit or explicit cultural-political agenda.

The plot of *Parade's End*, as well as of its nineteenth-century models, is driven by the interactions of contrasting characters against the backdrop of a changing social context, bringing about the typical unexpected 'reversals' of the nineteenth-century novelistic plot against which many leading Modernist authors revolted, choosing instead to delve deeper into the psychological complexity of characters at specific moments.[18] For all the subtle character psychology that Ford showed himself capable of in discursively synchronic narratives like *The Good Soldier* (1915) that occasionally comes up in the streams of consciousness of *Parade's End*, the latter novel is not primarily invested in presenting its characters as rounded individuals. Although dialogue and the novel's Modernist techniques give us insight into the complex mental states of the main characters, this is meant to show how the represented social types can be set off against each other within a specific historical context, and their minutely described anguish is not essential to themselves but triggered by crises that challenge their social roles. Similarly to the stock characters employed by a Scott, a Dickens or a George Eliot, the mannerisms of Ford's retrograde Tory landowner, slogan-shouting suffragette or Whiggish upstarts are types, with more than a hint of caricature. The very first sentence stereotypes Tietjens and his hanger-on Macmaster before we have so much as learned their names: 'two young men – they were of the English public official class' (*SDN*, 3). The characters represent social estates or institutions, and exemplify aspects of the spirit of their age, and when even heroes like Tietjens, or his typological prefiguration Edward Waverley, are allowed character development, the undergone change will be contingent with their original social identities.

In his later ground-breaking study on *The Historical Novel* (1962), Lukács explained that the construction of Scott's plots was inspired by his place 'among those honest Tories in the England [sic] of his time who exonerate nothing in the development of capitalism [...] yet who, precisely because of their conservatism, display no violent opposition to the features of the new development repudiated by them', which makes him seek out 'the middle way' between the two parties in the conflicts which he represents.[19] Elaborating on this, H. O. Brown believes that '[w]hat Scott demonstrates in his work, is that Scottish (and by extension: British) society is a long series of interchanging ruling groups, who have struggled, combined and recombined without any greater reason than the development of national history, and that this internal strife needs to be stabilized'.[20] *Waverley*, for instance, stages a dialectic sublation of the conflict between forward-looking (Hanoverian) Whigs and nostalgic (post-Jacobite) Tories that conveniently would help perpetuate the challenged Tory ideals. Scott is never so reactionary as to call for a second Restoration of the Stuart dynasty. Rather, Brown avers, '[w]hat seems to interest him most, even to the point of fascination, are instances of passage into some sort of modernity'.[21] The cultural nostalgia evident from Scott's novels is more constructive than has been admitted by his detractors. Apart from the antiquarian interest to which they were reduced in the late nineteenth century, his novels have an implicit political message that directly concerns the time that they are published: a turbulent period that had to negotiate the hazards of international strife (culminating at Waterloo), but also of domestic tumult (culminating in Peterloo). Narratives of national reconciliation set in the past might promote a similar mutual recognition between establishment and disaffected social groups. One century later, in '[Ford's] own time', similar social conditions came to apply.

Scott's rudimentary dialectics have major consequences for his plot construction, whereby the medium of the plot determines the message of the narrative. This is nowhere more apparent than in his predilection for so-called 'middling heroes'.

The 'hero' of the Scott novel is always a more or less mediocre, average English gentleman. He generally possesses a certain, though never outstanding, degree of practical intelligence, a certain moral fortitude and decency which even rises to a capacity for self-sacrifice, but which never grows into a sweeping human passion, is never the enraptured devotion to a great cause.[22]

The eponymous hero of *Waverley* stumbles into the major conflict of his day on the Jacobite side, not through careful deliberation or long-standing dedication to that cause, but through accident, manipulation and a boyish belief in romance. Likewise, Tietjens is despite his intelligence and book smarts often utterly naïve, or, in the words of Valentine, 'extraordinarily clear-sighted in the affairs of others, in great affairs, but in his own so simple as to be almost a baby', 'innocent as a child' (*SDN*, 287–8, 290). Also like Waverley, Tietjens does rise to the occasion, and shows a capacity for heroic self-sacrifice in the trenches, but he only enlisted in the first place out of frustration with his ignoble career in administration and the conflicts with his adulterous socialite wife Sylvia. He hereby hoped to find a new purpose for himself in this world, or (again according to Valentine) that his 'large hulking body will stop two bullets in front of two small anaemic fellows' (*SDN*, 289). As he has it himself, the battle that he wished could be fought out in the trenches was 'for the eighteenth century against the twentieth'. What he however soon realises was that Britain could not claim the moral high ground over the 'enemy nations': '[i]t was one part of the twentieth century using the eighteenth as a catspaw to bash the other half of the twentieth' (*SDN*, 287). This is almost a calque of the conclusions of Edward Waverley, no longer idealising his former fellow Jacobites after the failed Rising of 1745.

The in every sense romantic Waverley was receptive to Jacobitism because his education was based on chivalric romance and the inherited resentment of his debased family after their involvement in the previous Rising of 1715. Tietjens, despite the fact that he cannot claim such a pedigree as he descends from a family that occupied the country seat of the rightful Jacobite landowners after having come over with 'Dutch William' during the Glorious Revolution, for his implied belief in creeds such as Passive Obedience too appears closer to Jacobite Toryism. Scott's narrators and fictional manuscript editors blame the downfall of the Jacobites on their own historically backward feudalism and the absolutist stubbornness of the Stuart Pretenders, but still present them as respectable for their laudable disdain for political opportunism. The awkward Tietjens, too, nobly represents a vanishing class of disinterested landowners who did not need to connive themselves into power, and many petty nuisances suffered by him are caused by his unwillingness to deal with a new capitalist elite of newspaper magnates and bankers. As Saunders has noted, 'Ford's interest in Toryism was always paradoxical',[23] and whatever ambiguities are to be found in the character Tietjens may be enlargements of those in the author himself. Ford admitted that *Parade's End* was written that he had 'arrived at the stage of finding the gentleman an insupportable phenomenon'[24]; yet, he was infamous for only half-ironically playing the country squire.[25] It may not be entirely coincidental that a self-professed Tory Yorkshireman, who descended from Dutch usurpers, was devised by another self-styled Tory country gentleman, whose name had up until a few years before been 'Hueffer', tied ancestrally to a more recent national enemy. Tietjens is certainly a caricature, but rather than condemned for any reprehensible principles, he is shown to be the victim of his own unfounded purism. The cause of his tribulations is not that his ideals would be wrong per se, but that the institutions through which he can put them meaningfully into practice are in a state of decline. For the historical novel, unreasonable behaviour in a character is a productive commonplace that serves the inherent relativism of the subgenre, because it better shows that these individuals do not control their lives (fully) through their personal agency, but are determined by the historically contingent ideology of their class, time and place. Before the era under scrutiny is over, it is not fully possible to make sense of the ideological forces at work, which additionally makes the historical novel a rhetorically useful mode for politically conservative authors who aim to caution the reader about a (Whiggish) reliance on the historical agency of individuals, a strategy in Scott fittingly designated as 'Tory scepticism' by Andrew Lincoln.[26] The attitude of Ford, as well as that of his hero Tietjens, self-declared Tories who are adamantly against Imperialism and misogyny but also feel that social cohesion relies on tradition, could well go by the same name.

Nancy Armstrong has concisely stated that the nineteenth-century novel required that at the end of the narrative, 'two conditions are met: (1) the protagonist acquires a position commensurate with his or her worth, and (2) the entire field of possible human identities changes to provide such a place for that individual'.[27] After the hardships of battle, Tietjens, like Scott's heroes before him, returns to the family manor that by the outcome of the crisis has changed as much as he has, and is forced to find a way to make sense of this new reality. Like Waverley who weds Rose Bradwardine and builds a new home out of the ruins of the sacked Bradwardine estate of Tully-Veolan, Tietjens comes to live with his true love Valentine in *Last Post* (book 4) in the dilapidated family mansion Groby, which they will soon need to leave altogether. The ambiguous ending or *Parade's End*, implying resignation with a profoundly non-satisfactory and apparently hopeless situation, marks the shift of Tietjens's nineteenth-century reliance on social integration, to

Modernist isolation, and the necessity to construct a new context that can sustain his old ideals. *Parade's End* ends on Valentine's unanswered question: 'How are we to live now? How are we ever to live?'[28] What, according to Ford, will come after the previously ruling customs, and the social ritualism of parade? Although all the union of the suffragette and the Tory implies a dialectic mitigation between the best of the old and the new ways, what the future would hold for Tietjens and Valentine past the end of this final volume simply is not stated. Tietjens may be excused for being clueless, because he does not read novels written after the eighteenth century,[29] but there are plenty of nineteenth-century precedents for their relationship, and an intertextual reading of these links could suggest a possible outcome.

The 'Third Message' of Disraelian Dialectics

> Life's a bitter thing. I am an old novelist and know it. There you are working yourself to death to save the nation with a wilderness of cats and monkeys howling and squalling your personal reputation away... It was Dizzy himself said these words to me at one of our receptions. (Mrs. Wannop in *SDN*, 148)

Not going quite as far back as Scott, James Heldman has remarked that '[r]ead as one novel, *Parade's End* is very much the Victorian large fiction', going on to cite several examples of intertextual references between this novel and the Loose Baggy Monsters that may have provided Ford with plot elements.[30] One instance is the relationship between Tietjens and Valentine, tracked back to such salient precursors as Elizabeth Gaskell's John Thornton and Margaret Hale of *North and South* (1855). Arguably, the first instance in a Victorian novel of such a political odd couple, nevertheless, came from the most unmistakably Tory author of the period. Despite not being acknowledged as an important novelist in Ford's literary criticism, the Victorian politician and novelist Benjamin Disraeli gets four namechecks in *Parade's End*, and a number of more oblique references. At their simplest, the mentions of Disraeli the politician serve to remind us that the lingering Victorian age lay within living memory. This occurs most frequently in the first book, *Some Do Not...*, where the transition from the nineteenth to the twentieth century is treated most explicitly. However, Disraeli the novelist also furnished a trope that drives the development of the plot.

This first happens in the scene of the nightly cart drive, a pivotal event in *Some Do Not....* because at this point, it starts to dawn on Christopher and Valentine that, despite their different ideological profiles, they share a social background and have complementary values, from which a common intellectual and political programme may surface, and a strong emotional connection. In one of their increasingly flirtatious

exchanges, Valentine teases: 'I've never met a Cambridge Tory man before. I thought they were all in museums, and you work them up again
out of bones. That's what father used to say; he was an Oxford Disrae-
lian Conservative Imperialist...' (*SDN*, 169). This facetious juxtaposition between her father's Oxford background and Tietjens's Cambridge
education follows on an academic dispute about the differing Latin pro-
nunciation upheld at either institution. However, the mention of Oxford
does have a further relevance, because it hints at the Tory circles around
Lord Randolph Churchill, once warden of Merton College, to which
Professor Wannop is said to have belonged. Churchill, who presented
himself explicitly as a follower of Disraeli, in 1883 had founded the
Primrose League, which advocated the Tory Democracy line that sought
to recuperate the recently expanded electorate within a paternalist social
order.[31] The primrose was associated with Disraeli after Queen Victoria
had the flowers laid on his grave during his funerary service, and his
admirers for decades commemorated him on 'Primrose Day' (19 April),
the day of his passing. Professor Wannop is said to 'certainly have had
the friendship of Disraeli' and to have raised his daughter as a 'Primrose
Dame' (*AMCSU*, 58). In five instances, the very thought of Valentine
evokes for Tietjens the scent of that flower.[32] Finally, as quoted in the
motto to this section, her novelist mother Mrs. Wannop, to whom we
shall soon return, approvingly namedrops 'Dizzy' in conversation with
Tietjens. The insistent association of Valentine with Disraeli signals
that the suffragette Valentine may be socially forward-thinking, but she
comes from a conservative background, and we as readers are made to
reflect critically on the extent to which she deviates from it. Though
an unlikely wingman, Disraeli hereby forms a link between Valentine
and Tietjens. Beyond Oxbridge rivalry, what Valentine implies with the
juxtaposition of her father's and Tietjens's Toryism is that her father had
been part of a reformist Tory faction that sought to create a relevance
for itself in hostile socio-historical circumstances, whereas Tietjens is
content to be a reactionary 'Nenglish [sic] country gentleman and spin
principles out of the newspapers and the gossip of horse fairs. And let
the country go to hell, [he]'ll never stir a finger except to say I told you
so' (*SDN*, 170).

   This developing sympathy between Valentine and Tietjens is the most
important organising principle of *Parade's End* character-driven plot,
which gains additional importance when their relationship is compared
to that of Charles Egremont and Sybil Gerard in Disraeli's most influential novel, *Sybil, or The Two Nations* (1845). This was the centrepiece
to Disraeli's *Young England* trilogy, concerned with the three vestiges
of that parliamentary faction's programme, being a rejuvenation of the
Conservative Party (the central theme of *Coningsby*—1844), the appeasement of class struggle (*Sybil*) and a resurgence in the moral authority of
the Church of England (*Tancred*—1847). In *Sybil*, the rapprochement
between the aristocratic interest and the plight of the working class is

played out in the relationship between the conflicted young Tory noble-man Egremont and the radical activist Sybil Gerard for whom the novel is named. Not surprisingly for an opponent of liberalising tendencies in the Conservative Party, Disraeli has his narrator defend the idea that so-cial cohesion is primarily threatened by the Liberal Party and their sup-porters in the Peelite faction within his own party, and the working class and the responsible segment of the ruling classes alike should therein recognise their mutual enemy, at once trumping the more radically dem-ocratic Chartists in their bid for the hearts of the lower classes. Although Egremont and Sybil at the onset assess the mid-nineteenth-century Brit-ish social and economic situation from a completely different perspec-tive, they ultimately reach the same conclusions. While he is appalled by the lack of responsibility that his aristocratic peers show for their tenants, ignoring the social destitution caused by the liberalisation of the country's agriculture and the Industrial Revolution, she approaches the problem from the standpoint of the suffering workers, among whom her father is a leader who preaches reform but not revolution. With a stroke of luck straight out of Scott, at the end of the novel, Sybil conveniently turns out to be the descendant of an ancient family disaffected during the degenerate Tudor age, so nothing stands in the way of her nation-building union with Egremont. The union of Egremont the socially re-sponsible Tory and Sybil the conservative socialist stands for the class appeasement promoted through the novel, and Catherine Gallagher has identified here a rudimentary version of the Master/Slave dialectic that we have hinted at in the discussion of Scott, and which she feels would be the catalyst of this and other 'Condition of England' narratives of the mid-Victorian period.[33] Disraeli for his realist novel invented a syn-chronic alternative to the rudimentary diachronic (or historicist) dialec-tic of the 'middle way' sought out by Scott. Sybil, who represents all that is good and politically salvageable in the worker's struggle, loses militant radicalism after discovering that the more radical of her former associ-ates aim to turn the workers into a violent mob, and trusts to the parlia-mentarian agitation of Conservative MP Egremont instead. Indeed, the working classes / Slaves are hereby validating the authority of the upper classes / Masters, who—*noblesse oblige*—in turn have to deserve their dominance by facilitating the labour of the workers. However, rather than establishing fundamental differences to be overcome, *Sybil's* plot is invested in revealing the shared interest of the establishment and of democratic activists, a hot topic at the time of publication, right between the First (1832) and Second Reform Act (1867).

The relationship between Tietjens and Valentine is strikingly similar. Tietjens likes to dwell on the fact that despite Valentine's current finan-cial difficulties, the Wannops' is an old name, and she is 'of birth quite as good' as him (*SDN*, 131). One of his antiquarian musings teaches us in fact that 'the Wannops were first heard of at Birdlip in Gloucester-shire in the year 1417 – no doubt enriched after Agincourt', nearly three

centuries before Tietjens's ancestors landed in Yorkshire (*SDN*, 110).
In *Sybil*, it is hinted that the heroine's family is more rooted than the
Egremonts, who came into their estate in hazy circumstances, another
similarity between the two novels that is too strong to be coincidental.
While Gallagher is right to state that the radical position in *Sybil* is
largely neutralised in the dialectic pairing with Toryism, when Valentine
and Tietjens finally get together, there is no question of one political
position cancelling the other out; instead, their complementary profiles
bring out the best in either. There is perhaps no more plastic explanation
of dialectics in the whole of Western literature than Tietjens's following
plea to Valentine:

> You and I are like two people...' He paused and began again more
> quickly: 'Do you know these soap advertisement signs that read
> differently from several angles? As you come up to them you read
> "Monkey's Soap"; if you look back when you've passed it's "Needs
> no Rinsing." ... You and I are standing at different angles, and
> though we both look at the same thing we read different messages.
> Perhaps if we stood side by side we should see yet a third... But I
> hope we respect each other. We're both honest. I, at least, tremen-
> dously respect you and I hope you respect me.'
>
> (*SDN*, 284–5)

Mrs. Humphry Ward and the Role of Women

> Tietjens was about to say that Mrs Wannop, the mother, had written
> the only novel worth reading since the eighteenth century[.]
>
> (*SDN*, 94)

We have pointed out repeatedly above that *Parade's End* manages to be
'a historical novel of [Ford's] own time' because his own time happened
to be a period that was already then being interpreted as particularly
eventful, showing perhaps the first clear-cut break with a past period
since the French Revolution. The assertion and nuancing of this thesis
and its cultural implications is one of the core issues of Modernism.
In narratives of transition, be they Modernist, Victorian or Romantic,
family trees matter, because they map differences and likenesses across
generations. Edward Waverley feels obligations towards his Jacobite
forebears because of his apostate Whig father, Egremont and Tietjens
are conflicted about their questionable ancestors, and the nobler blood
of Sybil and Valentine asserts itself even in their reduced circumstances.
It is not just Tietjens's snobbery that insists on Valentine's lineage; the
adopted nineteenth-century plot needs to situate her seemingly modern
efforts for suffragism within a political tradition that is commensurate
with that of her Tory love interest. The artistic merits of *Parade's End*

lie precisely in the coincidence of such political histories with associated literary conventions. As described earlier, the links of Valentine's late father to Disraeli create a literary-historical framework for her later relationship with Tietjens and at the same time for an open-minded political project, but her mother may be equally significant. Ford's support for female suffrage is well-documented and much has been written on his portrayal of women, but for the final section of this essay, it may suffice to suggest that *Parade's End* again puts the cause of female emancipation in both political-historical and literary-historical perspectives by borrowing from nineteenth-century texts authored by a politically conservative woman: Mrs. Humphry Ward, who, according to Judith Wilt, '[a]s a late nineteenth-century novelist, [...] inherits a long and insistent tradition making her novel responsible for the representation of the phenomenon, and the phenomenology, of social change'.[34]

The political- and literary-historical context for Valentine's suffragism is provided by means of Mrs. Wannop, Valentine's mother, who is not only a novelist, but the author of the 'only novel worth reading since the eighteenth century', as Tietjens asserts when she is berated by the perpetually oblivious General Campion. Two plausible candidates have been suggested for the real-life model for Mrs. Wannop: the sensationalist novelist Mary Elizabeth Braddon, for whom Ford had a surprising fondness but who already passed away in 1915 and therefore would have furnished little material, or the now obscure Mrs. W. K. Clifford [Lucy Clifford], once a daring Victorian novelist who, like Mrs. Wannop, came to struggle tirelessly against a loss of popularity during the War years, and who too was the widow of an academic.[35] While Ford, unlike with Braddon and Clifford, has not left any record of his assessment of her, Ward too deserves to be considered as a third possible inspiration. Like Mrs. Wannop in *Parade's End*, Mrs. Humphry Ward too fell out of favour during the early twentieth century after a number of extremely successful novels such as *Robert Elsmere* (1888) that even secured the approbation of Ford's idol Henry James. Also like Mrs. Wannop, she worked as a propagandist during the War, and, most importantly, like her fictional colleague, she was opposed to female suffrage. While Ford must have disapproved of Ward's opposition to Votes for Women as a leader of the Women's National Anti-Suffrage League, there are important precedents for the character of Valentine in her novels.

The role of educated women in society is the theme of most of Ward's novels, which tend to amaze prejudiced newcomers to her work with their nuanced account of relevant debates, quite in contrast to the author's interventions in journalism and public speaking. In the typical conservative Victorian manner, Ward's novels acknowledge the justified complaints of her representative female protagonists, but present every political attempt that goes beyond gradual reform as dangerous, generally forcing her heroines to undergo a course of mortification in hands-on social work that is supposed to invalidate political theory and recommend private virtue. Two novels are particularly relevant to the depictions of Valentine, namely the bestselling *Marcella* (1894), on harsh lessons learned by a young woman with socialist convictions, and the later scathing anti-suffrage novel *Delia Blanchflower* (1915), that tellingly had been slighted as 'Victorian' when it came out.[36] In the latter, the titular young suffragette, whose rhetoric and more harmless exploits bear an interesting resemblance to the burlesque activism of Valentine described by Ford in *Some Do Not...*, sees the error of her ways after her violent associates plan an attack on the manor house of her conservative love interest that is described in much the same terms as Tietjens's hallowed Groby. With a cliché that has at least done the rounds since Jane Austen, it is such an identification with ancestral houses that often allows Ward's discontented women to reintegrate into society. This function should be clear: the manor stands for the historically sanctioned edifice of society, to be metaphorically inhabited by the body politic represented by the female heroine. She assumes a maternal role and administers privately to her family and tenants, thereby enabling her paternalist husband to structurally maintain the (e)state and outwardly assume control. This is a rigidly genderised philosophy, but Ward, who amongst other causes was active in the promotion of female higher education, always claims that this would permit educated yet virtuous women more challenges than the mere drudgery of household management. In the earlier novel, Marcella, after moving in 'Venturist' (probably Fabian) circles in London, moves to her father's country seat, and finds herself drawn to the life of the gentry, but also by the opportunities at social politics offered by the suffering cottagers on her neglectful father's estate. At first, she is puzzled by her respect and budding affection for her aristocratic neighbour Raeburn, an emotionally stilted squire with impeccable integrity who is uncannily like Tietjens, and who like Disraeli's Egremont is a young Tory who wants to stand for parliament and improve social policy in the Gentle Tory manner. Eventually, Marcella marries her awkward aristocrat, after disappointed experiments with reform and bad experiences with a caddish demagogue show her the fallacy of doctrinal radicalism and bring home the moral corruption of its proponents.

The final volume of *Parade's End* appeared in 1928, the year in which the Equal Franchise Act finally accorded the same vote to women as to men, though it is likely set soon after the end of the War and this was then by no means a settled matter.[37] During the War years, suffragist activism largely halted, and by his extensive portrayal of Valentine's efforts in social work, Ford perhaps wanted to give one final boost to the widespread view that the vote has been earned when women on the home front were of at least equal use as the men had been in the trenches. As Judith Wilt has emphasised, Ward in her novels confronts social ills with an often underestimated frankness, and some of her novels do imply that women should occupy a higher place in society, even if this awareness would have to be instilled through practice and example rather than imposed through governmental measures. The chastised woman is decidedly still the heroine of Ward's novels, because she enables the harmonisation of society by means of an alternative, indirect route. It is the old story of the dialectic plot: 'Woman enters the gap between Master and Man: first she sustains the blows of their angry alienations, as one or both turn on her, their true friend, and then she delivers each to the other across the bridge of her desire for the Man, and the Master's desire for her'.[38] Even though Ward's female characters have no legislative power and exert their influence in hardship and at a snail's pace, their very subjected position allows them to appreciate the side of the oppressed and instigate a move towards social cohesion which their male significant others—who invariably confess to have learned from them—by themselves could never have achieved either. For this to happen, the heroines have to pare down their initial views in order to fit into the social order envisaged by Ward, allowing continuity with the past in the process of political transition. Ford, by crafting with Valentine a heroine that readers would have recognised as highly reminiscent of Ward's, but expressly not humbling her, is again neatly updating 'Victorian' politics and novel plots by means of the one intertextual reference.

After first acknowledging their compatibility during the Monkey's Soap epiphany, Tietjens and Valentine still have to wait for two whole volumes before his fellow veterans are as surprised to find them together as they are themselves: 'You and old Tory Tietjens in the same room ... By Jove the war's over' (*AMCSU*, 216). If the announced 'third message' is then achieved, the reader is at the end of the third volume still left in the dark as to what exactly it would amount. This is the reason why Ford reluctantly consented to write a final volume, *Last Post*, despite the narrative closure of a happy ending in the preceding volume *A Man Could Stand Up–*, and despite the uneasy position that this final instalment has always occupied in the *Parade's End* canon. Although the current consensus is that it should not be considered a mere addendum but an intrinsic part of the novel, *Last Post* does not provide as many final answers as Ford's exasperated readers might hope. He states himself in the preface that this is not a demand that he could fulfil, because to provide a definite ending goes against his idea of the novel. We may add that speculating about the future would be anticipating history, and, of course, this novel treats 'of [Ford's] own time'. Tietjens and Valentine, or the political project for which their relationship functions as an allegory, do have an existence after the War that Ford would rather have left unaddressed. He can do little more than provide 'a slice of Christopher's later days', because 'the Affair that they set going would go on during the generations' (*Last Post*, 4). What this gnomic statement suggests, however, is that the open future will have some continuity with the past, and that the continued legacy will carry through as much of the old ways as is possible in the yet undefined hereafter of post-War society. The child that Valentine carries can only be considered, in the closing words of the narrator of *Sybil*, one of the 'the trustees of Posterity'.[39] As Ford's intimate friend William Carlos Williams concluded in his review of the first joint publication of the tetralogy, its last instalment might very well settle *Parade's End* as the account of 'the tragic emergence of the first Tory of the new dispensation'.[40]

Notes

1 David Priesland, 'The Gentle Tory is alive and well – On Television', *Guardian*, https://www.theguardian.com/commentisfree/2012/sep/03/gentle-tory-parades-end-yearning [last consulted on 13 February 2019].

2 Cf. Andrzej Gasiorek, 'The Politics of Cultural Nostalgia: History and Tradition in Ford Madox Ford's *Parade's End*', *Literature & History* 11.2 (October 2002): 52–77; Robert Green, *Ford Madox Ford: Prose and Politics* (Cambridge: Cambridge UP, 1981).

3 Qtd. in Max Saunders, *Ford Madox Ford: A Dual Life*, Vol. 2 (Oxford: Oxford UP, 2012), p. 206.

4 Ford Madox Ford, *The English Novel: From the Earliest Days to the Death of Joseph Conrad* (London: J. B. Lippincott, 1929), passim.

5 Ford Madox Ford, *A Man Could Stand Up —*, ed. Sara Haslam (Manchester: Carcanet P, 2011), p. 18. Hereafter *AMCSU*. Subsequent references to this edition.

6 Madox Hueffer Ford, 'Impressionism – Some Speculations', *Poetry* 2.5 (August 1913): 177–87, p. 179.

7 Ford Madox Ford, *It Was the Nightingale* (London: Lippincott, 1933), p. 180.

8 Saunders, *Ford Madox Ford*, p. 209.

9 Saunders, *Ford Madox Ford*, p. 226.

10 Marina MacKay, 'The Modernist Novel', in *The Cambridge History of Modernism*, ed. Vincent Sherry (Cambridge: Cambridge UP, 2016), pp. 307–26, p. 307.

11 Ford Madox Ford, *Some Do Not...*, ed. Max Saunders (Manchester: Carcanet P, 2011), p. 76. Hereafter *SDN*. Subsequent references to this edition.

12 Qtd in Donald Mackenzie, 'A Road Not Taken: Romance, History, and Myth in Ford's *Fifth Queen* Novels', in *Ford Madox Ford and Englishness*: International Ford Madox Ford Studies 5 (Amsterdam: Rodopi, 2006), pp. 97–118, p. 97.

13 Seamus O'Malley, *Making History New: Modernism and Historical Narrative* (Oxford: Oxford UP, 2015), p. 31.

14 Massimo Fusillo, 'Epic, Novel: The Obsession with Origins', in *The Novel*, Vol. 2: Forms and Themes, ed. Franco Moretti (Princeton, NJ: Princeton UP), pp. 33–34.

15 Georg Lukács, *The Theory of the Novel* (London: Merlin P, 1971), p. 80.

16 Georg Lukács, *The Historical Novel* (Harmondsworth: Penguin, 1962), p. 32.
17 Terry Eagleton, *The English Novel: An Introduction* (Oxford: Blackwell, 2006), p. 122.
18 Robert L. Caserio, Plot, *Story and the Novel: From Dickens and Poe to the Modern Period* (Princeton, NJ: Princeton UP, 1979), p. 57.
19 Lukács, *The Historical Novel*, p. 32.
20 Homer Obed Brown, *Institutions of the English Novel: From Defoe to Scott* (Philadelphia: U of Pennsylvania P, 1997), p. 141.
21 Brown, *Institutions*, p. 143.
22 Lukács, *The Historical Novel*, p. 32.
23 Saunders, *Ford Madox Ford*, p. 155.
24 Ford, *It Was the Nightingale*, p. 19.
25 Saunders, *Ford Madox Ford*, p. 154.
26 Andrew Lincoln, *Walter Scott and Modernity* (Edinburgh: Edinburgh UP, 2007), pp. 4–8.
27 Nancy Armstrong, 'The Fiction of Bourgeois Morality and the Paradox of Individualism', in *The Novel*, p. 349.
28 Ford Madox Ford, *Last Post*, ed. Paul Skinner (Manchester: Carcanet P, 2011), p. 203.
29 See *SDN*, p. 25.
30 James Heldman, 'The Last Victorian Novel: Technique and Theme in *Parade's End*', *Twentieth-Century Literature* 18.4 (October 1972): 271–84, p. 272.
31 Robert Blake, *Disraeli* (London: Eyre & Spottiswoode, 1966), p. 762.
32 Ford Madox Ford, *No More Parades*, ed. Joseph Wiesenfarth (Manchester: Carcanet P, 2011), pp. 31, 63, 64, 93, 255.
33 Catherine Gallagher, *The Industrial Reformation of English Fiction: Social Discourse and Narrative Form, 1832–1867* (Chicago, IL: U of Chicago P, 1985), passim.
34 Judith Wilt, *Behind Her Times: Transition England in the Novels of Mary Arnold Ward* (Charlottesville: U of Virginia P, 2005), p. 82.
35 *ODNB*.
36 John Sutherland, *Mrs Humphry Ward: Eminent Victorian, Pre-eminent Edwardian* (Oxford: Clarendon P, 1990), p. 343.
37 Paul Skinner, 'Introduction', in *Last Post*, p. xxvii.
38 Judith Wilt, *Behind Her Times: Transition England in the Novels of Mary Arnold Ward* (Charlottesville: U of Virginia P, 2005), pp. 87–88.
39 Benjamin Disraeli, *Sybil, or, The Two Nations*, ed. Nicholas Shrimpton (Oxford: Oxford UP, 1998), p. 422.
40 William Carlos Williams, '*Parade's End*', *The Sewanee Review* 59.1 (Winter 1951): 154–61, p. 161.

Selected Bibliography

Armstrong, Hamilton Fish, ed. *The Book of New York Verse*. New York: Putnam, 1917.

Baldick, Chris. *The Modern Movement, 1910–1940*. Oxford: Oxford UP, 2004.

———. *Literature of the 1920s: Writers among the Ruins*. Edinburgh: Edinburgh UP, 2012.

Bayley, John. *The Intellectuals and The Masses: Pride and Prejudice among the Literary Intelligentsia, 1880–1939*. London: Faber, 2002.

Beckson, Karl. *Arthur Symons: A Life*. Oxford: Clarendon, 1987.

Bell, Michael. 'An Analytical Note on Myth in Modernism: The Case of T. S. Eliot'. In *Religion and Myth in T. S. Eliot's Poetry*. Eds. Scott Freer and Michael Bell. Newcastle upon Tyne: Cambridge Scholars, 2016, pp. 65–76.

Benstock, Shari. 'Expatriate Sapphic Modernism: Entering Literary History'. In *Lesbian Texts and Contexts: Radical Revisions*. Eds. Karla Jay and Joanne Glasgow. New York and London: New York UP, 1990, pp. 183–203.

Bergonzi, Bernard. *Heroes' Twilight: A Study of the Literature of the Great War*. London: Constable, 1965.

Bizzotto, Elisa. 'Re-editing Arthur Symons, Decadent-Modernist Literary Ghost'. In *Reconnecting Aestheticism and Modernism: Continuities, Revisions, Speculations*. Eds. Bénédicte Coste, Catherine Delyfer, and Christine Reynier. New York: Routledge, 2016, pp. 31–44.

Bradbury, Malcolm and James McFarlane, eds. *Modernism: A Guide to European Literature 1890–1930*. London: Penguin, 1976.

Briggs, Julia. *Night Visitors: The Rise and Fall of the English Ghost Story*. London: Faber and Faber, 1977.

Brooker, Peter and Andrew Thacker, eds. *The Oxford Critical and Cultural History of Modernist Magazines*. Vol I, Britain and Ireland 1880–1955. Oxford: Oxford UP, 2009.

Chesterton, Gilbert Keith. *Collected Nonsense and Light Verse*. Ed. Marie Smith. London: Methuen, 1989.

Cockin, Katharine. 'Bram Stoker, Ellen Terry and Pamela Colman Smith: The Art of Devilry'. In *Bram Stoker and the Gothic: Formations and Transformations*. Ed. Catherine Wynne. Basingstoke: Palgrave, 2016, pp. 159–71.

———. *Edith Craig and The Theatres of Art*. London: Bloomsbury Methuen, 2017.

Coste, Bénédicte, Catherine Delyfer, and Christine Reynier. 'Introduction'. In *Reconnecting Aestheticism and Modernism: Continuities, Revisions, Speculations*. Eds. Bénédicte Coste, Catherine Delyfer, and Christine Reynier. New York and London: Routledge, 2017, pp. 1–15.

Dentith, Simon. *Parody*. London: Routledge, 2000.

DiBattista, Maria and Lucy McDiarmid, eds. *High and Low Moderns: Literature and Culture, 1889–1939*. Oxford: Oxford UP, 1996.

Disraeli, Benjamin. *Sybil, or, The Two Nations*. Oxford: Oxford UP, 1998.

Doan, Laura and Jane Garrity, eds. *Sapphic Modernities: Sexuality, Women and National Culture*. London: Palgrave Macmillan, 2006.

Eco, Umberto. *Lector in fabula: La cooperazione interpretativa nei testi narrativi*. Milan: Bompiani, 1998.

Edel, Leon and Gordon Ray, eds. *Henry James and H. G. Wells: A Record of Their Friendship*. Urbana: Illinois UP, 1958.

Eliot, Thomas Stearns. 'Reflections on Contemporary Poetry, III'. *Egoist* 4 (1917), pp. 133–4

———. 'The Metaphysical Poets'. In *The Complete Prose of T. S. Eliot: The Critical Edition: Volume 2: The Perfect Critic, 1919–1926*. Eds. Anthony Cuda and Ronald Schuchard. Baltimore, MD: John Hopkins UP, 2014, pp. 375–85.

———. 'Modern Tendencies in Poetry'. In *The Complete Prose of T. S. Eliot: The Critical Edition: Volume 2: The Perfect Critic, 1919–1926*. Eds. Anthony Cuda and Ronald Schuchard. Baltimore, MD: John Hopkins UP, 2014, pp. 212–25.

———. 'Tradition and the Individual Talent'. In *The Complete Prose of T. S. Eliot: The Critical Edition: Volume 2: The Perfect Critic, 1919–1926*. Eds. Anthony Cuda and Ronald Schuchard. Baltimore, MD: John Hopkins UP, 2014, pp. 105–14.

Ellis, Nadia. *Territories of the Soul: Queer Belonging in the Black Diaspora*. Durham, NC: Duke UP, 2015.

Feldman, Jessica R. *Victorian Modernism: Pragmatism and the Varieties of Aesthetic Experience*. Cambridge, New York et al.: Cambridge UP, 2002.

Fletcher, John Gould. 'Once More the Georgians'. *Poetry* 12.6 (September 1918): 332–7.

Forster, E. M. *Two Cheers for Democracy*. 1951. Middlesex: Penguin, 1965, repr. 1970.

Fussell, Paul. *The Great War and Modern Memory: An Illustrated Edition*. 1975. Oxford: Oxford UP, 2000.

Garber, Marjorie. *Academic Instincts*. Princeton, NJ: Princeton UP, 2001.

Gasiorek, Andrzej. 'The Politics of Cultural Nostalgia: History and Tradition in Ford Madox Ford's *Parade's End*'. *Literature & History* 11.2 (October 2002): 52–77.

Gorman, Herbert S. *The Procession of Masks*. Boston, MA: Brimmer, 1923.

Hotchkiss, Joyce. 'Romance and Reality: The Dualistic Style of E. M. Forster's *Maurice*'. *The Journal of Narrative Technique* 3.4 (1974): 163–75.

Howarth, Peter. *British Poetry in the Age of Modernism*. Cambridge: Cambridge UP, 2005.

Hynes, Samuel. *Edwardian Occasions: Essays on English Writing in the Early Twentieth Century*. London: Routledge, 1972.

Jaillant, Lise. *Modernism, Middlebrow and the Literary Canon: The Modern Library Series, 1917–1955*. London: Pickering, 2014.

James, Cyril Lionel Robert. *Letters from London: Seven Essays by C. L. R. James*. Port of Spain, Trinidad & Tobago: Prospect, 2003.

Laity, Cassandra. 'H. D. and A. C. Swinburne: Decadence and Sapphic Modernism'. In *Lesbian Texts and Contexts: Radical Revisions*. Eds. Karla Jay and Joanne Glasgow. New York and London: New York UP, 1990, pp. 217–40.

Leavis, Frank Raymond. *Mass Civilization and Minority Culture*. Cambridge: Minority, 1930.

Lee, Vernon and Clementina Anstruther-Thomson. *Beauty and Ugliness and Other Studies in Psychological Aesthetics*. London: John Lane, 1912.

Le Gallienne, Richard. 'On Re-Reading Walter Pater'. *North American Review* 195 (February 1912): 214–24.

Levenson, Michael. *Modernism and the Fate of Individuality: Character and Novelistic Form from Conrad to Woolf*. 1991. Cambridge: Cambridge UP, 1995.

Lewis, Wyndham. *Time and Western Man*. 1927. Boston, MA: Beacon, 1957.

———. *The Apes of God*. 1930. Santa Barbara, CA: Black Sparrow, 1984.

Lukács, Georg. *The Historical Novel*. Harmondsworth: Penguin, 1962.

———. *The Theory of the Novel*. London: Merlin, 1971.

Mahoney, Kristin. *The Literature and Politics of Post-Victorian Decadence*. Cambridge: Cambridge UP, 2015.

Majumdar, Saikat. 'The Critic as Amateur'. *NLH: New Literary History* 48.1 (Winter 2017): 1–25.

Mao, Douglas and Rebecca L. Walkowitz, eds. *Bad Modernisms*. Durham, NC: Duke UP, 2006.

———. 'New Modernist Studies'. *PMLA* 123.3 (May 2008): 737–48.

Marx, John. *The Modernist Novel and the Decline of Empire*. Cambridge: Cambridge UP, 2005.

Murphy, Patrick J. *Medieval Studies and the Ghost Stories of M. R. James*. University Park: Pennsylvania State UP, 2017.

Murry, John Middleton. 'The "Classical" Revival'. *Adelphi* (February 1926). In *T. S. Eliot: The Contemporary Reviews*. Ed. Jewel Spears Brooker. Cambridge: Cambridge UP, 2004, pp. 132–36.

Nicholls, Peter. 'At a Tangent: Other Modernisms'. In *Modernisms: A Literary Guide*. 2nd ed. 1995. Basingstoke: Palgrave Macmillan, 2009, pp. 189–218.

O'Connor, Elizabeth Foley. 'We Disgruntled Devils Don't Please Anyone: Pamela Colman Smith, *The Green Sheaf* and Female Literary Networks'. *South Carolina Review* 48.2 (2016): 72–89.

O'Neill, Michael and Gareth Reeves. *Auden, MacNeice, and Spender: The Thirties Poetry*. Basingstoke: Macmillan, 1992.

O'Neill, Michael. *The All-Sustaining Air: Romantic Renewals in British, Irish, and American Poetry since 1900*. Oxford: Oxford UP, 2007.

O'Neill, Michael, Sarah Wootton, Mark Sandy, eds. *The Persistence of Beauty: From the Victorians to the Moderns*. London: Pickering, 2015.

O'Neill, Michael. 'Poetry and Autobiography in the 1930s: Auden, Isherwood, MacNeice, Spender'. In *A History of English Autobiography*. Ed. Adam Smyth. Cambridge: Cambridge UP, 2016, pp. 31–44.

Orwell, George. *Inside the Whale and Other Essays*. London: Gollancz, 1940.

Patterson, Anthony and Yoonjoung Choi, eds. *We Speak a Different Tongue: Maverick Voices and Modernity, 1890–1939*. Newcastle upon Tyne: Cambridge Scholars, 2015.

Perkins, David. *A History of Modern Poetry: From the 1890s to the High Modernist Mode*. Cambridge, MA: Belknap-Harvard UP, 1976.

Pyne, Kathleen. 'The Photo-Secession and the Death of the Mother: Gertrude Kasebier and Pamela Colman Smith'. *Modernism and the Feminine Voice: O'Keeffe and the Women of the Stieglitz Circle*. Berkeley: U of California P, 2007, pp. 1–61.

Radford, Andrew and Mark Sandy, eds. *Romantic Echoes in the Victorian Era*. Farnham: Ashgate, 2008.

Sandy, Mark, ed. *Romantic Presences in the Twentieth Century*. Nineteenth Century Studies Ser. Farnham: Ashgate, 2012.

Sewell, Elizabeth. *The Field of Nonsense*. London: Chatto and Windus, 1952.

Sherry, Vincent. *Modernism and the Re-invention of Decadence*. Cambridge and New York: Cambridge UP, 2015.

Silkin, Jon. *Out of Battle: The Poetry of the Great War*. 1972. London: Ark, 1987.

Spender, Stephen. *The Destructive Element: A Study of Modern Writers and Beliefs*. London: Cape, 1935.

———. 'Poetry and Revolution'. In *The Thirties and After: Poetry, Politics, People 1933–1975*. Glasgow: Collins, 1978.

Squillace, Robert. *Modernism, Modernity and Arnold Bennett*. Lewisburg, PA: Bucknell UP, 1997.

Stallworthy, Jon. *Wilfred Owen*. 1977. London: Pimlico, 1988.

Stetz, Margaret D. '"To Amuse Intelligently and Cleverly": Carolyn Wells and Literary Parody'. In *Transgressive Humor of American Women Writers*. Ed. Sabrina Fuchs Abrams. Basingstoke: Palgrave Macmillan, 2017, pp. 17–36.

Symons, Arthur. 'Some Makers of Modern Verse'. *The Forum* (December 1921): 476–88.

———. *The Memoirs of Arthur Symons: Life and Art in the 1890s*. Ed. Karl Beckon. University Park: Pennsylvania State UP, 1977.

Tomlinson, Alan. 'Strange Meeting in a Strange Land: Wilfred Owen and Shelley'. *Studies in Romanticism* 32.1 (1993): 75–95.

Vaninskaya, Anna. 'The Political Middlebrow from Chesterton to Orwell'. In *The Masculine Middlebrow, 1880–1950: What Mr. Miniver Read*. Ed. Kate Macdonald. Basingstoke: Palgrave-Macmillan, pp. 162–76.

Wee, Valerie. 'The Scream Trilogy, "Hyperpostmodernism", and the Late Nineties Teen Slasher Film'. *Journal of Film and Video* 57.3 (2005): 44–61.

Woolf, Virginia. *Mr. Bennett and Mrs. Brown*. London: Hogarth, 1924.

———. 'The Novels of E. M. Forster'. 1927. *The Death of the Moth*. London: Hogarth, 1942, pp. 104–12.

———. 'Modern Fiction'. In *Selected Essays*. Ed. David Bradshaw. Oxford: Oxford UP, 2008, pp. 6–12.

Index

For Product Safety Concerns and Information please contact our EU
representative GPSR@taylorandfrancis.com
Taylor & Francis Verlag GmbH, Kaufingerstraße 24, 80331 München, Germany